What's the Story?

The Art of Writing and Communication

Revised First Edition

Edited by Beth Jannery and Daniel Walsch

George Mason University

Bassim Hamadeh, CEO and Publisher
Michael Simpson, Vice President of Acquisitions
Jamie Giganti, Managing Editor
Jess Busch, Senior Graphic Designer
Amy Stone, Acquisitions Editor
Brian Fahey, Licensing Specialist
Sean Adams, Interior Design

First published in the United States of America in 2015 by Cognella, Inc.

Printed in the United States of America

ISBN: 978-1-63189-962-1 (pbk)/ 978-1-63189-963-8 (br)

www.cognella.com 800-200-3908

Contents

II.
Getting from Here to There: The Evolution of Communication and Writing

III.
What is Good Writing, Anyway?

IV.
Journalists and Public Relations Practitioners and Good Writing

V.
Style Resources

VI.
Public Relations

VII.
Print

VIII.
Broadcast

IX.
Online Journalism

X.
Social Media

XI.
Legal Challenges

XII.
Effective Communication and Writing Skills in the Job Market

About the Authors

What to Expect

There are plenty of reasons not to write well. Lack of time. Lack of motivation. Generally, people do not read nearly as much as they used to, so who is there to write for anyway? Furthermore, what people do read these days is usually short, clipped, and easily disposable. So, you might wonder, why another book on writing? And why this one in particular? To us, the answer is simple. People are seekers of information. Wanting to know and understand more continues to be part of who and what we as living creatures are. While people may not sit down with the morning newspaper as much as they used to, they still seek out sources of information providing them with updates as to what is going on in their communities, regions, state, nation, and world. It is writers who provide us with that desired information. People may no longer write letters to friends or family members as much as they used to, but they still correspond just the same. This time it is electronically. Whether it is via a letter or a tweet, correspondence is only as effective as the quality of the words that are exchanged.

Writing remains a bridge between ignorance and enlightenment, isolation and engagement. We read writing to learn, and we attempt to write to inform as well as to engage. Here, in the second decade of the twenty-first century, that remains as true now as it did in the centuries preceding it. Thus, we present this book on writing because society, including students of higher education, need and demand it. The better people are able to perform this particular brand of communication, the better able they are to meet their own goals, connect with others, and position themselves as being of high value in their respective communities.

Journalists and public relations practitioners, specifically, and students of communication in general constitute the primary focus of this text. As a whole, the text is designed to provide you with greater insight into and understanding of the various aspects, including the mechanics of it and the rationale or purpose for it. In addition, the text, with its array of discussion questions, suggested readings, and insights into journalism and public relations, is geared to give those who wish that writing would remain an intimate and lasting presence in their professional and personal lives greater appreciation of just how challenging and vital being able to write well is. It is our hope that the body of this text will motivate those who read and make use of it to continue to be best they can be at this unique form of communication. Doing so is a matter of not only your own survival, but the ongoing advancement of society as well.

i

Effective Communication and Good Writing

A number of years ago, in the golden years of her life, a famous actress of yesteryear, Bette Davis, said, "Old age ain't for sissies." No question about it. As people age, they are more likely to take on aches and pains they never had and face a range of physical and even mental challenges that can and do make their lives a particular obstacle to over come challenge. Fortunately, more people these days are living longer and more productive lives than ever before. This, however, is not to say that they are not working hard at it. Such a perspective is also true when it comes to effective communication and good writing. Doing both is not without challenge, even as our birthdays accumulate. The bottom line: as is the case with old age, writing ain't for sissies, either.

The good news here is that communicating effectively and writing well are quite attainable. But as it is for those with a few years under their belts and who strive to continue being productive and active, commitment is definitely required. It is not unlike the old joke about the tourist in New York City who stops a pedestrian and asks, "Excuse me, sir, how do you get to Carnegie Hall?" The person simply and succinctly replies, "Practice." The same is very true of effective communication and good writing. They are attainable, yet require ongoing practice. It is one thing to connect with another person either verbally or via writing, but another to do it well and still another to maintain that connection. This is the ultimate challenge of any communicator.

In any discussion about effective communication and good writing, it is important to have a clear understanding of what each is and, just as important, how they relate. The two are not separate. Effective communication is all-encompassing, while good writing is one aspect of it. Other topics we will be discussing in this chapter will include why being able to do each well is important and what elements are needed for either one to occur. We begin with definitions.

Effective Communication

Communication is something we all do. Whether we are speaking or not, alone or with others, everything we do or say communicates some type of message. Communication to all of us is as basic and fundamental as breathing. It is what we do. The challenge, and one that we do not always meet successfully, is communicating the message we intend to communicate. We may know what we have in mind, but that by itself does not guarantee that the person or public to whom our message is intended recognizes or understands what we are trying to impart. A perfect example presents itself every day on our highways. The driver ahead of us slows down. But it is not clear to us, the driver behind that person, what the other driver is going to do. Is that person going to make a left or right turn or continue moving straight ahead? To us, there is confusion in that driver's action. But to that driver, she knows what she has in mind. To her, for instance, it is clear that she is simply slowing down as she approaches an upcoming intersection.

Such a scenario illustrates the complexity of communication. The front driver is not necessarily wrong in her actions. From her perspective, what she is doing and even why she is doing it are quite clear. Nonetheless, she has triggered confusion in the driver behind her because what she is communicating has been inadequate and confusing. Pardon the pun, but in this and so many instances, communication is not an easy street.

In the late 1940s, two mathematicians, Claude Shannon and Warren Weaver, working on a project for AT&T, created a communication model that outlined the flow of this act (Weaver & Shannon, 1963). Though simplistic at first glance, it inspired numerous communication scholars and practitioners to produce their own models and theories as a way of shining even more light and understanding on this thing we all do. Before mentioning any of these other models or theories, let us look at what Shannon and Weaver put together. According to them, following is a breakdown of how communication works:

Sender Encoding Message Decoding Receiver

The act of communication begins with the sender. This person starts the ball rolling by devising a message that he or she wishes to share with another. Encoding represents the sender's decision on how best to communicate the message. Finally, the sender "goes public" with the message. Obviously, the receiver is on the receiving end of the communiqué as, in the design of Shannon and Weaver, it is this person for whom the message is intended. Decoding represents the attempt to decipher or determine the meaning of the message. Following the introduction of their model, the authors added two more parts to the process: noise and feedback. Noise refers to any interference that disrupts, interferes with, or, in some cases, totally prevents the message from getting to its intended destination. Feedback, finally, is the response the receiver gives to the sender. When feedback occurs, the receiver and sender exchange roles, thus turning the communication act into a more circular exchange. Thus, rather than an act of talking at each other, the participants are talking with each other. When this occurs, the chances of the two developing a shared understanding of the message or information being exchanged are improved greatly.

There are two other communication models worth noting as they apply to both communication in a general sense as well as to writing. They are the transactional model of communication and the uncertainty and gratification model. The first of these two was created by Barnlund (2008). In it, he contends that in the communication process the sender and receiver of messages or communiqués are constantly receiving and sending messages simultaneously. With such a perspective, communication is depicted as a circular process involving ongoing exchange between those two primary players in the communication process: sender and receiver. In other words, these two are equal players or participants. The sender of the message, as one might be inclined to suggest, is not more important to the success of the communication effort than the receiver is. In such a scenario, the author or writer of a communiqué is equivalent to those who read it. They are, in a sense, equal partners or collaborators.

The uncertainty and gratification model is the brainchild of Berger and Calabrese (1975). In it, the two suggested that when it comes to interactions with others, all of us feel a bit uneasy with encounters, as we are unable to control the thoughts and behavior of people we might meetencounter. As a result, people constantly strive to achieve a tolerable balance between establishing a level of comfort and contending with any nervousness or discomfort they might be feeling. There is logic to this when one views any communication outreach or overture such as writing to be akin to stepping into the unknown. One does not know what the reaction or response to, say, an article or press release he or she has written will be. Scorn? Praise? Lawsuit? Anything is possible. Such a reality points to an additional challenge faced by communicators, particularly when they undertake writing as a strategy: contending with the consequences. Thus, when one writes or communicates in any other form, he or she is taking a risk. Will the outreach effort be accepted or rejected? Praised or scorned? Stimulate conversation or be ignored?

So, with all that, what is "effective communication"? Basically, we define it as the act of successfully exchanging messages and/or information with another. Straightforward? Yes. Simple? No. We view effective communication as an act involving dialogue or exchange. Ideally, it goes beyond one person simply talking at another, even though this is something we all do from time to time. "I'm going to bed." Or, "I think I ate too many chocolate chip cookies." We view such an exchange as technical communication. Yes, a message or information has been passed along from one to another. But there is little or no opportunity for the receiver of the message to respond. Thus, while the communicated message has been passed from one to another, little to no engagement has occurred. Such a scenario is like serving someone dessert and not receiving any feedback.

Effective communication should not be confused with receiving agreement or some sort of positive reaction. All of us express opinions on most any topic at times. While it may make us feel good or gain some sort of validation when the person or people with whom we share our perspective agree with us. But in terms of how we view "effective communication," being told that we are full of hot air does not make that act of communication any less effective. It would be akin to a person running for public office who loses the election and then views their experience as a failure of democracy.

It was in the twentieth century when scholars and practitioners began putting forth various models and theories to better explain and analyze the workings of communication. Such scholarly productivity corresponded with the rise of public relations as a profession and source of academic study. The benefit of this input helped solidify a more universal recognition of what makes for effective communication as well as the different strategies utilized by practitioners for the purpose of promotion, creating awareness, or establishing alliances. Perhaps the best known example of this insight was introduced in 1984 by James Grunig and Todd Hunt. As a result of their analysis of an array of public relations campaigns and strategic communication efforts, the two identified four public relations models (Grunig & Hunt, 1984). The models and a brief explanation of them are as follows: (1) press agentry model (designed to promote/publicize), (2) public information model (designed to inform or share information), (3) two-way asymmetrical model (designed to persuade), and (4) two-way symmetrical model (designed to establish partnerships). These models relate to the question of effective communication in that they illustrate various perceptions as to how it has been and is being perceived by professional communicators. The definition from which we are working in this text contains elements of each. Our working definition speaks to the sharing of information; prospective promotion of any kind of variable, including a cause, a product, or even a candidate; and attempting to persuade or influence another with some type of information. In addition, and perhaps most important, it speaks to reaching out to others for the purpose of establishing a connection. Reasons for such action can include addressing issues of mutual concern or combining resources to advance shared values. These objectives, it should be noted, can be pursued and achieved via oral or written strategies, or both.

Good Writing

The late composer and giant of jazz Duke Ellington was once asked what makes a good song. Ellington reportedly shrugged and said, "If you like it, then it's good." One cannot get much more direct than that. But can such a judgment be applied to writing? On the one hand, there is no question that one's preferences for music and writing are a matter of personal taste. We can sit through a song that is played flawlessly and with conviction and still not like it. At the same time, we can read a book where there are no errors in punctuation or sentence structure and the text is presented in a heartfelt manner and still not give it a thumbs-up, either. The same is also no doubt true for many people. The question then revolves around whether we can consider a particular book that we do not like still to be well written. Is it logical to not like something—anything—and still view it as being well done?

The answer to the above question, much like Ellington's response, is clear. While Ellington's answer regarding music is memorable, it is also a bit misleading and unfair to those who prefer certain kinds or styles of music. We do not know anyone, for instance, who does not like classical music yet, as a result, would then conclude that what Mozart or Beethoven wrote was not good. The simple truth is that those and other classical composers wrote pieces that do not appeal to everyone. Many of us just have different taste buds, yet can agree that while certain foods may be made well, that still does not mean we are going to eat them. (We are looking at you, okra.) The point is that everyone has different tastes and various preferences. This reality, despite Ellington's glib response, does not necessarily define good writing or distinguish it from that considered to be inferior. All of us can and probably do from time to time enjoy writings not necessarily as polished as they should be. While we all want what we write to be enjoyed, a worthy goal toward achieving that feeling is to t our readers view our work to be well written.

Let us look at this a bit more closely. To begin, we start with a quote regarding writing from Theodore Geisel, better known as Dr. Seuss, the most famous of children's writers: "You can get help from teachers, but you are going to have to learn a lot by yourself, sitting alone in a room" (1986). This bit of wisdom from the Pulitzer Prize–winning author is appropriate because while we are proud of this text and believe it will be of value to those wishing to pursue careers in communication, particularly in the writing aspect of it, it is essential that this or any other text should not be viewed as a substitute for the hard work required to become a competent writer. Like the person wishing to get to Carnegie Hall, good writing requires practice, practice, and then more practice. One who writes is always a student of this craft. Much as any athlete who trains to keep in shape, writers must continue to train and exercise their muscles. Just because a big leaguer leads the league in home runs does not mean that he stops taking batting practice.

With that in mind, let us define "good writing," just as we did "effective communication" earlier. Good writing is written communication that consists of interesting ideas that are well organized and told in a voice unique to the writer, and that follows the conventional parameters of basic and proper grammar. This definition applies to those who write fiction or those, as is appropriate to this text, who write professionally, such as public relations practitioners or journalists. Either way, to again quote from another famous writer, Sinclair Lewis, "Writing is just work—there's no secret. It you dictate or use a pen or type with your toes—it's still just work." One of the key aspects of our definition is that it is devised in the context of several rules for writers: knowing what you are writing about, knowing who you are writing for, and knowing what it is you want to say.

When public relations practitioners are hired by organizations or other entities to represent them, it is vital that they become as knowledgeable about that client as possible. This requires research. What does this research entail? The answer is doing what is necessary to become as familiar with the client's history, internal culture, vision/mission, strengths and weaknesses, and priorities and goals as possible. Specific tactics to collect this information may include talking with members of the organization or the entity's team, reviewing its budget and vital documents, assessing its goals and overall mission, and even conversing with its customers or those who utilize its services or who benefit from its efforts. Without such information, it is difficult for anyone to write about a client at least in any way even close to being considered substantive.

Knowing who one is writing for is another general but vital rule of thumb for those putting pen to paper on behalf of others. When one starts to write, the most fundamental question of all is the following: who is going to read this? Whatever answer you, the writer, come up with is the answer to the question of audience or desired readership. Without question, the answer should be more than "my client." The client or the entity paying for your services is only one part of the overall equation. Yes, they may be paying your salary, but as a writer you are performing this important function to connect with others on their behalf. These "others" include current customers, potential customers, competitors, stakeholders, internal members, and members of the general public. Remember: writing is not about you, the writer. It may seem that way, but the reality is that what one writes goes beyond his or her own interests. Writing, in many ways, is an act of "look at me!" Writers write to be read. At the same time, practically speaking, just as singers cannot and do not earn a living by singing in the shower, writers do not write without others in mind.

The third rule pertains to your sense of direction. Specifically, when you sit down in front of your keyboard, you must have a sense of what it is you are going to say. This is key if you are going to have any chance of keeping your readers with you. Readers, generally, value their time and do not suffer fools gladly. In other words, if they sense that what they are reading lacks a point or focus, they will quickly and without hesitation move on to something else. This is especially true if what you are writing is competing with other articles in, say, a magazine or other brochures on a coffee table. If you tend to wander in your writing, it is very likely that your readers will wander, too. Good writing keeps such wandering to a minimum. This is why it is key to let the reader know at the beginning of any article what it is about.

Where, then, does this sense of direction come from? The answer is tied to the amount of research and fact-finding you do regarding your client and/or subject. Such a step in the writing process should not be shortchanged. To do that also means that you are shortchanging your client. And to do that puts the credibility of the writer and public relations representative at risk. Should that ever occur, your effectiveness and reputation as a professional communicator comes into question. As has been said many times before, knowledge is power. Therefore, the more powerful you make yourself on a particular topic, the greater sense of purpose, confidence, and direction you will have when you sit down to write on that topic.

Putting the Two Together

By themselves, effective communication and good writing are important in that they are good skills for any of us to have. For professional writers, including journalists and public relations practitioners, these skills are essential to succeeding for the sake of one's own growth and professional standing and for the benefit of others. Numerous scientists, including Charles Darwin and Abraham Maslow, have written of the basic needs that we as individuals have in our day-to-day lives. Satisfying these needs is largely what drives us both in terms of working toward our own goals and in how we interact with others. Without question, the written word is one of the "horses" on which all of us ride in our efforts to better connect with others. This reality points to the primary purpose of communication in the form of effective writing. To illustrate this, we take a closer look at the theories of Darwin and Maslow.

Darwin, of course, is famous for his theory of evolution. In his classic *On the Origin of Species by Means of Natural Selection*, Darwin theorized that all living creatures, including people, are agents of change (1859/1958). They are constantly being called to adapt to their ever-changing environment. Failure to do so, he said, would it all likelihood result in extinction. In the context of various forms of communication, including writing, we do not refer to survival in the literal sense. Thankfully and realistically, the balance of your life is not part of the mix in the great majority of interactions or information exchanges that occur. However, how well you communicate can and does impact your various relationships, job security, and standing in the eyes of others. For example, when you get a new boss, communication is a key element that helps define your relationship with this person. In this scenario, "survival" refers to maintaining a positive connection with your boss, thus remaining employed. In fact, in so many aspects of life today, rather than "survival of the fittest," a phrase closely associated with Darwin, even though he never actually said it, it is actually more like "survival of the fittest communicator." This, it should be noted, applies to not just how well you interact with others but how well you present yourself in writing. As teachers, each year we review hundreds of written papers from students. Without question, a major part of our assessment of them is based on the quality of their writing and not just how they present themselves in person.

In the field of human behavior and the human psyche, Maslow has also gained his share of fame. More than a half-century ago, Maslow introduced his hierarchy of needs that everyone, he said, has (1954). The category of needs Maslow said we all share is, in descending order, as follows: self-actualization, esteem or self-esteem, acceptance or love, safety, and physiological needs. Collectively, they serve as great motivators for choices we make, actions we take, and how we communicate. Even more to the point, according to Maslow, they are behind everything we do. Self-actualization, for instance, represents our need to achieve or accomplish; esteem or self-esteem speaks to our need to gain recognition or some level of prestige; acceptance or love addresses our desire to belong; safety relates to our drive for security; and physiological needs speak more to our basic biological needs such as food, water and sleep.

If efforts to satisfy at least one or more of the needs articulated by Maslow define or shape our every move, it stands to reason that this includes how we communicate as well as how we react to what has been communicated to us. For the public relations practitioner, particularly when he or she utilizes the written word as an outreach strategy, being sensitive to the fact that others have these fundamental needs and then knowing what, specifically, they are becomes a major factor in terms of how to phrase or present information or messages. These needs, including the most fundamental one to survive, are among our most basic commonalities. Given the reality that they will never go away or cease to exist, the better we contend with them, the better it is for all. The communicator has a unique role to play in this context. If he or she has done the proper research, a respectful connection is more likely to occur.

Incorporating the theories of Darwin and Maslow into this discussion showcases the importance and even relevance of communication and all variations of it. Writing, as we will discuss in greater detail in chapter two, is a major aspect of that and has been for centuries. If it were possible to remove communication from man's behavior with and without others since the beginning of our species, any notion of advancement would be impossible to imagine. To paraphrase the old saying, "We are what we eat," we are and will continue to be how we communicate. Communication provides each of us with the ability to let others know our intent, our needs, our hopes, our concerns, and so on; for others, of course, communication enables them to do the same with us. Such information exchanges make possible connections between individuals and between publics. In addition, it paves the way for alliances and partnerships to be drawn. This, of course, is based on the premise that communication, no matter the form, is carried out in good faith and without any intent for dishonest manipulation. When that occurs, as it invariably has, positive ties devolve into negative ones. More globally, progress becomes difficult to achieve.

What elements, then, comprise effective communication and good writing? If you were to bake an "effective communication" pie or "good writing" pie, what would be the ingredients? The next section of this chapter addresses those points.

Elements of Effective Communication

Though we all communicate, it is clear that none of us communicate well all the time. Why not? Given that we communicate as often as we breathe, one might conclude or assume that rare is the day when we do not communicate effectively. That, of course, is nothing if not a pipe dream. If anything, rare is the day when we achieve our communication goals the majority of the time. The hard truth is that more often than not we fall short as communicators. Professional baseball players are a perfect example of this. In the major leagues, a good batting average is .300. That means that for every ten times at bat, a professional makes a hit three times. That, of course, means that he fails to hit seven out of ten times. Though hard data on the equivalent of this in communication have never been formally compiled, unofficially a similar success-failure ratio is very much an accepted truism. To gain a better understanding of what makes for successful and unsuccessful communication, it is appropriate to examine the steps followed by many practitioners in the traditional public relations process. In addition, we will look at a listing of barriers to communication and how best to overcome them.

Numerous variations on the process of public relations have been put forth over the years. Introduced by Guth and Marsh, one of the most popular and enduring revolves around the acronym RPCE (research, planning, communication, and evaluation) (2009). Others have included ROPE (research, objective, planning, and evaluation) and RACE (research, action, communication, and evaluation). One can easily see that there is little difference between any of them. For simplicity's sake, we focus here on the Guth-Marsh four-step model. Following is a bare-bones explanation of this process: research represents what is known as the discovery phase, in which practitioners attempt to gain a sense of history of what steps and results occurred in campaigns similar to one on which a practitioner is currently focusing. The planning phase is when practitioners take the information they gathered in their research effort and begin putting together their new strategies and tactics for their current campaign. The communication phase is basically when they begin carrying out or implementing their new plan. Finally, evaluation represents steps to measure the results of the current campaign and analyze reasons for its success or failure.

RPCE represents a systematic, step-by-step procedure for practitioners to follow as they formulate an outreach campaign. Public relations, despite an impression some may have about it, should not be conducted in a haphazard, seat-of-the-pants style. While this is not to say that some do not do it that way, at its best it is an act conducted in a deliberate, research-based, and well-thought-out manner. Furthermore, public relations is multidimensional in terms of its purpose and overall goals. An immediate goal, for instance, may be to increase a client's visibility or promote ticket sales to a particular event. Often underneath that is an effort to enhance goodwill, establish strong ties with other publics, and strengthen the reputation or image of that entity.

Scholars have, in fact, identified three levels of planning and practice in public relations: grand strategy, strategy, and tactics (Botan, 2006). When it comes to public relations, two distinct yet overlapping concepts are grand strategy and strategy. Grand strategy, as defined by Botan, is the policy-level decisions an organization makes about its goals, alignments, ethics, and relationship with publics and other forces in its environment. Two of the most important aspects of grand strategies are publics and issues. As defined by Dewey, a public is a group of people who see that they have a common interest with respect to an organization (1927). This, however, does not mean that any particular public has a long shelf life or lasts forever. The duration of a public varies greatly. People, for instance, may come together to form a public that works on behalf of a political candidate. Once the election is over, those men and women are likely to disband. Thus, publics are generally created as a result of folks having something in common, such as issues or concerns. This is particularly true when it comes to issues. As Crable and Vibbert noted, an issue is created when one or more individuals attach significance to a situation or perceived problem (1985). These then influence an organization when it devises its grand strategy.

On a more narrow scale, strategy is defined as campaign-level decision making involving the maneuvering and arranging of resources and arguments to carry out organizational grand strategies. Strategy feeds into or supports grand strategy. It is key in any effort toward effective communication to ensure that strategies are not inconsistent with an entity's grand strategy. If this happens, at the very least, the person heading up the public relations campaign should not be surprised if he or she is asked to step aside.

Where do tactics fit into this? As Botan explained, tactics, as one might guess, are the specific activities and outputs through which strategies are implemented. These include the specific press releases, purchased advertisements, flyers, blogs, or media events a public relations team might do as part of their outreach effort. These tactics, like the strategies that help shape them, must feed into the overall grand strategy. Tactics often give an organization's grand strategy a "face" in that they are visible, tangible objects. If done well, they serve as the first glimpse an organization provides a public regarding its position on issues of the day. Also, if launched in a timely manner, they can set the organization on a path toward communicating effectively within its environment.

Overcoming Barriers to Effective Communication

Earlier, we mentioned the reality of barriers that impede or get in the way of efforts to communicate effectively. What are they? What are these "things" that prevent communicators from hitting the bulls-eye every time people seek to connect with others or promote their client? Rather than simply list examples, we have come up several broad categories that cover the spectrum of barriers. Following are the categories with a brief explanation of each: (1) exposure—there is no guarantee that a message will reach its intended target because of such realities as limited funding or technical problems; (2) nature of media—incorrectly identifying the media habits of a targeted public; (3) nature of message—making a message too complex or too simple; (4) nature of audience—not knowing the audience's level of intelligence, areas of interests, level of education, or vocabulary; (5) audience's attitude—the audience may already have their minds made up over something, be apathetic, fear new ideas, and so on; and (6) opposition/competition—opposing competition may get in the way of or be more appealing to a public.

Overcoming these barriers requires gaining a thorough understanding of the public or publics an entity wishes to target. We have lumped such a step into the "five rights." They, along with a brief explanation of each, are as follows: (1) right people—knowing precisely who you wish to target or influence; (2) right channels—selecting the proper channel or channels, which can influence a given audience; (3) right time—being timely in one's outreach effort; (4) right message—make sure the message is believable, realistic, and pertinent to a targeted public; and (5) right words—making sure one uses words that can be understood and fit in with the lexicon of a public. Gathering this information requires thorough research that centers around specific publics. (As there is an endless number of publics, solid research is even more vital.) If adhered to, these measures will increase the chances of experiencing a successful public relations campaign.

Identifying these barriers and ways to overcome them is not in any way geared toward misleading practitioners—current or future—when it comes to their perspective on public relations. As we mentioned earlier, successful communication is a genuine challenge. Oftentimes whether a campaign is successful ends up being decided by elements or variables beyond the control of the practitioner. This is why public relations as a profession can be very frustrating at times. Think back to the analogy of the baseball player. When it comes to rate of success, there is little difference between it and public relations.

Elements of Good Writing

> "In order to be a good writer, I have to be willing to be a bad writer. I have to be willing to let my thoughts and images be as contradictory as the evening firing its fireworks outside my window." (Cameron, 1999)

The above is a timely quote that is quite pertinent to our focus as to what elements help make for what can be considered good writing. It points to a quality that makes children, for instance, so special. Often, they need to be given the latitude to make mistakes and fumble so that they will come to appreciate the benefit of doing something correctly. Memorable writing includes the writer's voice or personality to the extent that it takes a reader beyond simply reading coherent sentences. Children are not self-conscious about being silly in front of others. In putting words on paper, writers should strive to be equally uninhibited as they begin composing a piece. Even if a first draft turns out to be less than ideal, it becomes a foundation on which to improve, much like the child's early steps at walking or eating.

Perhaps a few exist, but one would be hard-pressed to identify a writer who never has to rewrite, edit, or touch up anything he or she does. Rewriting is part of the process, thus demonstrating that the road to satisfaction or perfection is rarely, if ever, a straight path. One must have the courage to be bad or not quite up to par. This is true even if an initial draft makes you cringe after reading and rereading it. But the good news is that oftentimes that initial draft inspires ideas as to how to make what you have done even stronger.

Later in this text, we will be outlining and discussing the mechanics of quality writing as well as many of the basics that are essential if one is to produce prose of merit. Thus, the elements of good writing referred to here are purposefully different from what is upcoming. What we are discussing now are elements of the emotional kind. Specifically, we speak of several key personality traits one must exhibit when attempting to produce writing of sustained quality. The above quote from author Julia Cameron got us off to a good start. Following are other desirable personality traits:

- **Courage:** As Cameron suggested, writers must have the courage to be bad. Determining the proper words to use in order to make a sentence flow and a concept easy to grasp is often a trial-and-error process. Give it a shot. Put something down on paper. Then build on what you have started.
- **Perseverance:** Serious writing should not be thought of as a hundred-yard dash. Even if one is given an assignment to turn around an article or press release within a short period of time, this particular task is a continuation of those before it and certainly ones that will follow. Thus, the challenge of writing is more like a long-distance run. As result, there will be times when the words flow easily and others when they do not. Such ups and downs are not new or unique to any one writer. The best way to contend with this is twofold: keep these times in perspective, as they happen to everyone, and persevere. Stick with it. Do not let whatever frustration you might feel at any given moment overpower your ability or compromise what it is you are trying to say.
- **Sense of humor:** Sometimes the time to laugh the most is when the situation calls for it the least. No, this does not mean that you should crack up at your favorite uncle's funeral. But what it does mean is that during those moments when you are searching for the right word or phrase, keep your internal door open to laughter. Good writing is a hard-won gift. Enjoy it. Rejoice in it. Anything that one does well, whether it is playing sports, parenting a child, being a friend, or pursuing a career, should have joy as part of the mix.
- **Self-confidence:** There will be assignments that are harder to write than others. Not every one will be easy. But the good news is that they will not all be a struggle, either. What all assignments and writing challenges have in common is you, the writer. That is no small thing. Each time you sit down in front of your keyboard, with you is your talent and the opportunity to help a client and your own organization. The better you do, the more benefit it brings others. This is an opportunity that not everyone has in the work they do. Furthermore, you would not have been given the assignment to write that media advisory, article for a newsletter, blog, or whatever it might be if people did not have confidence in your ability.
- **Ambition:** Good writing begets good writing. It also opens doors to career advancement, more career opportunities, wider professional and even social networks, and greater respectability. Is there anyone, particularly college graduates and new professionals, who does not want those things? Being a competent writer is one doorway to those baubles that lead to advancement. It is OK to want them and OK to be ambitious about wanting them and being willing to work toward them. Others may turn away from writing opportunities. Do not be one of them.

Readers of Writing

Before closing out this chapter, several words need to be directed to those on the receiving end of the written word: readers. Who are they, anyway? What kind of person, generally, do we find picking up a newspaper or magazine, checking out information sites on the Internet, or paying attention to the various communiqués produced by public relations workers? These questions are relevant, because if you are going to attempt to enhance your writing skills, it is important that you have a good sense of the person for and to whom you are writing. Readers are seekers of information. Generally, they are people in search of greater clarification, deeper insight, or confirmation. They are curious, inquisitive, and looking to expand their broad understanding of the world around them. With exceptions, they read because they want to and know that doing so will better their lot.

Those who read are brave. They pick up an article or go to a website knowing that there is a chance they may not grasp what they are about to peruse. Few of us like setbacks. Yet those who read face the possibility that an article—any article—may be something they do not understand even following an initial read-through. How determined they are often dictates whether they undertake a second review of the article. Thus, from the writer's perspective, those for and to whom they write are men and women with a purpose. The question, then, is how well the writer helps them meet their goal.

Wrap-Up

Throughout this chapter we have largely treated effective communication and good writing as separate topics. The two, obviously, are linked. Good writing is one aspect of the broader field that is communication. It is also a key component in the field of public relations. The primary focus of this text, of course, is writing, particularly as it applies to writing for a range of aspects of the media. Beginning with the next chapter, we begin focusing more on writing, its historical evolution, the mechanics of it, the legal challenges of which you must be aware if you choose to do it professionally, and how it relates to specific parts of the media, including the Internet, journalism, advertising, and public relations. What we touched on in this chapter, however, was important, as it places writing in context of the overall field of communication.

Effective communication is glue that helps keep societies and even individuals connected as they strive to address their own challenges and fulfill their own dreams. No one person has all the answers to everything. Yet it is communication that provides them with access to finding answers and/or resources that will help them face what they do not know. In addition, it is the communicator who is a vital part of this mix. This person helps present or showcase information in ways that others can easily access and understand. If a person is thirsty, often there is someone to hand her a drink of water. This is what communicators do when it comes to information. People have needs, and communicators help make it possible for them to get their needs met. Thus, while communication may be the glue, the communicator is the one who makes the application of it both possible and doable. How well things are written makes that all the more easy. To help drive these points home, at the conclusion of this chapter are several publications of interest that we recommend for your review.

Reading List

Though there have been many examples of effective communication and good writing throughout the history of mankind, really is there such an action of communication that is as embraced as heartily by society as a well-delivered act of written communication? Whether it comes in the form of the spoken or written word, it nonetheless is a deed with which people resonate. The act of communicating effectively carries with it the potential to inspire, dominate attention, and trigger action. It can and often does change thought and even behavior, sometimes permanently. The following publications address aspects of written communication as it stands today:

The State of English

By Wynford Hicks

Since the second edition of *English for Journalists* was published in 1998 there has been more public discussion about the state of the language than ever before. Newspaper and magazine articles, TV and radio programmes, website messages and individual emails pour forth an endless stream of information, comment and jokes about English.

Some newspapers now publish editions of their style guides on their websites as well as in book form. The *Guardian* has also published several highly entertaining collections of its corrected mistakes, particularly of English usage, with commentary by its readers' editor.

After the runaway success of *Eats, Shoots & Leaves* by Lynne Truss, many bookshops established a separate section for language guides and commentaries. Now there's no aspect of English too obscure to have a book devoted to it. Next to the dictionaries, usage handbooks and alphabetical lists of difficult words, there are anthologies of such things as clichés, rhyming slang, modern slang, insulting quotations, euphemisms, language myths ... Anybody looking for entertainment and enlightenment in the English language must surely find it.

But lively debate and spectacular book sales do not add up to a dramatic improvement in national writing ability. Take British university students, for example. The fact is that most of them lack the basic writing skills. This is the shocking but clear message of a report called *Writing Matters* published by the Royal Literary Fund in March 2006. It is based on the experience of 130 writers who worked as RLF fellows in 71 universities, offering students tuition in how to write a letter or an essay, how to draft a report or draw up a job application.

A similar—but wider—message was delivered in March 2003 by Bloomsbury, the publisher of the Encarta Concise Dictionary, who consulted 42 professors or teachers of English in Britain, the US, Canada and Australia. They reported strikingly similar problems among students in the four countries.

The RLF report emphasises that the problems apply across the whole range of ability—'from students aiming for a first to those struggling to avoid a fail'—and afflict those on arts courses as well as scientists. 'What is worrying,' one fellow reported of three particular students, 'is that these young people are students of English literature at an "elite" university. They ought to have attained, by this stage, a reasonably high level of written proficiency but ... they have genuine difficulty in writing a basic English sentence.'

Summarising the report's findings in an article in the *Sunday Times*, the biographer Hilary Spurling writes: 'The students' essays are muddled and clumsily expressed. They don't know where to start, how to organise their subject matter or follow a coherent chain of thought. They suffer, as another fellow succinctly put it, from lexical nullity and syntactical bankruptcy—their stuff is unreadable, and sometimes unintelligible as well.

> Meagre vocabulary, slack phrasing, tortured syntax, incompetent punctuation: these ... mean that teachers in higher education ... spend an increasing amount of their time correcting grammar, spelling and punctuation, and trying to explain how an essay is meant to be structured.

So who and what are to blame? 'Part of the trouble,' Spurling says, 'is that, until they reach university, most young people have never felt any need to write. They belong to a tick-box culture based on speeded-up electronic responses in education as in other fields.' Elsewhere in the *Sunday Times* the columnist Minette Marrin includes ticking boxes as one of a number of educational evils, pointing the finger of blame for students' poor writing skills:

> at bad schools, at bad teaching, at the shortage of able teachers now that able women have many other opportunities besides teaching, at failed methods of teaching reading, at child-centred learning and other disastrous educational orthodoxies, at the abandonment of grammar and learning by heart, at the distractions of computers, at tick-boxes and coursework, which encourage laziness and internet plagiarism.

To which could be added, surely, the bad example provided by much of the media. Just as journalism students are not immune from the general weakness in writing, so the practice of a newspaper like the *Sunday Times* can be said to be part of the problem. Mistakes of grammar, spelling and punctuation, peculiar vocabulary and clumsy constructions undermine attempts made elsewhere to raise standards—and certainly reduce the impact of those why-oh-why columns on students' terrible English.

How about this from the edition of the *Sunday Times* (26 March 2006) that reported on *Writing Matters*?

> I'm a great fan of the chef, John Williams, who once graced Claridge's. Which has been semi-desecrated. Although I dropped in recently and their Gordon Ramsay restaurant was very busy.

This is so bad it's stretching a point to call it writing at all. What was that about 'a basic English sentence'?

There's no attempt at construction here. The writer, Michael Winner, just plonks his thoughts down as they occur to him. And he keeps on doing it, scattering full stops like confetti:

> I've lost two and a half stone. I decline to use kilograms. Foreign muck. The vegetables were perfect. Even though they didn't have fresh peas.

The failure to write coherently in sentences is one of the most common faults in modern journalism. Another is the perverse use of language: how can Claridge's be 'semi-desecrated'? Either something is desecrated or it isn't. Yet another common fault is grammatical confusion between singular and plural. Describing Claridge's, Winner lurches from the singular ('*has* been semi-desecrated') to the plural ('and *their* Gordon Ramsay restaurant').

As well as mismatches of singular and plural, the *Sunday Times* of 26 March 2006 includes several dangling modifiers, such as this one in a reader's letter:

> Several years ago, while on a sightseeing pony and trap around New Orleans, the driver pointed out a large building which he told us was the House of the Rising Sun.

Is the driver sightseeing? No, it's the reader. And in the next example (from a political gossip column) money can't be 'like marriages':

> Like most rocky marriages, money is the problem.

Journalistic writing is increasingly informal, colloquial and so has a tendency to become ungrammatical. Here's another example of bad grammar (from a different gossip column):

> It is sad when streets—with the possible exception of Hogarth's Gin Lane—lose old associations; but as us scruffs learnt leaving Fleet Street, it can be a liberation ...

'Us scruffs' is wrong, ugly and, I think, pretentious. Are we scruffs trying to pretend we're proles not toffs? Anyway what's an expression like this doing in an edition of the *Sunday Times* that preaches the need to write well?

By contrast with what we might call the Michael Winner school of journalism, there are stylish writers who occasionally lapse. Simon Jenkins, a past editor of the *Times* and the London *Evening Standard*, has a column and a book review in the *Sunday Times* of 26 March 2006. In the column, about Tony Blair's foreign policy, he writes:

> Blair's attempt to bond Al-Qaeda, Saddam Hussein, Iran's mullahs, the Taliban and Hamas into some giant global conspiracy is both inaccurate and distorts coherent strategy.

The problem here is that with the emphatic expression 'both ... and ... ' the two phrases that follow must be grammatically equivalent, so to be correct, you would need something like:

> Blair's attempt ... is both inaccurate and a distortion of coherent strategy./Blair's attempt ... both is inaccurate and distorts coherent strategy.

The first alternative replaces a verb by a noun (usually a bad idea); the second sounds clumsy. There's a third option: lose the 'both' altogether.

The Jenkins book review includes a mistake that is increasingly common in words taken from French (other examples are émigré and pâté): 'résumé' meaning summary appears with only one of its accents as 'resumé', which is not a word in any language. (To show how difficult it is to get this right, the published version of the *Guardian* style book prescribes rather than proscribes 'resumé', though the error has been corrected in the website version.)

Hyphens are another problem area. While some writers omit essential ones, others put them in where they have no possible function, after an '-ly' adverb, as in:

> Bennett was poached from the Canberra Raiders to be appointed the first coach of the newly-formed Brisbane Broncos in 1988 ...

But the *Sunday Times* writer responsible for the redundant hyphen is in prestigious company. The 2003 edition of the Collins English Dictionary includes an unnecessary hyphen after an '-ly' adverb in its entry for 'pharming', which is quoted on the dust jacket:

> the practice of rearing or growing genetically-modified animals or plants in order to develop pharmaceutical products.

This is clearly a mistake rather than conscious policy for elsewhere in Collins, in the entry for 'genetically modified' for example, there are no hyphens; the example given is *genetically modified food.*

These are symptoms of a general malaise in publishing: book reviewers often complain about poor standards of editing and proofreading. But then there are those who say, about the state of English, 'Crisis? What crisis?' and attack the whole notion of correctness. The radicals, who tend to be academics in university departments of linguistics, say that standard English is only one dialect among many and should not necessarily be preferred to the others (for a fuller account of their position, see the introduction to my book *Quite Literally*). Their influence on public policy and the teaching of English—via the colleges of education where their views have been dominant—has been profound, extensive and malign.

But the popularity of *Eats, Shoots & Leaves* has undermined their position—and they seem to be aware of it. In a recent book called *How Language Works* David Crystal, a former professor of linguistics at Reading University, launches a wild attack on the presumption of prescriptive conservatives like Lynne Truss:

> Believing in the inviolability of the small set of rules that they have managed themselves to acquire, they condemn others from a different dialect background, or who have not had the same educational opportunities as themselves, for not following those same rules. Enthused by the Stalinesque policing metaphor, they advocate a policy of zero tolerance, to eradicate all traces of the aberrant behaviour. This extreme attitude would be condemned by most people if it were encountered in relation to such

> domains as gender or race, but for some reason it is tolerated in relation to language. Welcomed, even, judging by the phenomenal sales of *Eats, Shoots & Leaves*.

This is strong stuff from academe. Admittedly, the phrase 'zero tolerance' itself is pretty strong—and it does appear in the subtitle to Truss's book. But in fact her tone is more wry and whimsical than 'Stalinesque', which is one of the reasons why she has been so successful. Early on, she claims that she is not setting out to instruct about punctuation—'there are already umpteen excellent punctuation guides on the market'—and she often expresses doubt, even confusion, on particular points.

For example, she says that 'one shouldn't be too rigid about the Oxford comma' (sometimes it's a good idea; sometimes not). She concedes that hyphen usage is 'just a big bloody mess and is likely to get messier'. And on whether the possessive of names ending in 's' should have a second 's' (Truss' or Truss's), she says: 'There are no absolute rights and wrongs in this matter.'

She even says that St Thomas's Hospital in south London can make up its own mind whether it wants people to add the extra 's' or not. Well, no, I don't think it can: here Truss is being too tolerant. The sound argument (in every sense) is that where the extra 's' is sounded in speech, it should be included in writing. Because we say 'St *Thomas's*', I think we should write it.

But of course she is quite right to point out that the experts disagree on aspects of usage, particularly punctuation and grammar. Also, some words can be correctly spelt (or should that be spelled?) in more than one way and others create a problem because they mean different things to different people. This strengthens the argument for newspapers and magazines to decide on a house style to avoid irritating inconsistency.

House style can include everything from minor detail—whether to use single quotes or double, when to use italics—to major policy on things like four-letter words and political correctness. Published and internet style books also provide a very useful commentary on changing English usage.

For example, both the *Times* (online) and the *Economist* (published book) disagree with the *Guardian* (online and published) on accents. They both say we should keep accents, eg on café, cliché and communiqué, when they make a crucial difference to pronunciation.

The *Times* is pretty prescriptive about none, which 'almost always takes the singular verb', while the *Economist* is more relaxed: none 'usually takes a singular verb'. But the *Guardian*, which used to insist on it, now says: 'It is a (very persistent) myth that "none" has to take a singular verb.'

By contrast, on 'like' and 'such as', it is the *Economist* that now takes the liberal position. Whereas the *Guardian* and the *Times* still disapprove, the *Economist* bites the bullet: 'Authorities like Fowler and Gowers is an acceptable alternative to authorities such as Fowler and Gowers.'

I agree with the liberal view on both points. The entry on 'like' and 'such as ' has been changed in this edition of *English for Journalists*, as have the entries on 'hopefully', 'that' and 'which' and several others. A new entry, 'One word not two', includes examples like 'subeditor' and 'underway' and there are numerous additions and amendments.

The biggest change in this edition is to include many more examples of published mistakes to illustrate the points made. The general policy remains what it has always been: to promote a standard, but not stuffy, English.

Public Relations Writing Worktext: Preface

By Joseph Zappala and Ann Carden

About the Book

What's been happening in public relations since the last edition of our book in 2004? That's a question we had to answer as we began work last year on the third edition, now titled *Public Relations Writing Worktext.* Of course, technology has continued to have an impact, with the explosion of digital, new, and social media. The strategic role that public relations plays in organizations also keeps evolving. But one thing remains constant—the need for public relations professionals to write well. And that remains at the core of our book. In fact, in this edition, we've made some changes that put even greater focus on writing and the writing process.

The third edition of the book has the same "how-to" format we've been using in the past two editions: introductory text that explains the subject in an easy-to-understand, practical way, along with examples of professionally written materials and a variety of assignments that give students hands-on experience writing public relations materials that are used in practice today. This format seems to work; faculty members and students, as well as professionals using the book as a refresher or reference, tell us that the worktext is a great learning tool and resource. You'll also see changes that we believe make the third edition even stronger:

- expanded text sections with more detailed content on subjects such as research, planning, sales letters, proposals, advocacy writing, and legal considerations;
- more focus on writing for the Web, blogs, and electronic media, including information on writing social media releases and a new chapter entitled "Web Sites and Social Media";
- a new planning outline to help writers develop more effective messages;
- expanded checklists for writers to reference when working on assignments—one of the most popular features in the second edition;
- more and updated examples and reprints of effective public relations writing by leading companies in a variety of organizational settings, including Travelers, UPS, Burger King, Xerox, Frito-Lay, and many more;
- restructured content for better writing flow and consistency;
- new assignments based on topics, issues, and problems that public relations professionals in all sectors might find themselves facing today.

The parts of the book have been restructured to better reflect the public relations process:

Part One provides an "An Introduction to the Basics." Chapter 1 includes information on public relations as compared to marketing and advertising and introduces the different forms of public relations writing, as well as the concepts of communication and persuasion. Chapter 2 focuses on the basics of writing—spelling, punctuation, grammar, and style—as well as ethical and legal considerations. Chapter 3 introduces the four-step public relations process.

Part Two focuses on research. Chapter 4 reviews the importance of research and the various methods used.

Part Three provides an overview of the planning process. Chapter 5 includes a detailed look at developing public relations messages.

Part Four provides in-depth information on the various writing formats and techniques used in implementing strategic public relations plans, from news releases (chapter 6) and features (chapter 8) to business correspondence (chapter 10) and promotional publications (chapter 13).

Part Five completes the public relations process with a comprehensive look at evaluation methods in chapter 14.

Our Vision

This book provides students with the fundamental knowledge required for public relations writing, as well as the critical writing practice they need, allowing them to make mistakes in the classroom and receive feedback on written pieces before they enter a professional setting. Without this experience, students will have difficulty succeeding in field assignments and in that first job. Internship supervisors and employers want students and graduates who can "hit the ground running," and that means having the ability to write a variety of public relations materials competently and with minimal direction. We think this book will give students basic writing preparation to get started in their careers and be a useful resource "down the road" when they need a refresher on some aspect of public relations writing.

Although this book is primarily targeted to college students, we kept another audience in mind while preparing the text—the many people who, with little or no training, have found themselves in the position of performing public relations tasks. Before organizations make the decision to hire a public relations practitioner, they often turn to other people within the organization to write a news release, design a flier, or plan a special event. Nonprofit organizations often ask volunteers to complete public relations tasks. Although we do not suggest that this book replaces proper training in the field, it is hoped that it will provide some professional guidance to people who find themselves in these situations.

Acknowledgments

No book is assembled by the authors alone. There are many people involved in the writing process from beginning to end, and many people to thank for their contributions.

We are grateful to NTC/Contemporary Publishing Company and Lawrence Erlbaum Associates, Inc., who published the first two editions of the book, our new publisher, Routledge, of the Taylor & Francis Group, for seeing the value of publishing a third edition; to our editor, Linda Bathgate, for her direction and flexibility; and to other members of the publishing team at Routledge, including Katherine Ghezzi, Senior Editorial Assistant and Gail Newton, Production Editor; to Louise Smith, our capable copy-editor; and the production house, Florence Production

Ltd, where Senior Project Manager Fiona Isaac oversaw the production process that made this book a reality.

We are grateful for the time and comments of practitioners and educators throughout the country who generously agreed to review the proposal for the third edition.

We recognize the contributions of the many practitioners and educators who have developed, and continue to develop, a body of knowledge for public relations through books of their own, other publications, research, and practice. Their work, listed under "References and Suggested Reading" following each chapter, serves as a basis of this text as well as future works in the field of public relations.

This edition of *Public Relations Writing Worktext* includes dozens of excellent, and often award-winning, examples and reprints from leading companies. We thank these companies for providing access to their work and for their willingness to share.

Of course, there would be no book at all without readers. We are grateful to the instructors who selected the first and second editions of *Public Relations Writing Worktext* for use in their classrooms and expressed interest in a third edition. We appreciate their confidence in the material presented in the text and thank them, as well as future instructors and students, who will use the book.

On a Personal Note ...

Some years ago, when I was teaching full time at Utica College of Syracuse University, I began work on the second edition of our book. After completing the manuscript, I was faced with "publisher limbo." The original publisher decided to sell its college text division, and it was unclear if the second edition would find a publishing home.

When I finally learned, almost two years later, that a publisher had purchased the rights to this book, it was truly a day of celebration. At that same time, I made a major life and career change. After 13 years as a college professor, I decided to return to practice and accepted a position as a senior communications professional with Cornell University. When it came time to revisit the book and get the second edition completed, I have to admit, I started to panic, just a little. Working 50+ hours a week, plus juggling other commitments, I knew this would be an almost impossible task on my own. Fortunately, some colleagues connected me with Ann R. Carden, and here we are, now having finished our third edition. It has been interesting to complete the second, and now third, edition of the book as a practitioner, as I apply concepts shared in the book each and every day on the job—whether I am writing a high-level senior management correspondence, consulting with staff on Web and social media strategy and content, or working on a communications plan.

There are several people I need to acknowledge and whose guidance and support made it possible for me to complete this project. First, legendary PR educator Ray Simon, someone to whom I owe a debt of gratitude. When Ray asked me to assist him with the first edition, I was deeply honored, and a little scared. But his confidence in me made a huge difference, and I am thankful to him for all he did for me, both as a mentor and a friend. To this day, Ray's influence and his wise advice continue to shape my work as a professional and the way in which I relate to people and solve problems. I'm lucky that I had the chance to learn from him during my time at UC.

My co-author, Ann R. Carden, is an outstanding collaborator. There were many times that I lagged behind on a deadline, or when the demands of my job made it difficult to focus on the book. Ann was always there to keep the project on track and to pick up the slack when things got a bit crazy on my end, without complaint. This is the best possible co-author relationship, working with someone who has been successful in the field, but who also knows "what works" in the classroom right now. I couldn't ask for a better writing partner.

I also want to thank my former colleagues at Utica College, especially Kim Landon and Cecilia Friend, who saw me through both the first edition and the first draft of the second edition, and whose friendship meant a lot to me during those Utica years. I miss seeing them every day. And, of course, my thanks goes to all the students I have taught over the years, some of whom still keep in touch with me and still insist on calling me "professor." (At this point in time, I let them know that "Joe" is just fine.) I learned a lot from my students, both inside and outside the classroom. I hope this book proves to be a useful learning tool for the next generation of public relations students.

Finally, I want say thanks to my family and my parents for all their support through the years and three editions. I'd like to dedicate the book to them, and to my partner who saw me through many evenings and weekends trying to get this project done. He showed great patience and understanding when I had to devote "us" time to work on the book, and when stress levels got a bit high. Thanks, Billy. Much love to you and Olivia!

—J.Z.

I would not be writing this section had it not been for my co-author, Joseph M. Zappala, who graciously invited—with only a reference from a mutual friend to go on—a stranger to help with the second, and now third, edition of his textbook. Thank you, Joe, for your confidence in me and especially for your willingness to let me be a full partner in the writing process, which can be a deeply personal thing for the original author. While my co-author was leaving academe to return to the professional world, I was leaving daily practice to enter academe—and much has changed in the field since then! Joe was instrumental in making sure this edition included the most up-to-date and realistic information for today's public relations students and practitioners.

It has been my lifelong dream to teach at the college level and to someday publish a writing text. Knowing how important writing is to the practice of public relations, I wanted to do my part to ensure that future public relations practitioners developed strong writing skills. It is an area I'm passionate about, to which my students, both former and present, will attest. I thank them for letting me know (eventually) that, although I demanded much from them and made grade deductions for misspellings and poor grammar, they are now better writers.

My deep appreciation goes to my faculty colleagues in the Department of Communication at the State University of New York at Fredonia, who always expressed an interest in how the book was going, even though they must have gotten tired of my frenzied "I'm on deadline!" banter. Thank you for your support and indulgence.

My path to this point is the culmination of varied experiences and many influences along the way, and it is my honor to acknowledge them, beginning with my high school English teacher who talked me out of studying nursing in college because she thought I had a talent for writing. My thoughts on the practice of public relations have been honed through the years by every organization for which I have worked, by each co-worker in those organizations, and especially others in the public relations field. Whether it was a formal presentation, casual conversation, or a discussion over lunch (and there were many of those), I have learned much from my colleagues and am grateful to the members of the Buffalo/Niagara chapter of the Public Relations Society of America for sharing their expertise. Special thanks go to Ronald D. Smith, APR; Stanton H. Hudson, Jr., APR, Fellow PRSA; Donald J. Goralski, APR; and Bill Sledzik, APR, Fellow PRSA.

Lastly, I dedicate this book to my family and friends, who have been so supportive during a time of great transition in my life, and especially to my father, T. Guy Reynolds Jr., who instilled in me a strong work ethic, a thirst for knowledge, the belief that job satisfaction comes before money, and the attitude that there wasn't anything I couldn't do—all attributes that allowed me to stretch my wings and try new things; my sister, Vanda White, who has shown me what faith and courage really look like; and, my children, Maggie and Stephen. I love you and am so proud of the adults you have become.

—A.R.C.

An Invitation

A textbook is much like a snapshot in time. Different trends develop, theories evolve, and new case studies are introduced almost as soon as the book is published. With this in mind, we encourage our readers to provide us with feedback on the text so we may continue to develop it into a useful tool in the future. Please send your comments to:

Joseph M. Zappala, APR
Chief Communications Officer
ILR School
Cornell University
403 Dolgen Hall
Ithaca, NY 14850
jz76@cornell.edu

Ann R. Carden, APR, Fellow PRSA
Associate Professor
Communication
SUNY Fredonia
304 McEwen Hall
Fredonia, NY 14063
ann.carden@fredonia.edu

Chapter Highlights

- Effective communication is defined as the act of successfully exchanging messages and/or information with another person.
- Good writing is defined as written communication that consists of interesting ideas that are well organized and told in a voice unique to the writer, and that follows the conventional parameters of basic and proper grammar.
- The Shannon-Weaver model of communication illustrates the fundamental process or flow of communication.
- Three key points to good writing are that, as a writer, you should know what you are writing about, know who you are writing for, and know what it is you want to say.
- In the communication process, the sender and receiver of messages/information are of equal importance.
- The six categories of barriers to communication are exposure, nature of media, nature of message, nature of audience, audience attitude, and competition/opposition. The "five rights" are an effective way to overcome barriers. They are right people, channel, time, message, and words.
- Key personality traits for those who write professionally include having courage, perseverance, a sense of humor, self-confidence, and ambition.

For Discussion

1. Discuss the definitions of effective communication and good writing as provided in the text. Do you agree with them? Come up with your own and compare/contrast yours with those in the text.
2. What can communicators do to help ensure that those who send and receive messages/information play equal roles in the communication process?
3. We have listed several personality traits that good writers should possess. Do you agree with them? What others would you add to the list?
4. We have discussed how difficult it is for communicators to succeed each time they launch a campaign or outreach effort. Does this apply to your own personal life? Generally, do you feel that your communication efforts go over well with friends, family, coworkers, and others? Why/why not?
5. Do you believe that those who write well should be avid readers? Why or why not?

ii

Getting from Here to There: The Evolution of Communication and Writing

Rarely is the journey from a beginning to an end totally smooth or without unexpected turns and detours. This is especially true when the journey involves multiple travelers and success on advancement is linked to others. Such has been and continues to be the case of communication and a key element of it: writing. Communication, generally, has existed as long as mankind. Writing as a means to share information and exchange messages is, of course, not as old but close to it. With the exception of language, its length of existence as a means of communication exceeds all others. This chapter is not meant to provide a definitive history of communication or writing. Rather, we will provide a broad outline of their evolution, yet in a way that revolves around the purpose of each. As part of this, we will highlight the merging purposes of public relations and the role writers and writing play in helping them be fulfilled. This will include highlighting several notable events in history and a few key individuals and communication models and theories that, collectively, have contributed to the growth of communication and writing. In this journey, among the points we will be raising and attempting to address are differences between communication and writing at their beginning stages and today; whether these differences suggest improvement or simple change; differences, if any, between the challenges faced historically by communicators versus ones faced in current times; and future trends for professional communicators, in general, and those in the industry whose specialty is writing.

Both communication and writing are more than physical acts. For all of us, behind them are our ongoing efforts to address the psychological needs that propel all of us every day. This chapter, in addition to the above-mentioned objectives, will touch on the acts themselves as well as the forces behind them. Our purpose here is to provide students of communication and prospective professional communicators with a greater appreciation of what it is they will be doing throughout their academic pursuits and professional lives. For instance, when one sits down to write a press release announcing a new speaker's series, this action has more to it than simply the release itself. There is also what is motivating the series' sponsors to arrange it in the first place and the role these events play in helping the sponsors meet their basic needs as individuals, members of society, and business or social activists. For communicators, then, each action taken has more depth and unseen background than others might realize. This chapter will hopefully shed light on this reality and help provide prospective professional communicators with greater insight into just how important their role and duties are.

One final but related introductory point: in the eighteenth century, Sir Isaac Newton put forth a pronouncement he called laws of motion. The most famous of these laws stated that for every action, there is an equal and opposite reaction. Newton's vision has direct relevance to communication. Communication is never without purpose. This even applies to that person who we believe "talks for the sake of talking" or "loves the sound of her own voice." Though they may not have anything new to add to a conversation, this person speaks because it gives her a sense of esteem, a need we noted earlier that all of us share (Maslow, 1954). Also, every time we communicate—and, make no mistake, we do so all the time—it has impact. Whether what we communicate triggers laughter, eye rolls, anger, or some type of action, it affects others—even temporarily. We mention this to drive home the notion that there is no such thing as a superfluous act of communication. We speak and others hear, and for those moments they think about what we have just said. We write and others read and assess our words. We act and others react, either by moving out of the way, joining in our action, or continuing with their own actions. To paraphrase Newton, for every act of communication, there is a reaction. This, then, is the physics of communication, and it is a reality that pertains to everything professionals and even nonprofessionals do.

The Four Purposes

In the beginning days of communication, the primary purposes of this act stepped front and center almost immediately. They were as follows: share information, dialogue, persuade, and achieve collaboration. (Authors' note: One can easily argue that these purposes remain the key driving points today as well.) Communication, including writing, is not an act of isolation. You may respond to this by pointing out that often when you write, you do so in the privacy of your room. Even texting, to cite another example you might give, is often another act of isolation. Our response is not to argue that point. After all, much of this text was written in an equally quiet setting. Instead, we note that the purpose behind writing in those quiet settings falls under the heading of outreach. You write in your room to eventually share your thoughts, insight, and so forth with others. The text messages you compose are for others. This text also is for others. Thus, the composition phase of this act may have occurred without others present, but its final destination was and is for public consumption. Many of us might get dressed each morning without others present, yet we do so with the expectation, hope, or distinct possibility that others at some point during the day will see what we are wearing.

Also, there is the comment by some that at times they write only for themselves. For instance, many people at some point in their lives maintain a private journal or diary. They put pen to paper for no one but themselves. Never mind that invariably others either eventually see these writings anyway or, if not, are given hints as to what they are by the writer himself or herself. We are, after all, social beings. Remember: as we learned from Maslow, one of the needs that drives us is to gain acceptance. Part of achieving this end is self-disclosure. Again, our response is not to take issue with this point. Instead, it is to note that even such acts of isolation carried out are done so with others in mind. Thus, one who writes in isolation does so only in a physical sense. His or her thoughts, no matter how intimate, are in the context of others.

So, we proceed with our overview of the histories of communication and writing in the context of the four driving purposes of each. Our goal in what may seem like an odd approach to giving a history of something is to reinforce the notion that communication has always been and forever will be an intricate part of our fabric as living beings. Such a reality in terms of choices we have made over the years about how and why to communicate have not necessarily been ones we have made arbitrarily. Rather, they were and are driven by our very nature.

Share Information

Historians have traced the earliest uses of script back to 3200 BC, in the form of pictographic or syllabic systems as utilized by the ancient Egyptians and Chinese to a more phonetic one as adopted by various groups in Phoenicia and Palestine (Houston, 2004). Such phases or development stages as picture writing systems, a transitional system, and even a phonetic system in which early writers attempted to share information by illustrating words, symbols, and even sounds were part of the early years of writing as well. These represented the beginning of the effort to pass along or share information with others. Cave paintings, which we associate with early man, are estimated to have started around 30,000 BC. Other highlights in the early phases of writing include the first recorded use of homing pigeons to send messages in 776 BC; the first wooden printing presses invented in China in 305,AD in which symbols were carved on a wooden block; the first movable type, also invented in China; and the start of newspapers in Europe in 1450.

All these are interesting tidbits when it comes to looking at those early periods in the evolution of communication. As is the case today, of course, the primary currency in the more formalized form of communication known as writing was information. Perhaps more true back then than today, however, was the fact that information was more than simply a means by which to accumulate knowledge. Information was a form of power. Few people had access to it. This did not include the general masses but primarily only the wealthy and politically influential (Bernstein, 2013). Because of this, the powerful were able to maintain their high positions more easily as information and dictums they did share or hand down were accepted more readily and without challenge by the general masses, mainly because of the knowledge gap. People simply did not know as much as those of greater wealth and influence. Therefore, many of these so-called top-tier individuals were taken at their word no matter what they were sharing with those with lower socioeconomic status.

What books were written back then took months to reproduce and circulate, as they had to be copied by a single scribe (Drower, 1985). The result was that literacy outside the doors of the well-to-do was rare indeed. This is not to say that the masses were ignorant. Rather, they were simply devoid of information, certainly information the rich had on such topics as science, the arts, politics, philosophy, and religion. Thus, one of the significant results of the invention of the printing press in 1455 by Johannes Gutenberg (his used metal movable type) was that it did much to, in a sense, even the playing field when it came to information access. Suddenly, the powerful and influential could not count on the public's accepting whatever they had to say. There was now a real possibility that the keepers of information might be challenged or questioned. Plus, information could now be disseminated much more quickly and on a much wider scale than ever before. Thanks to Gutenberg, it was a new day for the sharing of information and those whose specialty it was to share and shape it.

This, of course, is not to suggest that upon Gutenberg's invention a great light shone down on the world and all wrongs were righted in the name of openness and transparency. Obviously, this was not the case. Nevertheless, the significance of the printing press cannot and should not be underestimated or treated lightly. What belonged to a few suddenly became available to many. For the first time the power of information, an element of communication without bias, preference, or hidden agendas, was raised to its full height. In the field of communication, in particular, it was a game changer.

At the same time, with its increased availability, what could be termed the battle over information took a new turn that, in many ways, continues to this day with a greater intensity than ever. Should all information be made public? If not, which information should be kept under lock and key? Who should have access to it? Regarding public information, how should it be disseminated to the public? Who should be responsible for ensuring that it is part of the public domain? Out of the debates regarding these and other pertinent questions, the role of the communicator was born. In the more than six hundred years since the printing press was invented, that role has taken various forms but also has continued to grow and be recognized as being vital to the matter of information and well-being of society. This truism is a key reason why this discussion on communication's history and its overriding purposes is germane to communicators and writers of today. They are part of a longstanding debate and challenge faced by governments and citizens throughout the world. Thus, to reinforce an earlier point, what may seem like a simple writing assignment is actually an opportunity to place one more rung onto a continuum of determining how best information fits into society and the most effective way in which to share it.

When a family plans a vacation, one of the first questions they ask is what the best way is to reach their desired destination. Who provides that information? While their neighbor may be the one who gives them direction, you can bet that at some point information was provided by a communicator. Furthermore, in all likelihood information was made available in written form. When other neighbors argue what was the best baseball team of all time, they turn to information that was gathered and made accessible by a communicator. The point is that writers are key caretakers and gatekeepers of information in ways that affect the day-to-day lives of those who are not necessarily in positions of power or influence.

In public relations, one of the early and more important proponents of information was Ivy Lee. A former journalist, Lee also was called the "father of public relations" by some. He came into prominence in the early twentieth century while working for the Rockefeller family. Unlike Edward Bernays, who was also given that title, Lee's feeling about information was different from Bernays's. Lee, in essence, believed that information should not be withheld from the public. It should be shared without interference, manipulation, shading, or any kind of editorializing. The public, Lee said, could and should be trusted to make a fair determination or assessment of information. While handling what was a dicey situation for the Rockefellers, Lee put into practice the tenants of the Declaration of Principles he had produced in 1906.

The circumstance revolved around the infamous Ludlow Massacre of 1914. Basically, men working for John D. Rockefeller went on strike to protest low pay and poor working conditions. Shortly afterward, members of the Colorado National Guard were called in to ensure that the strikers did not get out of hand in their protest. Guard members fired on the strikers. It led to the deaths of men, women, and children and triggered the killing of even more people .The public was outraged at what happened and held Rockefeller responsible. Lee was called in to help field media inquiries and calm the public outrage. As he done before in other situations, Lee worked closely with the media, providing them with key information in a timely manner. Lee's perspective and actions played important roles in transforming how practitioners were perceived. Many stopped seeing them as mere press agents or mouthpieces. Instead, these practitioners began to be viewed as important counselors who provided clients with guidance on all matters relating to communication.

Dialogue

Everybody talks with everybody. Right? We pass others on the street and smile "hello." We tell the person at the box office window how many tickets we want. We check our Facebook status and pass along information about ourselves and even toss out a comment or two to people we know about a party they recently attended or trip from which they just returned. As the day moves along, we make a few phone calls and chat with friends for a while. These and tons of other examples we could list are cases of typical encounters with family, friends, and acquaintances face to face, online, or on the air waves. They add up to nearly a full day of dialogue. These oral or written interactions reinforce our need and even desire to remain connected and, thus, ensure the acceptance we receive from those who know us on some level. Though none of these examples may seem all that vital or meaningful, each serves a purpose to satisfy our need for social membership and belonging. However, do these brushes with others represent the kind of dialogue that provides substance to, say, a public relations campaign? Not necessarily. At the same time, they do serve as examples of ongoing dialogues that we have each day, some of which are carried out in written form.

Nearly a half-century ago, noted entomologist Edward O. Wilson made waves when he theorized that human behavior is tied more to genes than it is to learned behavior. Much more recently, Wilson gained more attention when he said that there are rival forces within all humans that drive their behavior: group selection and individual selection (French, 2011)—march to the beat of one's own drummer, or be part of the group? What appear to be opposite forces are actually no different from Maslow's needs that we outlined earlier. We want esteem and want to be accepted. Can we do both? Can we strive to do our own "thing" while we try to receive nods of approval from others? The answer, of course, is "yes." When people start their own business, for example, they are definitely traveling on their own path. At the same time, their goal in doing this is to gain the acceptance of others in the hope that they will support this business in a manner that brings profit and even prestige to the venture.

How does this apply to communication and public relations, specifically to writing? Furthermore, why should writers even be concerned with these opposite forces within each of us? After all, the writer might wonder, "All I want to do is send out this media advisory. I don't see how this so-called individual selection versus group selection battle is even relevant." That is certainly a good and understandable point to raise. Several times in this text thus far we have alluded to the importance of knowing one's audience. If public relations practitioners, regardless of the form of communication they use, are going to connect with targeted publics or audiences in any kind of meaningful and lasting way, they must develop a thorough knowledge base and understanding of that group. The more communicators know, the better they will be able to craft messages and compose copy that speaks directly to the questions, wishes, needs, hopes, and so forth of the audience. This applies to media advisories as well as to paid advertisements and other outlets for which communicators will be expected to write. Thus, if you know what the audience's aspirations might be as well as the publics to which they align themselves, in your possession are some valuable pieces of information that should help you communicate more effectively either in writing or in some other format.

It is not uncommon, of course, for the goal of a public relations campaign or effort to be to trigger some action on the part of a public. Whether you want them to vote for your candidate or run right down and take advantage of the two-for-one sale of mattresses, your goal often is to ignite some type of action or response in the public. The fact is, however, that people will be reluctant to respond at all unless they have some degree of confidence in you, the sender of information, and trust you and what you represent. Also, on some level, they need to believe that you have their interests at heart. The first step toward instilling this belief in them is making the effort to do research and learn about them as individuals. This better enables you to make the targeted audience feel as if you are speaking directly to them. Part of "them," of course, is this group selection–individual selection dynamic that helps shape the choices your audience or public might make. Being aware of this internal debate helps you, the writer, compose your text. In the case of a mattress sale, a writer might highlight the sale that "everyone" is taking advantage of while emphasizing how these mattresses can help individuals sleep more comfortably at night.

Oftentimes, research includes entering into a dialogue with select or representative members of a population. One popular way of doing this is forming focus groups to gain a sense of what is on the mind of the very people with whom you wish to connect. Such a format requires that you, the communicator, who will in all likelihood be writing about what it is that these people might say, talk with and not at them. Meaningful dialogue is the key. We all know this regarding our personal lives. None of us enjoy being with people who do little or nothing but talk about themselves. On the surface, there appears to be little difference between this and when we are reached out to by companies or organizations. Who are they? What do they want? Do they even care about me? It is the challenge of the communicator to answer each of those vital questions in a manner that assures members of the public that while you have your own goals, you want to benefit each member of the public as well.

Meaningful dialogue with various public is not easy. As we know this to be true in our personal lives, we also know that trying to establish some type of level of comfort or trust within groups of people is also a challenge. It requires time, resources (which include a budget), commitment, and set goals that you, the communicator, wish to achieve in your interactions with these prospective customers or supporters. Establishing and maintaining such a dialogue requires a certain level of competence or, as Spitzberg and Cupach called it, "communication competence" (1984). These scholars defined this as the ability to interact well with others. Ingredients for success, they noted, include accuracy, clarity, comprehensibility, coherence, expertise, and effectiveness. These elements speak to individuals who happen to bump into each other as well as to organizations seeking to reach out to various publics. Adding to what Spitzberg and Cupach first put forth, Canary and Cody added other criteria to ensure such attempted dialogue: adaptability or flexibility, conversational involvement, conversational management, empathy, effectiveness, and appropriateness (2000). Specifics of these criteria range from being able to adapt to unexpected circumstances that might arise from dialogue and being attentive, exhibiting empathy, and being responsive to being able to control the flow of interaction and having specific goals or objectives for these planned encounters. For professional communicators, communication is a goals-driven act. Writers, note that this definitely applies to the establishment and facilitation of dialogue.

Before leaving this topic, it is important that we take a closer at the public themselves. Basically, there are two broad kinds: groups with a common interests and stakeholders. The conglomerations of folks with a common interest may not necessarily have an interest in the communicator's client. It, of course, is the challenge of the communicator to create one. Stakeholders, on the other hand, do have a vested interest in an organization or client. These people, by definition, are interested in the well-being of the organization and look to the communicator to be kept abreast of the entity's successes and challenges. This applies to you, the writer, not just to the general communicator. Thus, to encapsulate the difference between the two groups: all stakeholder groups are publics, but not all publics are stakeholders (Guth & Marsh, 2009).

Other publics can include the media, various levels of government, multicultural groups, customers or consumers, investors, employees, and businesses. These examples, of course, represent only a tiny fraction of the number of publics that exist or can be created depending on the circumstance. Regardless of the specific public, however, for communicators—and writers in particular—it is most helpful that they develop a good sense of the group's level of influence, how a possible connection or relationship with a client might benefit the group, what the group's demographic is, and what opinion, if any, the public has about the client. Obviously, if the communicator does not know the answer to any of these or related questions, finding them out is part of the goal when initiating a dialogue.

Persuade

All discussions of the beginning days of communication must include Aristotle. This Greek philosopher remains the ultimate communication pioneer. As a result of his vision and insight into how best to communicate with others, Aristotle planted seeds that led to resulted the eventual birth of public relations. Aristotle was an active and strong proponent of communicating with a purpose. Specifically, he claimed that the most effective act of communication resulted in the persuasion of others. As a recognized leader in the art of public debate, Aristotle said that persuasion came in three primary forms: logos (appeals to reason), pathos (appeals to emotions), and ethos (appeals based on personality or character) (Guth & Marsh, 2009). Knowing which form to use at any given time during a speech or debate, Aristotle said, was based on information on the audience as gathered by the speaker. Of the three forms, however, Aristotle identified ethos as being the most powerful. This one, he said, was based on the strength of the communicator's character rather than on just facts or emotions (Aristotle, 1954).

Any communicator, regardless of how she attempts to communicate with others, will attest to the fact that if she lacks credibility, her effectiveness as a communicator is compromised or, in some cases, completely gone. People will tune her out, stop reading what she writes, and move on to other sources of information. Credibility to all communicators is akin to oxygen. Professionally speaking, it is the difference between life and death. Aristotle recognized this immediately. No doubt, it one reason why he was such a firm believer in a values-driven approach to communication. Be honest. If you are recognized as such, audiences or readers will be more likely to listen to what you have to say or read what you have prepared and then give it genuine consideration. Even if they eventually disagree, the audience will continue giving you, the communicator, respect.

Credibility is enhanced by facts and accuracy. Sincerity, of course, is important, but when communicators present certain perspectives and can support their contentions or, in some cases, charges with facts, they are more credible and likely to succeed in triggering change. There are numerous examples of this throughout American history. Two of the more powerful ones are found at the time of the nation's founding and at the beginning of the twentieth century during a period of time known as the Progressive Era (1890–1917). Prior to the formal beginning of the American Revolutionary

War, Thomas Paine wrote *Common Sense*, a pamphlet designed to fire up the colonists to support a movement to break away from England (Salinger, 2010). It proved to be so influential that John Adams later said, "Without the pen of the author of *Common Sense*, the sword of Washington would have been raised in vain" (Adams, 2010). More than one hundred years later, Upton Sinclair exposed the horrors of the meatpacking industry with his novel *The Jungle*. It led to passage of the 1906 Pure Food and Drug Act and Mean Inspection Act (Oursler, 1964).

Following Aristotle's insights, the banner of persuasion as represented by Paine, Lewis, and many others was carried forth. While not all communicators and communication efforts adhered to his call for openness and honesty, many did. Efforts to persuade at times took on characteristics of manipulation and "spin," to coin a current descriptive phrase. A more recent public relations pioneer in the context of persuasion was Edward Bernays. Also called the "father of public relations" by many, Bernays wrote the first textbook on this subject and even taught the first class on it at New York University. One of the first to use the term "public relations," Bernays was a strong proponent of directing the actions of his clients as a way of swaying or influencing public actions and perceptions (O'Neill, 1991).

Throughout much of the twentieth century, a number of communication models and theories were put forth by scholars as a way of providing insight into the workings of communication. Specifically, many focused on why communication was so effective in terms of influencing people. One in particular—the N-Step Theory— recognized the value of opinion leaders. Its author, Wilbur Schramm, opined that making use of people with perceived credibility in various contexts provides much weight in helping sway others to a particular position (Guth & Marsh, 2009). Simple examples of this can be found when writers quote foreign policy experts when discussing international issues or economic experts when discussing financial matters. In our everyday lives, all of us follow this theory. For instance, if we are having car trouble, we often go to a mechanic for guidance, or if we need assistance on purchasing a new home, we often turn to a real estate agent.

Achieve Collaboration

Perhaps the most famous of poet John Donne's works is "No Man Is an Island." The first two lines of this classic are "No man is an island, entire of itself. ... " The poem is worth remembering for many reasons, one of which is its applicability to this final primary purpose of communication. Organizations do not function or exist in a vacuum. Their level of self-sufficiency has limits. This, of course, is also true for individuals. If nothing else, organizations or entities need the public either as a customer base or as users of whatever service they provide. The customers or users enable the organization to make a profit or, if profit is not the motivation, to provide justification for its service. Coinciding with the reality of this need on the organization's part are needs also possessed by those members of the public who utilize the organization. For instance, people like being recognized for the fact that they—the customers or service recipients—play a key role in helping ensure that the organizations are able to exist. This is one reason why many businesses, for example, have sales and customer appreciation days and why writers who work for those businesses make such a big deal out of them.

Given this, the question becomes what role or part can communication writers play in helping ensure that their organization or client is able to establish and maintain a level of collaboration with others? Upon first blush, their role may seem minimal. The fact, however, is that it can be quite significant, depending, of course, on how the public relations team is organized and how duties are assigned. Writers are part of the entity's public relations team. Often they perform other duties as well, including helping facilitate special events, working closely with reporters, and prepping the organization's leaders for press interviews. Even with these and other "duties as assigned," writing in the context of establishing and maintaining positive ties with the public is a key part of their normal workday and workweek. In essence, such a role for the writer falls under the heading of relationship management, an aspect of public relations or communication that has only recently begun to emerge as one vital to the sustained well-being of any organization.

With text messages, social media, and email now a regular part of people's lives, for many established entities or businesses, it is not unusual for them to receive an array of messages from customers, current and prospective, with questions and comments, both positive and negative. By following up on each of these communiqués in a timely and professional manner, writers can do much to help their clients maintain a strong image in the eyes of the public. People want to be heard and feel as if what they do makes at least a tiny difference in their lives and perhaps society's. Consequently, when they send out a message or put an idea in the virtual suggestion box, they do so with the expectation that what they are saying will be read, considered, and possibly implemented. The writer can give them this reassurance. It is the writer—and this includes those public relations practitioners who compose press releases that they feel no one will read, speeches for others that only a few will hear, or tweets whose shelf life is fleeting at best—who, as a result of her talent for putting pen to paper, has much more power than she realizes. This professional, in the words of historian Johannes Janssen, gives "wings to the human mind" (1896).

A listing or even partial listing of avenues by which writers can and do help their organizations or clients maintain viable bridges with their various publics is actually quite impressive. In no particular order, these include blogs, social networks, speeches, email, instant messaging, newsletters, news or press releases, media kits, advertisements, website copy, letters, public service announcements, backgrounders, fact sheets, annual reports, guest editorials, and media pitches. Collectively, all represent avenues by which the public relations representative can reach out and establish connections that might lead to collaboration or active partnerships.

In tapping into these various formats, one of the most challenging aspects of the job of writers is that oftentimes they have to balance the interests of their organization with those of the public (Ledingham, 2006). Such a challenge is as much of a part of a management function as anything else in public relations. Doing so requires being able to assess the cost of community outreach against the benefit of such effort. This type of management function, by definition, places more emphasis on building and maintaining collaborative possibilities than it does on what one might consider to be the more traditional role of public relations professionals: to generate publicity. Doing so involves stressing the potential benefit such a relationship can bring, not just to each partner but to the environment in which they all exist (Dozier, 1995).

In current times, recognizing the benefit being collaborative brings to any entity seems to be a no-brainer. But, actually, such awareness among communication scholars was only a recent occurrence. From a historical perspective, acknowledging the significance of relationships only started picking up steam over the past forty years. Relationships, Ferguson wrote, should be the unit of study of public relations (1984). This emergence has begun to be seen not just in the practice of public relations but also in the classroom where this social science is studied. No longer is public relations being taught only as an act of manipulation or persuasion. Rather, students are learning that it is also one of building, nurturing, and maintaining relationships (Ehling, 1992). This, of course, is a good thing. Not only does it add meaningful depth to the practice of public relations; it also highlights the value of collaboration. By joining forces on issues of mutual interest or concern, for instance, participants are more likely to direct their efforts toward serving the greater good rather than toward just their own interests.

Writers can and do play a key role in this effort. Part of their job is to conduct research on the various issues on which they write. This includes considering when a possible teaming between their client and another organization will occur. Thus, among the areas here that writers can explore are identifying what the two organizations have in common and how they are different, assessing the various publics each currently seeks ties with, and even the degree to which each other's position on a given issue can be predicted (Ledingham, 2001). The more in-depth the research is, obviously the more each partner knows about the other. Ideally, the result is a greater degree of openness and transparency between the two. Furthermore, it suggests a greater flow or exchange of resources and information between the partners. Not only does this level of trust enhance the collaboration; it also greatly improves the chances that such a joining will benefit the surrounding environment.

In communication, perhaps the sign that a particular perspective has achieved a certain level of acceptance is when models or theories begin being attached to it. The growth of relationship management is no exception. One interesting model was one put forth by Broom, Casey, and Ritchey. It stated, in part, that measurement of collaboration should be based on outputs that have the effect of changing the environment and of achieving, maintaining, or even changing the goals outlined by each of the participants in collaboration (Broom, Casey, & Ritchey, 1997). Such openness, as one might guess, is also helpful to the joined entities during times that go beyond the original purpose of their coming together. A time of crisis is an example. Depending on the circumstance, it is conceivable that one or both of the partners might need extra assistance in terms of resources and manpower. Another key element at such a time is information. Each organization may need assistance with supplying its employees as well as its external publics with timely and accurate updates on what is transpiring. Their respective communication teams can do this.

One dramatic example of this occurred in February 2008 at Northern Illinois University (NIU), located in DeKalb. On a quiet afternoon a graduate student walked into one of the institution's largest lecture halls and went on a shooting rampage. He killed five students, wounded eighteen others, and then turned the gun on himself. Word about the mass violence quickly spread, and a great deal of turmoil erupted on campus. A number of the university's partners, including local and state law enforcement officials and even the media, converged on the campus to provide assistance in the areas of security and information to those internal and external to NIU.

The institution's public relations team played a major role in helping respond to inquiries and comments and share information as to what was going on. In addition to the media reps who conducted interviews with reporters, that office's set of writers led the way in gathering and communicating vital pieces of information to the various publics. Later, the Public Relations Society of America recognized NIU's communication team, including its writers, for the effectiveness and quality of their performance during such a traumatic time. It was another example of the importance of information and those who are the providers and explainers of it.

Wrap-Up

One of the many pieces of advice to job seekers that continues to be passed along to those who are either in the market for jobs or looking to move from one they currently have to another is to find a niche and stick with it. Those who write and write well are examples of professionals who will always be needed by any organization, business, association, or company. Their niche is secure. Information is a vital commodity made even more valuable because of the increasingly complex world in which we live. It is an element needed by every aspect of our society. Thus, those who are able to access it and then explain it to others in ways that are accurate, understandable, inspiring, and/or usable are both needed and of high value. Writers are as vital in the field of public relations as are cooks in a kitchen or lifeguards in a public pool. Furthermore, if those same writers are able to help their communication or public relations units fulfill one, all, or several of the primary purposes of their outreach efforts—share information, be heard, persuade, or attain collaboration—their function is even more secure. Yes, companies want to make money, enjoy positive standing within their communities, and have dependable allies. But the reality is they cannot obtain any of these things without a strong public relations team in place. Furthermore, that team cannot perform well without solid writers comprising at least part of the operation.

Each era faces its own set of challenges that are often unique to the time in which they occur. But are they necessarily worse or more difficult than what is faced in other eras? Not necessarily. From the perspective of the writer, one thing different today is that this professional has more outlets through which to perform his or her skill. While we will be discussing this in greater detail in the ensuing chapters, suffice it to say now that never before have both the challenges and opportunities for those who write professionally been greater. Reflecting on his career as a professional communicator, John Echeveste, partner with Valencia, Perez & Echeveste Public Relations, said that one of the top qualities he looks for in rising professionals is their ability to write. "I can't overemphasize the importance of good writing skills," he said (Guth & Marsh, 2009, p. 51). As we have discussed in this chapter, such a reality has evolved from being important to a necessity for individual practitioners and the agencies or teams of which they are part. This is a key lesson provided to us by history as well as valuable insight into the realities of the present and the needs of the future.

Reading List

"You've come along way, baby" has evolved into a well-worn cliché that has been applied to countless topics, entities, and even individuals over the years. If it has not been applied to communication yet, that discipline is now officially the latest to receive this tagline. Communication, under which journalism, public relations, and, by extension, writing falls, has grown tremendously. While each of these off-shoots of communication have also evolved in dramatic ways, their metamorphosis continues and is experienced by millions on virtually a daily basis. It is what makes them so controversial, challenging, and fascinating. Following are articles that touch on pieces of this social science:

Before the Internet: Communications and its regulation through history

By John Mathiason

Before the Internet dominated the global communications system, there had been regulation by international organizations to ensure order in telecommunications and in intellectual property. While the Internet's borderless nature has rendered that old system ineffective, understanding how and why the old system was created can demonstrate why Internet governance is important now.

Communications was one of the first activities to have international regulation. For communications to cross borders, standards were needed and the economics of transnational commerce required agreements. Both were reflected in what is widely considered to be the first universal international organization, the International Telegraph Union (ITU). Then, property transmitted over communications channels also needed to be regulated. But before the Internet the processes, while technically complex, were conceptually simple.

The channel: the early history of international organizations

Although Samuel F. B. Morse had invented the telegraph in 1844, its initial progress was slow because telegraph lines did not run over national boundaries. Each country had different standards and to make the system work smoothly, many countries, especially in Europe, decided to create formal arrangements to facilitate interconnection. The countries decided to standardize equipment, initially by a large number of bilateral and regional agreements.[1]

The futility of trying to work out arrangements bilaterally, which had been the method used for most of previous history, was clear in this case. Unless there was an agreement on transmission standards, there would be no messages. Similarly, transborder communication raised issues of payment and compensation. While goods could be traded across borders based on negotiated prices and tariffs applied at the borders, information had to be paid for at either one end of the communication link or the other. While it would have been possible to collect fees from the sender, as a condition for putting a message into the system, and then collect fees from the receiver, as a condition for getting the message out of the system, this would be unwieldy, diffcult technically and would have probably killed the method.

The compromise was to collect fees only at one end—the sender—and then share the fees with the service that provided the message to the receiver. These are what are now called interconnection costs. How much to share has to be negotiated and agreed.

The initial treaty was only among continental European countries,[2] reflecting the importance of physical proximity for telegraph lines. The initial treaty dealt with principles and norms, including ensuring that messages are transmitted freely. They agreed in their Title II that all persons have the right to correspond by means of international telegraphs and that all states party agree to take all necessary measures to ensure the secrecy of correspondence and their good delivery.

In addition to general norms and agreement on definitions, such as what is a message, the treaty agreed on the tariffs to be charged in the national currencies of the states party. They also agreed that the treaty would be reviewed periodically to accommodate technological and economic developments.

In order to administer the agreements as well as to organize the review and amendment process the states decided to create an international organization, the International Telegraph Union. While this was a precursor of today's international organization, its secretariat was exclusively Swiss, who were considered by the other parties to be neutrals. The Swiss had also organized the International Committee of the Red Cross and had a precedent in providing secretariat services, including the Universal Postal Union (UPU). Both the ITU and the UPU were headquartered in Berne, Switzerland. Still, it reflected a functionalist model of international organization, where new organizations would be created because there was a need to preserve order when there was a change in technologies or other factors.[3]

An additional factor in the equation was that in some countries communication was a state-run enterprise, while in others, like the United States, the communication network was run by private corporations and, at the time, regulation was not considered a public responsibility. Even the United States decided to participate, at the Fourth Plenipotentiary Conference of the ITU in 1875. The ITU conferences provided an intergovernmental forum where both types of corporations could interact and agree.

As communications technology evolved, additional conventions were negotiated, to deal with telephony (as an amendment to the telegraphy convention), then radiocommunications, the latter culminating in the 1906 International Radiotelegraph Convention. As technology moved ahead the conventions were amended, or additional standards were adopted. In 1932, the Madrid Conference decided to merge the two basic conventions and rename the ITU as the International Telecommunications Union.

After the Second World War, like other previously existing international organizations, the ITU was reconstituted as a United Nations specialized agency. In addition to its plenary, the ITU set up, starting in the 1920s, consultative committees to coordinate technical studies, tests and measurements being carried out in the various fields of telecommunications, with a view to drawing up international standards. While many of the studies were done by private sector entities, whenever they had implications for global telecommunications, they became a responsibility of the ITU and its bodies. In 1956 the consultative committees were merged into a single Telephone and Telegraph Consultative Committee (CCITT). The ITU secretariat, since 1947 international rather than Swiss in character, organized the work and kept it going with its own research and analysis.

In addition to standards, the ITU also became involved in the allocation of frequency spectrums. Bandwidth for radio communications is a finite resource and to make sure that there were no competitors for the same frequencies, the ITU set up a procedure to allocate frequencies. Because the frequency spectrum is borderless, it has been considered a kind of global commons.

Similarly, when space satellites began to be launched for communication purposes, the ITU took the lead to allocate geo-stationary orbit slots, positions over the equator where satellites move at the same speed as the earth. Both spectrum allocation and orbit slots involved dividing up scarce goods among competing interests. Nevertheless, the ITU succeeded in doing so.

As long as telecommunications, considered "natural monopolies," were controlled either by government-owned enterprises or private enterprises with monopolistic rights, and the main channels were over landlines that passed over national borders much as telegraph lines in the nineteenth century, the ITU was able to maintain order through processes that were considered slow, but effective.[4] When technology and domestic politics in some of the larger industrial countries led to the breakup of the large telecoms and changes in standards had to be made quickly, the ITU began to experience problems.[5] When the Internet arrived full force in the mid-1990s, the ITU began to try to redefine its identity.

The content

Content of communication was regulated by three somewhat different regimes. One was the human rights regime that made guaranteeing freedom of expression an international obligation of states, where the United Nations Educational, Scientific and Cultural Organization (UNESCO) and the United Nations human rights program were especially concerned. The second was the regime for the protection of intellectual property, including that which could be sent over communication channels, managed by the World Intellectual Property Organization. The third was the World Trade Organization's (WTO) Agreement on Trade-Related Aspects of Intellectual Property Rights (TRIPS), negotiated in the 1986–94 Uruguay Round, which introduced intellectual property rules into the multilateral trading system

When the Universal Declaration on Human Rights was adopted in 1948, it included as one of its civil and political rights (Article 19):

> Everyone has the right to freedom of opinion and expression; this right includes freedom to hold opinions without interference and to seek, receive and impart information and ideas through any media and regardless of frontiers.

This was translated into international law by the International Covenant on Civil and Political Rights adopted by the United Nations in 1966 that entered into force in 1979. States party to that convention, numbering 160 by April 2007, have undertaken an obligation to ensure freedom of expression. However, Article 19,[6] while guaranteeing the right to freedom of expression including freedom to seek, receive and impart information and ideas of all kinds, regardless of frontiers, either orally, in writing or in print, in the form of art, or through any other media of his choice, provided for two exceptions. These are respect for the rights and reputations of others, and protection of national security, public order or public health or morals.

The second exception allowed states to tap telephone calls, intercept mail or censor newspapers, magazines or books. The first is more complex, because it depends on what "rights of others" means, but as international law has evolved, it has included intellectual property.

The Universal Declaration and its facilitative conventions are directed primarily at state behavior within a state's own borders. However, since they are international norms, all states are supposed to respect them and there is an "international interest" in how states comply. Over time, a compliance monitoring mechanism has evolved. In the case of the Covenant on Civil and Political Rights, the Human Rights Committee reviews periodic reports from states party on their compliance with the convention. The committee's independent experts ask questions of the presenting governments and review replies in what is called the constructive dialogue. The committee has prepared a series of general comments on the convention's articles as part of its work over the years, including one on Article 19 in 1983. The comment did not detect any general problems with state compliance with the article, but, of course the comment was written before the Internet.

The Covenant assumes that states can control their borders and that domestic law can ensure that compliance takes place. The same is true with intellectual property.

As analyzed by Christopher May in this series, "When knowledge becomes subject to ownership, IPRs [Intellectual Property Rights] express the legal benefits of ownership, most importantly: the ability to charge rent for use; to receive compensation for loss; and to gather payment for transfer."[7] Two elements of IPRs are relevant to communication: copyrights and trademarks. Copyrights refer to literary or artistic intellectual property, the ownership of the content of books, paintings, photographs, music and films. Trademarks distinguish the products of one company from another and can be made up of "one or more distinctive words, letters, numbers, drawings or pictures, emblems or other graphic representations."[8]

Intellectual property is protected under national laws, which initially differed according to the tradition of each country regarding property rights. Some countries took a very restrictive view of rights, while others were more generous. However, when intellectual property was traded, conflicts between national systems became evident. For example, in one country, the author of a book and his or her heirs would own the content in perpetuity, while in another country, copying of a foreign book was not considered an infringement of the author's rights. There were differences about what could be copied and how.

As a result, in the mid-nineteenth century, European countries, pressed by authors like Victor Hugo, worked to establish a multilateral agreement on copyrights. This was reflected in the Berne Convention for the Protection of Literary and Artistic Works (Paris, 1871). In its Article 2, the convention said: "The works mentioned in this article shall enjoy protection in all countries of the Union. This protection shall operate for the benefit of the author and his successors in title."

However, the protections provided would be determined by the laws of each state. In addition, "The protection of this Convention shall not apply to news of the day or to miscellaneous facts having the character of mere items of press information."

In order to administer the Berne Convention, as well as the companion Paris Convention for the Protection of Industrial Property (relating to patents), the states party decided, in 1893, to create what was called the Bureaux Internationaux Réunis pour la Protection de la Propriété Intellectuelle (BIRPPI) with headquarters in Berne, Switzerland. The main function of the organization was to assist in cross-registering patents and copyrights, compiling and publishing information on changes in state legislation and practice, assisting in modifications of the original conventions and in negotiating new ones to address technological changes.

In 1928, the states members of the BIRPPI, met in Rome to discuss the new broadcasting technologies. As May put it:[9]

> there were clear differences of opinion between states that wanted to reserve the private rights for authors as they already did for other technologies of distribution,

> and those countries like Australia and New Zealand that saw broadcasting as a public service that should be unencumbered by private rights, reflecting the emerging public service ethos of broadcasting in countries with vast distances between small communities. Once again, a compromise solution was concluded that, while setting the parameters of choice, allowed individual states to shape the measures that were appropriate for their societies.

This function continued when, in 1967, the Bureaux were converted into the World Intellectual Property Organization and switched from a Swiss to an international secretariat. The disputes about which types of intellectual property would be covered and by what national means continued but the regime, based on territoriality, functioned.

Most of the disputes on intellectual property were resolved nationally, especially in the United States. One of the major decisions had to do with the use of video recorders by individuals to tape programs being broadcast over television. In a 1984 landmark case in the United States, Sony Corp vs. Universal Studios (the Betamax case), a divided Supreme Court held 5–4 that owners of video recorders were not violating copyrights by copying programs to watch later.[10] The extent to which "fair use" of copyrighted material permits copying and sharing of music, films, radio and television programs or books was not completely clear, and depended on national legislation. The Berne Convention itself, in Article 10 (2), states:

> It shall be a matter for legislation in the countries of the Union, and for special agreements existing or to be concluded between them, to permit the utilization, to the extent justified by the purpose, of literary or artistic works by way of illustration in publications, broadcasts or sound or visual recordings for teaching, provided such utilization is compatible with fair practice.

Each state party was allowed to determine what constituted fair practice.

The creation of the World Trade Organization (WTO) added new dimension to content regulation when it negotiated the Agreement on Trade-Related Aspects of Intellectual Property Rights (TRIPS) during the Uruguay Round that led to the formation of the WTO. The need to include intellectual property as part of trade agreement was because the Berne and Paris conventions did not have clear enforcement provisions and, as the WTO itself says,[11]

> The extent of protection and enforcement of these rights varied widely around the world; and as intellectual property became more important in trade, these differences became a source of tension in international economic relations. New internationally-agreed trade rules for intellectual property rights were seen as a way to introduce more order and predictability, and for disputes to be settled more systematically.

While the reach of the TRIPS covered all intellectual property, and it took the Berne and Paris Conventions as starting points, its main focus was on tradeable goods. These were usually physical products like records, tapes, films, art, and books. Like all traded goods, it was within the power of states to stop illegal products (like counterfeit editions) at the frontier. The TRIPS allowed copyright holders access to national remedies, and this added teeth to the copyright protection system. Interestingly, TRIPS only included the concept of fair use with regard to trademarks, rather than copyright.

After the Internet: The RATS Problem

As long as IP protection was provided by the physical borders of states that joined the various international agreements, the system was essentially stable. The development of an essentially borderless Internet changed this, and was a major factor in creating a need for Internet governance. The effect of the Internet can be illustrated by what I will call the RATS problem.

In 1975, I was stationed in Islamabad, Pakistan with the United Nations Development Programme. One recreational activity in which I participated was the Rawalpindi Amateur Theatrical Society (RATS). Although Pakistan was a party to the Berne Convention, its enforcement was not very active, and RATS could put on any play without paying rights. If RATS had been in any of the many countries (like neighboring Afghanistan) that were not parties to the copyright conventions at all, any play—including those currently on Broadway in New York or the West End in London—could be put on without paying for the rights.

Before the Internet, this was not a real problem. It is highly unlikely that anyone would travel from New York or London to Rawalpindi to see a play put on by RATS. If they did, pressure could be put by the United States or the U.K. government to have the Pakistan government close down the play. Of course, if RATS put on its pirated play in Afghanistan, there would be no real recourse, but it is even more unlikely that anything would be done.

The same could be said for such IP violations as making illegal copies of records or books. The market in Pakistan was simply too small to worry about the problem.

The Internet changed all of this. If RATS decided to raise money by recording its production and then making it available for downloading, the product would be available globally, and would compete with licit examples. RATS could perform any play and video-stream it to the world and could archive it for downloading. Anyone, anywhere with a computer and suffcient bandwidth could see the play. RATS could charge for the download and pocket the money and none of it would go to the authors of the play or its publishers. If, instead of Pakistan, RATS was located in a country that was not part of the intellectual property regime, no one could bring RATS to court.

Of course, it is unlikely that many downloaders would be interested in a RATS production of a Broadway play, but suppose instead that it was putting the most recent release of the Dixie Chicks on its server. The same could be true of anyone making music, or films, or software, available for downloading without paying the owners of the copyrights. The Internet made the concept of broadcasting, or communication of content, completely different.

In short, the old system for regulating both communication and its content, based on international organizations who helped states deal with issues of interoperability and intellectual property based on national jurisdiction, was not clearly applicable to the Internet, and clearly some new form of governance would be required that took into account both the nature of the Internet and its different stakeholders.

Chapter Highlights

- All acts of communication impact others. As one form of communication, writing is no exception to this rule.
- The primary purposes of public relations are to share information, establish dialogue, persuade others, and achieve collaboration.
- Writers can and do play a key role in helping others fulfill their basic needs, including to gain acceptance, attain esteem, and survive as workers and individuals.
- Today, writers have more avenues for which to write and opportunities to reach a greater number of audiences than ever before.
- Information remains an increasingly valuable commodity in society. It is the responsibility of the writer to help share information but to do so in a way that is understandable.

For Discussion

1. We have identified four primary purposes of public relations. Do you agree with our list? Can you think of other purposes that could or should be added?
2. Identify examples of elements that have helped achieve each of the primary purposes of public relations as identified in this chapter.
3. Between social media and the more traditional media, there are more outlets to which writers can contribute than ever before. How has this helped public relations? Can you think of any negative consequences of this new reality?
4. Identify something you believe to be well written and then defend your choice. Identify something you feel is not well written. Explain this choice as well.
5. We have discussed the important role writers play in all public relations efforts or campaigns. Is such a comment valid?

iii

What is Good Writing, Anyway?

In the writing world there are three types of people: there are those who get good grammar, those who struggle with it, and those who wear the grammar expert hat proudly. At least in our experience we have found this to be true. Those who get it often have a grammar and punctuation guide or two by their side, and they easily flip through these books to guide them. Those who struggle with it often try to hide the fact that they are clueless. And the third type of people—we call them the Grammar Nazis—simply annoy the rest of us by insisting that they correct our bad grammar, usually publicly, and tend to show off how smart they are in the most condescending of ways.

The Grammar Nazis, and we all know at least one, will take every opportunity to show you their skill. You know who we're talking about. They have a dry sense of humor, and they make past and dangling participle jokes and jump at the chance to point out the first-person pronoun antecedent rule and how you are breaking it, or why your tense keeps jumping back and forth, or why your essential clause and nonessential clause are mixed up. They use big words on a daily basis that the rest of us tuned out and left behind in our middle school grammar lessons—words such as "compound adjectives," "plurals," "double possessives," and even "quasi possessives." They know the right and wrong time to use the dash and the ellipsis (...), and they know that "the comma may be dropped if two clauses with expressly stated subjects are short," according to the Associated Press Stylebook's Punctuation Guide.

Good News

The good news is that there is hope for all of us. We tell our students that they don't need to be grammar and punctuation experts, but they do need to know how to look up anything and everything. For example, how do we introduce direct quotes in a news article? The answer is simple, and it is found on the same page as the comma rule in the helpful AP Stylebook. Look it up. It will tell you exactly what to do. Use a common to introduce a complete one-sentence quotation within a paragraph: *Wallace said, "She spent six months in Argentina and came back speaking English with a Spanish accent."* But use a colon to introduce quotations of more than one sentence. All you need to do is look up the colon rule in the AP book. And now you know where to look for colon expertise. And, yes, we just used "and" at the beginning of the sentence. Professors like to break old rules sometimes, too.

In any newsroom in which we've ever worked, there has always been at least one Grammar Nazi. They are impressive with their vast knowledge, and they make the best editors. But it takes a strong person who will admit defeat, and we learned this lesson early on.

A Grammar Story

We decided to include a personal story from one of our journeys to show you that even professors and professional journalists stumble along the way. This is Beth Jannery's personal experience used to highlight some of the real-life challenges of being a writer.

Back in my twenty-something days, I was a journalist who covered the Pentagon. I wrote about the defense budget, what military weapons were being funded or cut by Congress, and how all the parts fit together. I loved what I did, and some of the most fun I ever had was attending briefings on Capitol Hill, interviewing admirals and generals at the Pentagon, and finding high-level sources who were willing to tell me what was really going on behind the scenes of a budget meeting so that I could break a story. This was the fun stuff filled with embassy parties and trips to war-gaming exercises and landing on aircraft carriers. But at the end of the day I was a journalist, and I was on deadline and my copy had to be submitted to my editor for review.

What I quickly discovered was that I was a great reporter, and I got good, breaking news, but I did not have a knack for the ins and outs of grammar. Fortunately, I worked with great editors who lifted me up and carried me along, but that could only last for so long. I got tired of the Grammar Nazi, who I secretly looked up to, spouting off why the sentence with the past participle didn't work with the prefix or the suffix and why I needed to avoid the duplicated vowels and tripled consonants (now I'm making this up to get a laugh, but you get the idea). Some time passed, and I realized that to be a better journalist, I had to study up and ask for help.

Asking for Help

Help came in the form of a sushi lunch, where my publisher at the time gave me a gift that I treasure today, and I take every opportunity to pass on this gift to young writers like you. It would be years before I actually opened this gift, which showed in my writing, but today it is a gift that keeps giving, and I am grateful for this seasoned journalist who pulled me aside and spoke directly and honestly to me. He said, "It's OK not to know something, but you need to know where to find it and take the time to look it up." This is a loose quote, but I get to take liberty with my own history from two decades ago.

My publisher at the time handed me a fresh copy of a gem of a book called *The Elements of Style* written by William Strunk and E. B. White. It is "the book" to get if you buy only one reference and writing guide—it is often referred to as the writer's bible—and it stands the test of time. I highly recommend Strunk and White's *The Elements of Style*, but, more than that, I recommend that you do what I finally did: open it and read it and use it in all of your writing today and every day. It truly is the gift that keeps on giving.

A good journalist, writer, or communicator can look up anything. The lesson here is twofold: you don't need to know everything, but be humble enough to know who you are. I am not a grammar expert—I will never wear the grammar-expert hat—but I do know how to admit defeat. There is no shame in having to look up something. The great part about being a journalist is that we get to know a little about a lot, but we don't have to memorize it all. We can ask for help, we can look up something if we don't know it, and part of our job is to ask questions. If there is something you don't understand about grammar, now you know where to look, and you know that it is OK to ask.

I remember this sushi lunch well because this publisher had a reputation for taking new reporters on staff out for sushi and ordering some kind of soup that contained an egg (with the shell), and it was gently encouraged that the young hack eat the egg and make a good impression on the boss. I managed to avoid eating this egg, and it was never addressed or held against me (at least I don't think it was), but I couldn't avoid the grammar discussion. It was something I had to face, as uncomfortable as it was. In high school English I managed to get by without facing too much scrutiny, but, being a reporter, this was part of my job. I could avoid it no longer.

Keeping it Simple

Today we like to keep our sentences simple and to the point. We are fans of constantly rewriting. They say that a good writer is a good editor. "Edit, edit, edit" or "Rewrite, rewrite, rewrite" are very familiar expressions to a journalist, writer, or communicator. "Practice, practice, practice." Sound familiar? In *The Elements of Style*, Strunk and White offer this advice: "Clarity, clarity, clarity. When you become hopelessly mired in a sentence, it is best to start fresh; do not try to fight your way through against terrible odds of syntax. Usually what is wrong is that the construction has become too involved at some point; the sentence needs to be broken apart and replaced by two or more shorter sentences."

The same rule is true of punctuation. When a sentence becomes littered by too many commas, dashes, or semicolons, the best thing to try is a rewrite. Break it down into short, clear, concise sentences, doing away with the overload of punctuation. In other words, keep it simple.

For those who *really* struggle with basic sentence structure and grammatical rules, there are additional resources. At our university we often refer students to our wonderful Writing Center. The Writing Center won't edit your work for you, but it has grammar refresher workshops as well as unlimited resource guides and online tools to use. But this takes time. We had to decide if we wanted to be a better writers or if we wanted to continue to hide grammar inadequacies. Today we believe that we can all write well; some of us simply have to humble ourselves enough to look things up. There is a life lesson in there somewhere. We hope you see it.

Making it Fun

Facebook is a fun place to post anything about grammar. We've put up a few witty posts about sentence structure, and they always get a lot of likes or comments. There are several funny ones floating around the Internet. We've included a couple of our favorites below (it's difficult to say who the original source is, so we're giving broad credit to open sources online). As you will see, the use of punctuation can completely alter the meaning of a sentence. Many of us grunt or groan when we hear the words "grammar" or "punctuation," but, simply put, *grammar* is the study of the way in which sentences of a language are constructed. And, simply put, *punctuation* is using a system of marks or characters in writing to make the meaning clear. That's it. Simple and basic.

When Systems Work Well

These systems are tools we can and should use to help our reader understand what we are saying. When it works, it works beautifully, but when the systems are not used, the outcome can be confusing and sometimes utterly funny. Let's take a look at how and why the systems work well (or don't work when not used properly).

Woman without Man

A professor wrote the following sentence on the board and asked the class to punctuate it:

Woman without her man is nothing.

Half of the class punctuated the sentence in the following way:

Woman: without her, man is nothing.

The other half of the class responded with the following:

Woman, without her man, is nothing.

See the importance of punctuation?

Who's Supplying Whom?

Say "No" to Drugs from the police D.A.R.E. officers.

There is a comma missing, which makes it look like the police officers are drug dealers.

Note: D.A.R.E. stands for Drug Abuse Resistance Education.

Commas Save Lives

Let's eat Grandpa!

Let's eat, Grandpa!

In this case, Grandpa needs a comma, or he's going to be eaten for dinner.

King George

King George walked and talked an hour after his head was cut off.

King George walked and talked; an hour after, his head was cut off.

Without proper punctuation, the entire meaning is changed.

The Panda

The Panda eats shoots and leaves.
The Panda eats, shoots and leaves.
The Panda eats, shoots, and leaves.
The Panda either likes to eat or likes using guns and leaving the scene of a crime.

Hot and Steamy Grandma?

Hot and steamy, Grandma took the turkey out of the oven.
Grandma took the hot and steamy turkey out of the oven.
We like the second sentence better; how about you?

I Still Love You!

I'm sorry I still love you.
I'm sorry. I still love you.
I'm sorry I still love you!
Uh oh! We could get in trouble here.

Two Dear John Letters

Letter One:

Dear John:
I want a man who knows what love is all about. You are generous, kind, thoughtful. People who are not like you admit to being useless and inferior. You have ruined me for other men. I yearn for you. I have no feelings whatsoever when we're apart. I can be forever happy—will you let me be yours? Gloria

Letter Two:

Dear John:
I want a man who knows what love is. All about you are generous, kind, thoughtful people, who are not like you. Admit to being useless and inferior. You have ruined me. For other men, I yearn. For you, I have no feelings whatsoever. When we're apart, I can be forever happy. Will you let me be? Yours, Gloria
What's Gloria trying to say to John?

Ugh! Why Write at All?

Why write at all? It can be such a painful process. There is not a modern writer who knows more about the process of putting the written word down on paper than best-selling author Stephen King. He took a short hiatus from horror novels to share his wisdom on writing. He wrote a wonderfully friendly book with the simple title *On Writing*. It is King's memoir of his craft. Remember that writing and communicating are considered to be a craft. We've selected a few of our favorite King quotes about writing in hopes that something will resonate with you and inspire you to do the work that it takes to write, and to be a competent writer. King also has a few things to stay about the challenge and importance of rewriting. According to King:

"I've written because it fulfilled me. Maybe it paid off the mortgage on the house and got the kids through college, but those things were on the side—I did it for the buzz. I did it for the pure joy of the thing. And if you can do it for joy, you can do it forever."

"You can approach the act of writing with nervousness, excitement, hopefulness, or even despair—the sense that you can never completely put on the page what's in your mind and heart. You can come to the act with your fists clenched and your eyes narrowed, ready to kick ass and take down names. You can come to it because you want a girl to marry you or because you want to change the world. Come to it any way but lightly. Let me say it again: you must not come lightly to the blank page."

"If you want to be a writer, you must do two things above all others: read a lot and write a lot."

"Write with the door closed, and **rewrite** with the door open."

"While it is impossible to make a competent writer out of a bad writer, and while it is equally impossible to make a great writer out of a good one, it is possible, with lots of hard work, dedication, and timely help, to make a good writer out of a merely competent one."

Nothing Wrong with a Li'l Motivation

If you worried that an entire chapter on punctuation and grammar and the basics of writing would be dull and dreary, here is a little motivational inspiration for you. These words of wisdom come from an incredible journalist named Steven Pressfield, from his book *The War of* Art. Pressfield talks about getting past the fear of writing and resistance. He tells us to simply show up and do the work we are meant to do. According to Pressfield:

"If you find yourself asking yourself (and your friends), 'Am I really a writer? Am I really an artist?' chances are you are. The counterfeit innovator is wildly self-confident. The real one is scared to death."

"Are you a born writer? Were you put on earth to be a painter, a scientist, an apostle of peace? In the end the question can only be answered by action."

"Do it or don't do it."

"It may help to think of it this way. If you were meant to cure cancer or write a symphony or crack cold fusion and you don't do it, you not only hurt yourself, even destroy yourself, you hurt your children. You hurt me. You hurt the planet."

"You shame the angels who watch over you and you spite the Almighty, who created you and only you with your unique gifts, for the sole purpose of nudging the human race one millimeter farther along its path back to God."

"Creative work is not a selfish act or a bid for attention on the part of the actor. It's a gift to the world and every being in it. Don't cheat us of your contribution. Give us what you've got."

Reading List

The following are readings that we selected to help you with the fundamentals of grammar, style, and punctuation.

Editing for Grammar

By Gerald J. Schiffhorst and Donald Pharr

The principles of grammar are means to an end: effective communication. They express the conventional practices followed by experienced speakers and writers of Standard English. Not following these conventions often results in writing that is not only technically incorrect but also confusing or misleading. Most of the time we follow the conventions of English without thinking about them. However, some errors are almost inevitable, and knowing the rules makes correcting those errors much easier.

If you find that you need to review any of the parts of speech discussed here, see Chapter 12.

Use Grammatically Complete Sentences.

A group of words that is punctuated as a sentence but that is not a grammatically complete sentence is called a *fragment* or *sentence fragment.* Although experienced writers sometimes use fragments intentionally, fragments are usually unacceptable in college writing. Unintentional fragments can create misunderstanding and distract your readers. A fragment is usually either a *phrase* or a *dependent clause.*

Complete sentence:	David is a talented artist. (independent clause)
Fragment:	Because David is a talented artist. (dependent clause)
Fragment:	Like a talented artist. (prepositional phrase)

Most fragments result from chopping a phrase or clause from the end of an adjoining sentence. It is usually a simple matter to correct them. You can reconnect the fragment to the previous or following sentence, or you can add the necessary elements to make the fragment a grammatically complete sentence.

Subordinating conjunctions such as *although, because, if,* and *when* (see the list on page 295) introduce subordinate (dependent) clauses, and such clauses cannot stand alone as sentences. The following examples show the most common types of clauses or phrases used incorrectly as fragments:

Incorrect: Although being left-handed has been seen as a minor misfortune. Many great athletes, artists, and political leaders have succeeded in adjusting to a right-handed world. (Subordinate clause introduced by *although* is not a sentence.)

Correct: Although being left-handed has been seen as a minor misfortune, many great athletes, artists, and political figures have succeeded in adjusting to a right-handed world. (subordinate clause connected to independent clause)

Incorrect: Science owes its system of plant classification and its double Latin names for flora and fauna to Linnaeus. The eighteenth-century Swedish botanist. (final noun phrase not a sentence)

Correct: Science owes its system of plant classification and its double Latin names for flora and fauna to Linnaeus, the eighteenth-century Swedish botanist. (noun phrase as an appositive connected to preceding sentence)

Incorrect: The Rattlers were disappointed once more. Having finished second in the city baseball tournament for the fifth year in a row. (participial phrase as fragment)

Correct: The Rattlers were disappointed once more, having finished second in the city baseball tournament for the fifth year in a row. (phrase connected to preceding sentence)

Correct: The Rattlers were disappointed once more. This was the fifth year in a row that they had finished second in the city baseball tournament. (phrase expanded to independent clause)

Incorrect: Collectively, they vowed to combine their efforts toward one goal. To win first place next year. (infinitive phrase as fragment)

Correct: Collectively, they vowed to combine their efforts toward one goal: to win first place next year. (infinitive phrase connected to previous sentence)

Incorrect: Practice sessions will begin immediately and will be held during the whole year. On the second Saturday of each month. (prepositional phrase as fragment)

Correct: Practice sessions will begin immediately and will be held on the second Saturday of each month during the whole year. (prepositional phrase inserted in previous sentence)

Exercise

A. Mark with *S* any word group that is a grammatical sentence; mark with *X* those that are sentence fragments. Explain why those marked *X* are fragments.

1. Maria's friend Jeff Reynolds who joined the football team.
2. Because the coach urged him to do so.
3. Good hands combined with better than average speed.
4. Jeff became a wide receiver, an assignment that he welcomed.
5. Although the quarterback and the running backs get the most publicity.
6. Because they are the ones who score most of the points.
7. Although Jeff was a sophomore, he started every game for Mippallaupa High.
8. Scoring five touchdowns on twenty-seven receptions.
9. Coach O'Reilly's philosophy of using rushing to set up the pass.
10. Coach O'Reilly believed in a balanced attack.
11. Hoping to keep the opponents on their toes.
12. Although, some teams handled the Mippallaupa Rattlers fairly easily.
13. Lake Parson High beating Mippallaupa four years in a row.
14. Absolutely Mippallaupa's most feared rival.
15. Gidneyville Consolidated, however, being something less of a challenge, losing to Mippallaupa 73–6.

B. Rewrite as sentences the fragments that you identified above.

Separate Two Independent Clauses with a Period, Semicolon, or Comma and Coordinating Conjunction.

If you fail to separate independent clauses properly, you will create one of two structural problems: a *fused sentence* (or *run-on*) or a *comma splice*.

An independent clause is a group of words that can be punctuated as a complete sentence. Whenever a sentence contains two independent clauses, those clauses must be separated by a semicolon or by one of the coordinating conjunctions *(and, or, nor, for, but, yet,* or *so)* plus a comma. A comma alone is not adequate punctuation, even if it is followed by a conjunctive adverb such as *furthermore, however,* or *moreover.*

Fused sentence: The arresting officer did not attend the trial the case was dismissed.
Comma splice: The arresting officer did not attend the trial, the case was dismissed.

Once you learn to identify fused sentences and comma splices, you can easily avoid them. Some of the most common ways are shown here:

1. Make each clause a separate sentence:
The arresting officer did not attend the trial. The case was dismissed.

2. Place a semicolon between the clauses:
   The arresting officer did not attend the trial; the case was dismissed.

3. Insert a conjunctive adverb between the clauses. The adverb should be preceded by a semicolon and followed by a comma:
   The arresting officer did not attend the trial; therefore, the case was dismissed.

4. Place a comma and coordinating conjunction between the clauses:
   The arresting officer did not attend the trial, **so** the case was dismissed.

5. Convert one clause into a dependent clause by beginning it with a relative pronoun (*whoever, whomever, whichever, whatever,* for example) or with a subordinating conjunction such as *because, after,* or *since:*
   Because the arresting officer did not attend the trial, the case was dismissed.

6. Rearrange the entire sentence into another pattern:
   The case was dismissed due to the absence of the arresting officer.

All of these revisions are grammatically correct. You will find that choosing the best correction is a matter of style. Note that each of the following fused sentences and comma splices can be corrected in ways other than the one shown:

Faulty: My old car has become too unreliable, I'm going to have to start looking for another one soon. (comma splice)
Corrected: My old car has become too unreliable; I'm going to have to start looking for another one soon. (semicolon)
Faulty: The old rancher perceived that a storm was imminent he turned his horse around and headed home. (fused sentence)
Corrected: The old rancher perceived that a storm was imminent, so he turned his horse around and headed home. (comma plus coordinating conjunction)
Faulty: There is one major problem with exercise, it is addictive. (comma splice)
Corrected: There is one major problem with exercise; it is addictive. (semicolon)
Faulty: Jack wanted to buy a camouflage outfit, he couldn't find one. (comma splice)
Corrected: Jack wanted to buy a camouflage outfit, but he couldn't find one. (comma plus coordinating conjunction)
Faulty: Many Americans believe that they are victims of the tax laws this attitude causes income tax returns to be highly creative. (fused sentence)
Corrected: Many Americans believe that they are victims of the tax laws, a belief that causes income tax returns to be highly creative. (sentence rearranged)

Exercise

In the following sentences, mark *C* for those that are correct and *X* for those that are fused sentences or comma splices. Then correct those marked *X*.

1. The district football tournament was held at Xanadu High the stadium was called the Pleasure Dome.
2. In the first round, Mippallaupa beat Gidneyville, Xanadu beat Lake Parson.
3. Maria attended the game with her parents, and they all sat in the visitors' section.
4. The Xanadu Kublas hadn't lost a game all season, however, their star running back was out with a broken ankle.
5. Maria could hear the chant of the Xanadu cheerleaders: "Beware! Beware! His flashing eyes, his floating hair!"
6. The game was tied at fourteen at the end of the third quarter, nevertheless Xanadu had a first down and goal to go at the Mippallaupa seven-yard line.
7. The Mippallaupa defense dug in, Xanadu scored two plays later.
8. The Kublas missed the extra point, with a Rattler linebacker coming through to block the kick.
9. Jeff Reynolds caught three passes in the Rattlers' final drive he would have scored a touchdown if he had not been caught by the free safety after the third catch.
10. The Rattlers were stopped, however, by an interception.

Make Each Verb and its Subject Agree in Number.

Use the singular form of a verb with a singular subject and the plural form of a verb with a plural subject:

Singular	**Plural**
She watches.	They watch.
The watch runs fast.	The watches *run* fast.
The team is playing.	The teams *are* playing.
The plan has changed.	The plans *have* changed.
He was especially kind.	They *were* especially kind.

Notice that the -s or -es ending makes nouns plural but makes present-tense verbs singular, except in the first and second person:

She goes.
I go.
You go.

Making subjects and verbs agree is usually easy in short sentences, but it can be more difficult in longer, more complicated sentences. Make sure that you do not let a prepositional phrase or other modifier influence your decision. Be careful to identify the subject so that your verb agrees with the correct word or words:

Incorrect: Ms. Gabriel's attention to time, efficiency, and savings deserve favorable consideration.

Correct: Ms. Gabriel's attention [subject] to time, efficiency, and savings *deserves* favorable consideration.

Incorrect: My supervisor's first priority in cutting departmental expenses are reducing overtime and sick pay.

Correct: My supervisor's first priority [subject] in cutting departmental expenses *is* reducing overtime and sick pay.

In a sentence beginning with *there,* the subject follows the verb:

Correct: There *is* an extra pair [subject] of shoes in the hall closet.

Correct: There *are* no good *concerts* [subject] at the Civic Center anymore.

Forms of the verb *be* agree with the subject of the sentence, not the complement, even when the subject is plural and the complement is singular, or vice versa:

Correct: Unsafe working conditions [subject] were the primary cause [complement] of the government investigation.

Correct: Mr. Jefferson's reason [subject] for early retirement was his health problem [complement].

Correct: Shopping [subject] on the Internet is her only reason [complement] for wanting a new computer.

50a With Compound Subjects Joined by and, Use a Plural Verb.

Incorrect: The movement of the tropical fish and the bubbles from the filter fascinates the young cat.

Correct: The movement of the tropical fish and the bubbles from the filter *fascinate* the young cat.

However, when *each* or *every* precedes the compound subject, use a singular verb:

Incorrect: Every boy and girl are required to have parental permission to go on the field trip.

Correct: Every boy and girl is required to have parental permission to go on the field trip.

Note: The phrase *as well as* is used as a preposition, not as a conjunction. It does not create a compound subject.

The Indian diplomat as well as the Pakistani was upset by the U.N. vote.

50b With Compound Subjects Joined by *or* or *nor*, Make the Verb Agree with the Subject Nearer to the Verb.

Use a singular verb when two singular subjects are joined by *or* or *nor:*

Incorrect: Either *Hamlet* or *Othello*, rather than the usual *Macbeth*, are going to be performed this year.

Correct: Either *Hamlet* or *Othello*, rather than the usual *Macbeth*, *is* going to be performed this year.

Use a plural verb when two plural subjects are joined by or or nor:

Incorrect: Neither Stephen King's novels nor Lawrence Block's novels seems to lose popularity.

Correct: Neither Stephen King's novels nor Lawrence Block's novels *seem* to lose popularity.

When *or* or *nor* joins a singular subject and a plural subject, the verb agrees with the subject nearer to the verb:

Incorrect: Gail could not decide whether her math class or her two science classes was harder.

Correct: Gail could not decide whether her two science classes or her math class *was* harder.

Also correct: Gail could not decide whether her math class or her two science classes *were* harder.

Incorrect: Neither the clerks nor the assistant manager were watching the register.

Correct: Neither the clerks nor the assistant manager *was* watching the register.

Also correct: Neither the assistant manager nor the clerks *were* watching the register.

In the last two examples, note that of the two correct sentences shown, the second sentence sounds much better. In this type of situation, placing the plural nearer the verb will produce a more natural-sounding sentence.

50c Each, Either, Neither, One, Everybody, Somebody, Nobody, and Anyone Require Singular Verbs.

Incorrect: Each of the development team's twelve members were given a portion of the bonus money.

Correct: Each of the development team's twelve members was given a portion of the bonus money.

Incorrect: Nobody from inside the company are ever given serious consideration for the top positions.

Correct: Nobody from inside the company is ever given serious consideration for the top positions.

50d Quantitative Words Such as Some, Half, all, Part, Most, and More are Singular or Plural Depending on the Nouns to Which They Refer.

Correct: All of the members *were* notified, and most *have* arrived.
Correct: All of the cake *has* been eaten.
Correct: Most of the committee's time *was* wasted in senseless wrangling.
Correct: One third of all meals eaten in this country *are* purchased in restaurants.
Correct: Two thirds of his diet *is* starch.

None usually obeys the same rule, although some writers consider the word's origin ("not one") and treat it consistently as singular:

I left messages for all of the members, but none *has* returned my call.

50e A Collective Noun that Refers to a Group as a Unit Takes a Singular Verb.

Nouns such as *class, committee, team, family, crew, jury, faculty, majority,* and *company* take singular verbs when they refer to a group acting as a unit:

Correct: The company *has* tried to diversify its investments.
Correct: If a majority *votes* in favor of adjournment, no further motions are allowed.

Occasionally you may need a plural verb to show that members of a group are acting as individuals:

Incorrect: If a majority votes according to their consciences, these amendments will be defeated.
Correct: If a majority *vote* according to their consciences, these amendments will be defeated.

In the incorrect sentence, the writer has been forced to shift from a singular verb *(votes)* to a plural pronoun *(their).* Once you have decided whether a collective noun is singular or plural, treat it consistently within the sentence as one or the other. Another example:

Correct: The jury *votes* by secret ballot, with twelve votes required for indictment. (*jury* treated as a whole)
Correct: The jury *have* taken their seats. (*jury* treated as individuals)
Incorrect: The jury has taken their seats.

Many writers of American English avoid using collective nouns in the plural. They say "members of the jury" when they treat the jury as individuals acting separately, or they use the singular: "The jury *is* seated."

50f Some Singular Subjects May Look Like Plurals.

Certain nouns look like plurals but function as singulars and require singular verbs. *News, economics, politics, physics,* and *mathematics* are common examples of words that cannot be made singular because they already are.

> **Correct:** Politics, unfortunately, often *affects* hiring decisions. (not plural verb *affect*)

Exercise

A. Study the sentences below for subject-verb agreement. Mark those that are correct with *C* and those that have faulty agreement with X.

1. In her junior year, Maria found that physics were a very difficult subject.
2. Neither her mother nor her father were able to help her.
3. All of the students in the class was having trouble.
4. Maria, along with April and Jeff, were planning to form a study group.
5. The group were composed of those three and April's friend Liam, who was making the best grades in the class.
6. Every one of them were responsible for checking the day's assignment on the class website.
7. Mr. Sterne, who had taught physics and chemistry for more than thirty years, were feared by generations of Mippallaupa students.
8. Liam believed that at least one of the study group members were going to fail.
9. A wide variety of problems was expected on the final exam.
10. However, most of the problems were based on those in earlier tests.

B. Correct the sentences above that you marked with X.

Use Singular Pronouns to Refer to Singular Nouns and Plural Pronouns to Refer to Plural Nouns.

Make each pronoun agree in number—singular or plural—with the noun or pronoun to which it refers. (This noun or pronoun is called the **antecedent.**)

> **Correct:** The flight instructor [singular antecedent] finished her [singular pronoun] lecture, but the pilots [plural antecedent] remained in their [plural pronoun] seats.

It is usually easy to recognize an antecedent as singular or plural and to decide whether the pronoun should be singular or plural, but some sentences are complicated. The antecedent may be compound, or it may be a collective noun or an indefinite pronoun.

51a Collective Nouns Such as *Team, Committee, Chorus,* and *Class* can be Either Singular or Plural Depending on how they are Used.

Avoid treating a collective noun as both singular and plural:

Incorrect: The interview committee is going to finish *their* deliberations tomorrow.
Correct: The interview committee *is* going to finish *its* deliberations tomorrow.
Incorrect: Our soccer team *has* not won yet, but Saturday *they* will be doing their best.
Correct: Our soccer team has not won yet, but Saturday it will be doing its best.

See **50e** for a fuller discussion of collective nouns.

51b Indefinite Antecedents such as *a Person, Each, Neither, Either, Someone, Anyone, No One, One,* and *Everybody* Almost Always Take Singular Pronouns.

Incorrect: There are too many issues raised by this petition for the officials to give each one the attention they deserve.
Correct: There are too many issues raised by this petition for the officials to give each one the attention *it* deserves.
Incorrect: When a student first registers for classes, they risk making embarrassing errors.
Correct: When a student first registers for classes, *he or she* risks making embarrassing errors.
Correct: When *students* first register for classes, *they* risk making embarrassing errors.

Avoid using *he, him,* or *his* with an indefinite pronoun unless the pronoun refers to an exclusively male group. Use *he or she, him or her,* or *his or her* instead, or rewrite the sentence so that the plural *they, them,* or *their* is appropriate. See **64a** for more on sexist language. See **50c** and **50d** for more on indefinite pronouns.

51c Compound Antecedents with *and* Take Plural Pronouns.

Correct: Beth and Eileen won *their* awards in tennis and swimming. (The pronoun *their* refers to Beth and Eileen, a compound or double antecedent.)

51d If a Compound Antecedent is Joined by *or* or *nor*, The Pronoun Agrees with the Antecedent Nearer to the Pronoun.

If both antecedents are singular, use a singular pronoun:

Incorrect: Neither the television station nor its radio affiliate had their license revoked because of the charges of corruption.

Correct: Neither the television station nor its radio affiliate had *its* license revoked because of the charges of corruption.

If both antecedents are plural, use a plural pronoun:

Correct: It was impossible to blame either the reporters or the editors. *They* did all *they* could to verify the story.

If one antecedent is singular and one plural, make the pronoun agree with the antecedent nearer to the pronoun:

Correct: Either the instructor or the students are responsible for turning off their classroom lights and projection equipment.

Avoid wasting time puzzling over intricate agreement problems with subjects or antecedents joined by *or* or *nor.* If following the rules in this section and in **50b** results in an absurd or awkward sentence, simply rewrite it. You may be able to join the subjects or antecedents with *and:*

Awkward: Neither Amanda nor Bob will be in [his? her? their?] office this afternoon.
Rewritten: Both Amanda and Bob will be out of *their* offices this afternoon.

Exercise

A. Mark with *X* those sentences with pronoun agreement errors. If the sentence is correct, mark it *C.*

1. Mr. Rodriguez announced plans to learn how to cook: "Every man should know their way around a kitchen."
2. After some reading, he found that each cookbook has a style of its own.
3. He soon discovered that one cookbook publisher aimed their books at men who were just learning.
4. He realized that an expert chef wouldn't waste their time on such a book.
5. Either Mr. Rodriguez or Mrs. Rodriguez cooked each night for his family.
6. In May, the Clickville Bakeoff was going to be held, and their entry rules were published in the *Clarion.*
7. Mrs. Rodriguez urged her husband to submit his recipe for Rutabaga Surprise.
8. "Anyone who submits their entry has a chance," Mrs. Rodriguez argued.
9. Neither Mr. Rodriguez nor Mrs. Rodriguez expected their recipe to win, however.
10. Both of them were pleased when a letter arrived in his mailbox stating that his recipe had gained second place, losing only to Rutabaga Milano.

B. Correct the sentences above that you marked with *X.*

Make Each Pronoun Refer Clearly to one Antecedent.

Because a pronoun takes the place of its antecedent, a pronoun's meaning is clear only when it points clearly to that antecedent. Two or more plausible antecedents will confuse your reader:

Ambiguous: Alex told Rafael that he should be earning more money.
Clear: Alex told Rafael, "You should be earning more money."
Or: Alex told Rafael, "I should be earning more money."
Or: Alex complained to Rafael about being underpaid.
Ambiguous: As soon as Dr. Angela Kennedy treated the porpoise, she was set free in the ocean.
Clear: As soon as Dr. Angela Kennedy treated her, the porpoise was set free in the ocean.

In the second pair of examples, sensible readers will know that the porpoise, not Dr. Kennedy, was set free, but because they will notice the comical ambiguity, the sentence is still ineffective.

52a Make Each Pronoun Refer to a Noun or to an Earlier Pronoun.

To keep references clear, make each pronoun refer to a noun used as a subject, object, or complement, not as a modifier or a possessive:

Ineffective: Mrs. Valdez questioned the investigator's honesty even though he had helped her.
Effective: Even though the investigator had helped her, Mrs. Valdez questioned his honesty.
Ineffective: At Sybil's office, she is the manager.
Effective: Sybil is the manager of her office.

Also be sure that a pronoun can logically refer to its antecedent:

Ineffective: I had tonsillitis when I was eight, so my doctor removed them.
Effective: I had tonsillitis when I was eight, so my doctor removed my tonsils.
Or: When I was eight, my doctor removed my tonsils because they were continually inflamed.

52b Make Each Pronoun Refer to one Word or to a Specific Group of Words Rather than to an Implied Idea.

Except in informal writing, use *you* when referring directly to your reader, not when referring to any person in general. Substitute *one* or an appropriate noun:

Ineffective: Many people believe that college should help you earn a better living.
Effective: Many people believe that college should help a person earn a better living.
Or: Many people believe that college should help one earn a better living.

Except in idiomatic expressions such as "It is cold," use *it* and *they* only to refer to specific nouns:

Ineffective:	On page 381 of our text, it says that Henry Clay was "the great compromiser."
Effective:	On page 381 of our text, the author says that Henry Clay was "the great compromiser."
Or:	On page 381, our text says that Henry Clay was "the great compromiser."
Ineffective:	They do not have many Catholics in Iran.
Effective:	Iran does not have many Catholics.
Or:	There are few Catholics in Iran.

52c Insert Nouns to Clarify the Antecedents of *this, that,* and *which*.

This, that, and *which* are often vague when they refer broadly to an idea expressed or implied in a preceding clause. To avoid confusion, change the pronoun to a noun or add a noun.

Vague:	The young residents did the actual cutting even though the surgeon received credit and payment for the operation. This is common in many hospitals.
Clear:	The young residents did the actual cutting even though the surgeon received credit and payment for the operation. This practice is common in many hospitals.
Vague:	The CPA reviewed tax returns after her interns prepared them, which is quite common.
Clear:	The CPA reviewed tax returns after her interns prepared them, a common arrangement.

Exercise

Underline all pronouns used inappropriately in the following sentences.

1. Maria enjoyed studying sociology, which led her to consider it as her major in college.
2. "It says in the newspaper that a degree in sociology can be used in many ways," Maria commented.
3. Maria told April that she could choose a major if she weren't so busy.
4. When Maria's father brought home a book that evaluated U.S. colleges, she read it eagerly.
5. "They charge more for tuition in the North than they do in the South," Maria said.
6. One of the reasons Maria liked choosing sociology was that it would gain the approval of her parents.
7. She might need to go through graduate school to finish her education, but she didn't mind this.
8. After Maria finished reading the book on U.S. colleges, she gave it to April.
9. April was in no hurry to plan her career; this is common in young people.
10. Maria and April agreed that she was not getting any younger.

Determine the Correct Case of a Pronoun by the Word's Function in the Sentence.

The personal pronouns *(I, we, you, he, she, it, they)* appear in different case forms depending on their function in the sentence: *I* liked *her,* but *she* hated *me.*

	Nominative	Objective	Possessive*
First Person	I, we	me, us	my, mine
		our, ours	
Second Person	you	you	your, yours
Third Person	he, she,	him, her,	his, her, hers,
	it, they	it, them	its, their, theirs

*Note that no apostrophe is used for the possessive pronouns.

The **nominative** (also called **subjective**) case forms are used for the subject and predicate nominative functions:

We were turned away. (subject)
This is *she*. (predicate nominative)

The **objective** case forms are used for direct objects, indirect objects, and objects of prepositions:

The modem gave *us* trouble all night. (indirect object)
The Cougars beat *us* badly in both games. (direct object)
Next year we will be ready for *them*. (object of preposition)

The **possessive** case forms are used to show possession:

Their product was no better than *ours*. (possessives)

Be especially careful of the pronoun case in compound structures. Note the following:

Incorrect: Me and Diane went on a cruise last year.
Correct: *Diane and I* went on a cruise last year. (compound subject. No one would say, "Me went on a cruise." Also, put the other person's name first.)
Incorrect: Mr. Edwards may try to get you and I in trouble.
Correct: Mr. Edwards may try to get you and *me* in trouble. (object of *get*)
Incorrect: The judge was unsympathetic to my mother and I.
Correct: The judge was unsympathetic to my mother and *me*. (object of *to*)

A pronoun used as an appositive (an explanatory word, phrase, or clause that clarifies a noun) should be in the same case as the noun or pronoun it refers to:

Correct: The culprits, Alice and *I*, were caught at midnight.
Correct: The police quickly apprehended the culprits, Alice and *me*.

Incorrect: Three contestants won prizes at the finale: Karen Turner, Kris Butler, and me.
Correct: Three contestants won prizes at the finale: Karen Turner, Kris Butler, and *I*.

Use the possessive form immediately before a gerund:

Incorrect: My parents are concerned about me working while carrying fifteen credit hours.
Correct: My parents are concerned about *my working* while carrying fifteen credit hours.

However, you can normally use a nonpossessive common noun before a gerund, especially if the noun is plural:

Correct: The officials attributed the rise in unemployment to *women entering* the job market.

Use the nominative case for the subject of an implied verb form:

Incorrect: No one on their team is as tall as me.
Correct: No one on their team is as tall as *I*. (understood: "am tall")

Use the nominative form as the subject of a clause regardless of the function of the clause:

Incorrect: Most Americans still show great respect for whomever is President.
Correct: Most Americans still show great respect for *whoever* is President. (*Whoever* is the subject of *is* in the final clause.)

In formal writing, such as research papers and theses, always use *whom* as you would *me* or any other objective form. Many people have stopped using *whom,* especially in speech and informal writing, but in most college writing it is best to use *whom* whenever it is called for.

Incorrect: Whom did you say was calling?
Correct: Who did you say was calling? (*Who* is the subject of *was*.)
Correct: Whom did you call? (*Whom* is the object of *call*.)
Correct: To whom was that call made? (*Whom* is the object of the preposition *to*.)

A quick way to determine the case is to rephrase such questions as statements—for example, "You did call whom."

As a relative pronoun, *whom* is often dropped from the sentence:

Correct: Commissioner Jackson is the only one [*whom*] we should reelect. (*Whom* is the direct object of *reelect*.)

Exercise

A. Study the following sentences. Mark *X* for those with improper pronoun case and *C* for those that are correct.

1. Maria believed that, out of her senior class, no one else wanted to go to college as much as her.
2. Few of the other students were as conscientious as she.
3. However, Bob and Marge Walker, the parents of April, believed that their daughter going to college was in doubt.
4. The school counselor was the person to whom they inquired.
5. The counselor could not find a record of April taking a college preparatory test.
6. "Who do you think is responsible for this problem?" Mrs. Walker asked.
7. "Her parents, Bob and me, would like to know."
8. The counselor replied that he would look through the online records again and would call Marge and Bob to inform her and him about anything that turned up.
9. "Whom will we talk to if you don't succeed?" Mrs. Walker asked.
10. The counselor replied that him losing anything that came into his office would be a rare event.

B. Correct the sentences above that you marked with X.

Use Adjectives to Modify Nouns and Pronouns, And use Adverbs to Modify Verbs, Adjectives, or other Adverbs.

Both adjectives and adverbs are modifiers; they limit or describe other words.

Adjectives: The *radical* changes of personnel were *unpleasant* but *necessary*.
Adverbs: The *highly* complex steering mechanism turned the glider *smoothly*.

Adverbs are usually distinguished by their *-ly* endings *(rapidly, formally)*, but many adjectives, such as *ghastly* and *heavenly*, also end in *-ly*, and many adverbs, such as *often* and *well*, do not. If you are in doubt whether a word is an adjective or adverb, check a dictionary.

In very informal writing and speaking, certain adjectives—such as *sure, real,* and *good*—are often used in place of the adverbs *surely, really,* and *well*. In more formal writing, however, the safer practice is to use the adverb forms to modify verbs, adjectives, and other adverbs and to use adjectives to modify only nouns or pronouns:

Very informal: I did so *bad* on my first calculus test that I thought about dropping the class.
More formal: I did so *badly* on my first calculus test that I thought about dropping the class.

Use adjectives for complements after verbs such as *feel, look, smell, sound,* and *taste,* which function like forms of the verb *be;* use adverbs to modify these verbs. A quick test to make sure that the complement is correct is to substitute *is, was,* or other appropriate forms of the verb *be.*

Complement: I must have been sick, but I did not feel bad. ("To feel badly" would mean to have a poor sense of touch, so using the adjective *bad* is the correct complement.)
Adverb modifying verb: He looked *angrily* at us, then stalked off.
Complement: I felt *nervous* as I approached the dark building. (Substitute *was* for *felt.*)
Adverb modifying verb: I felt *nervously* in my pocket for a match.

54a Use the Correct Comparative and Superlative Forms of Adverbs and Adjectives.

Most short adjectives add *-er* for the comparative and *-est* for the superlative. Longer adjectives and most adverbs use *more* and *most.* A few have irregular comparative and superlative forms. Check a dictionary when you are in doubt.

Positive	Comparative	Superlative
strong	stronger	strongest
happy	happier	happiest
surprising	more surprising	most surprising
happily	more happily	most happily
good	better	best
well	better	best
bad	worse	worst

Use the comparative form when comparing two items, and use the superlative for three or more:

Incorrect: Bill and Kathy are both excellent website designers, but Kathy has the most even temperament.
Correct: Bill and Kathy are both excellent website designers, but Kathy has the *more* even temperament.
Incorrect: Diamonds are the better sellers among the three stones most often picked for engagement rings.
Correct: Diamonds are the *best* sellers among the three stones most often picked for engagement rings.

Exercise

A. Mark the following sentences with *C* if they are correct; mark with *X* those containing incorrectly used adjective or adverb forms.

1. Maria sent applications to two schools, Harvard University and Click Memorial Union; Harvard was a great school, but C.M.U. was the closest of the two.
2. She felt pretty good about her chances of getting in either one.
3. However, the letter she got back from C.M.U. was worded very strange.
4. "Click Memorial Union accepts only the better students out of those who apply."
5. "Applicants who do good on their preparatory exams have the best chance of acceptance."
6. "We eagerly await further evidence of your skills."
7. Maria had the sudden thought that of her choices of attending Harvard, attending Click, or staying home, the last was not the worse option.
8. However, she knew that C.M.U. had to be better than what it first seemed.
9. She felt nervously about her choice of C.M.U.
10. But her parents were nervous about her going all the way to Massachusetts, so Maria chose C.M.U.

B. Correct those sentences above marked *X*.

Use the Verb Tense Appropriate to the Time of an Action or Situation.

Although English relies heavily on adverbs and adverbial phrases and clauses to refer to time *(now, tomorrow, yesterday morning, after the play had already started),* English also indicates time by changes in the verb. By using verb tenses accurately, you can help your reader keep track of time relationships in your writing.

English verbs have only two primary tenses—present and past—but by using auxiliary verbs we can create complex verb forms. Thus, we can list three simple tenses, three perfect tenses, and progressive forms for all six tenses.

Simple tenses The **simple present tense** is far from simple in the ways that it is used:

Present time:	I *hear* you calling. He *looks* anxious.
Habitual time:	I *hear* the train go by every morning. He *repairs* his old Volkswagen himself.
Historical present:	Brutus *hears* the mob hailing Caesar.
Literary present:	In "The Man That Corrupted Hadleyburg," Twain *exposes* the ability of money to corrupt us.
Future action:	The case *goes* to court next week. When the defense attorney *finishes* her remarks, the jury will retire.

In the present tense, verbs of third-person singular subjects require an *-s* ending.

The **past tense** is formed by adding *-ed* to regular verbs or by changing the spelling of most irregular verbs. The **future tense** uses the auxiliary *shall* or *will*. Traditionally, *shall* has been reserved for use with first-person subjects *(I shall go)*, and *will* is used with second- and third-person subjects *(you will go; she will go)*, except when the writer reverses the usage to show strong emphasis: "I *will* win; you *shall* obey me." Today, only the most formal writing observes that distinction, and *will* is regularly used with all persons.

The following box shows the forms for a regular verb *(play)* and for the most irregular and most often used English verb, *be*.

	Regular Verb *Play*	**Irregular Verb *Be***
Present:	I play	I am
	you play	you are
	he, she, it plays	he, she, it is
	we, you, they play	we, you, they are
Past:	I played	I was
	you played	you were
	he, she, it played	he, she, it was
	we, you, they played	we, you, they were
Future:	I will [shall] play	I will [shall] be
	you will play	you will be
	he, she, it will play	he, she, it will be
	we, you, they will play	we, you, they will be

Perfect tenses The perfect tenses indicate a relationship between two times. The **present perfect** refers to an indefinite time in the recent past or to a time beginning in the past and continuing to the present:

> Representative Green *has voted* with the conservatives more often than with the liberals.
> This five-dollar watch *has kept* perfect time for two years.

The **past perfect** indicates a time before some other specified or implied time in the past:

> The teams *had met* twice before the playoffs.

Similarly, the **future perfect** may be used to indicate a time before some other stated or implied time in the future:

> Before they return, the astronauts *will have broken* the record for time spent in space.

Note that *return* in the previous example is a typical case of the present used for future time. This use of the present is very common in dependent clauses.

The perfect tenses combine a form of the auxiliary *have* with the past participle of the main verb, as shown in the following box.

	Regular Verb *Play*	**Irregular Verb *Be***
Present perfect:	I have played	I have been
	you have played	you have been
	he, she, it has played	he, she, it has been
	we, you, they have played	we, you, they have been
Past perfect:	I had played	I had been
	you had played	you had been
	he, she, it had played	he, she, it had been
	we, you, they had	we, you, they had been
Future perfect:	I will [shall] have played	I will [shall] have been
	you will have played	you will have been
	he, she, it will have played	he, she, it will have been
	we, you, they will have played	we, you, they will have been

Progressive tenses Progressive forms of verbs indicate continuous actions:

> The candidates *are waiting* for the results of the election.
> I *was running* toward the corner when my knee gave way.
> I *shall be working* on my tax return all day tomorrow.
> Mr. Velkoff told me last week that I *had been using* the wrong database for at least six months.

There are progressive forms for all six tenses, as shown in the box.

Present progressive:	I am playing
	he, she, it is playing
	we, you, they are playing
Past progressive:	I was playing
	he, she, it was playing
	we, you, they were playing
Future progressive:	I, he, she, it will [shall] be playing
	we, you, they will [shall] be playing
Present perfect progressive:	I have been playing
	he, she, it has been playing
	we, you, they have been playing
Past perfect progressive:	I, he, she, it had been playing
	we, you, they had been playing
Future perfect progressive:	I, he, she, it will [shall] have been playing
	we, you, they will [shall] have been playing

Tenses of verbals Verbals (infinitives, gerunds, and participles) have present and present-perfect forms. Each participle also has a past form:

Present infinitive: to sink, to be sinking
Perfect infinitive: to have sunk
Present gerund: sinking
Perfect gerund: having sunk
Present participle: sinking
Perfect participle: having sunk, having been sinking
Past participle: sunk

Use the past or perfect form of a verbal to indicate a time before the main verb in the clause:

Amelia would like [now] *to have seen* last night's fireworks.
He could not get over *having failed* his teammates.
Having signed all the letters, she went home early.
But: The woman *addressing* the assembly will retire next month. (The present participle here indicates the same time as the speaking or writing of the sentence.)

Use the past participle to indicate a time before that of the main verb or to describe a condition that began before the time of the main verb:

Angered by the story, the apartment owner sued both the newspaper and the reporter.

In most other cases, use the present forms of verbals:

Emily decided to *play* selections from Sondheim. (The playing follows the deciding.)
Emily enjoys *playing* selections from Sondheim. (The playing and the enjoying take place at the same time.)
Writing about the film *Dick Tracy*, Pauline Kael remarked. ... (The writing and the remarking take place together.)

Voice English verbs show active voice (the butler committed the crime) or passive voice (the crime was committed by the butler). The forms presented in this section have all been in the active voice. Verbs in the passive voice combine a form of be with the past participle of the main verb, as shown in the box.

	Active	**Passive**
Present:	I know	I am known
Past:	I knew	I was known
Future:	I will know	I will be known
Present perfect:	I have known	I have been known
Past perfect:	I had known	I had been known
Future perfect:	I will have	I will have been known

Progressive verbs are sometimes used in the passive voice: "I *am being followed.*" Careful writers generally avoid the passive voice because it is wordy, indirect, and less natural than the active. For a thorough discussion of voice and style, see **23e.**

Exercise

A. Mark these sentences with *C* if they are correct and with *X* if they contain errors in verb tense.

1. In 2014 Click Memorial Union will have been operating for seventy years.
2. In 1974 the university was being celebrated as one of the South's leaders in the study of sociology.
3. C.M.U. invested a great deal of money in the sociology program when it had been described as lagging behind the other departments in Arts and Sciences.
4. When Maria took her first sociology class, she felt that she won't understand the instructor.
5. Edwin Click, a grand-nephew of Ezekiel, received his doctorate in 1985 and had started teaching at C.M.U. the next year.
6. Now Click puts his emphasis on teaching and decided to let his research wait a few years.
7. However, he still used a very abstract approach to sociology, and Maria had decided that he was hard to understand.
8. "My major problem at this point," she thought, "will be translating Clickese into English."
9. Professor Click had told the class that he will meet with students who had questions.
10. Having taken the midterm, Maria then faced the research paper.

B. Correct the sentences marked X.

Use the Correct Principal Parts of Irregular Verbs.

You must know the principal parts of verbs in order to form all the tenses correctly. English verbs have three principal parts: the infinitive (or present stem), the past tense, and the past participle. For regular verbs, the past tense and past participle are formed by adding *-d* or *-ed* to the infinitive: *walk, walked, walked; move, moved, moved.* Other verbs—the irregular verbs—form the past tense and past participle by various means, usually by changing a vowel in the infinitive *(win, won).* The list below includes the principal parts of the most common irregular verbs and a few regular verbs often mistakenly treated as irregular. Your college-level dictionary also gives the principal parts of irregular verbs. If your dictionary does not list the past tense and past participle forms, you can assume that the verb is regular.

Infinitive	Past Tense	Past Participle
awake	awaked (awoke)	awaked (awoke)
beat	beat	beaten
become	became	become
begin	began	begun

bend	bent	bent
bite	bit	bitten
bleed	bled	bled
blow	blew	blown
break	broke	broken
bring	brought	brought
build	built	built
burst	burst	burst
buy	bought	bought
catch	caught	caught
choose	chose	chosen
come	came	come
cut	cut	cut
deal	dealt	dealt
dig	dug	dug
dive	dived (dove)	dived
do	did	done
drag	dragged	dragged
draw	drew	drawn
drink	drank	drunk
drive	drove	driven
drown	drowned	drowned
eat	ate	eaten
fall	fell	fallen
fight	fought	fought
fly	flew	flown
forget	forgot	forgotten (forgot)
freeze	froze	frozen
get	got	gotten (got)
give	gave	given
go	went	gone
grow	grew	grown
have	had	had
hide	hid	hidden
hold	held	held
keep	kept	kept
know	knew	known
lead	led	led
leave	left	left
lend	lent	len
let	let	let
lose	lost	lost
mean	meant	meant
prove	proved	proven (proved)
read	read	read
ride	rode	ridden

(Continued)

ring	rang	rung
rise	rose	risen
run	ran	run
say	said	said
see	saw	seen
sell	sold	sold
send	sent	sent
sew	sewed	sewn (sewed)
shake	shook	shaken
shave	shaved	shaved (shaven)
shrink	shrank (shrunk)	shrunk (shrunken)
show	showed	shown (showed)
sink	sank (sunk)	sunk
speak	spoke	spoken
swear	swore	sworn
swim	swam	swum
take	took	taken
teach	taught	taught
tell	told	told
think	thought	thought
throw	threw	thrown
wear	wore	worn
win	won	won
write	wrote	written

A few verbs with two distinct meanings have different principal parts in each meaning:

bid (a price)	bid	bid
bid (an order)	bade (bid)	bidden (bid)
hang (execute)	hanged	hanged
hang (suspend)	hung	hung
shine (emit light)	shone	shone
shine (polish)	shined	shined

Three pairs of verbs are easily confused, especially in their past-tense and past-participle forms. The key distinction is that one of each pair is transitive (it takes an object) but the other is intransitive (no object).

Transitive

lay (place)	laid	laid
set (place)	set	set
raise (lift)	raised	raised

Intransitive

lie (recline)	lay	lain
lie (falsehood)	lied	lied
sit (be seated)	sat	sat
rise (rise up)	rose	risen

He *laid* his head on a rock and *lay* in the sun for an hour.
She *set* her pen on the desk and *sat* waiting for others to finish.
He *rose* from the bed and *raised* the window.

Exercise

Underline the correct verb forms in the following sentences.

1. Maria decided that the best topic for her paper (lay, laid) in the work of Émile Durkheim.
2. Durkheim (lead, led) the intellectuals of the twentieth century to (see, seen) the importance of sociology.
3. Today, many people have (forgot, forgotten) that Durkheim (set, sat) up the study of deviance as a primary field of sociological inquiry.
4. Maria had (dived, dove) into her research with a vengeance.
5. She had (wore, worn) out two pencils while taking notes in the library.
6. Her efforts that semester (lend, lent) credence to her parents' theories about the value of hard work.
7. When she received an A on the assignment, her face (shined, shone) with pleasure.
8. She (hanged, hung) the paper on her bulletin board.
9. The memory of Professor Click's difficult lectures (shrank, shrunk) with time.
10. Maria realized that by the time she finished school, she would have (wrote, written) many more essays.

Use the Mood Required by your Sentence.

English has three moods: **indicative** for statements of fact and questions about facts, **imperative** for commands, and **subjunctive** for wishes and demands or for statements that are contrary to fact.

Indicative: I *know* who he is.
Imperative: *Be* yourself.
Subjunctive: If I *were* you, I would avoid that subject.

The subjunctive is used far less now than earlier in the history of the language, but there are some situations in which the subjunctive is still the only choice:

Correct: She demanded that Thomas *finish* the work. (Desired action. Less formally, this might be expressed, "She told Thomas to finish the work.")
Correct: It is essential that I *be seen* at the boss's party.
Correct: Eddie drank as if Prohibition *were* being reintroduced. (contrary to fact)
Correct: Eve wishes that she *were* more talented. (contrary to fact)

Only a few forms of the subjunctive are different from the indicative forms given in **55.** Those forms are shown here in bold type:

Present:	that I walk	that I **be**
	that he, she, it **walk** (no -s)	that he, she, it **be**
	that we, you, they walk	that we, you, they **be**
Past:	that I walked	that I **were**
	that he, she, it walked	that he, she, it **were**
	that we, you, they walked	that we, you, they were
Present perfect:	that I have walked	that I have been
	that he, she, it **have** walked	that he, she, it **have** been
	that we, you, they have walked	that we, you, they have been

Exercise

Study the sentences below. Mark with *C* those that are correct and with *X* those that have errors in mood. Correct the sentences marked *X*.

1. Maria looked at her humanities class as though it was a harmless diversion.
2. However, the instructor, Mr. Santellini, insisted that humanities be seen as the "cultural repository of human memory."
3. If Maria were not interested at first, Mr. Santellini changed her mind.
4. He said, "If I was in your situation, I would explore the link between humanities and sociology."
5. He insisted that this connection be the topic of her research paper.

Be Consistent when using Verbs and Pronouns.

To present your information smoothly and clearly, be consistent in the tense, voice, and mood of verbs and in the person and number of nouns and pronouns. Unnecessary shifts—from past to present or from singular to plural, for instance—make awkward reading and can confuse your reader. Some shifts are necessary—to indicate passing time, for example—but it is best to make such shifts only when you have no other choice.

58a Avoid Unnecessary Shifts in Tense, Voice, and Mood.

A change in **tense** usually signals a change in time, so be sure not to give your reader a false signal by switching tenses unnecessarily. A shift such as the following is often just the result of carelessness:

Shift in tense: As he *turned* the corner, he *became* aware that someone *is* following him.
Corrected: As he *turned* the corner, he *became* aware that someone *was* following him.

Be careful not to shift time when you are using one of the perfect tenses:

Shift in tense: We had paid our dues and are ready to begin attending meetings. (past perfect with present)
Corrected: We have paid our dues and are ready to begin attending meetings. (present perfect with present)
Or: We had paid our dues and were ready to begin attending meetings. (past perfect with past)

See **55** for a discussion of verb tenses. Active and passive **voice** can be mixed in one sentence (she *ran* for senator twice and *was defeated* twice), but an unnecessary shift in voice can spoil the focus of a sentence:

Shift in voice: Electrolysis is used by Dr. Lambiase, and he also performs minor surgery.
Improved: Dr. Lambiase uses electrolysis and also performs minor surgery.
Shift in voice: The report showed that white-collar criminals almost never serve hard time, whereas long sentences are served by petty burglars.
Improved: The report showed that white-collar criminals almost never serve hard time, whereas petty burglars serve long sentences.

Active voice is usually more direct and natural than passive voice (see **23e**).

A change in mood should reflect a change in the way the writer views the action or situation being described: "If I *were* willing to lie, I *would tell* you I enjoyed the story, but I *am* not willing to lie." Unmotivated shifts are distracting:

Shift in mood: If I were the President, I would take action, not act as if I was still in Congress.
Corrected: If I were the President, I would take action, not act as if I were still in Congress.

58b Be Consistent in the Number and Person of Your Nouns and Pronouns.

Shift the number of nouns and pronouns (singular or plural) only to show a valid change: "I wanted to go to Europe, but *we* could not afford the trip."

Faulty: The class of 2006 was academically outstanding, but they were unusual.
Improved: The class of 2006 was academically outstanding, but it was unusual.
Faulty: The jury was given instructions by the judge before they were asked to start their deliberations.
Improved: The jury was given instructions by the judge before it was asked to start its deliberations.

Similarly, keep the person of your pronouns consistent. Be especially careful to avoid slipping into the universal *you* (second person) when you are writing in the third person *(she, he, it):*

Faulty: Deer hunters in the Ocala National Forest must wear bright clothing so you will not get shot.
Improved: Deer hunters in the Ocala National Forest must wear bright clothing so they will not get shot.
Faulty: Often, other hunters will shoot at you if they see movement in the brush.
Improved: Often, other hunters will shoot carelessly if they see movement in the brush.

Exercise

A. Mark *C* for sentences without awkward shifts and *X* for those with awkward shifts.

1. Maria was leery about her instructor for Sociology II, Ms. Chan, because students always have trouble with her class.
2. If a student had trouble early on in Chan's class, he or she is on a downhill path.
3. The class met in a building that was known by students as "Afterthoughts," and it is located near the Student Center.
4. The building had no air conditioning or any other amenity that invites attendance at classes.
5. Maria decided that if the class was held in any other campus building, the students would have a less difficult time.
6. Ms. Chan was feared by many of the students, but Maria excelled in Sociology II.
7. Each of her friends in the class struggled, but they were all passing at midterm.
8. The third exam was failed by seven students, but Maria received an A.
9. After the third exam had been successfully undertaken, Maria was ready for her next research paper.
10. If she had been allowed to choose her topic, Maria would have selected the work of Erving Goffman, but Ms. Chan insisted that Maria work on the early writings of Max Weber.

B. Reword those sentences above marked *X*.

Chapter Highlights

- Proper grammar and punctuation are key tools for a writer.
- The good news is that anyone can be a good writer because there are grammar, punctuation, and style book tools to help.
- All good writers stumble and fall from time to time. The key is to keep learning.
- You don't need to be a grammar expert, but you should be willing to ask for help. Try to understand the system.
- There are powerful writing tools in your toolbox. Open it.

iv

Journalists and Public Relations Practitioners and Good Writing

If there is one thing that journalists and public relations professionals have in common, it is that they are very partial to good writing. Hardly a day passes when both are not on the lookout for it or striving hard to produce it. If it is not what they do, at the very least it is what seek to do. These two students and practitioners of communication live and breathe by the written word. Writing is always part of how they communicate, even when what they do is largely broadcast-oriented.

One thing that makes such a commonality so interesting is the fact that often most of us rarely view journalists and public relations practitioners in the same way. Because they work in different or, in many cases, opposing camps, we tend not to focus on or give much thought to all they have in common. Ironically, the fact is that the two have more in common than not. We will be looking at this aspect of each professional more closely in this chapter. In addition, we will be examining the primary challenges each faces on a regular basis as well as how each perceives the other and what each one's expectations of the other are. Finally, we will relate all this to good writing and how that is defined by each in their respective professions. The bottom line for both the journalist and public relations practitioner is to connect with their intended audience. Without that goal being achieved, their work, no matter how much effort is put into it, is largely compromised. Such is the challenge each has been attempting to meet from the beginning days of their existence.

Journalism is viewed as the profession of gathering, editing, and publishing news reports and related articles for the array of media outlets that currently exist. Public relations, generally, is seen as the promotion of a favorable image or the practice of establishing, maintaining, and improving relationships, in part by making use of but not restricted to the media. One uses a one-way style of communicating—sender to receiver—while the other utilizes both one-way and two-way communication strategies, depending on the needs and wishes of the client that drives the communication. Generally, one strives to serve those who depend on an organization's product, while the other seeks mainly to serve those seeking to utilize the organization's expertise. At the same time, both depend heavily on maintaining a high degree of credibility in the eyes of the public in carrying out their main functions. As part of this, both operate under legal as well as ethical guidelines that, at least in theory, help ensure that practitioners operate within certain parameters and adhere to particularly social levels of responsibility. (Authors' note: We will be delving into this in greater detail later in the text.)

Both are also profit-driven. Scholars and even public relations practitioners do not always talk about this aspect of these professions, but the reality is that reporters and public relations workers do what they do to help turn a profit on behalf of the company that pays their salary. Such a truism, at times, can create a moral dilemma for workers. For instance, in the case of journalist, a reporter may come across a story that reflects negatively on one of the newspaper's biggest advertisers. What does the reporter and his or her editors do if the advertiser threatens to withhold its advertising with the paper unless the story is dropped or soft-pedaled? This can be a tough call, particularly if the paper very much needs all the revenue it can generate in order to remain afloat.

In the case of public relations workers, their daily job is to promote stories that reflect positively on their clients. Suppose, in doing their research, these workers discover negative information about the client—what then? Do they ignore what they know, even if such information compromises the positive image they are working to develop for this same client? Do public relations officers disclose this information knowing that their agency may lose the client and that the worker might even lose his or her job?

While such ethical questions may not be everyday occurrences, they happen and, as a result, take the reporters and public relations workers beyond simply, say, reporting a story or putting together a press kit. The mere fact that these dilemmas or crossroads do exist casts a shadow over the two communication professions in that they require their respective workers to carry out their assignments without rose-colored glasses. They must be realists. Sometimes the journalist and public relations worker may be called on to make difficult choices or told to take certain actions they do not like or with which they do not even necessarily agree. Balancing society's right to know with loyalty to a client and/or employer is not easy. Working in such an environment where something of this nature could happen almost any day may not be fun, but it definitely bonds the reporter and the public relations worker, even though they oftentimes seem to operate at cross-purposes.

The beginning days of journalism as we think of it today began in the fifteenth century when Italian and German businessmen began compiling what they believed were interesting news items and circulated them to their various business contacts (Morton & Copeland, 2003). It was then in the seventeenth century when someone had the notion of using the printing press as a way of distributing information on a much more broad basis. This began in, of all places, the Philippines. This, of course, is when newspapers became the dominant form of reporting and sharing timely information. Magazines joined the fray in the 1800s, radio and television made their debut in the 1900s, and the Internet became another major source of new and timely information during the latter part of the twentieth century. During those hundreds of years, journalism has gone through numerous guises and styles.

Interestingly, many of those styles and driving objectives of the work of the so-called press over the past 150 to 200 years remain active today. Specifically, these range from attempts at objectivity and subjectivity to editorializing and sensationalism.

Public relations, as a profession and social science, has also had a rich history, though one not as long as journalism. Even though, looking back, scholars have labeled various acts, activities, and written communiqués as early signs of public relations, this practice did not really get underway until the early days of the twentieth century. It was then that the first class in public relations was taught and the first book on this topic was written. Furthermore, we see the field's beginning in the efforts of Lee and Bernays as well as in the creation of numerous theories and models all designed to provide a greater understanding of what communication is and how and why it works. Over the past twenty-five years, the creation of programs of study at colleges and universities, the creation of scholarly journals for the profession, and the organization of numerous academic conferences, workshops, and retreats have added greatly to the emergence of this profession as one that is respected and accepted by the general public (Botan & Hazelton, 2006).

Historically and traditionally, journalists and public relations practitioners have been viewed as being about as compatible as the Hatfields and the McCoys or a mongoose and a cobra, none of which, according to conventional wisdom, you would want to invite to the same party. After all, who wants to have their path to the punch bowl blocked by a shootout or a death struggle? Under the banner of objectivity, and being champions of truth, reporters have been and are seen as ones who doggedly pursue a story regardless of where it might lead. Impeding their quest are public relations flacks who are not interested in the truth but, instead, want only positive stories about their clients covered by the press. Thus, the public relations flack does all he or she can to prevent reporters from doing their job in the name of the unvarnished truth. Such a scenario may make for a great story, but the reality of the dynamic between the two is not nearly as dramatic or so black-and-white, particularly given the economic realities today. The stars of the day have aligned themselves in such a way as to make the relationship between the two more collaborative than adversarial.

It is no secret that the number of newspapers in America and the world is shrinking. According to the Pew Research Center's Project for Excellence in Journalism, print advertising revenue generated by newspapers throughout the country dropped from $ million in 2003 to $189 million in 2012, while during the same period revenue more than doubled for online outlets (Mitchell, Jurkowitz & Gaskin, 2013). In addition, between 1990 and 2009, the number of newspapers in the United States dropped 14 percent, from 1,611 to 1,387. Furthermore, many of the newspapers remaining have had to reduce the size of their news departments and, in some cases, increase the amount of space they set aside each day for advertisements. What this means, then, is that their news hole has gotten smaller. Thus, what is left for many newspapers is a reduced news team with less space to fill and not nearly as many resources as they once had to give news as much attention as it often demands. Given their dwindling staffs, reporters have had to adjust to the reality that they are not able to pursue stories or interviews as easily as they were able to do in the past. Thus, they have turned to the one person working in many companies, organizations, and other entities in the best position of helping them gain access to key people and provide them with needed information or updates: the public relations worker. It has become a regular occurrence for reporters to turn more and more to the public information officer for assistance in collecting information or to attain access to key people whom they can interview. Furthermore, the hand of the public relations worker is strengthened by the fact that many of those so-called key people, including the CEO, welcome the existence of the PR officer, who can help control access to them from people such as reporters who might ask embarrassing or challenging questions.

So, where it used to be that the reporter could and would bypass the public relations practitioner, in much of today's climate the reporter is becoming increasingly dependent on that same public relations person. Furthermore, with the reporter more dependent on the public relations worker, representatives of the press are now more accessible to public relations practitioners than ever before. We will leave it to others to debate whether this turn is a good or bad thing. Either way, it has brought the reporter and public relations worker together like never before. The two, not unlike the tiger and young boy in *Life of Pi,* are thrust into an uneasy alliance in which they need each other to come even close to carrying out the work to which they have been assigned.

Historically, the dynamic or relationship between the two was not always as level as it is today. Well into the twentieth century, journalists had the upper hand when it came to interacting with public relations professionals. The publicists or public information officers needed reporters far more than journalists/reporters needed them. Newspapers and, later, the broadcast media were the primary way the mass public could be reached. This reality meant that public relations practitioners needed the goodwill and, ultimately, the approval of the press to have any of their press releases picked up or published. Thus, written articles authored by publicists had to conform precisely to the style followed by the press. This included adhering to not just the format of articles but also the kind of content print and broadcast outlets looked for in a story. It is no surprise, then, that in the beginning days of public relations, the great majority of its practitioners were former newspaper men and women. Not only did these people know how to write well; they also had a better sense of how releases should be written and the kind of stories reporters were looking to cover. This knowledge helped give many of the early practitioners the skills they needed to succeed. Nowadays, an increasing number of public relations workers are products of institutions of higher education with degrees in communication or public relations rather than professional experience in the news industry.

Game Changer

The advent of social media changed the reporter–public relations practitioner dynamic dramatically. In fact, many argue today that, as a result, it is now the public relations practitioner who is the alpha wolf in the relationship. Social media has made the public information worker far less dependent on the journalist as a way of reaching the general public. Social media allows publicists to speak directly to the masses or targeted publics within it. Instead of being the bridge separating the publicist from the public, the media is now only one possible option the public relations worker has to use. All of us have seen this change in the many social media outlets we utilize or follow, particularly during political seasons when tons of messages are sent directly to us rather than just by way of press coverage.

The public relations worker thinks, "Why should I have to seek a reporter's approval on my announcement when I can simply post it on our website, send it out over Twitter, put in on our organization's Facebook page, or do all of those things?" But this use of social media works both ways. It has also helped reporters pursue stories. The journalist thinks, "I am working on a story about mothers and daughters who work in the same company. Rather than make a bunch of phone calls, I will simply send out an email blast to my list of public relations contacts and invite them to send me names and numbers of anyone who fits this bill." This saves the reporter time and saves them the trouble of having to dig up people with whom they can talk after deciding on specific story ideas to pursue. Currently, one of the most popular examples of this kind of "outreach" by reporters is through Profnet. This national online service links reporters to experts on a range of topics or those who can put them in touch with experts. Its primary audience is public information officers working in higher education along with academic administrators and faculty members.

The question of which communicator is more dominant than the other, however, though interesting, is secondary to the communication challenges each professional faces on a regular basis, both in terms of their individual work and how that work impacts the other. Both still need to do what they do well and with strict adherence to the guidelines that define the qualities of effective communication and, of course, good writing. It is thus with the current relationship between the journalist and the public relations worker in mind that we provide a closer look at the work these professionals do and the expectations they have of each other, particularly when it comes to writing. While it is a given that the day-to-day work each does is different, what we will also outline are the many similarities found in their efforts. These commonalities paint a surprisingly similar portrait of each, despite the fact the primary purpose or job of each is counter to that of the other. Thus, we start with a general outline of the typical day in the life of a journalist and then that of a public relations professional. (Authors' note: For the sake of brevity, we present these days without specific timelines attached or other realities, such as travel time to interviews or other sources of information.)

A Day in the Life of a Journalist

The daily schedule of no two reporters is exactly alike. This, as you might guess, is particularly true when it comes to broadcast and print reporters. Also, some reporters primarily workday hours, while others work mainly in the evening. Also, not surprisingly, those working on weekends have a different tone to their days as well. However, there are enough similarities between journalists and public relations practitioners to present the workday of a composite field reporter. Because of the day-evening difference, rather than outlining the schedule in specific timeframes, we have broken down the day into blocks. It is as follows:

- Meet with editor/assignment desk. It is here when story ideas for the day are discussed. Sometimes the stories may be a continuation of the what has transpired the day before. Other times, new stories may be considered based on events coming up on this particular day or ideas from the reporter or editor. There are reporters who have specific areas of coverage, such as city hall, the police, the local school board, or local politics, such as the mayor and city council. Thus, their conversation and planning will revolve around their "beat." Other reporters, however, are viewed as being generalists in that they have no specific beat. Instead, they often are assigned stories that do not fall under any prescribed area or topic.
- Once a story idea has been agreed on, reporters go into reporting mode. They have to determine what information they need to acquire to give the idea substance. This includes identifying who they need to talk with or interview. Oftentimes, the story may have different perspectives or sides to it. Consequently, the reporter more often than not will need to talk with multiple people or sources, knowing that in all likelihood not all of these people are going to agree with each other. At times, these sources may simply be random people on the street. Other times, they may be specific individuals, such as a particular city council member or a particular member of the community. There are even times when it could be both.
- The research begins. Reporters begin to conduct their own fact-finding on their story. This includes collecting what they feel is the appropriate background data to give them a sense of

what has transpired up until now. Gathering this information may involve checking old newspaper clippings or videotapes, or identifying and reaching out to people who can speak with authority on the topic. As part of this step, it is not unusual for reporters to reach out to an organization or entity's public relations director for assistance in identifying an expert on a given topic. For instance, if they are doing a story on local education issues, they may contact their local college's public information office to see if they have anyone on the faculty who can, say, put the issue in some sort of perspective. Also, depending on the particular story, this may then require identifying others who can speak to the most recent developments in the story.

- More reaching out occurs. This time reporters begin making calls to set up times when they can interview their various subjects. This can be a frustrating experience requiring many stops and starts. Oftentimes reporters need to talk with these people as quickly as possible. Unfortunately, not everyone they may wish or need to talk with is available when the reporter would like them to be. This often requires much juggling in terms of working around the source's availability. On those occasions when the sources either are not available or simply refuse to be interviewed, reporters need to identify other sources and continue to reach out until someone is willing and available to talk.
- Interviews are alwayst a challenge. While it is most helpful if the subject is articulate and knowledgeable, just as vital is how well interviewers—reporters—are prepared. Have they done enough homework to gain a working understanding of the topic at hand? Have they prepared several insightful and stimulating questions that will challenge the subject enough to elicit meaningful responses? Ideally, interviews should be friendly yet always professional. While the reporter may genuinely like the subject and be sympathetic to his or her circumstance, it is essential that the reporter keep the interaction on a professional basis. Quotes drawn from interviews are designed to give stories color, emotion, and greater depth.
- Once reporters have completed their field work, which includes interviews and possibly attending an event or a meeting or two, now is the time for them to return to the office, where they can start the task of putting together the facts they collected via research and pertinent comments they received from their interviews. Even under the best of circumstances, such a task is a challenge. In the case of reporters, it is made more so because often they are under a tight deadline. Not only must they compose a tight, well-written piece; they must do so within the constraints placed on them by their editors and the production schedule of their producers.
- Not everything reporters write in a first draft is golden. Consequently, everything they do write is seen by others before it is given the green light to be aired, put in print, or posted on a website. It is not uncommon for reporters to be asked to redo their initial draft. Sometimes new information needs to be added. If so, this may mean another interview or two. Other times reporters may be asked to revisit some of the facts they collected in their earlier research. And then there are moments when the editor simply believes that the first draft needs to be improved because the writing is not as strong as it should be. When this happens, the good news is that reporters generally do not have to go back to square one. Rather, they simply need to do a better job of presenting the facts in a way that is more compelling. And, do not forget, this all has to be done under an ever-tightening deadline.
- The highlight of the day: the editor gives the reporter's story a thumbs-up. Even for those who have been journalists for many years, such a moment is always a high point. The story is now "put to bed." It will soon be made available for public viewing, assessment, and critique. Some may like it. Some may not. Some may not pay attention to it at all, while others may give it the kind of

close scrutiny one would devote only to examining a long-lost treasure map. Positive or negative, reporters and the company for whom they work will receive the brunt of the reaction—if there is any at all.

- In much of the twentieth century, receiving the editor's approval would signal reporters that the heavy lifting of their day was now behind them. In the twenty-first century, however, such is not the case. The work of a reporter is never completely done for the day. In addition to traditional stories, it is common for the reporter to have blogs to update and tweets to compose. News stories often need follow-up, updating, and revision as new information comes forth. In the day of social media and the Internet, this new reality means that the journalist is responsible for ensuring that the public remains up-to-date on the latest goings-on of a story. The result is that the reporter, like never before, is rarely off duty.
- Reporters finally go home with two thoughts: they are glad to have made it through the day and are fully aware that the challenge of doing it all over again is only hours away.

Summary

There are several key elements to the reporter's day. They revolve around fact-finding, research, reaching out to various contacts, connecting with a public relations officer, working under deadline, and the challenge of writing. While reporters can and often do a good deal of their work online or over the telephone, to enhance their effectiveness and to improve the quality of interaction with various subjects and sources, they spend a good deal of time making face-to-face connections with others. This is expected of them by their bosses, the general public, and even those they seek out for information.

As their day is driven by a series of deadlines, oftentimes reporters do not have much leisure time in their routine schedules. This reality makes the writing they are required to do all the more stressful. It also dictates that they conform to a certain style of writing that is not unlike what anyone else with limited time faces. Their writing must be crisp, to the point, fact-driven, and devoid of much, if any, overly descriptive verbiage. Furthermore, what they write should also follow a logical sequence, beginning with the most important element or fact of the piece. This is then followed by information of lesser importance, presented in descending order from most to least important. To better appreciate this style, one need look no further than how novels are organized. Their most important fact—the equivalent of a newspaper or press release's lead—comes at the end. (The hero and heroine live happily ever after, or the butler is revealed to be the killer.) In the case of press releases or news stories, the most important fact is at the beginning. This is called the "inverted pyramid."

Looming deadlines are alwayst a challenge. Even seasoned reporters have trouble writing under these circumstances. The tighter or shorter the deadline, the more challenging it is to produce a cogent article. Newspapers and television and radio stations have limited time or news holes for their stories. Producing stories that fit within these space limitations, yet are complete enough to present the public with a complete snapshot of what the news item is about, is a constant challenge for the press.

A Day in the Life of a Public Relations Worker

Nowadays, one would be hard-pressed to find an organization or association without some type of communication arm to it, someone onboard to handle promotional efforts, internal communication, membership drives, special events, community relations, and so on. In each of these scenarios it is not unusual to have someone who is called the "director of public relations." Interestingly, this person's specific responsibilities and duties often vary from organization to organization. This is because one reality of this profession is that many people have their own vision as to what functions a public relations professional should perform or be responsible for. At one organization, the chief communicator's primary duty may be to generate publicity. At another, it may be to oversee all publications. And at still another, it may be to handle all social media efforts. Such is the nature of the profession. To say the least, it does make it difficult at times for professional communicators to justify or explain themselves to their superiors when the vision of their job runs counter to how their bosses see them.

The above paragraph is meant to serve as qualifier in our outline of a typical day of a public relations worker. It is also our justification for setting certain parameters for such an outline. We do so under the premise that the public relations worker works for a mid-size organization. The primary job is to generate publicity for the organization and help strengthen ties with the entity's customer base.

- The workday for public relations professionals begins by their checking in with the organization's chief executive officer. If this person is not available, PR workers check in with the chief executive's office, along with those of other top officers. The primary purpose is to gain a sense of what the priorities for the day are, including any issues or challenges with which they might be concerned or feel need to be addressed. This information is important to public relations officers, as oftentimes the thrust of their day is driven by the priorities of others, especially those in top management.
- Rarely do public relations workers come to work with a blank slate as to what they are going to do on any given day. By definition, communication is a continuous, ongoing act. Thus, there is always a need on the communicators' part to ensure that all such efforts—internal and external—are running as smoothly as possible and coming close to achieving the objectives set for them. Depending on information they collect from the CEO or other top administrators, public relations workers may have to adjust what their own priorities are for the day. If no adjustments are needed, communicators review the status of their own communication initiatives to ensure that adjustments are not needed at that end.
- Assuming all is running smoothly and there is no crisis afoot, communicators can move forward with focusing on their primary duties: to generate publicity and maintain strong customer relations. To generate publicity requires having a thorough knowledge of all that is occurring within the organization. This enables public relations workers to keep abreast of anything happening that might be worthy of sharing with others, particularly the media.
- Taking on the role of a reporter, communicators begin reaching out to various mid-level managers and workers within the organization to see what they might discover. Are there goings-on that they might be able to pass along to reporters? Such stories can be timely and categorized as hard news, or they can be pieces one could view as being in the category of human interest and less time-sensitive. As luck has it, the communicator learns that not only is the organization meeting its numerous profit projections; it is surpassing them as well. This good news needs to be shared with the organization's employees, including its stakeholders, and the external public as well. The communicator prepares copy for the internal communication vehicle. Often, part of the text includes an appropriate quote from the CEO. It is not unusual for the communicator to actually prepare a quote for the CEO for that person to review and ultimately approve. This internal story is then disseminated to the workers via a range of outlets or vehicles. The communicator also prepares a letter under the CEO's signature for stakeholders.

- There is now the challenge of preparing the story for external distribution. Because communicators cannot control or dictate media interest in their story, a strategy must be devised to interest reporters in the story. This entails shaping the story in a way that speaks to the readers and/or viewers of the press. The communicator comes up with the following plan: make the announcement in the context that the profits represent an example of a larger regional story—efforts to turn the economy around. This good news speaks to that story. To sweeten the proposed story for the press, on the communicator's recommendation the CEO agrees to make himself or herself available for any press interviews to discuss the organization's performance and how it relates to the region. To help make the CEO more comfortable with these interviews, the communicator prepares a set of talking points. These points will better enable the CEO to reinforce specific pieces of information about the organization he or she wishes to be included in any articles being seen or read by the public. Depending on the CEO's comfort level, it is not uncommon for the public relations worker to conduct a mock interview with the CEO. This gives the CEO an opportunity to rehearse answers, thus better enabling him or her to come across in a more polished manner when meeting with a reporter. During these mock sessions as conducted by the PR worker, this communicator purposely asks difficult or awkward questions to enable the CEO to be better prepared for any unexpected or "hardball" questions.
- The communicator prepares an email to outline the main points of the announcement, including the availability of the CEO to select reporters. As the communicator knows some reporters better than others, he or she follows up the electronic communiqué with phone calls to those people. To the delight of the communicator, several of the reporters agree to pursue this story for their newspaper or station. When interviews occur, it is common for the public relations worker to actually sit in with the CEO during the interaction with the reporter. Reasons for this are several-fold: it makes CEOs feel more comfortable, the public relations worker is on hand to provide information at those times when the CEO cannot quite recall a specific fact, and it puts both the public relations worker and reporter in a better position to follow up with each other if additional information is needed at the interview's conclusion.
- Anytime the public relations worker can generate free and positive press on behalf of the client, it is a good day. Anytime a day passes without a crisis, this, too, is considered to be a good day. Thus, the above scenario has been a good for the public relations worker. As this communicator goes home, he or she knows that the next day could be totally different. Whether it presents an unexpected crisis or more opportunities to generate positive visibility, the public relations practitioner knows that he or she will need to keep doing everything possible to keep the client and its various publics connected.

Summary

Among the key aspects of the public relations worker's day is the initiative needed to collect and then share information. As much of what PR workers do is dependent on others, the fact is that they often serve as the one common denominator to which various publics turn for information. Furthermore, even though they may be writing about one thing, it is not uncommon for public relations workers to prepare different versions of the same story as a way of best connecting with various publics. Using the story on an organization's profits as an example, the public relations worker had to prepare it as a story for the internal newsletter, a letter on behalf of its stakeholders, an email for reporters, and talking points for the CEO for media interviews. Doing so is the communicator's attempt to personalize each communiqué and, therefore, reinforce the organization's ties with each public.

Public relations practitioners have deadlines, too, but often their deadlines are more self-imposed based on outreach strategies they help develop with their clients. In the above scenario, the communicator was operating in what we might refer to as a one-day-at-a-time clip. The person went into the day looking to see what could be done to generate positive attention for the organization. In this case, things worked out. Some days, however, nothing pops up. Generally, that is OK. In the case of a reporter, however, coming up empty-handed is not nearly as acceptable. Newspapers have holes to fill. Television and radio have air time to fill. It is the job of reporters to fill these gaps each and every day. Public relations workers generally do not experience that kind of pressure each day.

Mutual Dependency

During the course of an average workweek, journalists and public relations practitioners depend on each other. In the case of journalists, they look to their public relations "cousins" in several ways: as resources for supplying them with experts to interview and sources of information. In the case of public relations workers, they look to journalists as a way to help pass along information about their client to the general public. This mutual dependency requires that they establish and maintain a positive working relationship with each other, one that is based on trust, respect, and reliability. Without any one of those elements, such a semi-collaborative partnership will not happen. The written work of each professional plays a key role in this.

As we have stated, both professionals do a lot of writing. The success of their jobs depends on it. Consequently, it is essential that their writing be of the highest caliber. This means that it must be accurate, timely, well written, focused, and pertinent to the public. When public relations workers try to pitch a story on their client to a particular reporter, they do so with the expectation that if a story does result, it will be put together in a highly professional manner. Without that expectation, the PR worker would not approach the reporter. Oftentimes, as we outlined earlier, the journalist is approached in writing—in the form of a formal press release, email, or media advisory—to name a few options. The journalist expects these written communiqués to be well-thought-out, organized, succinct, and meaty. In other words, journalists are not looking for or interested in fluff. They do not want to be treated as mere extensions of the public relations officer. Thus, the written pieces sent to them must be substantive in content and speak to the needs and interests of the public, not just be articles that do little but sing the praises of the organization.

For both professionals, how well they write speaks to how well they do their respective jobs. Both count on the other to be highly skilled and professional in that regard. Even though the two may get along on a personal basis, it is essential that they communicate well, professionally speaking. This benefits their own performance as well as the performance of the other person. Furthermore, for this mutual dependency to work, a mutual appreciation must exist.

Wrap-Up

Journalists and public relations practitioners are professionals who communicate for a living. How they communicate largely revolves around the written word. This even applies to broadcasters whose reports in front of the microphone or camera come from written text. Ideally, the two strive each day to connect with various publics via copy presented in a way that is designed to be engaging, pertinent, timely, and, above all, truthful. What about journalists, you might ask, who report for a media outlet—print or broadcast—with an obvious political agenda? How truthful are their reports if they are slanted? And how can what public relations workers produce be anything but slanted, because they are paid to represent specific clients? Doesn't this, then, negate any notion of honest communication? These are good questions, no doubt driven by examples many of us see and read every day.

We are not going to pretend that dishonesty does not occur in the worlds of journalism and public relations. Is there any so-called profession where there is not some level of purposeful untruths being put forth? Sadly, we think not. At the same time, how effective are those who do, in a sense, lie for living? Granted, while they may have their hardcore followers, the reality is that the number of those who do subscribe to what the tellers and writers of untruths communicate usually reaches a plateau, levels off, and then rarely goes beyond that point. In fact, over time that number decreases. For communicators to succeed, maintain careers with a long shelf life, and enjoy the widespread respect of society, they must have credibility. What they write and share with others must be based on fact rather than information that has been twisted or distorted.

Journalists and public relations practitioners who establish a working relationship do so on the basis of a mutual, fundamental trust they have in each other. This truism is found in any meaningful relationship. The two communicators connect with each other based on the confidence they have in the other's work. While each may have their own agenda in terms of how they are slanting what they are writing and sharing with others, the professionals of the highest ethical quality do so with integrity and honor. Furthermore, these professionals know as well as anyone that by maintaining an unbreakable loyalty to honest reporting and communicating, they will be doing a great service to themselves and that which they represent. This all revolves around the written word of those in either profession. Communication only works when draped in the truth.

Reading List

When it comes to reading most anything, journalists and public relations practitioners are no different from anyone else. They, too, enjoy reading material that is well written, engaging, and informative. A primary reason for this is that this is what they try to achieve in what they write in their own jobs. They recognize that achieving such a goal is not easy and not always done on the first attempt. Thus, to encounter others who have accomplished such ends in their own work does give them a sense of professional regard.

The writing that journalists and public relations practitioners do is similar, yet different. It is similar in that they try to impart similar elements of information, including the famous "five W's," (who, what, when, where and how) yet different as defined by the purpose of what they write and, at times, the audiences for whom their work is intended. The fives Ws represent the basic questions a journalist seeks to answer in the course of any story they persue. Even with their similarities and differences, writing is a challenge for all who do so professionally. For the professional, past successes are nice and a source of comfort, yet sitting down in front of the keyboard is always like the first time. The following articles provide a glimpse into the mechanics of effective or good writing:

Understand the Demand for Good Writing

By Jack E. Appleman

Today, business moves at such lightning speed that writers at every level need to deliver information instantly and accurately to a wide array of tough audiences. Top executives demand that your documents get to the bottom line immediately. Prospective clients need your proposal to explain precisely what separates your firm from competitors. And rank-and-file employees need written communication with clear direction and explicit instructions.

Poor Writing Yields Poor Results

With the electronic tools at our disposal today—computers, wireless PDAs, and mobile Internet-linked devices—just about everyone writes. Practically gone are the days when most professionals dictated letters to their secretaries. You'd think that with everyone constantly writing, we'd get better at it—but that's not happening.

Most experts believe the quality of writing on the job has worsened over the past 30 years. They point to the lack of clarity and to carelessly written emails that ignore basic spelling and punctuation rules. It's unfortunate that the business world has come to accept such poor writing.

A recent survey by Cohesive Knowledge Solutions (www.cohesiveknowledge.com) revealed that working professionals spend 40 percent of their day on activities related to email—a third of which are considered wasted time. This translates into about 12 percent of the day or, financially extrapolated across the U.S. business landscape, more than $300 billion a year—wasted!

Getting people to send fewer emails is not necessarily the answer. One executive, responding to an Net Future Institute (NFI) Research survey, said the problem wasn't the number or frequency of emails; it was the inability of the writer to get to the point (*Hudson Valley Business Journal,* August 21, 2006).

If you're still not convinced about the impact of poor writing on productivity, consider these other reports:

- A third of workers in the nation's blue-chip companies write poorly, and businesses spend $3.1 billion annually on writing training. (National Commission on Writing, panel established by the College Board, *New York Times,* Dec. 7, 2004).
- "Poorly written business communications waste time, drain productivity and cause errors" (*HR Magazine,* June 2006).
- Eighty-five percent of respondents said weak workplace communication wasted time, and 70 percent cited lost productivity, according to a survey by Communicare, Inc. (*HR Magazine,* April 2006).

Plus, in a publication by its Public Policy Council, the American Society for Training & Development (ASTD) reported that one of the biggest knowledge gaps was in writing skills.

Why Don't We Like to Write?

Writing is hard, and it's one of the least-favorite activities for most employees. For many of us, the problem goes all the way back to elementary school when writing was that most-dreaded assignment. Instead of encouraging us to be creative and experiment with words, many teachers stressed correctness—pointing out every grammar and spelling mistake. That was no fun! Nor, for most of us, was high school or college English. Flashback: That 1,000-word essay is due tomorrow and you're still 400 words short! Crank up some more sentences. Plug in some fancy new vocabulary words—that'll impress the teacher (even if you're not sure what they mean). Don't worry about rephrasing ideas already written. Just keep churning out those words until you reach that magic 1,000.

That's a terrible and stressful way to write. Because too many workers haven't let go of that high school essay syndrome and other habits formed years earlier, their writing continues to suffer. For them, the consequence is worse than a poor grade: people will lose interest and stop reading their documents.

I apologize now to all teachers of composition, grammar, and vocabulary—those topics serve critical roles in our language. As business writers, we need to follow the rules of grammar to make our documents clear and readable. And we risk embarrassing ourselves before supervisors, clients, and colleagues when we ignore basic grammar rules. So I appeal to all teachers, from elementary school through college: stress clarity and brevity, the qualities your students will need when they write in the business world.

Effective Writing Can Be Learned

Forget those long and drawn-out essays with complex words to demonstrate your command of the English language (or to show how well you faked it). The rules have changed since you were in school. With business text, your objective is not to impress the reader. Typically, it's to explain a situation, to suggest solutions to a problem, to offer instructions, or to recommend action. If you convey these points in a clear, concise, and organized fashion, you become an effective business writer.

This goal is well within your reach; just follow the steps in this book. Plus, pay more attention to documents from other writers, everyone from authors and journalists to top executives, middle managers, and support personnel. Notice what's well written and what's not, what's clear and what's confusing. As the reader, determine how effectively information is presented to you—a process that will help you generate documents that are clear, concise, and easily understood.

Good Writing Pays Off

To a great extent, you are what you write in the corporate world. Co-workers, clients, vendors, and others may know you best by your writing, the most common means of business communication. Your words can convey anything from enthusiasm, intelligence, and empathy to laziness, selfishness, and ignorance.

Good writing helps demonstrate leadership skills. Company heads can shape the future of their organizations and inspire employees (see example 1.1). Senior-level supervisors can explain complex sales or management strategies. Mid-level managers can demonstrate or validate leadership abilities to subordinates and supervisors. And any employee who writes effectively will look better to the people who may play a role in determining his or her future with the company.

For example, a well-written document can show readers that

- you understand all aspects of the problem and can clearly convey them.
- you understand how the problem affects various people and departments.
- you've thought about potential solutions and can explain the options clearly.
- you know what steps different people should take and when they should take them.

Your Turn

1. Look through some recent emails from supervisors or executives at your company. Identify messages in which the language helped convey the writer's leadership skills.

EXAMPLE 1.1

Demonstrating Leadership Through Simple and Powerful Language

Here are excerpts from a CEO's letter to employees, shareholders, and clients, describing the positive results of a management style that some analysts considered controversial. In an effort to justify his management approach, the writer uses simple, compelling language and presents supporting data that illustrates the results of his leadership. The financial figures are stated simply (for example, *revenues rose 15 percent ... , earnings increased 19 percent ...*), so most employees can easily grasp them. Plus, phrases like *strongest results in the company's century-long history, energized by innovative e-commerce opportunities,* and *levels of performance and growth unprecedented in our company's history* drive home a simple and powerful message that credits all employees for the firm's success and inspires them to do even better.

To our employees, shareholders, and clients:

This last year was our finest, as 450,000 employees around the world helped us post the strongest results in the company's century-long history:

- *Revenues rose 15 percent, to $89.8 billion, a record.*
- *Earnings increased 19 percent, to $11.3 billion, the first time the company has broken the $10 billion mark in earnings from operations.*

- *Per-share earnings rose 22 percent.*
- *For the fourth consecutive year, our company was among* Fortune *magazine's most admired American enterprises.*
- *Shareholders—including our active and retired employees who own $17 billion of company stock in their savings and pension plans—were rewarded with a 48 percent total return on each share of company stock.*

We begin this new year completely focused on the customer, energized by innovative e-commerce opportunities, and poised to move forward to levels of performance and growth unprecedented in our company's history.

We thank you for all your support in helping make this future so bright.

---

2. Examine a few recent emails from your subordinates, especially those that discussed a problem, justified a recent action, or suggested next steps. Decide whether your opinion of each person's capabilities was influenced by how clearly she or he explained the situation in writing.

Why is Rewriting so Hard?

By Ellen Gilchrist

Why is rewriting so hard? why is it so hard to talk yourself into going back to a first draft and working on it? Why is it so hard to get started? Why do we procrastinate and procrastinate over this? I say WE on purpose because the main thing my students have taught me is that every writer seems to have the same problem. Here I am, twenty books and hundreds of magazine articles later, supposedly a grown woman, and when an editor sends me back a manuscript to have even small changes made, I go around in a huff for hours or maybe even days before I can sit down and get the work done. I would never rewrite anything unless I needed to make money.

I have thought about this long and hard since I have been teaching. Why do the students get that expression on their faces when told something has to be CHANGED? Why do I feel such trepidation when I open an envelope containing a manuscript returned to me from a LOVING editor who has been WORKING ON IT?

Why is Rewriting so Hard?

There is only one explanation that seems possible to me. We are all perfectionists and we can't stand to think we did something wrong EVEN IF WE KNOW HOW TO FIX IT AND DO IT RIGHT THE SECOND TIME. This is so childish. The expression on my students' faces when they don't want to go back to work is childish. My huffiness over editing is childish. It must be our parents' fault. Off with their heads.

Metaphorically we do have to assassinate the parents within us, whatever nasty complaining, correcting voices we hear. When we let another person read a manuscript we want complete and instant praise. The artist is a two-year-old child. She does not want to be criticized in any way. That's what you have to deal with to be a writer. You have to love and nourish the child within who writes the stuff. You have to give the little witch chocolate candy and feed her nasty little ego and then you have to get tough and tell her to sit down at the desk and act like a man or there won't be any money for next month's trip to the mall.

Except the students don't get money or publications and threatening to give them bad grades just makes the problem worse. Publish anywhere you can, I tell them. Get your name in print. Show the publications to your family and friends. Don't be a would-be author. It's too sad. Write things, rewrite them, get published anywhere. Or else, find something else to do. Don't pretend you are a writer. Be a writer.

Writing

Then I give them *On Writing*, a collection of small bits of advice by Ernest Hemingway. Once I copied a piece of it and put it on the first page of the worksheet. This is hard talk about a difficult profession but I thought they needed to hear it.

> *First there must be talent, much talent. Talent such as Kipling had. Then there must be discipline. The discipline of Flaubert. Then there must be the conception of what it can be and an absolute conscience as unchanging as the standard meter in Paris, to prevent faking. Then the writer must be intelligent and disinterested and above all he must survive. Try to get all these in one person and have him come through all the influences that press on a writer. The hardest thing, because time is so short, is for him to survive and get his work done.*
>
> —ERNEST HEMINGWAY

Advocacy Writing

By Joseph L. Zappala and Ann Carden

"As a rock star," says Bono, lead singer for the rock group U2, "I have two interests—I want to have fun and I want to change the world. I have a chance to do both." It can be argued that all public relations writers are advocates for change of some sort, and that all public relations writing advocates something in an attempt to influence or persuade. There are, however, specific tools—***letters to the editor, op-ed articles, position statements, talking points*** and ***speeches, public service announcements***, and ***public relations advertising***—you can use to more strongly establish a public position or express a point of view.

Letters to the Editor

Letters to the editor are primarily targeted to the opinion–editorial sections of print media. This includes newspapers, as well as many magazines. They have multiple purposes:

- When a negative or inaccurate story (or another letter to the editor) about your organization appears in the media, a well-written response can help your organization lessen the bad publicity or correct false information.

- Letters are used to respond positively to media coverage, as well. A hospital public relations person, for example, could send a letter to commend a reporter's series on health care or a health issue, and then use that platform to create further awareness of the hospital's services and to present the hospital as an information resource.
- Whether an article was positive or negative, letters to the editor can "fill in the blanks" and provide information that was not included in the media's coverage.
- Not-for-profit organizations write "thank you" letters to an editor after major fund-raising events to thank the community for its support.
- Organizations can promote a cause they have adopted or bring attention to important issues in their industry that may affect the community.

Newspapers are not required to print letters to the editor, but almost all of them do. Some suggestions for writing letters to the editor:

- Keep the letter short, about 250–300 words. Most newspapers publish letter guidelines on the op-ed page, so follow their rules.
- Each letter should begin with "Dear Editor" or "To the Editor," and conclude with the name, title, and organization of the sender. Sometimes, writing letters on behalf of senior managers and CEOs (with their knowledge and approval, of course) and signing their names can carry more weight and help you get published.
- The first paragraph of the letter should reference the specific article or issue to which you are responding. Mention the headline and date of the article. Other letters written about major issues should quickly identify the subject and indicate why this subject is timely.
- The remaining few paragraphs of the letter should give more background on the subject, making reference to hard facts and statistics when possible. Then, express your opinion or reaction, and conclude by summarizing your main point.
- Maintain a positive tone in the letter. Avoid name-calling and harsh criticism. When responding to a critical or inaccurate story, focus your energy on "setting the record straight" and creating a positive impression about your organization. Consider the consequences of "burning your bridges" with the reporter and publication.

Exhibit 4.1 illustrates the correct physical format and concise writing style of a letter to the editor. It addresses the reason for writing the letter in the first sentence, provides background in the subsequent paragraphs, and concludes by summarizing the main point.

Op-ed Articles

***Op-ed** articles* are longer versions of letters to the editor that allow you to comment on a subject in more depth. There are times when your response to an article or your opinions about an issue will be welcomed in a longer opinion piece, especially when the subject is timely or controversial. Op-ed pieces also are a good way to gain exposure for your organization and

Exhibit 4.1
Letter to the Editor: National Association of Counties

July 21, 2008

To the Editor:

I would like to take this opportunity to express my deep gratitude to Multnomah County Commissioner Lisa Naito for her hard work and dedication this past year as chair of the Justice and Public Safety Steering Committee of the National Association of Counties (NACo).

The committee is responsible for developing NACo policy regarding federal legislation and policy pertaining to criminal justice and public safety systems, including criminal justice planning; law enforcement; courts; corrections; homeland security; community crime prevention; juvenile justice and delinquency prevention; emergency management; fire prevention and control; and civil disturbances.

Commissioner Naito was especially influential in leading her committee's endeavors in developing solid NACo policy affecting counties during my 2007–2008 term as NACo President. Notably, she represented NACo at President Bush's April 9 signing of H.R. 1593, the Second Chance Act, a lop priority for NACo for several years. The bill authorizes $165 million per year in federal grants to local governments and states to provide ex-offenders with education, job training, substance abuse and aftercare treatment, and assist them with finding housing and employment upon release from jail and prison.The law is designed to help reduce recidivism, increase public safety and save local taxpayers money.

I believe with conviction that Commissioner Naito's strong leadership as the chair of the Justice and Public Safety Steering Committee has been of immeasurable benefit to the residents of Multnomah County. I hope she will continue to actively participate in NACo's efforts in Washington, D.C. to guarantee that all 3,068 counties in the nation have the tools, programs and information essential to achieving their goals.

Sincerely,

Eric Coleman, President
National Association of Counties

Eric Coleman is a county commissioner representing Oakland County, Mich.

Note: Reprinted with permission of Eric Coleman

position people within it as experts. In the article "And Now a Word from Op-Ed," David Shipley, the deputy editor for the *New York Times*' op-ed section, describes the format this way:

> Op-Ed is different from the editorial page in that it does not represent the views of anyone in the editorial division, even its own editors. It is different from letters in that it is not a venue to debate articles that have appeared in The Times.

With an estimated 1,200 op-ed submissions arriving weekly, Shipley says an op-ed is more likely to be selected to appear if the writer offers a fresh perspective or presents a topic that has not already been covered in the editorial section.

Op-ed pieces, which get their name from being "opposite the editorial" page, are set up much like technical articles in that they include the by-line of the company expert qualified to talk about the issue. Like technical articles, op-ed pieces should identify key message points or arguments and then use facts, statistics, and supporting evidence to back up those views. The end of the article, besides summarizing main points, should leave the reader with a clear solution to a problem, or state the best reasons for the organization and the public to show continued concern about an issue.

Exhibit 4.2 is an excellent example of an op-ed piece, written by the CEO of NRG Energy, Inc., a power company in New Jersey. It has an attention-getting opening and quickly gets into the main message: carbon dioxide emissions must be regulated by Congress. The writer supports his opinion with solid arguments presented in a persuasive writing style that is personable and easy to understand. The main point is reiterated at the closing—"Global warming should be at the top of Congress's agenda."

While most op-ed pieces have a news angle that reflects current events, organizations also distribute op-ed pieces to coincide with timely events such as a national day, week, or month. A university professor of social work, for instance, wrote an op-ed piece published during Hispanic Heritage Month to comment on the growing influence of the Hispanic/Latino community in the United States.

Like media pitches, op-ed pieces tend to work best when they are submitted to one publication at a time. In fact, some national publications, such as the *New York Times* and *Washington Post*, require that submissions be exclusive, so you want to make sure the publication you choose will best reach your target public. You might want to talk with the appropriate contact at the publication and gauge his interest in publishing the op-ed piece before taking the time to write it. Monitor possible publications and become familiar with the types of op-ed they run to increase your chances of success. You should pay close attention to the publication's submission guidelines, which will include the preferred length of an op-ed (the average length is 600–800 words) and information on how to submit your piece. There are no guarantees that your piece will be published, even if someone has shown interest or agreed to do so by phone or in an e-mail message. After submitting the piece, you should follow up to make sure it has been received, ask if there are any questions or if the piece could be improved in any way, and get a better sense of the intention to publish and when the article might be used.

Exhibit 4.2
Op-ed: NRG Energy

washingtonpost.com

We're Carboholics. Make Us Stop.

By David Crane

Sunday, October 14, 2007: B07

I am a carboholic. As Americans, we are all carboholics, but I am more so than most. The company I run, NRG Energy, emils more than 64 million tons of carbon dioxide (CO_2) into the atmosphere each year—more than the total man-made greenhouse gas emissions of Norway.

And we are only the 10th-largest American power generation company, Imagine the CO_2 emissions of Nos. 1 through 9.

Why do we do it? Why does America's power industry emit such a stunning amount of greenhouse gases into the atmosphere in this age of climate change?

We do so because CO_2 emissions are free. And in a world where CO_2 has no price, removing CO_2 before or after the combustion process is vastly more expensive and problematic than just venting it into the atmosphere.

Congress needs to act now to change our ways. Lawmakers should regulate CO_2 and other greenhouse gas emissions by introducing a federal cap-and-trade system, which would put a cap and a market price on CO_2 emissions.

If Congress acts now, the power industry will respond. We will do what America does best; we will react to CO_2 price signals by innovating and commercializing technologies that avoid, prevent and remove CO_2 from the atmosphere.

I emphasize the word "now." We are not running out of lime; we *have* run out of time. Decisions we make today in the U.S. power industry will have a significant impact on the size of the problem we bequeath to our children.

Without a price on CO_2, our industry will build a veritable tidal wave of traditional coal-fired power-generation facilities. Traditional coal plants are, and will be for some time to come, the least expensive and most reliable way to generate electricity on a large scale in the United States, China, India and much of the rest of the world—that is, so long as the CO_2 emissions associated with burning coal in these countries remain free.

We absolutely need to use coal for power-generation purposes. We probably even need to build a few more traditional coal plants in fast-growing parts of the country where there is no practical alternative. But we need to move as quickly as possible toward implementing the low-emissions ways of combusting coal that are under development or, in the case of "coal gasification" technology, are ready for commercial deployment.

A federal cap-and-trade system would push the power and coal industries toward deployment of CO_2 capture and sequestration technology, which is essential to reducing our domestic emissions and, ultimately, to weaning China and the rest of the fast-growring (and emitting) developing wrorld off traditional coal technology. Effective incentives for these new technologies could easily and readily be included in a cap-and-trade regimen. Lawmakers need to provide both the carrot and the stick to get the CO_2 out of coal.

continued ...

Exhibit 4.2
Op-ed: NRG Energy ... *continued*

Energy legislation under consideration in Congress focuses almost exclusively on renewables and conservation; both are worthy initiatives thai deserve our support. But in a world where a CO_2-emtting traditional coal plant is built every week, renewables and conservation are a sideshow at best.

The vast amount of CO_2 being emitted worldwide by coal-fired power plants is the heart of the global warming issue. Progress against those emissions depends on three critical initiatives: replacing traditional coal with "clean coal" plants, displacing additional traditional coal plants with new zero-carbon-emissions nuclear plants and implementing a federal cap-and-trade system on greenhouse gases.

Global warming should be at the top of Congress's agenda—because action by this Congress will turn the tide of climate change around the world. Never before have we faced the prospect of fandamentally damaging our global ecosystem by the day-to-day activities of each and every one of us. A cap-and-trade system is the place to start. America must act now to protect our future.

David Crane is chief executive of Princeton, N.J.-based NRG Energy Inc., a wholesale power generator. NRG, which owns power plants capable of serving 19 million households, recently filed for a license to build two nuclear reactors in South Texas.

Position Statements

Position statements are similar in their approach to letters to the editor and op-ed commentaries; however, they are more formal and represent official positions that have been adopted by an organization's governing body. In fact, they often include a statement in the heading or in the beginning paragraph that identifies who adopted the position and when.

Ranging in length from a paragraph to multiple pages, position statements deal with important, sometimes controversial, issues facing an organization and its publics and are often utilized by nonprofit organizations, especially professional associations. They may be distributed to the media, government officials, and other target publics, or posted online. The National Association for the Education of Young Children has issued position statements on topics such as curriculum, school readiness, and child abuse. The American Association of School Librarians has written a position statement on the confidentiality of library records, and the National Association of the Deaf has taken an official position on cochlear implants.

Position papers have many elements of a research paper (outlined in chapter 11) in that they identify an issue, provide a history of the issue, present data, and make recommendations. When writing a position paper, begin with a clear, objective statement of the issue, followed by background on the issue to provide context. The background should be thorough enough to offer readers who are not familiar with the issue an understanding of the subject matter. This paves the way for the writer to then state the organization's position, or opinion, on the issue. Position papers are persuasive pieces, so the position must be supported by logos appeals, such as facts, statistics, and scientific evidence, and pathos appeals, such as compassion, patriotism, or fear. It is also wise to address any opposition to your position; it is better to address opponents head on and refute their arguments, than to ignore them.

Writing a position paper presents a special challenge to the public relations practitioner. Not only is it a time-consuming project because of the research involved, but the practitioner must also take care to present information that can often be complex in a way the target public will understand.

Talking Points and Speeches

Public relations professionals also help organizations and their people express their points of view through the creation of ***talking points*** and ***speeches***.

Answers.com defines a talking point as, "Something, such as an especially persuasive point, that helps to support an argument or a discussion." Often, talking points are developed to ensure that consistent messages are delivered when organizations deal with difficult decisions and situations. For example, to explain a decision to implement lay-offs, talking points are crafted and provided to senior executives and others who communicate this news to stakeholders. These talking points are core messages that a company wants to repeat and deliver in the same way, using the same language, to help people understand why lay-offs are happening and to justify the company's course of action. If stakeholders hear differing messages, this can cause confusion and make people question the decisions, eroding trust. A talking point in this instance could be as simple as, "We need to take this action now to protect the long-term financial health of the company," emphasizing the importance of this decision as it relates to survival and future success.

Talking points help organizations in their efforts to increase public awareness of an issue and to build support around a cause. Blue Ribbons for Kids, a campaign aimed at community education and prevention of child abuse, offers several brief talking points on its Web site that could be used in presentations and conversations, or to generally guide thinking in the community about this subject. These talking points include:

- Everyone can do something to prevent child abuse. When you see an adult losing patience with a child, intervene but keep it positive. If a child is in danger, offer assistance or call for help.
- Get to know the children in your life, so they feel comfortable talking to you if they feel unsafe. Pay attention to changes in their behavior; this may indicate something is wrong.

Another advocacy-writing role you might be asked to play is that of speechwriter. Speeches take many forms: from brief remarks given at an awards presentation or to introduce another speaker at an event that are fully written for someone or delivered using a series of talking points; to longer scripts read word-for-word by executives who are asked to give keynote presentations at industry conferences or to speak at a commencement ceremony.

In either case, good speechwriting should always follow certain guidelines: know your audience in advance and understand what they expect or want to hear; establish a central theme and main idea that you want to communicate, and repeat that idea throughout the speech; and write an opening that will grab the audience's attention right away, a body that avoids trying to convey too much and focuses on just a few key points, and an ending that comes back to your central idea and leaves people with something provocative or encourages them to think differently.

As the speechwriter, of course, you also need to know the person who is delivering the remarks—how does she present herself, think, and talk? Speeches are meant to be heard, not read or seen, so the language and tone need to be conversational. Ask the person you are writing the speech for to talk through her ideas, and write down what she says. As you're writing, read aloud what's been written and ask yourself if it sounds natural or has the voice of the speaker. In the end, you want the audience to listen and be absorbed in the speech. If people are not engaged and entertained, then it's likely that the message will get lost, and the speech will fall flat.

Some public relations professionals can move through their careers and never write a speech. It's likely, though, that there will be occasions when someone asks for help coming up with brief remarks. Bill Cole, founder and CEO of Procoach Systems, says on the Procoach Web site that the writing for short speeches has to be even better than for longer ones, since you have "less time to get your critical message across." Other tips include:

- You must make sure the audience gets the central core theme and message right away. You don't have the luxury of "warming up" your audience. Get to the point quickly and "make the first impression the best." Keep the message to the point and on target.
- The logical flow of the talk must be tighter than in a longer talk, or the speaker risks being perceived as a "five-minute blatherer."
- If the speech is part of a series of brief remarks by other presenters, you need to "play off" the speaker before you to get the audience's attention quickly, or you might get tuned out. On the other hand, look for ways to write the remarks so that they stand out from the others and leave a memorable impression.

Public Service Announcements

It's a television image that many people remember. The shot opens on a frying pan. No sound. Then you see an egg and hear a voice saying, "This is your brain." The egg is cracked into the pan, you hear a sizzling sound for a few seconds, and the voice comes in again to say, "This is your brain on drugs." The egg continues to cook, followed by a brief closing remark: "Any questions?" This is an example of a classic ***public service announcement***, or PSA. It uses simple visuals, minimal voice-over, and the element of surprise to communicate a single, powerful message—drugs can "fry" your brain.

Not-for-profit organizations create PSAs to inform and educate audiences about important health, social, and public interest issues. Although the Federal Communication Commission no longer mandates stations to provide a certain amount of airtime to PSAs, the media still donate time to air these spots as a public service. Many stations have public service directors to coordinate PSAs and public service programming. Competition for PSA placement is stiff. A station may only air a few PSAs a day out of the many it receives each week. Attention to some fundamentals can help your PSAs succeed with the media and your target audiences:

- Come up with a strategic plan for your public service campaign that includes research of the issue, public attitudes, and media interest in the subject; goal setting and targeted message development; production techniques and costs; and distribution and evaluation methods.
- Create and send a variety of formats and lengths—:10, :15, :20, :30, and :60 spots. For radio, you can create prerecorded spots with voice-overs and sound effects, as well as simple announcer scripts that cost nothing to produce and can be read on the air by deejays between songs to fill time.
- Focus on one main idea and reinforce that idea a few times in the spot. Use a memorable theme line (e.g., Friends don't let friends drive drunk). Do something at the start of the spot using voice, visuals, or sound that will get the audience interested and make them ask, "What's coming next?"
- Include a call to action such as a phone number or Web site where people can get more information or make a donation.
- Incorporate a local angle, such as a local phone number to call or a statistic that relates to the geographic area targeted. Many nationally prepared PSAs provide room at the end to include local information. Keep minority audiences in mind, and prepare targeted versions or scripts with content that will appeal to diverse groups and ethnic media.
- Track PSA usage. As with VNRs, SIGMA encoding can be used. Send reminder cards or make follow-up phone calls to the media to build interest.

The Ad Council, founded in 1942, has produced numerous memorable public service ads, many of which have become part of popular culture. Its campaigns have included "Only You Can Prevent Forest Fires," "Take a Bite Out of Crime," and "A Mind is a Terrible Thing to Waste." The council conducts campaigns on health and safety, community, and education by bringing together advertising agencies and the media; ad agencies donate their time to create the spots, and media donate advertising space. The award-winning "Think Before You Speak" campaign sponsored by the Ad Council and the Gay, Lesbian and Straight Education Network includes three television PSAs, three radio PSAs, and six print PSAs. See Exhibits 4.3 and 4.4 for examples from the campaign, which is aimed at reducing and preventing homophobic language among teenagers.

Public Relations Advertising

Organizations wishing to take a public stand on an issue or express a point of view in the media can also create ***public relations*** or ***institutional advertising***. Editors can choose to print your op-ed letters and articles, or they can reject them completely. The advantage of running an ad is that you pay for the space, which means your message will appear in print exactly as you want it to. Ads produced by Anheuser-Busch and other beer companies asking you to drink responsibly and to use designated drivers are public relations ads. They advocate a corporate point of view, not the product.

Exhibit 12.3
PSA Print Ad: Gay, Lesbian, and Straight Education Network

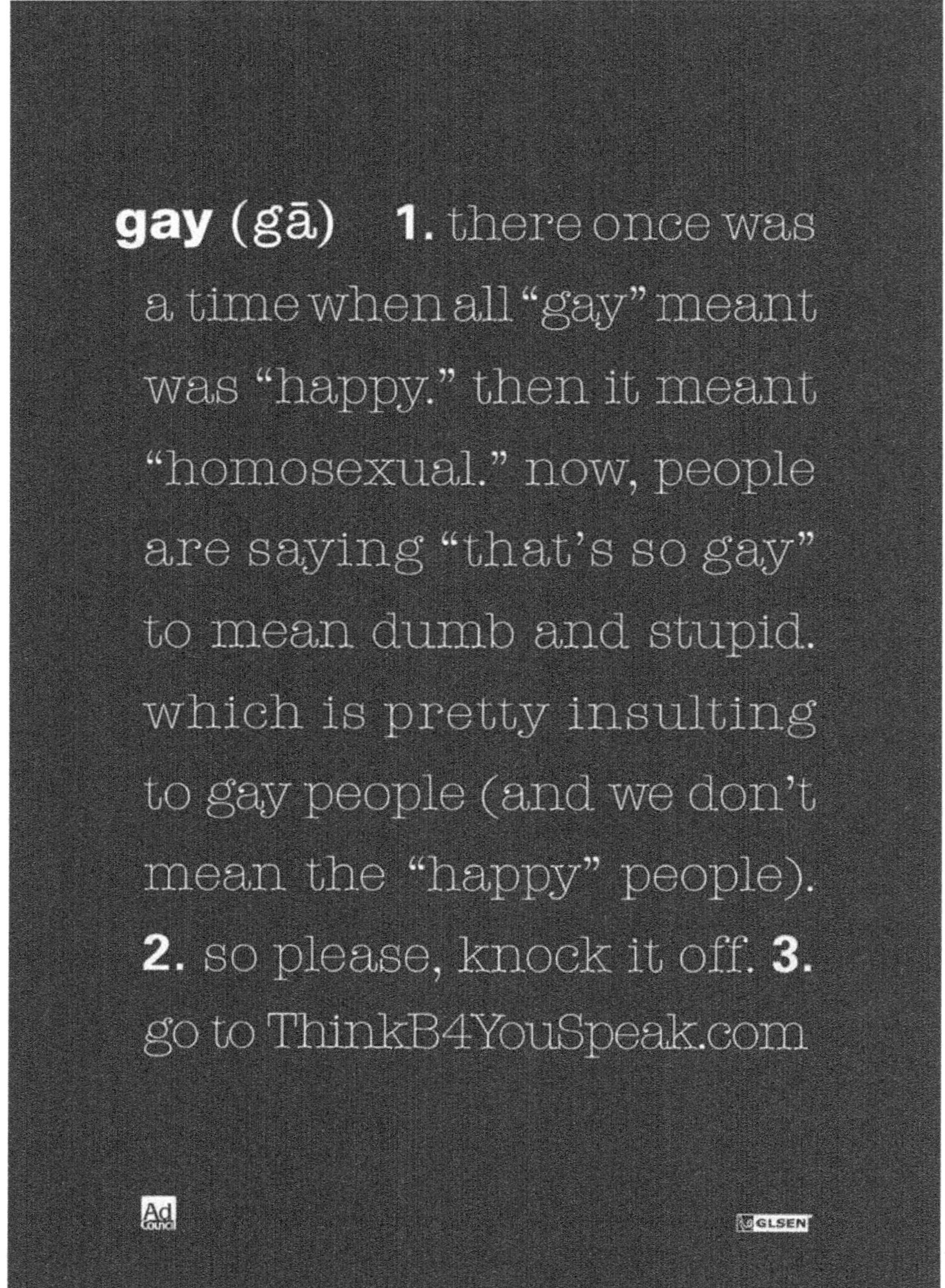

ThinkB4YouSpeak, from Educator's Guide: For Discussing and Addressing Anti-Gay Language among Teens, p. 14. Copyright © 2008 by Gay, Lesbian and Straight Education Network (GLSEN). Reprinted with permission.

Public relations advertising is produced in much the same way as a public service announcement. When creating copy for public relations ads:

- Put some thought into the headline. Raise a provocative question or recommend that the reader think a certain way or do something specific about an issue. Some ad headlines have impact when written more like news headlines. Whatever the case, make the headline strong and catchy. A public relations ad placed by Verizon carried the headline: "When One Million People Get Together, a Million Good Things Happen." The ad promoted Verizon's $1 million donation to five major charities in celebration of the company's one millionth long-distance phone service customer.
- Make the first paragraph an extension of the headline. That first sentence in the body of the ad needs to build off of the idea presented in the headline.
- Write simple body copy, use active voice, and keep sentences and paragraphs short. It is acceptable to use incomplete sentences in ad copy for emphasis.
- Recap the main point at the end. Effective ads do that creatively, and bring the reader back to the key idea raised in the headline and first paragraph. Some ads include a final statement that asks the reader to take a desired action. The Verizon ad concluded by informing customers about a letter being sent to them about the company's $1 million charitable donations and encouraging visits to its Web site to learn more about the campaign.

Advertising is very expensive. To make sure your dollars are spent wisely, media outlets should be chosen based on: your target public; ***reach***, which refers to how many people are exposed to the medium during a specific time period (such as "sweeps weeks," certain times of the year when television and radio stations are measured for viewership and listenership in order to establish their ratings in the market); and ***frequency***, which refers to the number of times those people were exposed to the message.

ASSIGNMENTS

Assignment 12.1—Primo Pizza Advocates Safer Driving

According to the Centers for Disease Control and Prevention, "Motor vehicle crashes are the leading cause of death for U.S. teens, accounting for more than one in three deaths in this age group." The risk of being in a car accident is higher for 16–19-year-old drivers than it is for any other age group, and the risk of a crash is much higher during the first year teenagers are able to drive. For each mile driven, teen drivers ages 16–19 are about four times more likely than other drivers to crash.

Your state has enacted a graduated driver licensing system. Graduated licensing is designed to delay full licensure; it allows beginning drivers to get their initial experience under lower-risk conditions in three phases. Under this system, full driving privileges are given to young drivers after meeting age and other requirements that demonstrate safe driving ability.

Primo Pizza, a chain of more than 50 pizza shops operated exclusively in your state, also has a special interest in teen driving and safety on the roads, since many of its delivery people are older teens. Anthony Roe, the president of Primo Pizza, has asked to meet with you, the company's new public affairs and community relations manager, to talk about ways in which the company can align with this issue.

"As you know, Primo has a special interest in teen driving and safety on the roads. We hire many younger drivers, and if they come to us with well-developed driving habits, that would certainly benefit our business," Roe says. "As we move into the winter months, when driving can be a lot trickier, I think it would be good for us to publicly say something about safe driving and how critical it is for people and to the way we do business."

"What's also really great about this is the fact that we've become known for our concerns about safe driving, so there's a genuine interest on our part," you say. "But, of course, it does bring with it some public relations and marketing benefits, there's no question about that. Can you refresh my memory about some of the steps we take to promote safe driving?"

"Sure. We start by looking closely at people's driving records before we hire them, and new drivers never start driving right away," Roe explains. "We usually have them go out with another, more experienced driver for the first week or so. Then, after that, a manager or a senior driver goes out on a delivery with a newer driver every few weeks for a two-month period to monitor how well that person is doing behind the wheel."

"Don't the drivers have to attend some courses, as well?" you ask.

"Yes, we call them safe-driving workshops. We sponsor a few of those during the year and all of our drivers are required to attend. Those are interesting because they expose our drivers to real-life driving problems they might encounter on the road, and ask them to act out how they would respond to certain hazardous situations. Local police and AAA staff run those for us in each town or city where we have shops," Roe says.

"I definitely see some opportunities for us to get some positive media exposure around this issue. I know the company was a big advocate for the passage of the graduated licensing system laws, so we could weave that into any messaging, too. I did some research, and it looks like those laws have been contributing to a drop in auto accidents that involve teens."

Exercises

1. Write a letter to the editor for distribution to statewide print media. Your focus should be the importance of safe driving during the winter months and Primo's position on teens and safe driving. The letter should be about 300 words and be signed by Anthony Roe, president of Primo Pizza.
2. Write copy for a Primo Pizza public relations advertisement that establishes the company's position on teens and safe driving and the importance of this issue to the company. Your ad copy should begin with a creative headline and a brief description of any appropriate visuals. Limit the copy to no more than three or four short paragraphs.

Assignment 12.2—The Humane Society's PSA Campaign

With more than 10 million members and constituents, the Humane Society of the United States (HSUS) is the nation's largest and most effective animal protection organization. The HSUS serves the animal population in many ways. It advocates for public policies to reduce animal suffering, investigates animal cruelty and works to enforce existing laws, and helps educate the public about animal issues, among other programs and services. The HSUS provides direct care for thousands of animals at sanctuaries and rescue facilities, wildlife rehabilitation centers and mobile veterinary clinics.

You work as a public relations specialist for the HSUS and have been speaking with staff members in the organization's regional offices about their public relations needs. You share feedback received from regional staff with your supervisor, Mary DeFreitas.

"The regional operations are saying that they're getting more requests from individuals and local shelters for information on animal cruelty," DeFreitas says. "It seems that many of the local communities have seen an increase in cases involving pet owners who have seriously neglected their animals. There are more reports of malicious attacks on animals—cats that have been set on fire by kids who said they were playing a practical joke, dogs beaten and left for dead. The regional offices told me that they would like to have some new materials to help better educate people about animal cruelty, in hopes that more people will report abuse and neglect and discourage others from committing these acts."

"We've been thinking about creating some new public service announcements," you add. "This might be a subject we could focus on. There's an interesting tie-in here, too, with the increase in youth violence that we've seen lately. We know that young people who have been involved in violent acts, like school shootings, often have a history of being cruel to animals. On some level, maybe our efforts could contribute positively to a more serious social problem."

"PSAs are a good idea," DeFreitas says. "The local media in these areas have covered many of these animal cruelty cases, and in some instances that coverage got residents to rally around this issue and take a stand. It would be great to bring even more visibility to this issue."

DeFreitas continues. "While you're here, I wanted to talk to you about another project. I've been asked to give some brief remarks at the opening of the new animal shelter in town. I'd like to make a few key points about the importance of shelters, but also about the work we do, in general. The Pet Smart store has donated some food products and toys for the shelter, so I should say something about that in my remarks. The overall remarks don't need to be too long. Besides HSUS staff, we're inviting volunteers and donors, and we'll see if we can get a few local government officials to show up."

Exercises

1. Prepare scripts for the following HSUS public service announcements. At the top of each script, state the goal of the spot and the audience targeted.

   - 20- and 30-second versions of an announcer-only radio PSA on animal cruelty;
   - a 30-second produced radio PSA on animal cruelty;
   - a 60-second television PSA on animal cruelty.

2. Prepare DeFreitas's remarks for the opening of the new animal shelter. Her remarks should be at least three but no more than five minutes in length.

Assignment 12.3—Defending Home Health Care

You handle public relations for PersonalCare, the oldest home health care agency in a medium-sized city. PersonalCare offers three levels of service: companions, who assist the elderly and disabled with dressing and personal hygiene and handle household activities such as light house-cleaning, meal preparation, and shopping; home health aides, who perform household activities, but who also have the training to take vital signs and assist with patient exercise routines; and registered and licensed practical nurses, who can provide more involved medical care for those recuperating from major surgery or others with chronic illnesses, such as cancer and Alzheimer's disease. All of PersonalCare's companions and aides are supervised and trained by registered nurses. The person receiving home health care enjoys the comfort and security of his or her own home, which can have emotional benefits and speed the healing process.

Recently, the morning daily newspaper ran a story on the front page of its local section with the headline, "Home health care aide convicted of stealing from elderly woman." This led to a few more stories on the risks of hiring home health aides to care for the elderly and disabled in their private homes. After reading these negative stories, you approach Luke Shaw, the agency's executive director, to discuss the impact of this media coverage.

"Even though this incident didn't involve us, I feel like we have a responsibility to respond to all the negative press," you say. "If people start perceiving that it's dangerous to bring a home health aide into their homes, and that all people who work as home health aides are criminals and can't be trusted, it could hurt our business. Unfortunately, that's the picture that the local media have been painting, and it's an undeserved stereotype that we need to correct, since most home health aides are responsible people."

"So far, we haven't had any problems with aides committing thefts. But I see what you mean. The average person will not necessarily separate one home health agency from another. It gives all of us a bad name. What do you think we should do?" Shaw asks.

"I'd like us to put together a public information program that informs people in our community about the value of home health care, but also helps them to become smart consumers when it comes to selecting a home health care agency. People might not know, for instance, that many agencies, like ours, are licensed by the state, and that all employees are required to go through an intensive screening, and their references are carefully checked. We screen employees to see if there is any criminal activity in their background before anyone is placed in a person's home. It's also pretty easy to get information on an agency's reputation by checking with the Better Business Bureau or a chamber of commerce. Consumers should find out if the agency is insured for general and professional liability and how that protects them. Those are some of the tips we could offer."

"I like this idea and I like the fact you're suggesting we be proactive and take a leadership role on this issue. We can provide an important service to the community and strengthen the agency's reputation in the community and in the home health care industry at the same time. It might even bring us some new clients," Shaw says.

"True. I think we have an excellent opportunity to show people just how critical home health care has become, and how it will be even more critical as the elderly population grows in size. We do a lot of good for people. Many sons and daughters tell us that they don't know what they would have done without this service and the companionship it provides day-to-day for their elderly parents. That's a story we need to tell," you say.

Exercises

Prepare the following pieces for the PersonalCare public information program:

- A fact sheet that outlines 10 tips for selecting a reputable home health care agency. Do research to gather information for the fact sheet.
- A 500-word op-ed article to be sent to the local media that explains the positive aspects of home health care and dispels negative images of home health care workers. It should be signed by Luke Shaw, PersonalCare's executive director.
- A three-page feature/human-interest story on the important role of home health care and the benefits it provides to home health care users and their families.

References and Suggested Reading

About Ad Council (n.d.). Retrieved December 11, 2008 from http://www.adcouncil.org/default.aspx?id=68.

Bivins, T. H. (2007). *Public relations writing: The essentials of style and format* (6th ed.). New York: McGraw Hill.

Fink, C. C. (2004). *Writing opinion for impact.* Ames, IA: Wiley-Blackwell.

Newsom, D. & Haynes, J. (2007). *Public relations writing form & style* (8th ed.). Belmont, CA: Thomson & Wadsworth.

Public Service Advertising Research Center, www.psaresearch.com.

Sample talking points (n.d.). Retrieved January 16, 2009 from http://blueribbonsonline.wi.gov/Download%20resources/WI_talking %20points.pdf.

Shipley, D. And now a word from op-ed. (2004, February 1). *The Washington Post.*

Smith, R. D. (2007). *Becoming a public relations writer* (3rd ed.). Mahwah, NJ: Lawrence Erlbaum Associates.

Top ten tips for writing and delivering very brief speeches: Be good, be brief and be sected (2005). Retrieved January 16, 2009 from http://www.mentalgamecoach.com/articles/BriefSpeeches.html.

Wilcox, D. L. (2008). *Public relations writing and media techniques* (6th ed.). New York: Allyn & Bacon.

Writing for writers: Speechwriting (n.d.) Retrieved January 16, 2009 from http://teacher.scholastic.com/writewit/speech/index.htm.

Chapter Highlights

- Good writing is a major component in the work of journalists and public relations practitioners.
- Both journalists and public relations practitioners devote much of their energy toward fact-finding and then communicating that information—in writing—to various publics.
- Despite the different foci of each profession, to maintain credibility, what the journalist and public relations practitioner communicate must be accurate and fact-based.
- These two professional communicators share a mutual dependency based on accessibility, responsiveness, the quality of their work, and openness.

- The dynamic between the journalist and the public relations practitioner has shifted over the years. In the beginning, the public relations worker was much more dependent on the journalist. The rise of social media has caused a major shift in the dynamic, as no longer does the public relations worker always need the journalist to reach various targeted publics. Still, the two continue to interact on a regular basis.

For Discussion

1. How would you describe the dynamic between the journalist and the public relations practitioner? Do you agree with us that each professional is equally dependent on the other?
2. How are journalists and public relations practitioners similar? How are they different?
3. The authors describe how the work of journalists and public relations practitioners must be steeped in facts and an honest presentation of them. Do you agree that in real life this is the case? Why or why not?
4. Select several examples of journalistic and public relations writing. Compare and contrast the two.
5. Discuss the writing challenges that journalists and public relations practitioners face in the course of what they might view as a normal workweek.
6. At present, would you say that either one of these professions makes a greater contribution to society than the other? Why or why not?
7. A primary purpose of journalistic writing is to inform, while for public relations writing it is often to persuade. Is one more effective than the other?

V

Style Resources

One of the most valuable tools for an editor, journalist, or writer is a good style book. *The Associated Press Stylebook* is the one we use in our classrooms when teaching. To fully understand what a stylebook is and why it is one of our most valuable resources, we turn to the Associated Press to understand more.

First, what is the Associated Press (AP), and why should we care? Pulling from the AP's website (www.ap.org), we take a closer look: "The Associated Press is the most trusted source of independent news and information in the world. Founded in 1846, the AP is a not-for-profit cooperative of news organizations, and it is solely focused on finding, reporting and distributing news. The AP is independent and objective and has a deep and active commitment to freedom of the press. It is headquartered in New York and has about 3,700 employees globally—about two-thirds of them journalists and editors—in more than 300 locations worldwide, including every statehouse in the U.S."

The Associated Press Style

The AP uses a certain style in writing, and all the information is compiled in a very handy book we use in our classrooms. The stylebook is used in almost every newsroom we've worked in.

The Associated Press Stylebook is also available online. We enjoy the spiral-bound version for easy and fast flipping as well as the online version, which can be found at www.apstylebook.com.

The good news for students is that acquiring knowledge of AP style is a tangible skill that students can put on their résumés. We've had several students put this skill down on their résumés, and it helped them obtain jobs in journalism and public relations. Editors know that a working knowledge of AP in writing is a valuable asset. The best part is that students don't need to know everything about the style; they simply need to know how to use it and be well-versed in accessing the information in the stylebook. In fact, in AP tests in our classrooms, we allow students to use their AP books, just like they would in a newsroom or at their offices.

We require that students use *The Associated Press Stylebook* for our journalism courses. Inside the stylebook students will find everything they ever wanted to know about the writing style for social media, food guidelines, sports guidelines, editing marks, caption writing, broadcast guidelines, business guidelines, a briefing on media law, and even a statement of news values.

AP Sample Test

Here is an example of an AP test to take as a sample test. We will include two versions. First, the test itself, and, second, the test with the answers in bold. This exam is based on the most recent edition of the AP stylebook. When taking the test, you may look up the answers in your current edition of *The Associated Press Stylebook*.

Grade: __________

1. Circle the sentence if it is in correct Associated Press style.
   She was entitled to the promotion.
   The book was titled "Gone with the Wind."

2. What term is used for an intoxicated driver, and what is the adjective/noun rule?
3. Is it ever appropriate to abbreviate WMD? If so, what is the rule?
4. When referring to the weight of a person or object, do you spell out the numbers or use figures?
5. When writing an article about Queen Elizabeth II's Diamond Jubilee, how do you correctly write her name and title?
6. Is it proper to use swear/curse words in an article?
7. What numbers do you spell out? What's the basic rule of thumb?
8. Regarding addresses, what is the rule of thumb for abbreviating street names?
9. You are writing an article about the TLC television program *Little People, Big World*. According to AP style, what is the correct way to refer to a "little person"?
   a. little person
   b. dwarf
   c. midget
   d. short-statured person
   e. pint-size person
   f. none of the above are appropriate

10. In your article, you are writing about the demise of the yellow pages to smartphones, technology, and mobile access to the Internet. What is the proper way to cite within the article?
    a. Yellow pages
    b. yellow-pages
    c. yellow pages
    d. Yellow Pages
    e. Telephone Book
    f. Yellow-page business resource

11. When describing a person by hair color, which of the following is acceptable?
    a. red-haired
    b. redhead
    c. redheaded
    d. fire-engine-red hair
    e. all of the above

12. If you are writing movie reviews, which style is correct to use when writing about ratings?
    a. The movie has an R rating.
    b. an R-rated movie
    c. The movie is R-rated.
    d. an R-Rated movie
    e. all of the above
13. What acronym is acceptable in all references to "absent without leave"?
14. The use of "irregardless" and "regardless" are both fine—true or false? If false, why?
15. When is it appropriate to use "port" and "starboard"?
16. If you are writing about the Olympics, when do you uppercase the season? What is the rule on this?
17. What is the correct style when describing a woman's gender?
    a. female
    b. woman
    c. girl
    d. chick
    e. lady
    f. all the above

18. Which car reference is correct?
    a. 4 × 4
    b. four by four
    c. four-wheel drive
    d. fourwheel-drive
    e. four wheel drive 4 × 4 vehicle

19. You are writing about the terrorism events on September 11th. Circle the correct style references.
    a. September 11, 2001
    b. September 11th
    c. Sept. 11

d. 9-11
e. 9/11
f. 911
g. all of the above

20. When is the use of "FIFA" acceptable?
 a. on the first reference
 b. only on the second reference
 c. never
 d. always spell out the French acronym

AP Answer Key

When looking up the answers, please refer to a recent edition of *The Associated Press Stylebook*. The sample tests were created using the 2012 AP book, but you can also find the answers within a few pages if you are using an older version of AP.

1. Circle the sentence if it is in correct Associated Press style.
   She was entitled to the promotion.
   The book was titled "Gone with the Wind."
   Answer: Both sentences are correct. See page 93: entitled/titled.

2. What term is used for an intoxicated driver, and what is the adjective/noun rule?
   Answer: "Drunken" is the spelling of the adjective used before nouns—for example, "drunken driver" or "drunken driving." See page 85.

3. Is it ever appropriate to abbreviate WMD? If so, what is the rule?
   Answer: Yes, "weapons of mass destruction" is abbreviated as "WMD" on the second reference. See page 291.

4. When referring to the weight of a person or object, do you spell out the numbers or use figures?
   Answer: Use figures—for example: The baby weighed 9 pounds, 7 ounces. See page 288.

5. When writing an article about Queen Elizabeth II's Diamond Jubilee, how do you correctly write her name and title?
   Answer: The word "queen" is capitalized only when it comes before the name of a royal individual. Therefore, the first time you write "Queen Elizabeth II," the "Q" must be capitalized, and you must include that she is the second Queen Elizabeth. In subsequent references, it is appropriate to reference the queen only as Queen Elizabeth. See pages 223, 186, and 264 of the 2012 AP stylebook.

6. Is it proper to use swear/curse words in an article?
   Answer: It is not proper to use vulgar language in an article, unless it's in a direct quote. See pages 279, 192, and 72.

7. What numbers do you spell out? What's the basic rule of thumb?
   Answer: Spell out the numbers below ten. See page 191.

8. Regarding addresses, what is the rule of thumb for abbreviating street names?
   Answer: Use "Ave.," "Blvd.," and "St." only with a numbered address. See page 4.

9. You are writing an article about the TLC television program *Little People, Big World*. According to AP style, what is the correct way to refer to a "little person"?
   a. little person
   b. dwarf
   c. midget
   d. short-statured person
   e. pint-size person
   f. none of the above are appropriate
   Answer: The correct answer is (b) "dwarf." See page 86.

10. In your article, you are writing about the demise of the yellow pages to smartphones, technology, and mobile access to the Internet. What is the proper way to cite within the article?
    a. Yellow pages
    b. yellow-pages
    c. yellow pages
    d. Yellow Pages
    e. Telephone Book
    f. Yellow-page business resource
    Answer: The correct answer is (d) "Yellow Pages." See page 293.

11. When describing a person by hair color, which of the following is acceptable?
    a. red-haired
    b. redhead
    c. redheaded
    d. fire-engine-red hair
    e. all of the above
    Answer: The correct answer is (a) "red-haired." See page 228.

12. If you are writing movie reviews, which style is correct to use when writing about ratings?
    a. The movie has an R rating.
    b. an R-rated movie
    c. The movie is R-rated.
    d. an R-Rated movie
    e. all of the above
    Answer: Answers (a), (b), and (c) are acceptable. See page 174, regarding movie ratings.

13. What acronym is acceptable in all references to "absent without leave"?
    Answer: The acronym "AWOL" can be used. See page 24.

14. The use of "irregardless" and "regardless" are both fine—true or false? If false, why?
    Answer: "Irregardless" is a double negative. "Regardless" is correct. See page 137.

15. When is it appropriate to use "port" and "starboard"?
    Answer: These are nautical terms for "left" and "right" (when facing the bow, or forward). "Port" is left. "Starboard" is right. In writing, change the nautical terms to "left" or "right" except in direct quotes. See page 210.

16. If you are writing about the Olympics, when do you uppercase the season? What is the rule on this?
    Answer: Use "Winter Olympics" and "Summer Olympics." See page 240, regarding seasons. Uppercase these words if they are part of a formal title.

17. What is the correct style when describing a woman's gender?
    a. female
    b. woman
    c. girl
    d. chick
    e. lady
    f. all the above
    Answer: The correct answer is (a): use "female" as an adjective, not "woman." See page 103. For example: She is the first female governor of North Carolina.

18. Which car reference is correct?
    a. 4x4
    b. four by four
    c. four-wheel drive
    d. fourwheel-drive
    e. four wheel drive 4x4 vehicle
    Answer: The correct answer is (c) "four-wheel drive." See page 109.

19. You are writing about the terrorism events on September 11th. Circle the correct style references.
    a. September 11, 2001
    b. September 11th
    c. Sept. 11
    d. 9-11
    e. 9/11
    f. 911
    g. all of the above
    Answer: Both (c) "Sept. 11" and (e) "9/11" are acceptable. See pages 185 and 241.

20. When is the use of "FIFA" acceptable?
    a. on the first reference
    b. only on the second reference
    c. never
    d. always spell out the French acronym

Answer: The correct answer is (a). "FIFA" stands for "Federation International de Football Association." See page 413 regarding sports guidelines. "FIFA" is acceptable on the first reference. Refer to it as the international soccer governing body rather than spelling out the French acronym.

Grammar is Power

Grammar is power, according to the grammar and style expert for *The Washington Post*. Not too long ago, *The Washington Post* ran a wonderful article about why AP style is important. What follows is this clever piece (written by journalist Paul Farhi) that you will enjoy about the real-life application of AP style and grammar. Take a look at your own knowledge and see where you come up smelling like roses but also where you may fall short just a bit. It is our hope that you will come to enjoy the art of style and grammar. We can all improve our writing; this is just one valuable resource or tool to help you through the years, in college and in your career.

The Grammar Expert

In its modern, digital forms, writing has become something like an untended garden. It's overgrown with text-speak and crawling with invasive species like tweets and dashed-off e-mails. OMG, it's a mess.

So think of David Minthorn as a linguistic gardener, doggedly cultivating this weedy patch in the hope of restoring some order and maybe coaxing something beautiful out of it.

Minthorn's mission is the maintenance of English grammar, the policing of punctuation and the enforcement of a consistent written style for one of the world's largest news organizations. As the Associated Press's deputy standards editor, he's the news wire's word nerd, the go-to guy for settling all manner of niggling usage questions. Is it "e-mail" or "email"? "Smart phone" or "smartphone"? "Tea Party" or "tea party"? According to Dave Minthorn, it should be the latter in each case.

His distilled wisdom is the AP Stylebook, the bible for correspondents and editors and a best-selling volume in its own right for the past three decades. Minthorn and two colleagues, Darrell Christian and Sally Jacobsen, are the Stylebook's editors. They spend all year arguing about what to include, updating the book to take account of new words and phrases such as "geotagging," "unfollow," and "Internet-connected TV."

For the past four years, Minthorn has also been the author of AP's "Ask the Editor" feature, in which perplexed writers from all walks of life (and all corners of the globe) seek his counsel on such pressing matters as the placement of commas and the appropriate use of an apostrophe. Since taking over the column from its founder, Norm Goldstein, Minthorn has answered more than 8,000 of these queries, offering brief but definitive responses to questions such as:

- "What is the plural of meatloaf? Meatloafs? Meatloaves? It isn't in the dictionary." Minthorn replied that AP's style is "meatloaves," noting that this "makes sense because the dictionary lists loaves as the plural of loaf, the food."
- "Is it redundant to call the language Mandarin Chinese? Nobody uses the term Cantonese Chinese." Mandarin is sufficient, Minthorn decreed.
- "Is the short form of microphone mic or mike?" The informal form of microphone is "mic," he responded. (The Washington Post, which has its own word-usage and style committee, disagrees, sticking with "mike," no matter what the manufacturers print on your electronic devices.)

In fact, Minthorn is frequently asked how bulleted items, like those above, should be presented in a letter or formal presentation. (We're not sure we did it right.)

"I feel a little bit of an obligation to answer as many of these questions as I can," says the mild-mannered Minthorn. "I don't get to all of them. But I try my best. People really want to know."

"We get hundreds of suggestions a year [for changes]. We adopt the ones that we think have reached a critical mass."

All told, Minthorn, who is 69, exerts a subtle yet profound influence on the way words appear online and in print. His judgments guide AP's dispatches, which is no small thing. The New York-based news service, a nonprofit cooperative owned by member news organizations, has 3,700 employees in 300 bureaus around the world. On a given day, it claims, its work is seen by half the world's population. Because of this ubiquity, Minthorn's Rules of Order are about as close to a universal code of English usage as there can be.

And like any code, this one has its own breed of code-breakers. The somewhat Olympian pronouncements by AP have led to a Twitter phenomenon called "The Fake AP Stylebook," whose existence may be the only way a lot of people know there is such a thing as the AP Stylebook. Making fun of some of the tenets journalists hold dear, "Fake AP" has tweeted commands such as telling writers always to use the word "allegedly" to avoid accusations of bias: "the allegedly wet water," "the allegedly poisonous poison." Even those who enjoy the humorous wordplay, though, probably look to the real AP Stylebook when word decisions have to be made.

"You can imagine the sense of assurance you get when Dave Minthorn himself is doing the editing on a memo or a story for the wire," says his immediate boss, Tom Kent. "It's like doing math and having Einstein check your work."

The most common "Ask the Editor" question is about the use of italics and quotation marks when citing books, movies or TV shows. Does one use them on some titles but not others, or not at all? Minthorn's answer: AP puts quotes around titles (exceptions: the Bible and standard reference works, which get neither) and it never uses italics. This is for practical reasons more than anything. AP doesn't transmit copy with embedded italics because not all computer systems can send or receive them.

The questions Minthorn fields from the public come from just about everywhere and everyone. Newspaper copy editors write to him, as do public-relations executives, students, teachers, corporate and military types, librarians and "just plain word nuts."

And, yes, they can be a little nutty about this stuff. Minthorn, Christian and Jacobsen kicked up quite a ruckus recently when they agreed to refer to electronic mail as "email" instead of "e-mail." The pro-"e-mail" faction protested the hyphen-ectomy, but the AP style mavens declared that the extra character was unnecessary because it slowed writers down, if only by a fraction of a second. "We spend a lot of time debating these things," Minthorn says. (The Washington Post prefers "e-mail.")

Conversely, the punctuation gods ruled that the proper form of "bed and breakfast" is "bed-and-breakfast," a change sure to please the hyphen lobby. Go figure.

You'll get an argument, too, about the plural of "octopus." Minthorn's preference: "octopuses." Fans of "octopi" will probably take exception.

Whatever his pronouncements, Minthorn doesn't rule merely by fiat or whim. He has 42 years of experience as an AP correspondent and editor, so he's hardly a novice at this. Besides, it's not just his say-so. Minthorn consults references such as the American Heritage Dictionary of the American Language, the Concise Oxford Dictionary, Roget's Thesaurus and "The Elements of Style," the classic Strunk and White volume that is the Torah, New Testament and Koran for writing style.

When a reader asked him whether female softball players are basemen, Minthorn did some legwork before answering. Webster's was of no use, so he investigated how AP's sports department refers to women in other sports. In women's basketball, he learned, when a team switches out of zone defense it is said to be playing man-to-man. Hence, the Minthorn-ian judgment: Position players in softball are basemen.

This may all seem arcane and trivial to a world moving rapidly away from linguistic formality—C U L8tr, m8—but not to Minthorn. "We take this very seriously," he says. "We're not a bunch of old fogies sitting around in our ivory tower. We're alive to changes and new ideas. We have a real sense that new words and changes in language reflect the culture and give us inkling to where society is headed."

AP's senior managing editor, Michael Oreskes, argues that precision and clarity and "other hallmarks of proper style" are vital in an age in which rules seem to matter less and less. "Times of change are when standards matter most," Oreskes says. "The faster the eye flits across the words, the more vital it is that language be immediately and abundantly clear. The world of journalism is lucky to have Dave. He is an asset for the whole profession."

Minthorn's love of words springs from boyhood. He attended the Lakeside School in Seattle, where two memorable teachers, Frederick Bleakney and George Taylor, instilled in him the joy of writing and reading. Naturally, he went on to get a degree in English (Whitman College, '64) and a master's in journalism (University of Oregon, '65).

Along the way he picked up an appreciation for more than just the finer points of English. During his long career at AP, he spent 16 years as a foreign correspondent, including 12 in Germany (where he met his wife). He became fluent in that language and now regularly tweets breaking-news alerts in German.

"Everyone has a passion," says Oreskes. "Dave's is writing that cannot be misunderstood. He is a true believer in the power of the well-used verb, the properly ordered infinitive and the non-dangling participle. He sets rules so the rest of us will rise to them."

Test Your Smarts

The online quiz reproduced below can be found at the following link. The idea is to go online to The Washington Post and take this quiz. Here is the link and then you can check your answers and see how well you did.

The AP Stylebook guides newsrooms in creating consistent standards for language and usage. Test your inner copy editor by answering the questions below. Credit: *The Washington Post.*

1. Representatives received hundreds of ____ about the debt ceiling.
   - e-mails
   - emails
   - E-mails
2. The _____ was down after a denial-of-service attack.
   - Web site
   - web-site
   - Web-site
   - website
3. The ___ District Court will hire ___ law clerks this year.
   - Second, 2
   - second, two
   - 2nd, 2
   - 2nd, two
4. Which of the following social-media terms is not in the AP Stylebook?
   - tweet
   - mash-up
   - app
   - unfollow
   - geotagging
   - All of these words are in the book
5. The fire on Main ____ in Fort Worth, ___, was quickly extinguished.
   - street, Tex.
   - Street, Texas
   - st., Tex.
   - St., Texas
   - Street, TX
6. After the tornado, people rushed to apply for _____ disaster assistance.
   - Federal
   - federal
7. The two witnesses' stories didn't ___.

- gibe
- jibe

8. Martha Minow, ___ of the Harvard _____, was quoted.
   - dean, law school
   - Dean, Law School
   - dean, Law School
9. She moved into the house, ___ its poor condition.
   - despite
   - in spite of
10. The California and New York _____ will consider the amendment.
    - legislatures
    - Legislatures

Reading List

1. Wire-service style summary:

The Associated Press was founded in 1848 as a cooperative effort among six New York newspapers that wished to pool resources for gathering international news. Today, with more than 3,700 employees in 121 countries, the AP is the world's single largest news organization. Every day, more than one billion people read, hear, or see AP news.

From the beginning, AP reporters have written their dispatches for readers from diverse social, economic, and educational backgrounds and a wide range of political views. The AP therefore strives to keep its writing style easy to read, concise, and free of bias.

The Associated Press Stylebook, first published in 1977, clarified the news organization's rules on grammar, spelling, punctuation, and usage. There are many style summaries available for a quick check. We are including this one to help with some basics for quick and easy referral: The Boston University COM Writing Center/Quick Associated Press Style (from BU's site for educational purposes).

> **Quick Reference**
>
> *The Associated Press Stylebook.* *See chapter* "Briefing on Media Law" (328).

Chapter Highlights

- A valuable tool for any editor, journalist, writer, and communicator is a good style book.
- *The Associated Press Stylebook* is used in many newsrooms. As a journalist or communicator, you will want to learn this valuable skill.
- Inside the AP stylebook you will find guidelines for social media, food, sports, and much more.
- You can take an online grammar and style quiz to test your knowledge.
- You have read an article about grammar, policing of grammar, and consistent style used in one of the world's largest news organizations.

For Discussion

1. *The New York Times* doesn't use AP style. Take an article from the front page and edit it into AP style.
2. Look at the last five emails you received. Edit them for grammar. Rewrite the emails. Don't let the email senders know that you are editing their personal emails, of course.
3. Look at the food guidelines and the social media guidelines in your AP stylebook. What surprises you? Recently hashtags have been added to our culture's vocabulary. What else are you seeing in everyday language that may make it into the AP book in the near future?
4. Pull out the sports guidelines of your AP stylebook. How do you reference scores? Why is a sports guidelines section necessary? If you enjoy writing about sports, take a local sports story, or even a national sports story from *The New York Times*, and rewrite it using the AP style you have now become familiar with.
5. Come up with an AP exam question of your own. Submit it to the professor and make a game show–style class lecture out of it. What a fun way to learn together. If you're lucky, perhaps the professor will have candy for prizes.

vi

Public Relations

Even though not all of us play golf, we are familiar with the image of the golfer carrying his or her bag of clubs down the fairway contemplating the next shot. What is the position of the ball? Which club in the bag should be used to get the ball onto the green? Public relations practitioners are not unlike golfers in that they, too, wrestle with what "club" they should use in helping a client advance toward achieving its goal of better connecting with a targeted public, gaining greater visibility, enhancing its image, or all of the above. Instead of a two-iron, a driver, or a putter, in the case of professional communicators, their "clubs" range from press releases, pitch letters, and op-ed pieces to fact sheets, press kits, media advisories, and even advertising campaigns. Used correctly, each can do much to help the practitioner achieve his or her ends in successful fashion. And, to make one more analogy with golf, often more than one club is needed to ultimately drop the ball into the hole or, more to the point, to achieve a communication objective.

The trick with each of the tools is that not only must each be well written; each must be composed in a manner that best speaks to or fits a specific audience. Generally, communication tools are not designed to speak to the masses. Even when their intended destination is a publication of general distribution, their purpose is to speak to a specific point: press releases revolve around a singular topic, press kits focus on a particular event, op-ed pieces speak to one point, and so forth. Communication tools impart the warmth of an office receptionist yet the aloofness of a ticket-taker at a public arena. Ideally, they should be engaging, stimulating, and easy to understand and invoke in their intended audiences a desire to learn more. Just like the public relations representative himself or herself, they should represent their client in the best possible light. Thus, they need to exhibit both style and substance as well as the organization's values. In essence, communication tools are important public relations tools that can and do much to advance the owners' reputation and goals.

Communication Tools

Which communication tool to select in any given scenario, of course, is a matter of professional judgment. To add to the complexity of choosing the correct tool to use, many times it is not a matter of one being "wrong" and another being "right." If done well, they all move the client toward its goal. Instead, for the communicator, it is often a matter of selecting the tool that is "most right"—the one that best fits a given challenge or situation. Any number of the tools might be acceptable, but only one works best. This is where being an experienced professional comes into play. Through trial and error, having a thorough knowledge of the intended audience, being well versed in the needs and background of the client, and having a good understanding of the production challenges of each of the tools are factors that help the professional communicator determine which one to select. While such a challenge may not be hard science in the traditional sense, there is no doubt that research and fact-finding are key elements in such an undertaking. One final note: readers should know that none of these tools, no matter how well executed, are guaranteed to bring about the results for which they might be intended. As forms of communication, they, too, are subject to being overlooked, misinterpreted, or overshadowed by outside elements. In keeping with this, not all communiqués are read or even seen by their intended audiences; not all generate action as one might hope. This is why it remains advisable for communicators to utilize more than one of these tools during the course of their various outreach efforts or campaigns. Such is the nature of public relations.

In this chapter, we will be analyzing eight of the more popular and utilized communication tools that are part of the arsenal of professional communicators. We will discuss the specific purposes of each as well as provide pointers to the dos and don'ts of what makes for ones that can be considered to be well crafted. To begin, however, it is important that we present them in the proper context. After all, each is designed to strengthen the public relations effort. Thus, we need to define the term "public relations" so that we are clear on what it is the tools are being used to support. Since the beginning of the twentieth century, more than five hundred definitions have been put forth by practitioners and scholars. Do not worry; we are not going to drop all five hundred on you here, nor are we going to give you several from which you can choose. Instead, the one definition we will use, on which this chapter is based, was introduced in 2012 by the Public Relations Society of America (PRSA), the largest professional association for public relations practitioners in the world.

In 2011–2012, PRSA leaders authorized a comprehensive research drive to produce a definition that best fits where this social science is today. Following is the final result of their effort: "Public relations is a strategic communication process that builds mutually beneficial relationships between organizations and their publics." As explained by those same PRSA executives, a key word here is "process," in that it suggests cooperation between entities rather than one attempting to manipulate another. Furthermore, the PRSA suggested that other key aspects of public relations must be considered as well in terms of the interpretation and ultimate implementation of this definition. These include interpreting public opinion, counseling management, conducting research, and planning and implementing efforts to influence targeted publics or audiences. Thus, it is in this context that we discuss the following public relations tools: press releases, media advisories, backgrounders, pitch letters, speeches, letters to the editor, op-ed pieces, fact sheets, and press kits. One is not any more important than another. Rather, it is the situation or circumstance that often determines which one is the most appropriate. This is why readers should not misinterpret the order in which each is analyzed. Readers should also remember that often more than one of these tools is utilized in a campaign and that they are geared to complement each other. In our analysis of these tools, we will be discussing the purpose, format, and parts or elements of each. Also, we will touch on their intended audience or distribution and how you can measure the effectiveness or success of each one. Finally, we will share some dos and don'ts when it comes to each tool. Let us begin.

Press Releases

Without question, this communication tool can probably be considered the granddaddy of all that are at the disposal of the professional communicator. In fact, oftentimes, "press release" is used as a to decribe r any form of communication that should be created and distributed to the public. It is the oldest of the communicator's tools. At the same time, there is some truth in the notion that press releases are considered by many to be the first among equals in the practitioner's bag of weapons. It is the press release, after all, that generally provides targeted publics with specific quotes from key individuals relevant to a story, full explanations of the topic itself, and a description of the organization and/or client behind the release. None of the other communication tools, generally, do this—certainly not with the detail that can and often is contained in a press release.

This tool should be written in an active voice in order to provide a sense of immediacy to what is being announced. Not only is such a style often more engaging to the reader; it lends itself to members of the press who are looking for news that is timely and fast-breaking. The reporter's job is to provide the audience with the latest on any given topic. An active press release feeds into this need.

Purpose

Why are press releases even necessary? What is behind them? What does a client hope to get out of these articles? Are the expectations realistic? Press releases are designed to provide entities with a written vehicle through which to share information about themselves. Not surprisingly, the information often is favorable or positive. But it can also be designed to enlighten intended audiences.

Press releases often represent the official "word" on a particular topic. For instance, if a major company is announcing a significant restructuring in how they are organized, oftentimes it is the press release that communicates their official explanation as to what the changes are and the reasons behind them. It is not unusual for these communiqués to include direct quotes from key officers within the organization. Such a composite of items is put together to provide outside members of the public, particularly the media, with what they will need to do their story on this announcement. In this case, depending on the CEO's attitude toward speaking with the press, the release can either protect those so-called key individuals who may not actually want to talk with reporters from doing so or serve as an unspoken invitation for reporters to call for further comment. Either way, press releases often contain direct quotes from individuals significant to the topic of the release. Working from instructions from that CEO, the public relations professional knows which "signal" the direct quotes are giving and, as a result, knows how best to showcase them to the press. (It is not unusual for those statements to have been prepared by the same public relations officer who writes the actual release.) This is not to say that individual reporters will not want more direct quotes. Dealing with these requests represents another aspect of the public relations practitioner's job that is not directly part of the challenge faced in putting together a viable, timely, and well-written press release.

The press release, then, can have one or two distinct purposes: (1) serve as the organization's official and only public comment about an issue; and (2) serve as a tip or tease to motivate reporters to want to take the essence of the story and then do their own piece on it while using the facts provided in the release as the foundation for their own version. Either way, the press release represents the public relations office's attempt to generate positive coverage for the client.

Format

One common question many have revolves around the length of a press release. How long should it be? Generally, there is no exact answer to this, though conventional wisdom suggests one to two pages, double-spaced. However, we view this as a judgment call on the part of public relations workers. If they believe the release needs to be longer than that because of the inclusion of information deemed vital to what it is they are announcing, they should not fret over the length.

Different press offices have their own way of formatting press releases they produce. Generally, such designs are geared to showcase the press office and to provide the media with pertinent information geared to help them follow up on the release itself—should they choose to do so. Specifically, this information includes the name and contact information of the author of the release, a headline giving the reader a sense of what the release it about, and a boilerplate description of the organization or client whom the release is about. Also, it is important to include information as to where readers can turn for more information on the story itself. This information, such as a phone number or web address, is usually different from the contact information of the release's author. These, then, are the primary ingredients that comprise the release.

The beginning of all releases is called "the lead." Generally, writers should confine them to approximately thirty words and one to two sentences in length. Such a length better showcases the point of the release as well as gives its beginning more punch. This first paragraph captures the essence of the story by highlighting the most important fact of the piece. Paragraphs that follow should not be overly long, either, perhaps no more than three sentences. Much like how a journalist would write a story, the public relations writer should seek to answer the traditional who, what, when, where, why, and how ("the five W's") in what they depict. This is done because media outlets are the primary destination of press releases. This is why public relations writers should adhere to the Associated Press style of writing, as we discussed in the previous chapter.

Examples

Example 1

XYZ University will not raise tuition for in-state and out-of-state students for the coming 2014–2015 academic year.

The institution's board of trustees made the announcement at its final regular meeting of the year. Director Jane Doe said that the university's governing body was unanimous in its conviction that they must do all they can to keep the cost of a college education affordable. "We are sensitive to the many economic challenges people are currently facing," said Ms. Doe. "Our decision is designed to put our conviction into action and to help ensure that the university's overall enrollment numbers will remain strong."

Example 2

"Thanks to the great support of our many customers, our sales totals this year are the highest in our company's twenty-five-year history," announced John Doe, chief executive officer of XYZ industries, at the annual meeting of its board of directors.

XYZ Industries enjoyed a 35 percent increase in profits over its total of the previous year. According to Doe, this year's profits exceeded $35 million in revenue. He attributed the company's success to their innovative marketing strategies, which included making greater use of social media, and "our outstanding product."

Comparison/Analysis

The examples above focus on the beginning of two press releases. Though the specifics of each are different, their tone is very similar. Each is straightforward in that it begins with the most important information or fact. The obvious difference is that example two begins with a direct quote from the chief executive officer, while example one begins in a more traditional way: with a clear statement of fact. Each is equally appropriate. Beginning a press release with a quote is normally done only when the writer has an interesting comment to work with, particularly if it is given by a person key to the story.

In the standard press release, information that follows what is showcased in the lead rests on the judgment of the writer. What is the second most important fact, the third most important, and so on? Such decisions are ones both journalists and public relations workers grapple with. Such a style is the essence of the "inverted pyramid" style of writing that we have mentioned previously. How creative can or should a writer be in presenting the information in a press release? Such a decision also rests on the judgment of the writer. However, when making a choice between being too creative and presenting information in a straightforward, understandable manner, one should always let the facts take the lead. It is important that the writer remember that the primary purpose of any press release is to share the information, not showcase his or her writing style.

Distribution

Obviously, press releases are geared for the press. In a perfect world—from the perspective of the press offices—they would love seeing newspapers reprint their releases without any changes or have radio and television stations simply read the releases to their audiences. Realistically, the chances of this ever happening are virtually nonexistent. Nevertheless, the releases are written with the press in mind, as the public relations workers know that these communication tools represent an important element in their outreach efforts. Realistically, the primary intent of press releases is for them to generate media interest in a particular story so that they—reporters—will pursue stories on them. Releases, as we have suggested, are often designed to announce initiatives, share new information, and highlight organizational achievement, to cite a few reasons. But press releases are not prepared exclusively for reporters. It is not uncommon for them to be prepared for and distributed to other targeted audiences, including the general public. An organization's stakeholders, such as its governing or advisory board, is a good example of a public other than the press that often receives press releases.

Measurement

How do you know whether a press release is successful? The best answer is found in the response to it. If reporters call wanting additional information or want to expand on what is shared in the release, this speaks to the effectiveness of the release. If members of other publics call wanting more details, this, too, is a positive indicator of the release's overall merit. One should not fall into the trap of judging the quality of a release only by how well it is written. While this is no doubt important, the bottom-line purpose of a release is to generate active interest and media coverage. Press releases that are well written and show creative flair are important. As we have mentioned, they do not always result in press coverage. Such a result is never a certainty, regardless of the quality of the release or timeliness of its focus. Sometimes reporters are pursuing other stories and simply do not have time to react to your release. Without doubt, this is frustrating, but it is a reality that speaks to the challenge faced each day by public relations workers: they can make all the right moves for all the right reasons and still not achieve the end they seek. That is why these communicators use more than one communication tool in their campaigns.

Dos/Don'ts

As is the case in so many other aspects of life, there are certain ways to proceed when it comes to press releases and certain ways not to proceed. To begin, as we have stressed, press releases must be well written and free of typos. They must also be factually accurate. In the world of journalists, of course, it is equally vital what is written be accurate, too. However, in the world of media, rarely, if ever, are drafts of what reporters have written shared with their sources for fear of the source(s) might change the tone of the piece. From their perspective, it is a matter of safeguarding the integrity of their work. This is not the case for the public relations writer.

Remember: what public relations writers compose is ultimately designed to showcase their clients in a positive light. Thus, it is rare when they do not first give their sources or clients the opportunity to review the release before it is distributed. Such a review helps ensure that their facts and quotes are accurate and true to the values and goals of the client. Such extra steps can often make the preparation of a press release a more time-consuming venture for public relations writers than it is for journalists. For their part, while journalists must ensure that what they have composed is also accurate, they have the added challenge of doing so without actually letting anyone other than their editor see the fruits of their effort before their article is published.

Media Advisories

Most of us have received invitations or save-the-date cards to various events over the years. Whether it pertains to an upcoming wedding, a graduation ceremony, or a party, we receive notices of this kind to give us a "heads-up" about a special or noteworthy activity. Media advisories are similar to these kinds of invitations. They almost always allude to some type of media event, such as a press conference, ribbon cutting, ground-breaking ceremony, or what an organization considers to be a significant address. The activities and events to which advisories refer are rarely, if ever, hastily thrown together. Much like weddings and graduation ceremonies, they are well-planned activities designed to showcase the host.

Purpose

As is the case with any upcoming special event, media advisories are designed to give reporters and key members of the general public an opportunity to plan ahead for these activities. Oftentimes, upon receiving an advisory, reporters will then start contacting the person listed on the advisory to try to obtain details about this upcoming event. This is when public relations workers should be very careful. If they say too much, they may end up giving the reporters enough information for them to go ahead and do a story in advance. The result is that the reporter then may not deem it necessary to attend the actual event at all. On the other hand, public relations officers should not ignore those early media inquiries. They need to be prepared to discuss the advisory's content without giving away too much information. (For example: "We will be discussing next year's budget projections. The mayor will get into specifics at the press conference.") Again, it is situations like these that help make the public relations practitioner's job so challenging.

Format

How these communiqués are organized is straightforward. All a writer has to do is start with a headline and then follow it up by answering the five W's. This is not written in a traditional prose or paragraph style. Rather, the writer simply lists each W and then answers them. For instance:

- Headline: City Mayor to Outline Economic Measures
- Who: Mayor of City
- What: Speech on the Economy
- Where: City Hall
- When: 2:00 p.m. on Friday, September 5
- Why: To outline new strategies for the coming fiscal year
- How: Introducing new legislation that will be presented to the city council for discussion and approval.
- For more information, contact Paul Agent at 703-555-1212 or pagent@cityhall.gov.

Distribution

Media advisories are almost always distributed only to reporters and other members of the media. However, occasionally they may be used as notices to an organization's or a client's stakeholders.

Measurement

For much of public relations, the name of the game is positive visibility. The more the public relations worker can generate, the happier the client is. Ideally, the advisory will generate enough media attention that, in turn, will result in multiple stories that present the client in a favorable light. Media advisories can contribute to this effort.

Dos/Don'ts

Whoever first said "timing is everything" possibly had media advisories in mind. As it is with invitations, these should not be sent out to the press too early or too late. Rather, they should be distributed to give reporters enough time to plan for the event, yet not too far in advance where they have time to pursue their own stories on the topic before the official event. This is one reason why public relations workers should let others within their organization see these communiqués in advance before they are actually sent out, either in the traditional mail or electronically. Because all that public relations workers do is in the name of others, any tactics they perform need to be shared with those with and for whom they work.

Backgrounders

This communication tool can be considered to be a close cousin of the press release. As its name indicates, this document provides background information to reporters on a particular topic—information the reporters will find useful in putting together their own story on the subject. An example might be information on a scientist's recent research findings. While the actual story might focus on the findings themselves, the backgrounder provides supporting information designed to give the reporter a better, more detailed understanding of the overall subject matter, including research conducted leading up to these newsworthy findings.

Purpose

If done properly, this tool can be a major help to those seeking to build their own article or story on the topic being showcased. Its primary purpose is to provide important supporting information around which an actual article or story can be composed. In a loose sense, while the information these tools share may not necessarily provide advice on a given topic to those for whom they are intended, they do give those people helpful information from which they can work. Generally, public relations workers utilize this tool when reporters have indicated a strong enough interest in a story and wish to conduct one or several interviews regarding it. Such a tool moves the reporter a bit further along in helping them make the desired commitment to actually put together a story for publication or airing.

In terms of actual writing, this tool should be written with an active voice. While the author should not exaggerate any of the facts, the goal with the backgrounder is to instill enthusiasm in those who read this document. "Hey, I want to find out more about that! Let me at least check it out," is the kind of response the writer is shooting for from the reader (i.e., reporter). Backgrounders are also very helpful when it comes to stories that are a bit technical. This tool enables the public relations practitioner to explain the piece in layman's terms. Doing so not only helps the reporter better understand the story, but also helps that same reporter more easily explain it to his or her readers or viewers. In this kind of process, something that professional communicators should never forget is that all effective communicating begins with establishing a basic level of understanding. Such a goal is a basic tenant of competent communication.

Example

Example 3

For more than twenty-five years, Dr. Victor Frankenstein has been experimenting with ways to bring back life. Recently, by harnessing a powerful natural energy source—lightning—Dr. Frankenstein was able to give life to an inanimate body that he had constructed from body parts. The new being, which Dr. Frankenstein is calling "The Creature," is approximately eight feet tall. While The Creature contains the same physical features of all humans, Dr. Frankenstein cautions that its appearance may still be considered grotesque by many. He says that The Creature is articulate, intelligent, powerful in strength, and highly sensitive.

"What we have done is completely unique. It opens the door to possibly extending life as we know it," says Dr. Frankenstein.

Dr. Frankenstein is available for interviews. He is also willing to make The Creature available to members of the press. He stipulates, however, that any interviews with The Creature be conducted under specific guidelines. Reporters wishing to follow up are asked to contact John Doe of Press Talk, Inc., at either 202-xxx-xxxx or johndoe@gmail.com.

Analysis

Obviously, the above example is tongue-in-cheek. That aside, it does provide you with a viable sense of how backgrounders are written. What we have done is provide reporters with a glimpse of this story and how they can follow up on it. As backgrounders go, this one is shorter in length than most. But length of this communication tool is not as important—nor should it be—as how the piece is able to attract members of the press to doing a story on it.

Format

While the press release is designed to be prepared and sent to the media so that it could be printed or aired as it is received, this communication tool is not. Rather, it can be considered an eyes-only document in that those working from it must compose their own stories. Similar to the press release, this tool should include some type of descriptive headline or tagline telling the reader what it is about, a phone or email address of the author of the advisory, and, of course, several paragraphs—no more—that provide an overview of the story's history.

Distribution

Similar to the advisories, the primary recipients of these communiqués are the media. As these tools represent another way to generate interest among reporters, the challenge for public relations workers is to provide reporters with enough insight into a particular topic to make them want to learn more. Thus, backgrounders should be geared with reporters and only reporters in mind. Of course, this is not to say that others may not see or even receive a backgrounder. But the reality is that only members of the press can provide entities with the kind of free publicity that helps strengthen an organization's image and reputation.

Measurement

This is an area of similarity with the media advisory. If the background generates positive media coverage, that is the ultimate bulls-eye for the public relations practitioner. Everything else is a distant second.

Dos/Don'ts

Backgrounders should be prepared and distributed in a timely manner. Furthermore, they need to be written in a way that is easily understood. Writers should assume that whoever reads this communiqué knows nothing about the topic and then write accordingly. Is what you, the writer, are saying understandable even to the layperson? For the writer, it is better to err on the side of simplicity in writing style. Public relations professionals are in the business of communicating; that means being understood. Backgrounders represent an opportunity for public relations workers to demonstrate that they can do this.

Pitch Letters

When you write a book or put together a book proposal, it is an unwritten rule that you should approach only one prospective publisher at a time. The problem in approaching several publishers at the same time is that it creates problems if more than one actually likes the idea and agrees to publish the book. Once a certain publisher learns that other publishers have agreed to do this, it is not uncommon for that publisher to rescind its offer. Rightly or not, publishers do not like being placed in a position where writers are playing them off one another. They believe in exclusivity. The situation is similar when it comes to pitching stories to the media. Reporters are a competitive lot and strive to best their competitors with stories that are unique or exclusive to them. Public relations workers often use this reality to enhance their ties with specific reporters. Reporters, generally, are flattered when given a first opportunity to consider pursuing a particular story. While they may not always accept the offer, they do tend to think more favorably of the public relations professional who gives them the opportunity to "one-up" their fellow reporters. In the course of their strategic planning, public relations practitioners should constantly be on the lookout for story ideas they can pitch to specific members of the press. For instance, if a public relations officer knows that a particular reporter has a special interest in family-oriented stories, when the communicator uncovers one (such as two sisters working in different departments of a company who both receive "employee of the month" awards), they can directly approach that reporter with this story idea. Such a strategy complements efforts that are more targeted, where press releases are sent to multiple reporters at once.

The key here is for public relations practitioners to do their homework. Offer story suggestions and then be prepared to provide official interviews and access to reporters wishing more information or details on your story idea. This way, you are being of help to the reporter and not a time drain.

Purpose

Pitch letters are an effective way of presenting story ideas to specific reporters. Generally, they are informal in tone and provide the public relations worker with an opportunity to "sell" an idea rather than merely present something in a more subdued, objective manner as represented by a press release. Reporters do not mind seeing (or should we say "reading") this side of the public relations worker, so long as he or she is upfront about the intent. Obviously, the purpose of such a communiqué is to convince a reporter to do a story on this idea.

Format

Pitch letters, generally, are not very long—two or three paragraphs at the most. Given the heavy use of computers, rarely do public relations practitioners send their story ideas via traditional mail. Nowadays, pitches are usually sent in the form of an email. The formality of the tone of a particular pitch is usually dictated by the relationship public relations workers have with the reporters to whom they are pitching. If they have a close working relationship, the tone can be a bit looser or informal. If their relationship is either not close or, up to this point, nonexistent, the tone of a pitch should be very formal and respectful. (It is not unusual to approach reporters you do not know with an idea. This can even be a good way to begin establishing a connection with a reporter.) An example would a public relations officer working for a chemical research agency that wants to connect with the science reporter of, say, National Public Radio. When one of the agency's researchers makes a notable discovery, the communicator uses this achievement as a way to reach out to that reporter. Here is another example: "Hello (name of reporter). I saw your recent story about (topic), and I thought you might be interested in (brief description of your client's efforts)."

Distribution

As we have mentioned, pitch letters usually go out to one reporter at a time. If public relations workers truly believe that their idea is a good one, they should not hesitate to take it to a second reporter if their first choice turns it down. Of course, if a story on what is pitched is done, the story idea becomes fair game to any and all wishing to do their version of this item.

Measurement

Either the reporter does or does not accept the idea. Sometimes reporters will say they like the idea and want to do a story on it, only they do not have time to do it in the timeframe preferred by the public relations worker. If this happens, it is professionally ethical for the public relations worker to let the reporter know that he or she is taking the idea to another reporter. The main thing is to not go behind the reporter's back. As all relationships are built on openness and trust, it is important for public relations workers to be upfront about their actions. One other note: it is not uncommon for story ideas pitched to reporters to never be picked up. Assuming a story idea is actually quite good, there are times when reporters simply do not have time to pursue them. This is part of the challenge that public relations practitioners face. Public relations workers should not give up on their ideas just because one or even several reporters turn them down. If necessary, repackage the idea or save it for another day. But do not let a reporter's rejection be a source of discouragement. Generating press coverage is a constant challenge involving variables that sometimes are beyond the practitioner's control.

Dos/Don'ts

In addition to what we have already mentioned, it is important for public relations workers to be economic in their pitches. By this we mean to have the best chance of having their ideas seriously considered, public relations practitioners need to give their idea serious thought and go forward with those ideas that are of high caliber and match the interests of the reporter to whom they are pitching. Pitch letters, if done well, can be a powerful tool with a high success rate. But if too many ideas are pitched, the quantity of their ideas tends to detract from the ones that are actually of high quality. If you have several story ideas, you can pitch each one to as many reporters as there are ideas. Understand that we are not suggesting that public relations workers should not think of as many story ideas as they can. We do believe, however, that pitch letters are most effective when used sparingly.

Speeches

Author Ralph Waldo Emerson once wrote, "Speech is power; speech is to persuade, to convert, to compel" (Bosco & Myerson, 2010). In the hands of an effective speaker working from a well-written and well-researched speech, such a communication tool can be highly effective. Speechwriting is an important aspect of any comprehensive public relations plan. It is also a skill that not every public relations worker—no matter how gifted as a writer—is able to do. Some are able to transition from writing speeches to press releases and other communication tools, and some are not. Oftentimes, to cite one reason for this, writing speeches requires being able to establish a close bond with specific people, something not all public relations workers have the time or opportunity to do. It is the challenge of the speechwriter to become the "voice" of a specific person, such as the organization's chief executive officer. This requires time and a willingness on both individuals' part to make that effort. Such a commitment is not always practical, particularly if an entity's communication team is limited in size.

Purpose

A speech actually has several key purposes: (1) it is a way of showcasing the speaker, (2) it accents the importance of the topic that is the focus of the speech, and (3) it clearly and publicly defines the organization's attitude or position in the eyes of its intended audience. Furthermore, if done well, a solid speech can enhance the overall image and reputation of the speaker and the organization. A good speech is enhanced by the delivery, of course, but more often than not, it is the words that drive its shelf life and determine its impact.

Format

The question of a speech's format revolves more around its tone than its actual look or design. Tone is largely driven by the speaker. Does the speaker want the speech to be light or very serious? Is it to be inspirational or informative? Is it celebratory or commemorating a specific event? Is it to be scholarly or more conversational? These are among the fundamental questions the speechwriter should settle with the speechmaker before sitting down to write. Once that is done, depending on the preference of the speaker, the actual text should be either double- or triple-spaced, with the size of the type itself also conforming to the wishes of the speaker.

Distribution

This is not as obvious as you may think. Obviously, in one sense, the speech is for the speechmaker. But in another, there is an audience or public beyond the speaker for whom the speech is intended.

In this case, the speech is generally distributed orally. Speechwriters must familiarize themselves with the audience for whom the speech is intended. Is it being given to an internal audience, or will outsiders, including members of the press, be on hand to hear it as well? Such knowledge helps dictate the content of the speech as well as its tone. For instance, an address before stockholders—even on a similar topic—would be considerably different in tone than one given at a graduation ceremony. Particularly if a speech is of high quality and memorable —as defined by the audience—copies of it may be requested.

Measurement

There are areas of measurement when it comes to speeches: immediate and long-term. Besides the audience's immediate reaction, the public relations team can be on hand to conduct an informal poll on whether opinions were swayed, support strengthened, or attitudes shifted. If members of the press were part of the audience, the kind and amount of coverage is another form of measurement. If appropriate, the public relations team can also make copies of the speech available to groups or individuals. Such a strategy gives the speech a longer shelf life and helps elevate its level of importance.

Dos/Don'ts

It is important for the speechwriter to remember that the speech is not about him or her. It is about the speaker. Thus, the speech should reflect the speaker's thoughts, vision, and style of talking, not those of the speechwriter. The longer a speaker and speechwriter work together, the easier it becomes for the writer to talk with the speaker's voice. This takes time and requires the establishment of a firm level of trust between the two. Good speeches, from the perspective of the writer, are much more than simply words on paper that someone else recites to room a full of people. A speech unveils the essence of the one who delivers it. The challenge of the writer is to depict that essence in a way that accurately reflects the person and the topic on which they are speaking. Speechwriters should not take what they do lightly. By approaching a writer to compose a speech, that person is putting himself or herself in the hands of that writer. Allowing another person to write words that he or she will then carry forth as his or her own is a significant act of confidence and trust.

Letters to the Editor

Though not utilized nearly as much as they used to be, there remains a place for letters to the editor as a key communication tool. Letters to the editor generally refer to the editorial sections of local or area newspapers or publications, including magazines. This space is reserved for laypeople wishing to submit their thoughts, perspectives, and so forth on various issues. They can pertain to current events, matters having little to do with what is in the news, or topics relating primarily to them, personally or professionally.

Purpose

Because a fundamental goal for public relations practitioners is to generate positive visibility for their clients, letters to the editor help achieve this end. Such communiqués are generally written in response to an article that may have appeared in an earlier edition of the newspaper or as a comment on an issue of local or regional importance. These communiqués give entities an opportunity to speak out on a given issue. It is not unusual for public relations writers to pen them but then have the letter sent out under the name of another member of the organization, such as its chief officer. An added benefit when these communiqués do appear in print is that they take on an air of added credibility by the mere fact that they are part of a publication's editorial page. Examples would be a letter calling for action on local traffic congestion issues or strengthening of graduation standards for area high schools.

Format

Letters to the editor are not long. Generally, they are a few hundred words in length. In writing them, it is important to be direct. Newspapers and other written publications encourage their readers to share their opinions. In order to publish as many of these letters as possible, they prefer brevity. In fact, the newspapers will even go as far as to edit or reduce the size of entries if they are deemed too long or not as succinct at they should be. Also, timing is critically important when it comes to letters. These tools are examples of an idea that must be acted on quickly.

Distribution

As is the case with pitch letters, letters to the editor do not have a general or broad distribution. They are written with a single publication in mind, as they are usually done in response to article or story that publication has previously covered or an editorial position it has taken on a particular issue. It should be noted that not all submissions are published because of such reasons as a lack of space or the fact the publishers might not deem the letter's content to be timely or the letter itself to be well written.

Measurement

Obviously, if the letter is not printed, the worthy effort did not succeed. But if it is, a direct benefit may not be readily apparent. The good news, however, is that people do read these letters and take note of their source. Thus, there is secondary benefit to the successful placement of this outreach tool.

Dos/Don'ts

Without question, the letter must be well written, even if it is short in length. Also, writers should not be skimpy with pertinent facts in these pieces. Writers should stick closely to the point of their letter and touch on any points that others may deem to be irrelevant or off-subject. Remember: the space publications set aside for letters to the editor is limited in size.

Op-Ed Pieces

This communication tool can be viewed as the big brother or sister of the letter to the editor. These articles appear opposite the editorial page of a newspaper and are the result of that publication's policy of allowing and encouraging outsiders to share their perspective on various issues of the day. As the average length of these pieces is 750 words, they are longer and more substantive than typical letters to the editor. Also, individuals or representatives of various entities are free to lay out their views on most any topic they wish—topics that do not necessarily have to be tied into current events.

Purpose

It is not unusual for the general public to equate an organization with its most visible representative. In many cases, this is the organization's chief executive. If that person's image/reputation is positive, most likely the general public will have a favorable impression of the entity this person oversees. An op-ed piece or guest editorial/column enhances the reputation of its author and that which he or she represents. Even more than that, however, it presents this person and the organization as being actively engaged in issues of the day and elevates the author as a thinker who contemplates matters beyond the welfare of the organization. An example would be a university professor who writes on a national issue, such as college affordability rather than his or her own particular institution. Such an image resonates well with the general public. It is typical for the organization's public relations director to write the piece for the group's chief executive or, at least, provide him or her with a detailed outline and supporting documentation to give him or her what is needed to write the piece. Even if the chief officer himself or herself writes the piece, often the public relations worker provides assistance with editing the initial draft. The public relations worker must never lose sight of the fact that this article is an extension of the chief officer and, therefore, of the organization itself.

Format

The format is straightforward: double-spaced, with a suggested headline, brief biographical information on the author, and contact information as to how the outlet can contact the author for purposes of confirmation and in case its staff have any questions.

Distribution

As is the case for a letter to the editor, an op-ed piece has a very narrow distribution: one outlet. Many newspapers refuse to accept a piece that has appeared in another paper or, in some cases, been submitted for consideration to other papers. Only when a paper formally turns down a request should the public relations worker consider submitting it to another outlet. Larger city newspapers are harder to get published in than their smaller counterparts. Generally, such major outlets as *The New York Times* or *The Washington Post* receive submissions from national and international leaders. For the sake of their circulation and own prestige, they are more likely to publish entries from those sources than they are ones from unknown people. Thus, reality suggests that while you would love to have your byline in a paper of that caliber, it is usually wiser to submit entries to smaller, more local outlets. These can be just as effective, if not more so, than being published in a more national outlet, simply because people you want to read your piece are among those in your own region.

Measurement

Op-ed pieces may not generate immediate reaction. For instance, such a piece may not necessarily result in greater sales. But that is not a bad thing. Having your chief executive officer's name attached to an op-ed piece brings prestige to that person and the organization or company he or she represents. It represents free publicity designed to enhance an image or public standing. Such a boost does not hurt the standing of the organization in the eyes of the immediate public.

Dos/Don'ts

Even though this piece is approximately 750 words in length, prospective authors should not view this as a license to wax philosophic about their topic. In other words, they need to make their point quickly and then spend the bulk of the piece defending and/or justifying their perspective with facts. An op-ed piece is not something you "wing" or makes up as you go along. The newspaper editors who review and ultimately decide to approve the piece as worthy of running are not interested in a soapbox rant. Yes, they want people to take a stance on an issue, but they also look for these articles to be informative and stimulating. Remember: the quality of this communiqué also reflects on the newspaper or media outlet that runs it.

Fact Sheets

Many years ago one of the more popular television shows revolved around hardworking yet unglamorous police officers going about their day-to-day jobs of dealing with the public and enforcing the law. Their catchphrase when getting statements from witnesses was that all they wanted was "just the facts." This is what fact sheets provide. Generally, they comprise little else but a listing of pertinent yet bare-boned information designed to give reporters the basics without corresponding paragraphs of explanation or quotes from key individuals. Arguably, fact sheets are also the most popular of tools in the public relations officer's arsenal.

Purpose

Oftentimes, reporters do not look for or wish to see information they view as being extraneous to what they need to put together a story on a particular topic. Fact sheets meet this need. If a new building is being dedicated, for instance, information the reporter wants may simply include the facility's cost, size, and funding sources, the name of architect, and a listing of the kind of rooms, offices, and so forth to be housed within it; also, contact information is helpful, in case they need additional details. Such information comprises the fact sheet. Nothing else.

Format

Fact sheets are not fancy. In fact, this may be part of their appeal. Generally, this communiqué is topped off with a heading. What follows that is a list of basic information (see the following example). Once they have the facts, reporters, to coin the common expression, can "take it from there." While putting together a fact sheet may not necessarily require the kind of writing we have been discussing throughout this text, this tool does require research and fact-checking. It is essential that the public relations worker be thorough in his or her fact-finding.

Example

Example 4

XYZ UNIVERSITY'S 2013 COMMENCEMENT

Graduates: 8,000

Degrees:

Undergraduate: 6,000

Graduate: 1,800

Doctorate: 200

Most Popular Programs:

Nursing: 855

Computer Science: 627

Communication: 525

Commencement Speaker: U.S. Congressman Jeffery Talbot (D-KY)

Size of 2012 Graduating Class: 7,600

Total Number of Graduates in institutions's history: 53,000

Analysis

Granted, on the surface, there may seem to be little that is creative about a fact sheet. That in no way detracts from its effectiveness Reporters and other interested people, including internal personnel, find them most useful. Once done, they are great resources.

Distribution

Another great thing about fact sheets is that they can be and often are distributed to any and all members of the public interested in the topic on which they are focused. Though they are designed primarily for members of the press, they are perfect handouts to any or all who want to learn more about something.

Measurement

As fact sheets are supporting documents, there is no formal form of measurement attached to them. However, public relations workers are wise to informally ask reporters if they find a fact sheet to be of use. Also, reviewing coverage of a particular event and seeing how many, if any, of the facts are included in the story is another gauge.

Dos/Don'ts

It is essential that any specific information included in a fact sheet be double-checked before its inclusion. Any errors not only detract from this tool's usefulness but also detract from the credibility of the communicators who produced them.

Press Kits

This tool is actually a compilation of a number of the other above-mentioned tools, virtually a one-stop-shop for reporters seeking details about a particular subject. Press kits are a key element in most any event open to the press. In fact, reporters come to expect them when attending or covering an event. Press kits are not unlike packets that real estate agents provide to families looking at prospective homes when they attend open houses. The trick when it comes to compiling a press kit is in deciding which information to include in the kit and which to exclude. It is not unusual for press offices to go overboard in this regard. This should be avoided. (This is why it is good to have another person review the press kit before it is made available for public consumption.) It is this kind of overkill that leads some to criticize press kits. Overall, particularly when material compiling the press kit is spot-on, they are quite beneficial to reporters.

Purpose

If it is agreed that the primary responsibility of a public or media relations officer is to work closely with reporters, one need look no further than the press kit as an instrument designed to help a public relations operation serve the interests of a client or organization. Thus, press kits also are designed to help reporters do their job.

Format

All press kits are the same in purpose yet different in content. They are similar in that they contain information that speaks to a specific event or subject, different in that the supporting material comprising each varies. Again using a fictional commencement as an example, a press kit would likely contain the following items: a press release on the ceremony itself, a fact sheet on the graduating class, a fact sheet on the college or university, a bio with a photo of the commencement speaker, possibly mini-profiles on several of the more interesting graduates, and the commencement program. There would be no introductory message on the contents of the press kit, as it generally speaks for itself. But should there be another event, such as a building dedication, the next day, content for the press kit for that event would be different. Generally, press kits are built to order rather than being all-purpose or generic.

Distribution

Press kits are distributed at the site of the event or activity. Rarely are they made available elsewhere or at other venues.

Measurement

In this area, press kits are similar to fact sheets. Informal feedback from reporters and looking to see if any information from this compilation of materials may have been used or alluded to in the press coverage are the primary ways to assess the effectiveness of a particular press kit.

Dos/Don'ts

It is easy to fall into a trap of slapping together a number of materials, including brochures, and then view them as a cogent, coherent press kit. Ideally, however, press kits should be put together with as much care as a seating chart for a dinner at the White House. Each piece of material should have a specific purpose for its inclusion and should complement other documents that are also part of this packet. Such attention speaks to the level of professionalism of a public relations operation. Reporters do notice when little attention has been given to the production of these packets. Consequently, they can and do influence the level of trust in and respect for a public relations office that members of the media have.

PR Extras

One of the challenges of a public relations specialist is to get the attention of a journalist, with the goal of having an article written about the brand or issue the PR specialist is promoting. We encourage personal communication and relationship building between PR specialists and journalists to help build trust, and this takes time. Let's say that as a PR specialist you have to contact journalists whom you don't know; we suggest that you never send a blanket email or cold call without doing some research first. Find out who you are contacting, and be sure you are targeting the right reporter. For example, you would not contact a science writer for a healthcare issue, and you would not contact a technology writer for an education issue.

Casual Pitch via Email

If you must send a pitch letter or an email to a writer you don't know, try this approach. It has worked for PR specialists we know and admire, and we think it may work for you, too: "Hello __________. I saw your story about ____________, and I thought you might be interested in ________________." One of our former PR students went on to graduate school at a top university, and he learned this script technique in class and swears by it, terming it the "rock star" pitch letter. We happen to like it because it is written casually and it shows the journalist that the PR specialist did some homework first. Journalists appreciate help on stories that will advance their work toward their deadlines. Here the PR specialist is offering a story idea, which is helpful, and not a waste of time.

In essence, do your homework and offer useful story suggestions, then be prepared to provide an official to interview to further the story if the journalist contacts you for more information or sends a request for an interview. This way you are being of help to the writer and not a time drain. It is a skill that is much appreciated. Follow the simple script above, and you may get your story idea heard.

Also, we suggest keeping a pitch letter short and simple, not using more than three paragraphs. If the journalist is interested, the PR specialist will be contacted for more information. Finding an angle to a story that is not obvious to the reporter can be very helpful in grabbing a reporter's attention. This, combined with figuring out what a journalist covers and what topics the journalist is interested in (before contacting the reporter), will go a long way.

One of the most fun assignments we do in class is a PR campaign. Students do such a great job on this project that they are able to add it to their writing samples and résumés. We have seen it help students get the edge over other potential hires for positions after graduation, and we have seen it used as part of supplemental materials to help students get into graduate school. We begin by taking a look at a couple of fun branding campaigns that were extremely successful to help change an image, by using the media to get the word out about a particular product or brand. Next, we look at a viral video that doesn't mention the brand whatsoever, but it was popular with consumers, specifically with your "connected generation." Then we will include the actual PR campaign assignment, and if your professor chooses to have you do it, you will get to work and begin the process of research and brainstorming ideas and ways to use the media to get the word out.

Two brands that changed significantly are Sperry shoes and Vera Bradley bags. Sperry shoes are very trendy and popular today, but they once were very generic-looking brown boat shoes with a bland image. Vera Bradley bags today are popular and come in many fabrics with colorful lines in addition to added products from wallets to calendars to lunch bags, but Vera Bradley bags were once seen as somewhat frumpy and resembled more of a grandmother's quilted knitting needle bag than a hip middle school backpack. These product images were changed through incredible branding and PR campaigns. Take a look at both:

- Sperry: www.sperrytopsider.com
- Vera Bradley: www.verabradley.com

An effective PR campaign that was done by Chipotle involves the use of a scarecrow, a game, and a digital animation clip that went viral. We will show this and discuss it in class and talk about creative social media tactics for getting a brand talked about in a word-of-mouth campaign as part of the PR. The use of the Chipotle clip is especially interesting because the Chipotle brand is not once mentioned in the digital video, yet audiences know that the scarecrow represents Chipotle. The slogan asks viewers and customers to "join the scarecrow on his quest for better food." A very clever PR strategy, indeed. To see the game, the film, and the facts, visit www.scarecrowgame.com.

Chipotle: www.chipotle.com

PR Campaign Assignment

PR campaign elements include a three-page strategy, several writing samples, and a presentation. This assignment is in three parts.

Part one: a three-page PR strategy. We suggest breaking down your three-page strategy into the following elements: research, product/brand info, print (magazines, newspapers), broadcast (radio, TV, other), social media, advertising, Internet (blogs, online outlets), and so on.

Part two: writing samples. Create a one-page writing sample for each area listed above (examples may include scripts, press releases, pitch letters, facts sheets, ads, ad copy, newspaper articles, magazine articles, social media writing examples, radio copy, and TV segments—the ideas are endless). Two to three per sample is acceptable.

Part three: presentation pitch. Use visuals (PowerPoint is one option) for your five-minute (or shorter) presentation to provide the class with an overview of your PR campaign. A well-rounded campaign will include a strategy, plus at least a handful of writing samples, and successful visuals that keep colleagues interested. The focus should be on using "writing across the media" to market your product or brand.

Ultimately, each student will submit a three-page PR strategy on the day of his or her five-minute presentation, plus writing samples that complement the ideas discussed in the strategy. The PR campaign is a pitch that provides an overview of your brand or product, to include how you will successfully promote your brand or product using several different mediums (print, broadcast, social media, magazines, TV, Internet, blogs, newspapers, etc.).

Timing: You must keep your pitch to five minutes or fewer. You will be cut off at five minutes. No exceptions. If you do not meet your deadline (presenting and submitting your PR campaign and writing samples on the day you are scheduled), you will not have a chance to present again. Please take this deadline seriously, as if you are taking an exam.

Your grade will reflect organization, an emphasis on strong writing style, creativity, vision (think outside the box), and following the assignment in detail as explained above. Have fun!

Advertising

This particular "tool" is different from the others we have mentioned, even though you may consider it to be the first cousin of public relations and marketing. It is often initiated and carried out independent of any public relations event or announcement. Furthermore, it, in many ways, is as far-reaching and extensive as public relations is. In 2010, for instance, according to eMarketer Research, more than $142 billion was spent in advertising within the United States. Worldwide that same year, the total surpassed $465 billion. Companies and individuals advertise so extensively because it is the one form of public outreach that can be controlled as much as any other while providing the advertiser—depending on how much is spent—with potentially national and even international visibility.

Advertising is considered to be a controlled medium. By this, we mean that the words and images within it are controlled by its creator. This control also includes where the advertisement is distributed and how often it is displayed. In fact, a working definition of advertising is that it represents the use of controlled media in an attempt to influence the actions of targeted publics (Guth & Marsh, 2009). This type of communiqué, of course, is paid for. How much an organization spends dictates the frequency in which the ad is aired or run as well as its location and/or time spot. As a comparison, while entities can determine the content of their press releases, they cannot dictate how much of that content will be aired or run by the media, its location, or whether it will be picked up at all.

As its definition suggests, advertising falls under the umbrella of controlled media. As we suggested, an advantage to this is that the content and placement can be controlled by the entity doing the advertising. However, the flip side is that at times publics can be skeptical of paid advertisements because they know that the advertiser is saying what it wants to say without interference from the vehicle in which the advertisement is appearing or—in the case of issue-oriented or political ads, for instance—without being challenged by those on the opposite side. Controlled media speaks to such as outlets as television and radio that cannot be told what to report or instructed on which angle to cover in a story. Other examples would include magazines and online news providers.

In terms of copy or text for an advertisement, as much attention and care is needed for it as is required of any other communication tool or effort. Just because an organization is purchasing the space in which the ad will appear does not mean that it should not make its message as strong and dynamic as possible. The client is paying for this space or air time, so you can bet that the client is going to want to get its money's worth. The person playing a vital role in making that happen is you, the communication officer. For many entities, a high-stakes, expensive advertising campaign is important in the overall scheme of their efforts to remain connected and visible to the public. Before delving into the challenges of writing copy for various forms of advertising, let us review the primary reasons why companies, organizations, or even individuals advertise. Such an understanding helps communicators—in the realm of advertising commonly referred to as copy writers—better frame their various messages.

Purposes of Advertising

Imaging

For any entity to turn a profit or succeed over an extended period of time, its general public must think of well of it. A positive image or reputation is something that the company must establish and then do what it can to hang on to. Whether it is sponsoring a local little league soccer team or being actively involved in the area's chamber of commerce or a service organization, a business must strive to assure current and potential patrons that it is committed to serving the community as well as to turning a profit each quarter. Specific advertisements can help foster and perpetuate such an impression.

Promotion

This is among the more common reasons why companies purchase advertisements. A retail store such as Macy's has a Labor Day sale. A grocery chain such as Giant has special deals on various food items. An airline offers low prices for a roundtrip flight to and from Chicago or New York. The list of examples is endless. Advertising is a popular way to let the public know about such promotions.

Announcement

Major corporations are known to utilize advertisements to inform their followers when they have something significant to announce. For instance, if General Motors has just selected a new chief executive officer, it is not uncommon for the company to purchase a large ad in a prestigious publication such as the *Wall Street Journal* to let the public know of this decision. You can also find numerous examples of these type of advertisements from the motion picture industry. For instance, if a film company has just cast leading actors in a major film, one way it often lets the public and potential moviegoers know is via advertisements in relevant media outlets. Is there a promotional aspect to such announcements? No question about it. The difference, however, is that in these ads no specific "opening night" or individual product is being touted. Rather, the company or entity is sharing what it considers to be a significant decision on its part. You can bet that the promotional ads will follow.

Editorial

In the world of advertising, editorial or issue advertisements are relatively new. In these ads, the advertiser purchases space in a publication's editorial section. It then runs an editorial on a particular issue or topic. An example of such advertisements can be found in *The New York Times*, in which a major corporation such as Texaco will outline its position on such topics as the rising cost of gasoline, fuel efficiency vehicles, or climate change. Some consider such advertisements to be risky because not everyone may agree with the company's stand on a particular issue and, thus, some people will be turned off by the company. However, many believe that such advertisements help position the advertiser as a major force in society, thus enhancing its image and reputation.

Tips for Writing Ad Copy

Those who write copy for advertisements are in a tough situation because the competition they face is fierce. To illustrate, let us look at any commercial on television. Television viewers are watching a favorite show when a commercial comes on. What follows is not that atypical: the viewer goes to the kitchen to get a snack, perhaps goes to the bathroom, flips channels, or fiddles with his or her iPhone until the show is back on. None of these scenarios includes watching the commercial. And even those folks who do watch the commercial do so with the hope that it will be over as quickly as possible. This is not all that different from commercials or advertisements that appear in print. A person leafs through a magazine or newspaper in search of interesting articles to read or pictures to enjoy. Often when they come across advertisements, they quickly turn the page, as their interest is elsewhere.

Thus, the ad copy writer competes not necessarily with other ads but with normal priorities of those for whom the ads are intended. Not only is what they write—no matter how clever or creative—going to be overlooked; this will be done purposefully. To add to such a daunting reality, there is the challenge of producing copy or text that fits into a prescribed block of space or time constraint. Ad copy writers do not have the luxury of writing on their subject until they have nothing more left to say. For those who write for television or radio, they have seconds in which to state their case. For those who write ad copy for magazines or other print outlets, their space is equally limited, to the point that they may not even be able to write in complete sentences. Without question, ad copy writers have a tough and challenging gig. It is also true that they remain among the most talented of those who write under the umbrella of public relations. After all, while many people do, in fact, ignore the fruits of their work, many do not. Obviously, enough of us pay attention to their advertisements and commercials to keep the advertising industry alive and quite profitable. While there are numerous reasons why ads are successful, good writing tops the list.

This, then, takes us to the question of what actually makes for effective writing for advertisements. What characteristics are found in these situations that capture the attention of readers and viewers and help turn the expense of purchasing advertising time and/or space into a profitable venture? Before addressing those fundamental questions, it is important to acknowledge that with the bulk of all successful advertisements there exists a powerful visual and sound component. Ads for television and print, for instance, must be carefully designed and choreographed to be visually appealing to the reader or viewer. Regarding radio, the ad must have a strong and engaging voice that appeals to a listener's sense of comfort. Thus, the look and sound need to do an effective job of showcasing the written or spoken word that serves as the advertisement's heart and, ultimately, substance. It is in the best of advertisements where the two components showcase each other perfectly, thus creating an harmonious appeal to those for whom they are intended.

Following, then, are key writing tips for ad copy:

- **Tell what it is you want to say.** Do not by shy about this. If you are selling toothpaste, you want your potential customer to go out and buy your toothpaste. If you are political candidate and want a potential voter to vote for you, say so. The point is that by the advertisement's conclusion, there should be no doubt as to what it is you want the reader or viewer to do.
- **Be economic/do not linger.** There is only so much space or time in an advertisement. Make your point, support it, and then remake it. Advertisements are no place for words not essential to the fundamental point of the ad itself. In-person pitches are a different matter, as in those scenarios you can afford to expound on your point. Writers do not have that luxury.
- **People have needs.** All of us want to feel good about ourselves, want to be our own person, and want to be accepted by our peers and those with whom we interact. Such needs help define us as human beings and are with us every day. As a result, attempts to effectively communicate with us should carry messages that speak to those fundamental needs.
- **Repeat, repeat, repeat.** This is especially true of advertisements on the radio. Many people listen to the radio when they are driving or occupied doing something else. As a result, they usually do not have a pen and paper handy with which to write, say, a phone number down. This is why it is important to repeat whatever a key element within the ad is. Many times, it is a phone number to call. Other times it is a key date. Repeating this information gives listeners the opportunity to either remember this information or get to a note pad so that they can write it down. The same, though to a lesser extent, is true of television. While viewers may not be driving a car while watching TV—at least we sure hope not—they need to have key information reinforced to give them a chance to write it down or, better, remember it. This is not quite as important when it comes to print ads, such as one would see in a newspaper or magazine. In these cases, it is much easier and more convenient for readers to make note of important information that you, the writer, are trying to impart.
- **Be serious but with a twinkle.** Even advertisements with dark messages have a light tone. For instance, over the years there have been numerous public service announcements on cancer and its relation to cigarette smoking. Some have been downright grim. However, even those have offered the audience hope in the form of how to address the problem, how the challenge can be met, and so forth. This is the "twinkle" to which we refer. Writers need to give the public either the solution to a circumstance or information on what they can do to find the solution.
- **Be mindful of the basics: be clear, accurate, and respectful.** Rarely do electronic ads last more than sixty seconds. More, in fact, are half that length. Print ads are also limited in space, whether it is a full page or less or even the size of a billboard. In either venue, space is a premium, and it is up to the writer to make the most of it. While traditional rules of grammar do not always apply, writers must focus on being understood in what they convey, yet in a way that is not offensive. People under any circumstances do not wish to be mocked or belittled. Advertisements can be serious yet not harsh at the expense of the audience.

Branding

This is a key aspect of advertising that deserves its own mention. What, you might ask, is branding? One way to think of it is advertising on steroids. A successful advertising campaign will make customers want to buy a particular product. A successful branding effort will make those same customers need a particular product. For instance, many parents may want their child to receive a college education, but some want their son or daughter to get their degree at a specific university or college. While the reasons for such strong feelings may be many and vary from family to family or person to person, the common denominator is that the specific college or product has done an effective job of instilling that need in its user or consumer. For such people, not any brand of toothpaste will do. It must be Crest or Colgate, for example.

Creating such a feeling of driven, uncompromising loyalty among customers is not something done overnight. It is usually done—if at all—over months and months of consistent, well-coordinated effort by advertising and marketing experts. It involves raising an acute awareness of a product, for instance, as well as establishing a personality or lifestyle of a product or service in the eyes of the public (Klein, 2008). More to the point, branding is about getting customers or prospective ones to see a specific product or service as the only one that provides a solution to a need they might have (Lake, 2013). Achieving such an end entails having detailed knowledge and understanding of a particular public, including their needs and wants, and then integrating one's brand through every aspect of the company's or organization's contact with the public.

Public Relations Campaign Assignment

Life for the public relations practitioner being what it often is, professionals do not always get to choose their own assignments. In fact, more often than not this is the case. Consequently, flexibility is the name of the game for practitioners. Usually, their boss at the agency or in the organization will call or pass along a written request for the practitioner to either connect with a current or prospective client or perform a particular task, such as drafting a press release or media advisory or making some phone calls. Given such a reality, however, this is not to suggest that the work of public relations practitioners is always in response to the whims or wishes of others. In truth, it is a mixture of proactive and reactive decisions and actions.

It is important to remember that as a professional public relations practitioner, you wear the cloak of "professional communicator" or "communication expert." Thus, while you may not always dictate the challenges or assignments dropped in your inbox, in many ways, you do determine and/or oversee the specific solutions and strategies to which the client will follow or adhere. Professional communicators are in the business of relationships: helping establish and then maintain them. In other words, while practitioners may not always determine the song to be played on the jukebox, they do play a major, even indispensable, role in deciding how that same song it will be showcased and shared with others. Such a position is no small thing.

In a field such as communication, for you to expect that you can and will always dictate each aspect of outreach or the need to establish or strengthen a connection dooms you to workdays of constant frustration. Remember: public relations practitioners work on behalf of others. By definition, such a posture contains a large portion of reaction. An easy example of this is a crisis. If you are the top communicator for a board of education and you receive a call that a shooter has entered one of the local high schools and has wounded several students and is holding others hostage, your duty is to respond as quickly and effectively as you can. No question, this is a challenge, and without one doubt this puts the practitioner at the disposal of others. Such is the cross a go-to person carries.

Wrap-Up

Scholars and practitioners alike view public relations as a social science not unlike sociology, psychology, or even history. As we know, public relations revolves around the workings of communication. The focus of this chapter, however, pertained more to the actual mechanics of this vital aspect of human relations. More specifically, we looked at a range of tools communicators use to help promote their clients as well as strengthen their ties with reporters. The various communication tools, including the press release or the fact sheet, represent more than a desire on the communicator's part to help a reporter do his or her job. Make no mistake, each of the tools we outlined is designed for the express purpose of advancing information about a client and the image of that client. The fact that many of these tools provide assistance to reporters or even members of the general public is an add-on.

Prior to the introduction and rise of computers, public relations practitioners made good use of press kits. This has not changed with the profession's greater use of and dependency on new technology. Press kits, in this sense, remain timeless. Where press kits were packets of information handed out at events—and they still are—in the current culture of the communication profession, there are electronic press kits that reporters have access to. The difference with the electronic version is that reporters are more free to pick and choose what supporting material they might need. Nevertheless, the same principles of writing apply as much to electronic versions as they do to the more traditional ones.

Regardless of the communication tool, even if it is something as comprehensive as the press kit, these various communiqués are also designed to better enable public relations practitioners to control their messages. By compiling and/or determining the facts being included in each tool, the public relations worker better sets the parameters within which reporters will pursue their stories and, ultimately, showcase the organization. Granted, this does not always work, as at times reporters will often incorporate their own perspective or story angles into how they tell or write their piece. Still, the communication tools, from a more global perspective, are part of the subtle and sometimes not-so-subtle efforts public relations workers make to ensure that those they represent are depicted favorably.

Advertising remains the one communication tool that stands apart from the other tools identified and discussed in this chapter. Its primary focus is on the general public rather than the media. More than those tools, advertisements speak to an entity's image. Also, they represent a one-way communication overture designed to promote or enlighten. Though more expensive to produce and place in a public forum, advertisements serve as a surefire way of gaining visibility to all with the budget to afford them. The other communication tools listed in this chapter fall under the umbrella of uncontrolled media.

Reading List

The following articles provide a solid overview of public relations writing as it pertains to composing copy for various communication tools as well as take a close look at the challenges of public relations writing itself:

What is Public Relations Writing?

By Joseph M. Zappala and Ann R. Carden

> A song that sounds simple is just not that easy to write.
>
> —Sheryl Crow[1]

> I don't know what real childbirth is like, but writing songs seems as close as I'm going to come.
>
> —Billy Joel

You may think that songwriters and public relations writers have little in common. But songwriters, poets, novelists, and other writers, including public relations writers, will tell you that writing is hard, even painful. Most writers know the frustration of staring at an empty computer screen or a blank sheet of paper, waiting for the right words to come, and public relations writers are no exception.

The songwriter faced with writer's block might take a long drive or meditate to stimulate the writing process. As a public relations writer, you don't always have that luxury. In a crisis, when you need to communicate quickly and accurately about a threatening situation, there's little time for leisurely drives or meditation. Consider, as well, that public relations professionals write for many different audiences, for many different media, and in many different forms and styles, sometimes all in the same day. This is no easy task.

Songwriters, like poets, novelists, sculptors, and other artists, often create works that are deeply personal; they are not always creating a work of art to please someone else, but more so to express something important they need to say. This is not so for public relations writers. Public relations writing has an organizational purpose. You must write with the interests of a specific group of people in mind, and balance that with the interests of the organization you represent. Public relations writing succeeds when people respond by doing something your organization wants them to do, whether that be learning something you want them to learn, adopting an attitude or position you want them to adopt, taking a positive action you want them to take, or simply thinking good thoughts about the organization. In the public relations world, writing without such a purpose is a waste of time.

As a public relations writer, you are not aiming to create works of art. Don't make the mistake of thinking that good public relations writing is like a song, or like poetry or prose, full of descriptive phrasing and obscure thoughts. There are times when creative writing is necessary, but creativity should never overshadow what's most important about a public relations message: its ability to communicate information in a way that people will understand. It's about simple words and clear messages that inspire a desired change in thinking or behavior.

Joseph M. Zappala and Ann R. Carden, "What Is Public Relations Writing?" *Public Relations Writing Worktext*, pp. 3-12.

While those brochures and news releases you write may not be on the artistic level of a classic novel or an Academy Award-winning film script, they do require special skill and finesse. And that makes public relations writing a fine art.

What is Public Relations?

Before discussing the role of a public relations writer, it's important to give that role some perspective by first defining the public relations function, and then explaining how public relations differs from and integrates with marketing and advertising (as illustrated in Exhibit 6.1). While each of these functions has a distinct purpose, they also work together and share the common goal of helping an organization communicate to its publics—groups that are critical to the organization's survival.

Exhibit 6.2 presents some of the classic definitions of public relations by some of the industry's most respected educators and professionals. In sum, public relations is a strategic function that manages and builds relationships with an organization's publics through two-way communication. Public relations professionals promote two-way communication by providing an open flow of idea exchange, feedback, and information between an organization and its publics. They counsel management on how to best shape policy and establish programs that are mutually beneficial and sensitive to public concerns. Public relations builds goodwill and an understanding of organizational goals among various internal and external publics to help the organization operate smoothly and conduct its business in a cooperative, conflict-free environment.

The goal of *marketing*, by contrast, is to develop, maintain, and improve a product's market share; attract and satisfy customers; and cause a transaction in order to build profitability. Public relations professionals support marketing staff by providing promotional services. One common marketing communications activity is *publicity*, which may involve placing news stories in the media about products and services. The most common form of publicity is the news release, an announcement from an organization written in news style.

If a newspaper publishes your product news release, it does so at no cost to you. Once your publicity material is received by the media, however, you lose control of the content. The media is free to use it in any form they choose, or they can decide not to use it. This differs from *advertising*, which is paid promotional messages that you can control. When you supply an advertisement to the media, they run it as you've written it. Advertising copy has a creative flair, with language and phrasing designed for the "hard sell." Publicity materials are more subtle and read more like news articles. To illustrate the difference, look at the lead from a product news release that appeared on the Verizon Wireless Web site and the opening of a commercial for the same product:

> *Product News Release:*
> The BlackBerry® Storm™ (model 9530) from Research In Motion (NASDAQ: RIMM)—the first touch screen BlackBerry smartphone with the world's first "clickable" touch screen—will be available beginning Nov. 21 in Verizon Wireless Communications Stores and online at www.verizonwireless.com for $199.99 after a $50 mail-in rebate with a new two-year customer agreement.

Exhibit 6.1
The Integration of Public Relations, Marketing, and Advertising

Public relations is a strategic function that manages and builds relationships with an organization's publics through two-way communication.

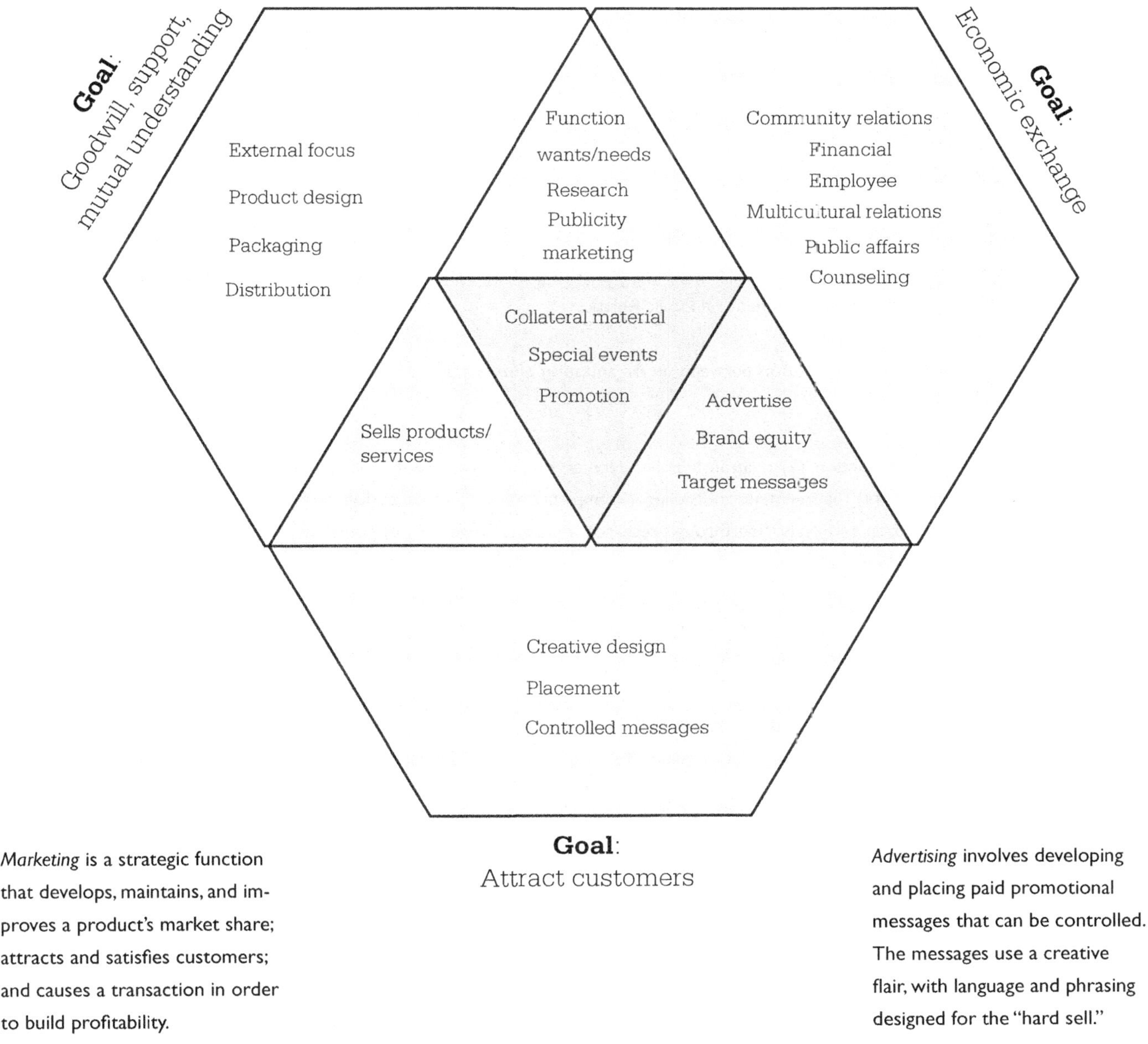

Marketing is a strategic function that develops, maintains, and improves a product's market share; attracts and satisfies customers; and causes a transaction in order to build profitability.

Advertising involves developing and placing paid promotional messages that can be controlled. The messages use a creative flair, with language and phrasing designed for the "hard sell."

Note: Adapted from *PR Reporter*, Ragan Communications, Inc.

Exhibit 6.2
Defining Public Relations

"Public relations practice is the art and science of analyzing trends, predicting their consequences, counseling organization leaders, and implementing planned programs of action which will serve both the organization's and the public interest."—First World Assembly of Public Relations Associations and the First World Forum of Public Relations

"Public relations is a distinctive management function which helps establish and maintain mutual lines of communication, understanding, acceptance and cooperation between an organization and its publics; involves the management of problems or issues; helps management keep informed on and responsive to public opinion; defines and emphasizes the responsibility of management to serve the public interest; helps management keep abreast of and effectively utilize change, serving as an early warning system to help anticipate trends; and uses research and sound ethical communication techniques as its principal tools."—Harlow, "Building a Public Relations Definition," *Public Relations Review*

"Public relations helps our complex, pluralistic society to reach decisions and function more effectively by contributing to mutual understanding among groups and institutions. It serves to bring private and public policies into harmony."—PRSA Official Statement on Public Relations

"Management of communication between an organization and its publics."—Grunig and Hunt, *Managing Public Relations*

"(1) Management function, (2) relationships between an organization and its publics, (3) analysis and evaluation through research, (4) management counseling, (5) implementation and execution of a planned program of action, communication and evaluation through research, and (6) achievement of goodwill."—Simon, *Public Relations Concepts and Practices*

"Public relations deals primarily with advice on action, based on social responsibility."—Bernays, *The Later Years: 1956–1986*

"The management function that establishes and maintains mutually beneficial relationships between an organization and publics on whom its success or failure depends."—Cutlip, Center, and Broom, *Effective Public Relations*

"(1) deliberate, (2) planned, (3) performance, (4) public interest, (5) two-way communication, and (6) management function."—Wilcox, Ault and Agee, *Public Relations Strategies and Tactics*

"PR involves responsibility and responsiveness in policy and information to the best interests of the organization and its publics."—Newsom, Scott, and Turk, *This is PR: The Realities of Public Relations*

"Public relations is the management function which evaluates public attitudes, identifies the policies and procedures of an individual or an organization with the public interest, and plans and executes a program of action to earn public understanding and acceptance."—*Public Relations News*

"Public relations (PR) is the practice of managing the flow of information between an organization and its publics."—Wikipedia

Product Advertisement:
Whoa! It has no keyboard. And did it just click? You never clicked a screen before. Is that supposed to happen? Is it supposed to feel so right? It feels like a keyboard, just no keys. What kind of mad genius designed this?

In addition to supporting the marketing function with promotional efforts, public relations practitioners offer advice on the social implications of products and help counter attacks from consumer and special interest groups. For example, some years ago, tuna companies faced protests from environmental groups concerned about the number of dolphins getting trapped and killed in nets used by tuna fishermen. Protests and negative media headlines created a serious public relations problem that, in turn, had an impact on product sales. To regain public trust, tuna companies opened up dialogue with environmentalists and began making changes in their fishing practices to avoid doing harm to dolphins. After these changes were made and communicated, tuna companies began declaring their products "dolphin safe" and restoring their reputations through good public relations, while avoiding a marketing disaster.

Types of Public Relations Writing

Public relations writers are among the most versatile of writers. While a magazine journalist writes each article for a single mass audience—the people who read that magazine—the public relations writer prepares many pieces for a wide range of publics. A corporate public relations professional, for example, writes for employees, customers, media, and stockholders. Writing for each of those publics can require variations in message and style. Among the types of writing assignment handled by public relations professionals are:

- ***Business correspondence***—internal memos that inform others in the organization about the status of projects and other subjects, external business correspondence and e-mail messages that confirm agreements and solicit support, and proposals to clients and internal supervisors that outline recommended public relations campaigns.
- ***Corporate and internal communications***—news and feature stories for publication in newsletters, company magazines, and other employee publications; content for Web sites, intranets, and digital social media; scripts for training and corporate video programs; and annual reports directed to shareholders and the financial community.
- ***Publicity writing***—news releases, background materials, and other written pieces designed to produce print and broadcast media coverage.
- ***Marketing communications***—written materials that support marketing efforts, product promotion, and customer relations, such as product publicity, product brochures and catalogs, posters and fliers, sales literature, direct mail pieces, and customer newsletters.
- ***Advocacy writing***—writing that establishes a position or comments on an issue, endorses a cause or rallies support, such as letters to the editor and articles sent to the opinion pages of print media; speeches written for executives that are delivered at industry conferences, media events, or business meetings; and corporate or "image" advertising that "sells the company," not a specific product (e.g., a corporate ad from a utility company publicly thanking the community for its patience during a power outage).

Communication and the Public Relations Writer

Public relations writing, regardless of what the specific piece is or who it is written for, is always purposeful. Its primary goal is to communicate information that will influence people. Mass communication literature identifies four mass communication goals that also have relevance to public relations writing:

- to ***inform*** people of threats and opportunities and to help them better understand their environment;
- to ***teach*** skills, knowledge, and appropriate behavior that help people adapt to their environment and feel accepted;
- to ***persuade*** people to adopt desired behaviors and see them as acceptable; and
- to ***please*** people by providing entertainment and enjoyment.

These goals have much in common with those of the public relations writer, especially the first three—to inform, to teach, and to persuade. Some public relations writing certainly has entertainment value. For example, many college public relations and communication programs across the country produce alumni newsletters. Graduates say they enjoy reading the newsletter and especially like knowing what former classmates are doing, if they have changed jobs, gotten engaged or married, had babies, or received an award for their work.

But, in addition to entertainment, this information has greater value. Publishing alumni updates helps graduates stay connected to one another and to the program. Over time, this builds loyalty and support and increases the perceived value of their college degree. The newsletter is more than just an interesting, entertaining read. It has a positive, long-term influence as a communication vehicle.

Like any good communicator, public relations writers must get feedback from their targeted publics to measure the true success of their efforts. The receiver of the message must respond in some way to indicate the message was received, processed, and understood. If you send a news release to a newspaper and the newspaper publishes the release, have you communicated with your public? Not necessarily. You have merely interested an editor enough in the subject to use the material. You can estimate the potential number of people who may have read the story by looking at the circulation figures for the newspaper. But you cannot assume that communication took place, or that people even saw your message, unless they tell you. If the goal of your news release is to inform and to encourage people to learn more about a subject, include a toll-free number in the release and ask them to "call for more information." This technique generates feedback you can measure and provides some assurance that communication occurred.

Public relations theorists and behavioral scientists point out that the traditional S-M-R communications model—sending a message through a specific channel to a desired receiver—is not effective if the intent of communication is to change behavior. They say this model is best used for publicity and awareness building. It is most effective when sending information to people who have little resistance to your message, such as consumers who already use and like your product and whose positive feelings are simply reinforced through the communication. But if the goal is to get people to form an opinion, or to reduce negative public opinion, building awareness alone is not enough.

According to the diffusion of innovations theory, people adopt new ideas as the result of a five-step process that begins with ***awareness***. They must first learn about the idea. Next, they must develop further ***interest*** in the idea and gather additional information on the subject. Then come ***evaluation*** and ***trial***, weighing the pros and cons of the idea and discussing it with others, followed by testing the idea to see how well it fits into their lives. If the trial is successful, the result is ***adoption*** of the idea.

Think about buying a car. You might first see a television ad or article in the "Auto" section of the newspaper about a particular model (awareness). Thinking this car has potential, you visit a Web site, collect brochures, and read *Consumer Reports* to get more details (interest). With more information in hand, you talk to associates at work, people you know who own the car, "friends" in a chat room or through your Facebook page, and maybe parents to get their opinions of the car's quality, value, and performance. You also look carefully at your budget to determine if this is a realistic purchase (evaluation). Their positive remarks may motivate you to visit a dealer, talk to a salesperson about the car, and take a test drive (trial). After negotiating an agreeable price, you buy the car (adoption). The late Patrick Jackson, one of the most widely known and respected public relations practitioners, developed a behavioral model of communication to explain this process as it relates to public relations (see Exhibit 6.3). According to this model, once people are aware of a product, service, or issue, they will begin to formulate a readiness to act; an event then triggers this readiness into actual behavior.

As the car example shows, publicity and public relations writing have the greatest impact in the awareness and interest stages. Well-placed media articles about the car, a creative Web site, and informative brochures, all produced by public relations writers, play a significant role. These written tools become less influential in the later stages, when personal communication and the opinions of family, friends, and peers have the most impact; it is important to keep this in perspective. Public relations writing plays a part in the acceptance of new ideas and behavioral change early in the process, but face-to-face communication and personal experience make the difference in the end. In addition, your written materials are competing with those of other organizations for someone's attention, so these pieces must do more than just communicate—they must communicate persuasively.

Exhibit 6.3

Jackson's Behavioral Communication Model

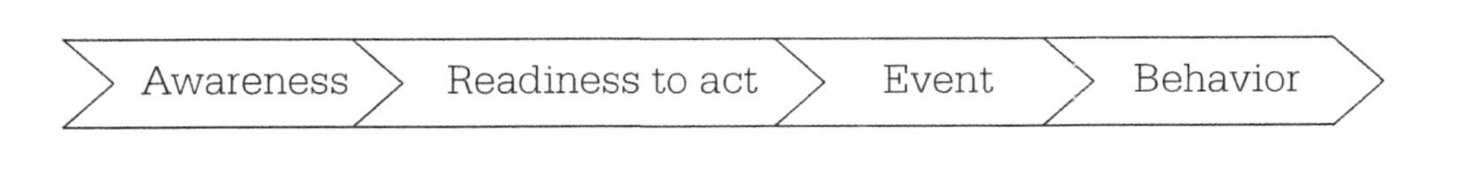

Note: Reprinted with permission of PR Reporter, Ragan Communications, Inc.

Persuasion and the Public Relations Writer

Persuasion is not a dirty word. "Persuade" means influence, move, motivate, convince, win over. Those aren't bad words. When you think about it, many of the things you say or do as a college student in an average day—asking your roommate if you can borrow her car, calling your parents in hopes they will send money, convincing your professor to extend an assignment deadline—are all done in an effort to influence, motivate, or persuade. Persuasion "goes bad" when you purposely mislead someone or tell a lie to get what you want. If you tell your parents you need extra cash to buy some textbooks, but they find out you used the money to buy a DVD player or new music from iTunes, those checks from home will probably stop coming.

Some people may perceive persuasion as negative because they confuse it with propaganda. While persuasion and propaganda may use similar techniques, such as symbols, stereotypes, and testimonials, the goal of ***persuasion*** is to provide new information or existing information in a fresh light to enable people to make up their own minds. ***Propaganda***, on the other hand, seeks to manipulate the public's thinking by deliberately providing misinformation.

Public relations professionals are in the persuasion business. They are advocates for their organizations; every conversation, every proposal, every media event, and every piece of writing is intended to influence, build rapport, and win support. But winning support at any cost is never an option. There may be pressure to twist facts, omit details, or say something that just isn't true, but *do not bow to that pressure*. Once trust is lost, it is hard to regain. In a statement made at Utica College when he delivered the Harold Burson Distinguished Lecture, John Reed, an international public relations consultant and veteran practitioner, defined public relations as "ethical persuasion." Keep that definition in mind as a writer, communicator, and protector of an organization's reputation—and your own.

There are honest and reasonable techniques to make communication more persuasive. Messages that genuinely appeal to a public's self-interests, that come from trusted sources, and that suggest a beneficial course of action can be highly persuasive. These principles are illustrated in The Air Bag Safety Campaign launched by the National Safety Council. In response to an increasing number of automobile air-bag-related fatalities, the campaign stressed the importance of properly restraining children under 12 when riding in a car.

Public opinion research showed that many parents did not know the risks air bags posed to their children, and that the majority of parents did not take the necessary steps to buckle up their children. In addition, national crash test data confirmed that the greatest risk was not the air bags themselves, but the potential for injury should an air bag deploy when someone is riding without a seat belt. The campaign appealed to the most fundamental of interests: parents' desires to protect the lives of their children.

The campaign, "Air Bag Safety Means: Buckle Everyone! Children in the Back," or the ABCs of air bag safety, communicated a simple and clear call to action. The key message was, if you and your children use seat belts, you can avoid injury and a possible air-bag-related fatality. Information provided to adult drivers also clearly explained how air bags work and what can happen if someone is unrestrained and too close to the air bag when it deploys. To strengthen message impact, the National Safety Council partnered with professional organizations such as The American Academy of Family Physicians, The National Highway Traffic Safety Administration, and respected safety groups to help educate drivers about air bag safety. The campaign led to a significant increase in the number of adult drivers properly restraining children before transporting them in cars and thus to a reduced number of air bag fatalities. Follow-up surveys indicated greater awareness of the risks of air bags. Here are other tips for persuasive communication that are supported by behavioral research:

- Use a blend of rational and emotional messages. The National Safety Council's campaign shared facts, statistics, and results of air bag safety public opinion research, but it also used the media to publish stories about individual tragedies. This made the problem real: it added a human face to the problem to which other families could relate. Generally, messages directed to high-involvement audiences—those already connected to or inclined to support your organization or cause—might call for a more rational or factual approach. Low-involvement groups may need to be targeted with more emotional messages.
- Select the most appropriate media based on message content and the preferences of your target publics. Print media are best when attempting to explain complex subjects, but visual messages usually have greater influence on attitude change. Know your public and how it prefers to receive information. The fire department of a northeast city, concerned about the growing number of inner-city fires, provided information to local newspapers in hopes of educating residents about fire safety, but with minimal effect. Upon closer inspection, the department discovered a high rate of illiteracy among residents in those areas of the city where fires broke out most often. This prompted a change in strategy that involved using more face-to-face communication and broadcast media.
- Begin and end your writing with the most important messages. Studies indicate that people have higher recall of information that appears in the opening and closing of a message.

At the start of this chapter, we described public relations writing as a fine art, one requiring special skill—a skill that can be learned. To hone that skill, public relations writers must know all aspects of their organizations; have in-depth understanding of their publics and the media that reach those publics; possess finely tuned research skills and expertise in communication and persuasion theory; and be creative, strategic thinkers who can take complex, detailed material and make it simple and easy to understand.

Note

1. Malloy, 1995, pp. 148–149.

References and Suggested Reading

Bernays, E. L. (1986). *The later years: Public relations insights 1956–1986*. Rhinebeck, NY: H & M.

BlackBerry Storm (2008). Available in US, November 21, exclusively from Verizon Wireless. Retrieved November 16, 2008 from http://news.vzw.com/news/2008/11/pr2008-11-13.html.

BlackBerry Storm commercial (2008). Retrieved November 16, 2008 from http://www.youtube.com/watch?v=GmyVzoyY9Jo.

Broom, G. (2008). *Effective public relations* (10th ed.). Upper Saddle River, NJ: Prentice Hall.

Caywood, C. L. (1997). *The handbook of strategic public relations and integrated communications.* New York: McGraw Hill.

Cutlip, S., Center, A., & Broom, G. (1994). *Effective public relations* (7th ed.). Englewood Cliffs, NJ: Prentice-Hall, Inc.

Gordon, J. C. (1997). Interpreting definitions of public relations: Self assessment and a symbolic interactionism-based alternative. *Public Relations Review, 23 (1)*, 57–66.

Grunig, J. E. (Ed.) (1992). *Excellence in public relations and communication management.* Hillsdale, NJ: Lawrence Erlbaum Associates.

Grunig, J. E., & Hunt, T. (1984). *Managing public relations.* Fort Worth, TX: Holt, Rinehart, & Winston.

Harlow, R. (1976). Building a public relations definition. *Public Relations Review, 2 (4)*, 34–42.

Jackson, P. (1990). *PR Reporter, 33 (30)*, 1–2.

Kitchen, P. J. (1997). *Public relations: Principles & practice.* Stamford, CT: International Thomson Business Press.

Lesly, P. (1998). *Lesly's handbook of public relations and communications* (5th ed.). St. Louis, MO: McGraw Hill/ Contemporary Books.

Malloy, M. (Ed.) (1995). *The great rock 'n' roll quote book.* New York: St. Martin's Griffin.

Newsom, D., Scott, A., & Turk, J. V. (1989). *This is PR: The realities of public relations* (4th ed.). Belmont, CA: Wadsworth.

Newsom, D., Turk, J. V., & Kruckeberg, D. (2006). *This is PR: The realities of public relations* (9th ed.). Belmont, CA: Wadsworth.

PRSA Official statement on public relations (n.d.). Retrieved January 24, 2009 from http://www.prsa.org/aboutUs/officialStatement.html.

Public relations (2006). *Merriam-Webster's collegiate dictionary* (11th ed.). Springfiled, MA: Merriam-Webster, Inc.

Public relations (n.d.). Retrieved January 24, 2009 from http://en.wikipedia.org/wiki/Public_relations.

Seitel, F. P. (2006). *Practice of public relations* (10th ed.). Upper Saddle River, NJ: Prentice Hall.

Simon, R. (1984). *Public relations concepts and practices.* Englewood Cliffs, NJ: Prentice Hall.

Smith, R. (2004). *Strategic planning for public relations* (6th ed.). Mahwah, NJ: Lawrence Erlbaum Associates.

Wilcox, D., Ault, P. H., & Agee, W. K. (1989). *Public relations: Strategies and tactics* (2nd ed.). New York: Harper & Row.

Wilcox, D., Ault, P. H., Agee, W. K., & Cameron, G. T. (2001). *Essentials of public relations.* New York: Longman.

Wilson, L. (2000). *Strategic program planning for effective public relations campaigns* (3rd ed.). Dubuque, IA: Kendall/Hunt Publishing Company.

Media Kits

By Janet Mizrahi

PR professionals are routinely called on to put together media kits, a collection of materials providing facts about an organization, its leadership, its products, an event, or an issue. As the name denotes, media kits are intended for use by the media and should not be confused with packets designed for sales support. Although a kit put together for sales may contain many of the same elements as a media kit, its purpose is entirely different.

Media kits are used to supply the media with background about an organization or the necessary facts to cover an event. That event may be a speech given by an organization explaining a product recall (think Toyota); it might be an introduction to a new product (think iPad); it might be a public relations disaster (think BP in the Gulf). In all cases, the organization would provide a media kit containing salient information.

Traditional media kits are hard copy, but increasingly this is changing. Some organizations provide digital versions of a print media kit in PDF format. Many organizations simply post information on their websites that is accessible to any interested party. The benefit of this approach is that information can be updated regularly, thereby making it more timely and less expensive than a print media kit. Still, the hard copy media kit continues to be a staple of the PR function.

Media Kit Audience

Media kits are put together to provide information to those in print, radio, television, or Internet-based media. As we have previously discussed, editors and reporters form an uneasy alliance with public relations practitioners; both need one another to exist, but both are skeptical of the other's motives. Knowing this, the PR professional must serve the organization while not antagonizing or alienating the media. The contents of a media kit should be well written to appeal to a discerning audience and objective to appeal to this audience's sense of ethics.

Media Kit Purpose

Media kits are designed specifically to provide background material a reporter or news entity needs to cover an event or feature a subject in an article or radio or television broadcast. Therefore, this material should be complete, well written, factual, and objective. Nothing will make a reporter less inclined to write a good story than a self-serving media kit.

Janet Mizrahi, "Media Kits," *Fundamentals of Writing for Marketing and Public Relations: A Step-by-Step Guide*, pp. 79-84.

Media Kit Appearance and Contents

The materials in print media kits are placed into an attractive one- or two-pocket folder. An image of the product being promoted or the company's logo is often affixed to the cover. The stock quality, cover image choice, and printing of these folders all work to create an image. A folder with a glossy, four-color photograph and metallic touches connotes a glitzy event or product, whereas a folder made of high-quality stock with matte finish and embossed with a company logo produces a more conservative image. Folders vary vastly in price, but if kept simple can be relatively inexpensive to produce.

Often organizations print a large number of folders to have on hand for various purposes. Sometimes the folder is designed to be multifunctional. Other times an organization may create a separate folder for a specific event. In both cases, this shell for the contents is the first thing the media sees and should be created with the tastes and needs of the media in mind. All folders should include a die cut in which a contact person's business card is placed.

The contents of media kits vary but all tend to include the following:

1. **Fact sheets.** A tersely written overview, the fact sheet has boldfaced headings and bulleted points. It may include an overview of the organization with names of principals, number of employees, address, location(s), contact information, and the like. A fact sheet may be about a new product with product specifications; it may provide the facts of an upcoming event. It will answer the standard news questions: who, what, where, when, and why.
2. **News releases.** The specially prepared news release about the event or subject may be accompanied by previous pertinent news releases.
3. **Bios.** A one-page description of each of the organization's main players accompanied by a headshot of reproducible quality. Bios can be straightforward and simply discuss the executive's experience and accomplishments at the organization, or they can be narrative and include more personal details.[1]
4. **Nonprint items.** If broadcasters are covering the event, they will require a video. Print media will need photographs. Visuals should be included in the media kit and be produced with the media's needs in mind.
5. **Backgrounder.** The backgrounder provides an explanation of the mission, history, and strategic vision of an organization written in paragraph style with an objective tone. This document can go into depth about the organization, even explaining day-to-day operations.

Optional items or those items that would only be included for a specifi c event include the following:

1. **White paper or position paper.** *A white paper* is a technical report that educates readers about an issue or a topic. A *position paper* is opinion based and conveys an organization's stand on an issue.
2. **Past news articles.** Any time an organization has had press coverage, the organization has tear sheets of those articles reproduced. These are often included in a media kit to illustrate that the organization has been worthy of media coverage.
3. **Spokesperson's statement.** A spokesperson's statement is a quote or quotes from an individual speaking on behalf of the company or organization designated to go on the record. These include the spokesperson's contact information.

4. **Pitch letter**. Pitch letters are persuasive letters to an editor or writer of a specific media vehicle proposing an idea for a story. (This is discussed in more detail later in the chapter.)

The organization and placement of the items in a media kit should be logical and easy to follow. If there are many pieces, a list of included items similar to a table of contents could be used. In addition, the media might find it helpful to have all the materials reproduced on a CD, which should also be placed in the folder.

When I worked at a software firm, we had a media kit area in our offices. In it were dozens of printed pieces in separate slots. These pieces included various news releases, reprints of articles about the fi rm and its leadership, product information sheets, brochures, director bios, and more. These sheets were available to the staff for both sales and marketing purposes. It was a popular spot!

Pitch Letters

A pitch letter is crafted to capture the interest of the most jaded of readers: an editor or reporter. Pitch letters are used by organizations to prod an editor or reporter to cover a story featuring the organization's product, service, or event. For example, a foreign country might hire a U.S. PR firm to raise awareness of its nation. As part of the overall PR strategy, the PR representative might write a letter to a travel magazine writer or editor hoping that the idea pitched in the letter would stimulate interest in writing about the destination.

If it sounds impossible, it's not … but it is difficult! Good pitch letters contain an angle that will appeal to both the editor and the readership or viewing audience. A successful pitch requires not just thinking the way the media thinks but also understanding that media's needs.

Pitch letters work best when the PR professional analyzes the publication (or television show) to understand the type of stories that are typically covered. Back issues or shows should be read or viewed to make sure the idea has not been done previously. Target a writer or producer who specializes in covering stories related to the idea being pitched. The better the background research, the better the chance the idea will be picked up.

A good pitch letter is tightly written and error free and includes the following elements:[2]

- Name of specific individual to whom the idea is being pitched.
- A professional tone. Don't become effusive or imagine that you are the writer's pal. That will just irritate a journalist.
- A first paragraph that reads as if it were the lead of the article; it should hook the reader with its captivating, feature article style.
- A second paragraph that describes how and why the story will appeal to the readers or viewers of the particular media, illustrating an understanding of both the publication or show and the reader or viewer.
- A third paragraph that provides the terms of the offer: Is the story an exclusive? If so, for how long will you hold it? Discuss how you can help with setting up interviews or obtaining original art. Do *not* offer to write the story!
- The date by which you'll need to have a definitive answer. Be polite and thank the addressee.
- A sign-off with a simple "Sincerely."

The sample in Figure 6.1 illustrates how a PR writer might pitch an idea to a writer.

Conclusion

Media kits continue to be indispensable in public relations. Whether they are sent as a PDF or handed out at an event, media kits are versatile tools that help an organization promote its message. As with all writing for public relations, media kits require the writer to be acutely aware of the audience's needs while simultaneously serving the organization's purpose.

April 13, 2011
Mr. John Doe
Staff Writer
Travel on a Budget
11111 Park Place
New York, NY 10001

Dear Mr. Doe:

Brad Smith and his buddies are such hardcore campers that they plan their monthly weekend getaways a year in advance. But after repeatedly visiting the same old location near their homes in San Diego, they needed a new spot. The guys were pretty picky, though. Brad insisted on pristine hiking trails. Mario needed clear streams with plenty of fi sh. They all wanted rugged bicycle paths and untouched natural surroundings. Then Brad found Idyllwild. And things got a little, well, wild! Did I mention the bear? Never mind, the story has a happy ending.

I think readers of *Travel on a Budget* would enjoy hearing about the camping adventures of Brad and his friends in the little-known gem of Idyllwild, California. Nestled halfway between LA and San Diego in the San Jacinto Mountains, Idyllwild gave these working men a weekend they'll not soon forget. Such an article would complement your recent series on weekend getaways in Northern California and would appeal to active readers who want to learn about affordable destinations with lots of exciting activities.

We can offer you this story as an exclusive and provide you with access to Brad and his colorful camping cohorts as well as exquisite still and video footage of Idyllwild's natural surroundings, but I'd have to know your intention by [date]. We even can give you a shot of Brad and the bear! Please give me a call at 555–111–1234 or email me at xxx@xxx.com to let me know if I can be of any help.

I'll follow up with you on [date] to see how I might be able to assist you. Thanks for your consideration.

Sincerely,
[Name, Position]

Figure 1. Sample pitch letter.

Chapter Highlights

- Professional practitioners have at their disposal a number of communication tools designed to provide external publics, including the media, with pertinent information on a specific topic.
- The various communication tools are designed to help public relations workers control the information that reporters have to work from in putting together their stories.
- Not all of the primary communication tools require original writing. Some call for facts and figures. Still, all demand thorough research and close attention to detail.
- he various communication tools call for collaboration. Public relations workers should not put any of them together or make them available to the public without their having been reviewed by others within the organization.
- The communication tools reinforce the notion that the public relations operation is an organization's primary gatekeeper of information and messaging. The communicators work closely with all levels of an organization, including its top officers, to ensure that what is made known to the public presents the client in an accurate and, ideally, favorable light.
- All communication tools are subject to constant updating and revision. Public relations workers should not allow out-of-date information to be disseminated to the public, especially to reporters. This can be just damaging as information that is inaccurate.
- In scope and outreach, advertising goes beyond many of the traditional communication tools. It is the tool that communicators can control best in terms of content, placement, and frequency of display.
- The primary purposes of advertising include enhancing an entity's image; promoting an event, product, or service; announcing a key decision or moment on the part of an entity; and putting forth a position on a particular issue.

For Discussion

1. Discuss the pros and cons of communication tools.
2. Think of an event that you recently attended. If you had been assigned to produce a press kit for it, what material or documents would you have pulled together?
3. Using any issue of your choice, draft the following: a letter to the editor and op-ed piece about it.
4. Discuss how each of the communication tools identified in this chapter supports the outreach efforts of a public relations officer. What factors would help you determine which tools to use?
5. Are there occasions when a specific communication tool might not be appropriate?
6. Is it ever possible for a company to over-advertise?

vii

Print

Back in the day, there were separate tracks for journalists. There was the print journalist, and then the broadcast journalist came along, and the unwritten rule seemed to be "never the two shall meet." There were two very different schools of thought. As authors of this book, we have experienced the transition. One of us started out in print journalism and went on to the field of public relations, and one of us started out in broadcast journalism and went on to print and public relations, and then we both incorporated online and social media into our work.

We see this transition as over. There is no more one path to take; instead you will be expected to do it all, and we see this textbook as a great way for you to learn a little about each path. Eventually what you will find is that all the paths merge, and you will be best equipped for the journalism, writing, and communication world if you can do a bit of everything. In this chapter we will explore writing for print, and much of what is said can now be applied to online writing as well.

We think that as time goes by there will be no separate paths defined by labels such as print, online, or broadcast. Instead you will simply be a journalist or a writer, and you will know the fundamentals of what is required for all mediums, and you will be a blend of all the formats. This is crucial to securing work today—to be able to have knowledge and understanding and skills in each medium will be mandatory for journalists and communicators graduating from colleges and universities. You may already be seeing this in your internships. You must be able to work across platforms as a journalist today.

Print journalism made huge headlines recently with the sale of *The Washington Post*. Is print dead? Will newspapers disappear altogether? What is the new model for revenue? How will print journalism thrive and profit, if at all? We certainly have our opinions about this, and we can all be in agreement that the world of journalism has changed. What it will look like exactly is a great question, and one that we don't need to worry about for this class, although it makes for a great discussion. The thing to remember is that if you can write like a print journalist, and really understand and value the fundamentals of writing that are used to write a basic news story, you are well on your way. These are much-needed skills that will transition into any medium you choose. The format and technology of journalism may change over the years—it certainly has evolved over the past few decades that we have been in the field of communication—but the fundamentals of writing remain. You are on your way to being a cross-platform journalist.

A handful of years ago, there were passionate discussions in our classrooms and in the news about social media outlets such as Facebook and Twitter. Questions were raised, such as the following: Are these credible outlets for breaking news? Will the face of journalism change forever? Will the credibility of reporting change? How will sources be attributed? Is there a place for news on Twitter? As time goes by, we find out the answers. News (wars, classroom shootings, and terrorist attacks) break on social media. This isn't a one-time phenomenon. It is a fact of breaking news coverage in our world today.

There will always be a new medium in town (newspapers were once widely read, and now papers fold frequently), but news will never die. Neither will your valuable writing skills. So it is important to learn how to write a clear, concise news article, whether it is for print or online publications or linked to social media or even for another medium we cannot even imagine. Let us not worry whether print will soon be a journalistic dinosaur; instead, let's focus on the basics and fundamentals of writing. We can promise you that there will always be a need for good, solid, strong, clear, and concise writers and reporters. Before you begin to write a story, you must do the research and reporting. Although this text focuses on the aspect of communication and writing, we stress the importance of research. Do not begin to write an article or cover a story before you have done your research. With social media we are able to watch the news-gathering process unfold, which has proven to be fascinating and frustrating. Above all else, research, research, research; understand the facts of your story before reporting; and talk with as many credible sources as you can to check your facts. Only then will you be ready to write a solid news story or lead. Let's get started.

Leads (or Ledes)

Here is a fun piece to enjoy that dissects the different types of leads. Full credit for this goes to the quirky and insightful editors at *Stuff Journalists Like*, a cool blog you may want to check out. And we must preface this by saying that we aren't recommending that you go out and drink; we simply thought it was a fun way to think about the different styles of lead cocktails (or ledes, as you will sometimes see … same thing).

When it comes to writing ledes, journalists have a number of different weapons in their arsenal.

There's the tried-and-true summary lede, which gives readers the five W's and how. It's simple and takes the least amount of effort, but usually it's duller than a journalist's wardrobe. For even lazier journalists, there's the quote-and-question ledes (these should be avoided 99 percent of the time). [Side note: This is where the writer takes the easy approach and uses a direct quote or starts the sentence off with a question. We suggest you do more work than that.]

There's a lede for those adventurous journalists who want to give their stories a bit of zest, color, and flavor—the anecdotal lede. Sure, it's easy to dismiss the anecdotal lede as too playful, too "feature-y," but it's the one lede that gives most journalists the greatest satisfaction.

Generally, news writing doesn't call for too much creativeness from journalists. Journalists cover an event or issue, write down who said what, report what happened, then slap on their byline and go on the next story. But when the story calls for it (and when there's enough time before deadline), a journalist will try to dust off that last remaining creative brain cell and try to punch out an anecdotal lede.

All journalists should try the anecdotal lede every now and again. But, like Indiana Jones, choose wisely. When an anecdotal lede is good, it's good, but when it's bad, it can make editors cringe, make readers skip the story, and force journalists into hiding. Journalists shouldn't be discouraged from giving the anecdotal lede a shot. But, of course, not every story calls for an anecdotal lede. The story about the grandmother who has met every president since FDR—sure. The triple homicide piece—maybe just stick with the hard news lede.

If the hard news lede is a stiff shot of whiskey, the anecdotal lede is the refreshing, colorful, girly drink served in the playful glass with an umbrella. Though most nights you just want the stiff drink, it doesn't hurt to try something else on the menu (just make sure the veteran journalists aren't looking).

The Basics—Anecdotal Leads and Other Stuff

We are fans of the lead that contains the most compelling information. If after reading the first paragraph, the reader says, "Oh, wow, I want to know more about this," you know you have written a strong lead. Ultimately, the goal of a well-constructed lead is to capture readers' attention so that they keep reading. It's fairly basic. A poorly written lead is confusing, chaotic, and rambling, and it leaves the reader wondering what the news is. Do the work for your reader; don't make your reader do any work. We suggest giving the anecdotal lead a shot, rather than always writing in the inverted pyramid style. It's not that the inverted pyramid is bad, it can just get a tad dull because it is so formulaic. Given the growth of online journalism, the inverted pyramid model is also outdated. No longer are there a certain number of columns and inches to cut based on what a newspaper's spacing requires. It is outdated. That said, we are still a fan of putting the most important information first, with the less important information in progression. It is always a smart and simple approach, and not wrong by any stretch of the imagination; however, with the anecdotal lead, writers have a bit more room for creativity to pull the reader in. If you are looking for "just the facts," by all means, write in the basic formula of who, what, how, when, and why, and you will be on track.

To get a good description of how to write a successful, anecdotal lead, we look to an expert newspaper journalist named Bob Baker. Baker was at *The Los Angeles Times* for a quarter of a century, and he has some simple and compelling tips for the journalist who wants to master the anecdotal lead. More of Baker's work—he writes articles to help journalists better do their work—can be found at www.newsthinking.com.

We appreciate the use of his questions for our educational purposes, and we encourage you to visit his site and become a subscriber to his work. We try to help out fellow journalists whenever possible. First, let's define what an anecdotal lead is and why we should use it. Personally, we feel this style of lead is much more effective and interesting and more current than the use of an inverted pyramid style lead (a loaded and just-the-facts approach). We believe that a more effective lead is an anecdotal lead, which often begins with a brief story that contains a quick anecdote to pull readers in. With an effective and interesting anecdote that highlights the writer's larger point, this approach can be helpful to draw a reader in. If this style of lead is used, it should illustrate the broader angle of the story. When it works, it can be wonderful to read and it engages the reader, but often it can fall short, and then the article falls apart.

A Handful of Questions to Ask before Starting the Anecdotal Lead: How to Make Sure the Anecdote Doesn't Cause More Problems Than It Solves

Nothing winks more seductively at a reporter with a complex news-feature than an anecdotal lead—the promise of a way to quickly personalize the abstract and set the stage for a broader proclamation of the story theme.

And nothing falls apart more quickly.

The reason is the problem that sent you to the Anecdote Solution in the first place: life is so damned complicated. Too often, the anecdote requires too many grafs to make it work. Still other times, even when the anecdote can be compressed into a couple of grafs, it may simply be a trick to hide from the awful truth: You've got a news story on your hands, and you ought to tell it like one.

What follows are several considerations you ought to apply every time you are toying with using an anecdotal lead: Should I delay it? Should I distill it? Should I reject it? Do I really need that quote inside the anecdotal lead? What would The Wall Street Journal do? And, Am I using the right language to stitch my anecdote to my nut graf? Please note, that in journalism a nut graf (or nut graph) is the short version for explaining something "in a nutshell." Particularly in a feature story, a nut graf explains the news value of a story.

Question: Should I Delay my Anecdote?

Consider a story my newspaper published last October, at the height of the Ford Explorer/Firestone scandal. Until about 9 p.m., the top of the story read like this:

(First, the anecdote)

> On the day Christy McKinney turned 21, she was running an errand with her 7-month-old son, Conner, in her Ford Explorer when the tread on her left rear tire peeled loose, causing her car to sail off an embankment on Interstate 40 near Alma, Ark.
>
> The sport-utility vehicle rolled over twice. Conner was ejected from his baby seat, suffering cuts and bruises to his face. He was the lucky one. His mother was thrown from the vehicle—even though she was wearing her seatbelt, according to her attorney—and landed on the highway's grassy shoulder. McKinney and her son were rushed to a hospital in nearby Fort Smith, where doctors declared her a quadriplegic.

(Then the news)

> The toll from defective Firestone tires mounted on Ford Explorers has largely been measured by the 101 deaths compiled so far by the National Highway Traffic Safety Administration. But

as investigators delve into about 400 injury cases, story after horrific story emerges, some involving people who have become paraplegics or quadriplegics.

These victims will have to cope with the fact that their life expectancies have been shortened as they face the prospect of raising enough money—sometimes millions of dollars—to pay looming medical bills. The costs also include an emotional toll, changing the lives of these victims' families who must now grapple with caring for their loved ones.

(Then back to the anecdote)

In McKinney's case, her mother, Sheri, was recently forced to give up her job, leave her own 13-year-old son behind, and borrow money from friends and relatives so that she could watch over Christy, who has been transferred to Northwestern Memorial Hospital in Chicago.

Christy cannot speak, but her mother can read her lips.

"Every day I dry her tears [that] roll down her cheeks when she says, 'I miss my baby,'" said Sheri, 39. "I try to hold myself together. I can't let her see me fall apart. But she is my baby and her crying makes me cry."

(Then back to the news)

NHTSA officials said they don't know how many people have ended up like Christy–seriously injured as a result of an accident involving defective Firestone tires.

The 101 reported deaths and 400 injuries over several years are a small fraction of the 41,611 deaths and 3.2 million injuries caused by traffic collisions last year alone. About 8,000 of those injured are people who will never walk again, according to officials with the National Spinal Cord Injury Assn., who say the numbers of people left paralyzed in Firestone-related crashes has shed new light on the financial and emotional costs associated with such debilitating injuries.

The rising toll of casualties is also bringing fresh attention to the tendency of some vehicles' roofs to cave in during rollover accidents, which can cause fatal or crippling head and neck injuries. Consumer safety advocates ...

And so it went until an hour or so before the home-edition deadline, when Deputy Managing Editor Leo Wolinsky decided that the back-and-forth shuffle between poignancy and news should be replaced by a more direct, clearer approach. Leo felt we had published so many stories about the human tragedy of the Firestone/Ford controversy that this story would unfairly suffer from a feeling of sameness.

So the published story proclaimed the news first:

The toll from defective Firestone tires mounted on Ford Explorers has largely been measured by the 101 deaths counted so far, but as investigators delve into about 400 injury cases they are finding horrific tragedies that have left some victims paraplegics or quadriplegics.

These victims will have to cope with shortened life expectancies as they face the prospect of raising enough money—sometimes millions of dollars—to pay looming medical bills. The costs also include an emotional toll, changing the lives of these victims' families who must now grapple with caring for their loved ones.

The focus on the news allowed a third graf that explained the causes of the maiming more fully, giving the piece more immediate perspective:

> The number of people left paralyzed in these crashes is also bringing fresh attention to the tendency of some vehicles' roofs to cave in during rollover accidents, which can cause fatal or crippling head and neck injuries. Consumer safety advocates have criticized the auto makers for not strengthening roofs and the National Highway Traffic Safety Administration for not toughening the roof-crush standard.
>
> A close look at some of these tragedies, alongside an analysis of government crash data, shows that in many cases the human cost was raised by occupants simply not wearing their seat belts. But in others, the violence of the crash—and the damage to the vehicle—was so extreme that wearing a seat belt was not enough to save passengers or drivers from death or crippling injuries.

Then, in the fifth graf, having established the institutional context, the story gave us the Christy McKinney story in five consecutive grafs:

> Consider the case of Christy McKinney.
>
> On the day she turned 21, McKinney was running an errand with her 7-month-old son, Conner, in her Ford Explorer when the tread on her left rear tire peeled loose, causing her car to sail off an embankment on Interstate 40 near Alma, Ark.
>
> The sport-utility vehicle rolled over twice. Conner was ejected from his baby seat, suffering ...

From there, the story returned to the macrocosm.

The lesson is that if you have real news, use real news. As the writer, Davan Maharaj, puts it:

> Although the anecdote was gripping and maybe powerful, it still couldn't cut to the chase fast enough. My humble feeling is that we often try to play on readers' emotions to draw them into stories. They would read on if you were honest with them from the start, and if they were interested in the topic. I'm now a convert to the belief that any time you can use a straight lede instead of an anecdotal one, go with the straight one. Reader reaction to this piece also confirmed that it worked.

Question: Can I do a Better Job of Distilling my Lead Anecdote?

Bill Rempel and Rick Serrano's investigation of Texas' concealed-handgun law, published shortly before the 2000 presidential election, was another example of balancing news and color. No one anecdote could serve this story, because it was about the cumulative effect of the law. And yet the key to understanding the impact was the litany of what various individuals did with their gun permits. So the story hit you hard, with the essential contrast between goal and result, for two grafs ...

> AUSTIN, Texas—In 1995, four months into his first term as governor, George W. Bush signed a bill ending a 125-year ban on concealed handguns in Texas. The new law, he vowed, would make the state "a safer place," and he promised Texans that license applicants would undergo rigorous background checks.

> But since the law took effect, the state has licensed hundreds of people with prior criminal convictions—including rape and armed robbery—and histories of violence, psychological disorders and drug or alcohol problems, a Times investigation has found.

... and then, for the next two grafs, distilled the bare-bones details about six cases that would be detailed later on:

> James W. Washington got a license to carry a concealed weapon despite having done prison time in Texas for armed robbery. So did Terry Ross Gist, who left a trail of threats and violence in court records from North Carolina to California. A license also went to an elderly Dallas man with Alzheimer's disease.
>
> Still others committed crimes, ranging from double murder to drunk driving, after they were licensed. A frustrated commuter, Paul W. Lueders, shot and severely wounded a Houston bus driver. Audi Phong Nguyen ran with a Houston home invasion ring. Diane Brown James helped her husband kidnap a San Antonio woman to be their sex slave.

Then back to the macro to continue establishing the sweep of the problem:

> About 215,000 Texans are currently licensed to carry concealed weapons. The state concedes that ...

Jennifer Oldham's first draft of her scoop about the danger of certain home furnaces employed a semi-featurized lead because the concept was unfamiliar to most readers. She graciously shares the draft with us:

> On chilly nights this fall, tens of thousands of unsuspecting California homeowners will turn on attic furnaces similar to those that fire investigators say sparked numerous catastrophic blazes across the state over the last 10 years.
>
> Federal safety experts and furnace makers and distributors have known for years that horizontal attic furnaces manufactured by Consolidated Industries ignited dozens of fires in single-family residences, townhomes and condominiums from San Jose to San Diego.
>
> Yet the government, the manufacturer, and the 30 distributors who sold these attic furnaces under various brand names in the state from 1984 to 1992 have never issued a recall or a formal warning urging homeowners to get these units inspected and replaced.
>
> "These things are latent time bombs in peoples' attics and they don't know about them," said Dan Mogin, a San Diego attorney who this summer filed a class action lawsuit against Sears, a Consolidated distributor. "The Consumer Products Safety Commission has absolutely dropped the ball on this."

But Jennifer switched to a hard-news approach after recognizing the quality of her material. Notice that in the published version that follows, she used five grafs of news before a quote (rather than three in the first draft), and that she found a better quote—one that provided a more satisfying transition from the news. You'll also notice that by the time the story was published, Jennifer's inquiries had pushed the product safety commission into action, reflected in the third graf:

> Defective attic furnaces manufactured by a now-bankrupt firm have caused scores of residential fires in California in the last decade, fire inspectors and federal investigators said.
>
> Hundreds of thousands of unsuspecting homeowners may be at risk from these furnaces, made by Indiana-based Consolidated Industries and sold under various brand names in California from 1984 to 1992, these sources said.
>
> The Consumer Product Safety Commission, the independent federal agency responsible for warning citizens about defective products, has known about the problem since the mid-1990s. It said Tuesday it will issue a warning today about the furnaces.
>
> The commission's staff said it didn't issue a warning earlier because federal law prohibits it from doing so while it is in negotiations seeking a product recall. The agency said it had hoped to issue a recall, but was unable to do so when Consolidated—which would have been required to finance this action—went out of business.
>
> The lack of a recall or warning to date had created a sense of foreboding among many fire-prevention officials.
>
> "Every time we have a cold snap we have a furnace fire," said Michael Freige, a senior fire inspector for the Torrance Fire Department, who said Consolidated furnaces have caused seven residential fires there since 1994.
>
> The issuance of a warning without a recall means that homeowners probably will have to foot the bill …

Similarly, Greg Miller eschewed the temptation for an anecdote when writing about the frighteningly sophisticated ways companies are snooping on employee computer use. The trend was important enough to be recognized directly. So Greg gave it to you like this:

> Moving beyond merely monitoring employees' Internet use, many of the nation's largest companies are quietly assembling teams of computer investigators who specialize in covertly copying employees' hard drives and combing them for evidence of workplace wrongdoing.
>
> These high-tech investigators employ tools and techniques that originally were devised for law enforcement to catch criminals but that are now spreading rapidly in the private sector at Microsoft, Disney, Boeing, Motorola, Fluor, Caterpillar and dozens of other major companies.
>
> The development, little known outside the narrow community of corporate security experts, is sure to raise tensions over workplace privacy in an age when the lives of millions of workers are inextricably tied to their office computers.
>
> Employers say that their rush into the field known as "computer forensics" is a matter of self-defense, that being able to retrieve computer evidence is essential to their ability to catch employees engaged in everything from spending too much time surfing the Internet to stealing company secrets.

One basic test is: Does the anecdote actually represent the greater truth of the story? Watch the problems you get into when that doesn't happen:

> LAS VEGAS—This was the end of Martina Bauhaus' job interview for one of the most sought-after positions in town:

> She put on black velvet high-cut briefs and a tight, low-cut bustier. When her name was called, she walked out of the fitting room to pose in front of a mirror—and half a dozen silent, staring men who measured her up like cattlemen at a livestock auction.
>
> She didn't get the job. "Maybe," said the slender 28-year-old, "they didn't like my body in their outfit."

Know what the story's about yet? You'll have to keep reading.

> Bauhaus, a law student with a master's degree in public administration, wasn't seeking a job as a model, but as a cocktail waitress at the new Suncoast Casino. Nobody asked her the difference between a screwdriver and a rusty nail. She just had to have the right look.
>
> Indeed, despite the supposed "Disneyfication" of Las Vegas, widespread unionization and the arrival of politically correct corporate casino owners, the image of the sexy cocktail waitress remains as vital here as a one-armed bandit.

Here comes the point:

> But while young drink servers are still willing to don revealing outfits, there's something of a rebellion afoot—literally: growing discontent over the use of high heels.
>
> Led by a cocktail waitress named Kricket Martinez, members of an impromptu labor organization dubbed the Kiss My Foot Coalition are campaigning against shoes that they say can rack their bodies. After a rally in May, several casinos in Reno agreed to allow lower heels, and the loose-knit group now hopes to …

It's not just that the story requires 168 words to get to the point (the 6th graf). It's that most of those words (the first four grafs) don't lead you to the point. The story is about discontent over the use of high heels, but the anecdote doesn't contain a single reference to footwear. Thus, the story virtually starts over at the 5th graf by building a contrast so that the 6th graf will have something to bounce off. In other words, we wind up with two leads: an anecdotal lead, and a contrast lead. That's one lead too many.

Why not dump Martina Bauhaus, exploit the central contrast—the (shortened) fifth and sixth grafs—and start the story this way:

> LAS VEGAS—Despite this city's supposed "Disneyfication," the image of the sexy cocktail waitress remains as vital here as a one-armed bandit.
>
> But there's something of a rebellion afoot—literally: growing discontent over the use of high heels.
>
> Led by a cocktail waitress named Kricket Martinez …

Question: Do I really need that Quote Inside my Anecdote?

One indulgence that frequently sabotages anecdotal leads is the quote. By trying to give the anecdote a "voice," the writer pushes down the key grafs that define the story. Consider this New York Times story from last year, with the questionable quote grafs underlined:

> Kevin Heebner, owner of a building supply store in Temple, Pa., got a call four years ago from his longtime stockbroker recommending an investment in short-term bonds. Assured the bonds were safe, Mr. Heebner invested $100,000.
>
> Three months later, Mr. Heebner received a stunning phone call. The broker told him the money he had put into the bonds was gone. The president of the broker's firm, Old Naples Securities, had stolen it.
>
> With his wife about to deliver their third child, Mr. Heebner, 36, reeled at the thought of a $100,000 loss. Then he remembered with relief that his account was insured by the Securities Investor Protection Corporation, created by Congress in 1970 to protect investors' brokerage accounts from just the sort of theft he had been a victim of.
>
> "I knew that if they didn't find the money from Old Naples Securities, I was insured through S.I.P.C.," Mr. Heebner recalled. The broker's "business card and letterhead all had S.I.P.C. logos on them; I figured S.I.P.C. would cover it."
>
> Mr. Heebner figured wrong. For more than four years, the corporation maintained he was entitled to nothing—even though three federal courts ruled that S.I.P.C. should pay him $87,000. Only last week, days after a reporter interviewed the lawyer representing the corporation about Mr. Heebner, did the investor receive a check in the amount of $87,000.
>
> "I never got the sense that S.I.P.C. was in any way trying to help my client," said William P. Thornton Jr., a lawyer at Stevens & Lee in Reading Pa., representing Mr. Heebner against the corporation. "They are very aggressive in attempting to prove that investors' claims do not come within certain legal definitions within the S.I.P.C. statute. And the loser is the investor."
>
> At a time when millions of United States citizens have taken their money out of federally insured banks and put it into brokerage firms, the Securities Investor Protection Corporation's charge of protecting the investing public has never been more important. Officials of the S.I.P.C. defend the corporation's record and say they must be vigilant in protecting against invalid claims by investors.
>
> But a close look at this little-understood organization shows that the safety net that investors believe the corporation offers is in fact full of holes.
>
> Industry-financed but not government-backed, the corporation is a far cry from the agency on which it was loosely modeled, the Federal Deposit Insurance Corporation, which protects bank customers against losses.
>
> Created three decades ago …

You can see why the writer used the first quote: It allowed him to move seamlessly from the end of the quote to the third graf, playing off "figured" with "figured wrong." But was it worth it? It ate up 39 words, delaying us from understanding what the hell the story was about.

Even less functional was the second quote, which ate up 64 words to underscore a thesis that the writer had yet to introduce: the S.I.P.C. is full of holes. It took 351 words before you got to that proclamation graf—a trip made 29% longer by the two quotes.

Even without the quotes, the story used an unusual amount of length—248 words—to make its general point. If you think you don't lose a proportion of your readers by that kind of dawdling, you're kidding yourself. Make your point first, then let your characters talk.

It's not that quotes can't be used before the story gets to the point, but they tend to work better with a simpler story. Read this one, which also used parallel language to link quote and syntax. The difference was, this story linked the quote to the point of the story, not just to a less crucial passage in the anecdote:

> SAN LUIS OBISPO—Amy Hutchcraft, 18, and her dorm mates set up housekeeping in a lounge next to a laundry room. Ashleigh Boslet, a freshman from Pennsylvania, was crammed into a conference room with five others.
>
> They were luckier than Birgitte Marthinsen, who arrived at Cal Poly San Luis Obispo two weeks ago from Norway and still had not found a place to live when school started Monday.
>
> "My mother was crying on the phone last night," Marthinsen said as she dejectedly scanned the housing bulletin board in the campus union. "She said, 'What's happening to you?'"
>
> What's happening is that students here and at other coastal universities in California have been caught in the jaws of a serious housing crunch. From Berkeley to Santa Barbara, stories of students employing desperate strategies to find places to sleep have become the stuff of local legend.
>
> The crunch reflects the same conditions, if aggravated, that have afflicted the broader housing market across California. Too many people are chasing too few beds, especially in desirable coastal areas where slow and no-growth pledges have become as much a litmus test for political office as a hatred of taxes.

Words used to get to the point (the third graf): 93.

Question: What would the Wall Street Journal do?

The Journal offers cheap eight-week introductory subscriptions. Get one. Look at the front page news features for a week. You will notice that the Journal seems to virtually command its writers to bring anecdotal leads into focus by the fourth paragraph.

The Journal is mocked in some quarters for a formulaic approach to its anecdotal leads, but that's about as valid as complaining that Sam Phillips used a formula because all those Sun Records rockabilly hits of the '50s were between 2:25 and 2:50. In both cases, the trick was letting great ideas unfold creatively within a disciplined setting.

You can almost set your watch by the efficiency of the Journal's anecdotal leads. By the fourth paragraph you have sampled great density of detail, or a scene, or a quote—or possibly all three. You know quickly whether you want to go along for the ride.

Like this 1999 Journal piece, an e-commerce story which needed only 122 words to get to the point (paragraph 4, sentence 2):

> Toby Lenk, founder of eToys Inc., is sure he knows the secret behind e-commerce: Build a single-focus Internet site, laser in on one swath of the marketplace, and don't let customers get confused by clutter from other goods or services.
>
> Jeff Bezos, founder of Amazon.com Inc., is just as confident about his strategy: Build the world's biggest online department store, then offer everything from Milton to modems, so shoppers can get whatever they want with one click on their Web browsers.
>
> Messrs. Lenk and Bezos are true pioneers, Internet innovators with astonishing net worths. So if they're both so shrewd, how could they take such widely disparate gambles?
>
> That question, in one form or another, is on the minds of executives everywhere. In businesses ranging from aerospace to telecommunications, CEOs are making big strategic bets, trying to position their companies to take advantage of productivity and technology trends that they are only beginning to understand. And very often, major players are making completely divergent bets within the same industry.

Or this from the Journal, which needed only 114 words to do both the set-up and the nut in three graphs:

> BERLIN—As Nick Jackson hawks tickets for his morning walking tour of the city, a Chilean woman approaches, her parents in tow, and spits out three questions in a single breath: "How long is the tour? Do you have senior-citizen discounts? Do you go to see the Wall?"
>
> "Three-and-a-half hours. It's 15 marks [$8] for everyone. And, yes, I'll take you to the Wall," the guide replies. "Not that there's much left," he confides to someone else.
>
> As the Chileans will discover, the Berlin Wall is hard to find in Berlin today. In fact, its remnants are more prominently displayed at Honolulu Community College than in the heart of the city it once divided.
>
> Of the roughly 28 miles of wall that bisected Berlin, less than a mile remains standing, and most of that is in an out-of-the-way …

You are also likely to find a stronger writer's voice in many of the Journal's anecdotal leads than other papers, because the Journal's devotion to compression forces the writer to employ his own devices rather than the journalese of standard anecdotal leads. Like this one, which took 133 words to get to the point (graph 4, sentence 2):

SAN FRANCISCO—There was romance in the resumes: She, a computer consultant turned fashion model; he, an Apple Computer engineer turned Silicon Valley entrepreneur. They were young, beautiful, wired for love.

> But caution fell between them. During a yearlong courtship, Alfred Tom held back, wary of revealing too much. Then it happened. After an afternoon with friends, Mr. Tom took Angela Fu back to his car. There, on the front seat of his 1994 Integra, he went for it.
>
> "Naturally, I flinched a bit," Ms. Fu says. But in a stroke it was done: a signed nondisclosure agreement, or NDA, in the parlance of the Net set. Henceforth, Ms. Fu would be sworn to silence about her boyfriend's trade secrets.
>
> DNA, meet NDA, your twisted, alphabetical cousin in the world of baser instincts. Long the province of lawyers, investment bankers and other traffickers in corporate secrets, non-disclosure agreements have gone mainstream.
>
> Propelled by Internet frenzy, an epidemic of secrecy pacts is …

Former Journal editor and writer Bill Blundell puts it this way in "The Art & Craft of Feature Writing," a wonderful book based on the Journal's in-house writing guide: "We do try to engage the reader's attention immediately. We do try to give him a clear idea of what we're up to early on. And we do try to prove our assertions in detail throughout. If these add up to a formula then I suppose we have one. But it offers the reporter enormous latitude, and it's the same one successful storytellers have used for centuries."

So beat yourself up a little more. Be more purposeful, more unforgiving of your tangents. Play a game with yourself: Draw the line at four graphs per anecdotal lead—and that includes the graph that tells the reader what the story's about. See whether it forces you into some positive habits—better distillation, better use of your own voice as a writer, a stronger sense of urgency in your work, and greater clarity.

Question: Am I Effectively Connecting my Anecdote to the Nut?

Does the anecdote flow seamlessly into the grafs that proclaim the story? Too often, writers use anecdotes to evade that responsibility.

In the three examples that follow, the writers achieved a precise fit. The underlined language illustrates the glue between the anecdote and the proclamation.

First, a news story—almost a consumer expose—that used the anecdote to give you a picture:

> The letter from Ralphs Grocery Co. to its fruit and vegetable suppliers began cordially enough. Addressed "Dear Valued Supplier," it laid out Ralphs' plans to add 44 stores in Northern California and build a warehouse to service them.
>
> Then came the hard sell: To help pay for Ralphs' growth, suppliers would have to pony up thousands of dollars in shelf fees, either in cash or by surrendering dozens of cases of free products. The implication was that if they didn't, there would be no space on the chains' shelves for their goods.
>
> Ralphs' letter is one demonstration of a dramatic escalation in the grocery industry's demands for so-called slotting fees, which food companies pay to get supermarket shelf space for new products. Manufacturers shell out $9 billion a year in shelf fees, representing more than half of the supermarket industry's total profits, analysts estimate.
>
> Mergers have sharply consolidated supermarket ownership in recent years. Five giant companies account for 40% of U.S. grocery sales, and the mega-chain share of the Southland market is even higher.
>
> With grocers using their newfound clout to expand the "pay for space" system to the produce aisle, and to charge $25,000 or more to place new products, small suppliers say they can't compete.
>
> Regulators are watching with concern. Three federal investigations ...

The second example is a feature, written during the 2000 New Hampshire primary, about how that state's citizens have become spoiled by the disproportionate attention presidential candidates pay them:

> MANCHESTER, N.H.—John McCain is sweating. He has just downed an entire bowl of three-alarm chili and half a bottle of fizzy water.
>
> Twenty Manchester firefighters are lunching with the Republican presidential hopeful at a long table in the central station's glassed kitchen, called the fishbowl. It would be a cozy respite from the freezing cold if not for 100 reporters crammed in a corner, staring.
>
> With the nation's first primary on Tuesday drawing ever closer, McCain is shopping for votes the New Hampshire way—one at a time. The senator from Arizona puts down his spoon and asks in a low purr, any questions?
>
> "I've got one," Firefighter Mike Lawrence pipes up. "How do you like ... "
>
> The room falls silent. The cameras zoom in for tonight's sound bite. How does he like—what? The flat tax? Russia's new president? The threatened deportation of the little Cuban boy?
>
> "How do you like ... the chili?"
>
> Therein lies the essence of New Hampshire, where a citizen's sway is off the scales and the ratio of people to political clout is wildly out of proportion. With the Iowa caucuses out of the way and less than a week to go before New Hampshire's all-important contest, this

> tiny state of 1.2 million—one-thirtieth the population of California and roughly the size of San Diego proper—has assumed its place at the center of U.S. politics.
>
> No candidate since 1952 has won the White House without first winning his party's primary in the Granite State—except in 1992, when next-door-neighbor Paul E. Tsongas of Massachusetts beat Bill Clinton. ("An aberration," one local insisted, "and everyone should just forget it.")
>
> It is here that working-class people have regularly humbled political aristocrats, creating a searing photo album of electoral gaffes: Former Tennessee Gov. Lamar …

Finally, an example of connective language that links the right kind of quote to the right kind of generality:

> SEOUL—Han Mi Sook, a 37-year-old company worker in Seoul, has owned a Daewoo sedan for several years. But riding around town with "Daewoo" on your hood has become a lot less prestigious since last August, when the entire industrial group was brought to its knees financially.
>
> "It's still running," she said with a laugh. "But it's a bit noisy."
>
> The same might be said for the entire South Korean auto industry these days. Headlines blare daily every step and misstep of an intricate ownership dance that promises to reshape this once-proud South Korean industry for decades to come.
>
> General Motors and Ford have already declared their interest in buying Daewoo Motor, a subsidiary of Daewoo Group, amid reports that Volkswagen …

Exercises

1. One of our favorite exercises to do in the classroom is to dissect articles. Select any article from your favorite print publication. Be sure the article you select is written in AP format. What's the story? A really good writer will answer the question the reader asks in his or her head. It is a true talent. In class you will look at each graph, from the lead graph down to the final graph, and discuss why the article is written in this way. You will come to see that the reporter was very thoughtful about what information was used in the first two graphs and so on.
2. Your professor will list ten facts for you. Consider each fact and decide what are the most important elements of the news. Put the details in a list and then sort the elements of news into order of most important to least important. Once you have completed the organization, begin to work on the first graph. Keep in mind, not all of the facts need to be included in the article. Sometimes deleting the least important information helps make the news article more relevant and timely. Just because you have tons of research and information doesn't mean you have to include it all. Learn to cut. Sometimes less is more.
3. Your professor will provide the class with several paragraphs of news. Take a look at the notes. Read it all and then find the who, what, where, when, and how.
4. Take a look at five articles about politics in Washington, DC. Perhaps the stories are about lawmakers on Capitol Hill or about policy at the White House or the Department of Defense. Read the first few graphs of each article. Notice the names and titles of people in the news. These articles should be written in AP style. Observe how names and titles are used.

5. What's the story: introductions. It's time to get personal. There is news right here in our very own classroom. Now, the fact that you are students majoring in communication or in another field is factual, but this isn't the news about who you are. It is a given that you are a student. You will need to figure out what the story is and get to the heart of the matter of each person. Here's how: Divide into pairs. One student will be the reporter/interviewer and the other will be the source/ interview subject. First make a list of questions, and really probe. Then begin asking questions. Give yourself fifteen minutes to conduct the interview, and then switch roles. In the end you will both have a lot of facts to write a short news story. Focus on the lead. Ask yourself, "What's the story?" Write up the lead. Remember that you will have many facts and a lot of information, but the "news" is the most interesting and critical piece of information. We will share these stories in class. It will be a fun way to get to know each other.
6. Write a news article and focus on the top two lead graphs. Take your copy and share it with your colleague next to you. In this exercise you'll have a chance to play researcher, reporter, writer, and editor. You or your professor will decide on the news story, and you decide on the angle after doing your research and conducting an interview. Focus on writing one paragraph with five to six sentences. Before beginning, be sure to know what your news hook, peg, or angle is. Then pass your copy to your colleague for editing, and you take his or her copy. Your goal here should be to cut down the sentences to be short, clear, and concise. Remember, more is less. Also, the news hook, the peg, or the angle should be crystal-clear to the reader once you are done with this exercise.

Reading List

Bolt Newspapers: Is There a Future in Print Media?

By Gregory B Fairchild and Brianne Warner

Jane Darcy stared in dismay at the spreadsheet. As the editor of *Bolt*, a free daily newspaper in Richmond, Virginia, Darcy had been working since January 2007 to build a devoted readership. Published Monday through Friday, *Bolt* featured topics such as local news and sports and was written in a snappy style for readers between 18 and 34 years old. Advertising had been steadily climbing. Everywhere Darcy went, she heard: "I love *Bolt*!" A few advertisers told her that their teenage kids were reading a newspaper for the first time. Darcy thought *Bolt* was on its way to success.

But the economy had not cooperated. It was November 2008, and over the past year, as businesses had tightened their budgets, newspaper advertising declined. The pace was frightening: Newspaper advertising was down an estimated 14% in a single year.[1] *Bolt*'s advertising had been slowly growing, but its parent company was suffering. And that meant it might not be able to support fledging publications created to capture future readers.

The directive from *Bolt*'s publisher was clear: *Bolt* had to make money in 2009. Any publication in the red would be cut. The original business plan gave *Bolt* three to five years to break even. *Bolt* was not yet two years old and in the worst economic fall the United States had seen since the Great Depression. The publisher had laid out three options:

1. Reduce *Bolt*'s circulation from five days a week to one day a week.
2. Move *Bolt* entirely online, and close the print publication.
3. Close *Bolt*—both print and online.

Most likely, *Bolt* was on the chopping block. Still, the publisher wanted Darcy's opinion. Which was the best choice? Was there another way?

The State of Print Media, Circa 2008

The newspaper industry had traditionally been very profitable. In 2004, its peak year, newspapers brought in $47 billion in advertising.[2] In the 20th century, margins at some papers reached 30%. The news of the day drew a large audience, which was very valuable to advertisers—and translated to big profits for newspapers.

In the early years of the Internet, the user base was too small to attract much notice from newspapers. As more Americans began going online, media companies started building websites with stories and ads. These new online readers helped offset a declining print readership (see **Table 1** for data on print readership). According to a Pew Research Center report on American journalism, "Unduplicated Web audiences are now estimated to add 8.4% to the average newspaper's readership, making up most, but not all, of the audience decline."[3]

The bigger problem for publishers was not shifting readership, but shifting ad revenues (see **Exhibit 1** for ad revenue trends). Businesses were not willing to spend the same amount online as they were in the print newspaper. Author and media columnist Ken Auletta said:

> The rule of thumb is that an online ad brings in at most about one-tenth the revenue as the same ad in the newspaper. There are two reasons for this: readers spend much less time reading a paper online than they do a newspaper, and because ad space is not scarce on the Web, advertisers pay lower rates."[4]

One of the biggest concerns for newspaper publishers was the loss of classified advertising revenue to sites such as Craigslist. In the fourth quarter of 1997, for example, newspapers

Table 1. Daily print newspaper readership.

	Percentage of Total Adults
1998	58.6%
2000	55.1%
2002	55.4%
2004	52.8%
2006	49.9%

Data source: Scarborough Research, *Top 50 Market Report 1998–2007*, prepared by the Newspaper Association of America.

Exhibit 1
BOLT NEWSPAPERS: IS THERE A FUTURE IN PRINT MEDIA?

U.S. Newspaper Industry Advertising Sales
(in thousands of dollars)

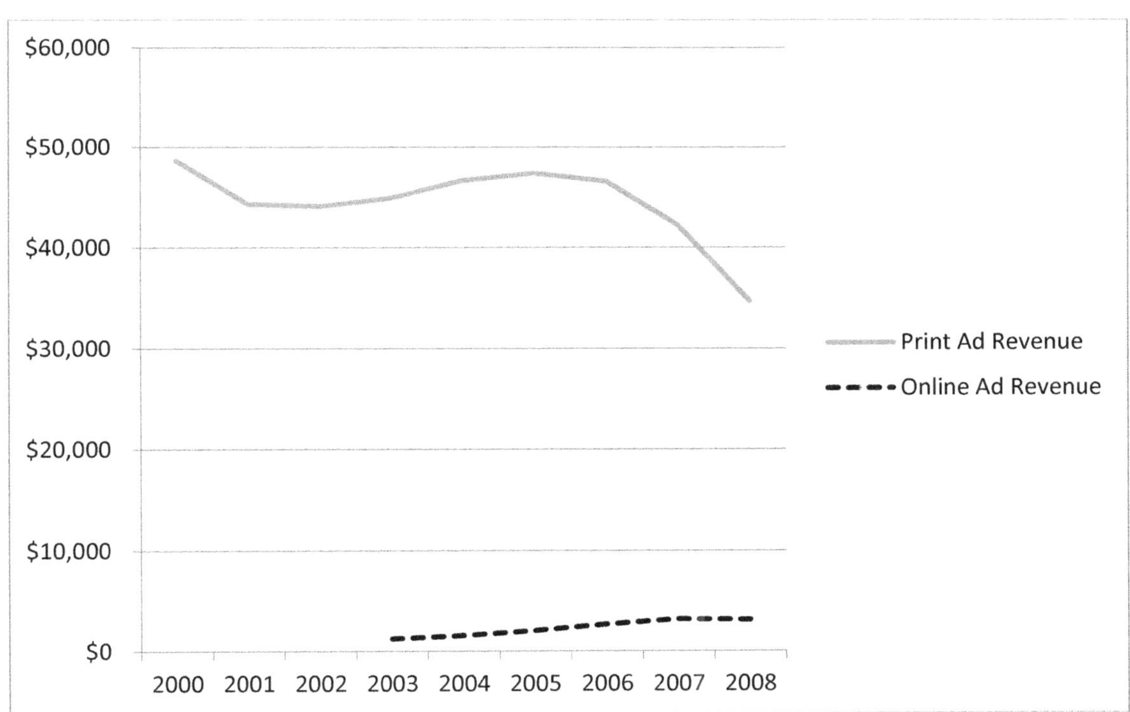

Data source: Newspaper Association of America.

Table 2. Demographics for Richmond metro area.

	Richmond-Petersburg MSA	United States
Population in 2000	1,096,957	281,421,906
Change since 1990	15.6%	9.1%
Persons ages 25–45	44%	42%
Per capita income	$40,286	$38,615

Notes: Richmond-Petersburg MSA includes the City of Richmond and Chesterfield, Hanover, and Henrico counties plus the cities of Petersburg, Colonial Heights, and Hopewell and the counties of Amelia, Caroline, Charles City, Cumberland, Dinwiddie, Goochland, King and Queen, King William, Louisa, New Kent, Powhatan, Prince George, and Sussex. The MSA was redefined and enlarged following the 2000 Census and this table uses the new definition. Source: "An Online Resource for Information about Greater Richmond." The Greater Richmond Partnership, Inc. http://intranet.grpva.com/intranet/Brochures/JTF/jtf_page_3.asp.

Data sources: http://www.census.gov and http://www.grpva.com (all accessed April 19, 2012).

reaped $5 billion from classifieds. By the third quarter of 2008, classified advertising revenue had declined 53%, to $2.36 billion.[5] There did not seem to be a solution anywhere in sight.

The Emergence of Free Dailies

With the erosion of their print audience, daily newspapers began searching for new business models. Young adults with disposable income were highly desirable readers. A successful model emerged: free dailies. (Though called "free dailies," these papers were typically published Monday through Friday.) Free dailies were often tabloid-size (e.g., *Parade*), rather than broadsheet-size (e.g., *New York Times*). The tone was typically youth-oriented, and contents included celebrity gossip as well as local, national, and international news.

Metro, a free daily, entered the Philadelphia market in 2000 and later expanded to New York and Boston.[6] Soon, large city newspapers were trying the formula out too. Large newspapers could designate a few copy editors and designers to take some of the same stories from their own newspapers, trim them, lay them out in a tabloid format, and create a new, lighter version. This free edition could be handed out to young on-the-go readers and could lure advertisers interested in a different audience. The *Chicago Tribune* launched its free daily, *Red Eye*, in 2002. A year later, the *Washington Post* debuted *Express*.

"The reason these things are cropping up is they seem to be working," Mary Glick, associate director of the American Press Institute, told the *American Journalism Review*. "I find the ones that I've been reading are well-written. They're boiled down to the essential point— which is really what I want anyway."[7]

The Opportunity in Richmond

By 2006, the free-daily model had been proven to be a consistently good bet. Beacon Media, the owners of the *Richmond Chronicle*, saw potential to launch a free daily in the Richmond market. With a daily circulation of 158,000, the *Richmond Chronicle* could easily repurpose some of its stories into a quicker read.

Further, Richmond mirrored the demographic makeup of the United States. Acxiom Corporation, a marketing intelligence company, named it one of the top 10 test markets in the country.[8] The Richmond metro area included slightly more than one million people, according to the census of 2000—a 15.6% increase from the previous census in 1990.

As a private company, Beacon Media had a reasonably strong balance sheet. It owned several publications across the Richmond-Petersburg area, including a monthly business journal, a weekly entertainment listing, a weekly conservative paper, and a weekly targeted at the African American community (**Exhibit 2**). In 2006, when Beacon Media had begun planning for the launch of a free daily, the owners had understood it would lose money for several years before it turned a profit. "We viewed *Bolt* as a long-term investment," explained the publisher.

Bolt launched in January 2007. The newsroom consisted of 10 journalists: 4 copy editors, 3 designers, 1 reporter, 1 managing editor, and the executive editor. Each night, copy editors combed through hundreds of stories from the *Richmond Chronicle* and the Associated Press and other wire services, selecting the stories they thought would interest *Bolt* readers. They would cut each story into a fraction of its original length. The designers would then lay out the stories on the page and pick out photos from the *Richmond Chronicle* and the news services. By midnight, the entire paper had been designed, edited, and proofed. The presses ran 25,000 copies, and distributors began arriving at 4:00 a.m. to pick up papers. More than 80% of papers were delivered between 5:00 a.m. and 9:00 a.m.

Exhibit 2
BOLT NEWSPAPERS: IS THERE A FUTURE IN PRINT MEDIA?

Beacon Media's Publications

Name	Subject	Circulation	Est. 2008 Net Income	Change from 2007	Years in Existence
Richmond Biz	local business news	70,000 monthly	$248,000	−2%	34
Go Out!	entertainment listings	60,000 weekly	$729,000	−8%	8
Richmond Dish	food and dining	100,000 quarterly	$183,000	−9%	12
Richmond Chronicle	daily newspaper	118,000 daily	$2,432,000	−18%	121
Richmond Chronicle Online	daily newspaper's website		$378,000	−3%	10
Bolt	the "free daily" version	21,000 Mon–Fri	−$897,000	25%	1
The Republic	conservative weekly news	32,000 weekly	−$122,000	−20%	31
African American Today	local African American community	19,000 weekly	$387,000	−10%	10
TOTAL			**$3,338,000**	**−10.62%**	

Source: Created by case writer.

The general manager/publisher of *Bolt* oversaw five ad reps and two ad designers. The *Richmond Chronicle* shared its staff to help with the rest of *Bolt*'s needs (e.g., marketing and legal issues). Distribution was outsourced to a contractor who hired people to hand out 25,000 papers five days a week. These "hawkers" would stand near places of high foot traffic, such as outside of busy downtown office buildings, and give passers-by a free copy of that morning's paper. Other papers were bundled and placed in free racks in restaurants, hair salons, office building lobbies, and so on.

Despite the terrible economy in 2008, only two of Beacon Media's publications were on track to lose money: the *Republic*, the conservative weekly, which lost $122,000 in 2007, and *Bolt*, which lost $900,000 in 2007. *Bolt* had lost nearly $1,200,000 in its first year of publication, but that had been expected—building a stable of advertisers took time, and printing and distributing a paper five days a week was expensive.

Going Online

Beacon Media had focused on *Bolt*'s print product first. *Bolt Online* launched in July 2008. One of the difficulties of the online format, though, was that 95% of *Bolt*'s articles were *already* online—they were, after all, mostly shortened versions of the *Richmond Chronicle*'s articles. Who would want to read the trimmed version online?

Darcy struggled with how to handle the *Bolt* website. All *Bolt*'s original stories went online too, but with just one reporter, that was hardly enough to fill the site. She set up three blogs and encouraged the staff to add to them. The ad department had not sold any online ads—with little traffic to the site, there was no audience to monetize yet, and online ads brought in so little revenue compared with print ads.

The publisher advised that the ad team needed to focus on the print ads. The online focus would come later.

The Decision

After reflecting on the past year, Darcy turned back to the three options before her. Traditionally, labor had constituted about 50% of a newspaper's expenses; production/distribution comprised 30%.[9] As a free daily, *Bolt* flipped those ratios. Because most of the stories and photographs came from wire services or *Bolt*'s parent newspaper, the *Richmond Chronicle*, *Bolt* had a much smaller staff. Production and distribution made up 65% of costs; staffing was around 25%; wire services were another 5%; and other expenses made up the remaining 5%.

The costs of paper and printing and distributing *Bolt* could not be easily cut. The only way to make substantial changes would be to reduce the number of days it was produced. The publisher was proposing changing *Bolt* to a weekly and potentially merging it with the *Republic*, a weekly that was also at risk of being closed. This way, both could be salvaged.

Darcy had a few worries. *Bolt*'s weekday distribution allowed it to be timely. As a weekly, *Bolt*'s news might be seen as stale. "Perhaps *Bolt* could shift into feature pieces," Darcy ruminated, "but that could conflict with the proven concept of bits of news for readers on the go." Further, *Bolt* had worked hard to be middle of the road when it came to politics. Merging with the *Republic* could change how it was perceived. Would that matter? And goodness, what would the name even be—the *Bolt-public*?

If *Bolt* did become a weekly paper, the newsroom staff would need to be reduced. After much agonizing, Darcy concluded that one copy editor, one designer, and one editor would be the bare minimum. The second option was to go all online. In theory, *Bolt*'s demographic would be ideal for a shift to the web. Younger people were reading more of their news online. While *Bolt*'s online audience was tiny, Darcy knew they had not marketed *Bolt*'s website much. There was definitely room to grow. The real problem was what to offer online. For wire-produced news, readers could go to Yahoo!, Google News, or a multitude of other sites. Why go to *Bolt*? Would they need more reporters?

Darcy dreaded the last option: Close *Bolt*. The publisher had emphasized that the company was bracing for a down 2009. Beacon Media could not afford to lose almost $1 million again on one publication. If *Bolt* closed now, the staff would all receive a severance package. Instead of reducing the staff to three, and then potentially having to close *Bolt* anyway later, perhaps it was better to face the awful economic reality and cut Beacon Media's losses now.

Notes

1. Newspaper Association of America, "Trends and Numbers, Advertising Expenditures," http://www.naa.org/Trends-and-Numbers/Advertising-Expenditures/Annual-All-Categories.aspx (accessed April 19, 2012).
2. Newspaper Association of America.
3. Pew Research Center's Project for Excellence in Journalism, *The State of the News Media 2009: An Annual Report on American Journalism*, http://stateofthemedia.org/2009/overview/key-findings/ (accessed April 19, 2012).
4. Ken Auletta, "Chasing the Fox," in *Googled* (New York: The Penguin Press, 2009), 165, via Dana Scherer, "Newspaper Advertising: Paper Dollars vs. Digital Dimes?," Future of Media blog, http://reboot.fcc.gov/future-ofmedia/blog?entryId=142770 (accessed April 19, 2012).
5. Duncan Riley, "Understanding the Fall of Newspapers in Revenue Numbers," *Inquisitor*, November 30, 2008, http://www.inquisitr.com/10201/understanding-the-fall-of-newspapers-in-revenue-numbers/ (accessed April 19, 2012).
6. Sharyn Vane, "Hip—and Happening," *American Journalism Review* (April/May 2005), http://www.ajr.org /article.asp?id=3854 (accessed April 19, 2012).
7. Vane.
8. "Richmond, Virginia: One of the Top Ten U.S. Test Markets," June 2004, Southeastern Institute of Research, http://www.sirresearch.com/assets/documents/top10.pdf (accessed April 19, 2012).
9. Suzanne M. Kirchhoff, "The U.S. Newspaper Industry in Transition," Congressional Research Service, September 9, 2010, 8, http://www.fas.org/sgp/crs/misc/R40700.pdf (accessed April 19, 2012).

Comparing Reporters' Work across Print, Radio, and Online: Converged Origination, Diverged Packaging

By Zvi Reich

This paper compares how eighty reporters from three media—print, online, and radio—obtained a sample of their items, seeking to establish which of two schools of thought is closer to reality: scholars who contend that each news medium embodies a unique "regime" of content creation, or those who argue that the different media maintain similar news reporting standards. A series of face-to-face reconstruction interviews with reporters from nine leading Israeli national news organizations suggests that the three media are not unique factories of news, but rather unique packing and distribution houses of similarly obtained materials.

Introduction

It has only been about fifteen years that news has been produced and consumed in four distinct media[1]—print, radio, television, and online. Obviously, these media are diverse in terms of their final products, as well as in their modalities, sensory experience, ways of dissemination and consumption, and even in their perceived credibility among audiences.[2] Their diversity probably extends one step backwards when medium-specific features, such as photos, video, audio, multimedia, hyperlinks, and the like, are inserted into the items.[3] Even farther back, the presence of medium distinctiveness at the start of the news assembly line—during the news reporting stage—is less obvious; as shown below, the issue is disputed among scholars and has received little attention in comparative research.

Exploring what happens at the reporting stage is both theoretically and normatively consequential, highlighting the essence of what a news medium constitutes: Is it an original factory of raw news materials, a unique "regime of content creation," as Boczkowsky suggests regarding online news,[4] or merely an original packing house for similarly obtained raw materials? Second, exploring what happens at the reporting stage may indicate whether journalists constitute a coherent community of practice or a federation thereof, each entitled to its own sociology of journalism, as Deuze suggested regarding online news and others have done regarding TV news.[5] Third, findings may identify gaps among reporting standards in different media, suggesting hierarchies of meticulousness in newswork that bear important lessons for journalists, educators, scholars, and the general public regarding all that concerns media literacy.

Zvi Reich, "Comparing Reporters' Work across Print, Radio, and Online: Converged Origination, Diverged Packaging," *Journalism and Mass Communication Quarterly,* vol. 88, no. 2, pp. 285-300.

This paper seeks to help resolve the scholarly dispute regarding distinctiveness of reporting patterns across media by studying how reporters actually obtain their news information and determining whether these processes embody different reporting efforts, different source relations, skepticism toward sources, and unique structures of news processes, as explained below. The paper focuses on print, radio, and online reporters, who were studied comparatively and concurrently with parallel news beat mixes. Television was excluded to enable focus on information-oriented media and avoid the "noise" of that distinctively visual, teamwork, and production-oriented medium.[6]

A brief description of the media studied follows:

Print. The three studied papers published a single daily edition, representing a non-updatable product, based on relatively long textual items (typically hundreds of words per item), presented in clear hierarchies, and accompanied by graphics, photos, and illustrations. They employ relatively large reporting staffs (eighty to one hundred reporters per newspaper at the time of the research).

Radio. The three studied stations aired an hourly bulletin (plus shorter news flashes on the half hour throughout most of the day), comprised of extremely short news items.[7] News bulletins are read by anchors and—in one case—accompanied by brief inserts of interviewees' voices. Although updated hourly, many items are aired across a few bulletins. The case study involved twenty to forty reporters per station. One station's reporters also work for a television station.

Online. The three websites publish items that are closer in length to those of print media than radio, accompanied by the largest variety of medium-specific features. One website employed a 100% dedicated reporting staff (about forty reporters), another employed a nucleus of eighteen reporters (with the support of eighty newspaper reporters), and a third double-jobbed its newspaper reporters.

Data were gleaned through a series of face-to-face reconstruction interviews in which a sample of reporters from these nine leading Israeli national news organizations detailed—source by source—how they reported a sample of their recently published items.

The studied organizations constitute a valuable case study, not only as viable, leading, and competitive national news organizations, but also as employers of substantial staffs of dedicated reporters—a feature rather uncommon at radio and online news organizations.[8]

Source Work Across Media

Comparative cross-media studies that seek to determine medium differences are still scarce even outside the specific context of journalism studies. According to two meta-analysis projects (of the 1980–1999 and 1993–2005 time periods), only 10%–20% of the papers in leading communication journals focused on more than one medium, with only 10%–13% of them on the Internet.[9] Many of the bi/multimedia research projects that did study news tended to focus on journalists[10] or their final output,[11] while only a few focused on news processes.[12] These journalist-centered studies found personal characteristics that may play a role in shaping news work, the content studies found similarities between print and online news, and comparative studies that focused on work processes discovered strong lines of continuity between offline and online news, although with some measure of increased workload and time pressures.

Whether different media report their news distinctively or similarly is disputed by those in two major opposing "camps," dubbed *particularistic* and *generic* in this study. According to the particularistic camp, reporters in each medium employ particular or unique practices to obtain their raw information, following their unique "medium logic"[13] that is manifested in various ways, including unique production methods.[14] Dahlgren[15] wrote: "[...] Media logic points to specific forms and processes which organize the work done within a particular medium. Yet, media logic also indicates the cultural competence and frames of perception of audiences/users, which in turn reinforces how production within the medium takes place."

This position gained momentum with the rise of online news, described by some of its pioneering scholars and advocates as a "fourth kind of journalism" and "new regimes of content creation" with "distinctive media logic" and terminology, a change in the face of journalism, if not its soul.[16] According to Kolodzy: "print, broadcast, and online news operations have developed different cultures in which they do news."[17] A particularistic position does not necessarily entail technological determinism, as the specific patterns of reporting may be shaped by cultural, social, and economic factors, such as journalistic orientations, editorial policies, prevailing routines and standards, availability of news holes, and news staffs, etc.

On the other hand, according to the generic camp, which emphasizes general aspects or the common denominator of news reporting, journalists across media report their news rather similarly.[18] As Gans noted: "Despite the differences between the electronic and print news media, the similarities were more decisive."

The generic camp is supported by the "institutionalist" school of thought that views journalism as a monolithic phenomenon,[19] as well as by some major books on the sociology of news that are not only dominated by a generalizing tone but also dedicate limited space—sometimes less than one page—to their principal discussion of medium differences[20] (although other medium differences are mentioned occasionally). While Deuze considers such tendencies to reflect "print bias,"[21] they may reflect a broader inclination toward overgeneralization that is typical of news ethnographies.[22]

The generic camp does not necessarily ignore medium differences and technological innovations, but rather contends that they are counterbalanced by a series of converging forces: the "isomorphism" of different media organizations; equivalent practices and routines; coverage of same sources under similar definitions of newsworthiness; "pack journalism"; cross media production; "homogenization"; and convergence of norms, standards, people, and content.[23]

Research Questions

To explore the patterns of news reporting in the three media, the study focuses on four research questions (specific variables are mentioned below each question, including categories of variables that are not self-evident):

> **RQ1:** Do print, radio, and online reporters invest similar reporting efforts in obtaining raw news information?

The extent of journalistic effort invested in news reporting is not always measurable and may be misleading at the individual news item level at which an item may be based, for example, on a single source yet may demand considerable reporting effort to locate it and convince it to cooperate. Across large samples of items, however, it is reasonable to expect that more reporting effort will be largely a function of more news sources, initiative, negotiation-enabling contacts, and firsthand witnessing, representing more authoritative and less source-dependent coverage.[24] Following Reich's method,[25] channels of communication such as outgoing telephone calls and Internet searches are considered reporter-initiated contacts, while incoming calls and e-mails are considered source-initiated.

RQ2: Do print, radio, and online reporters maintain similar source relations?
This question addresses the extent to which the reporters in the studied media rely on a similar mix of sources—including PR practitioners, spokespersons, and ordinary citizens—and leaks. The "diversity" score measured the extent to which the reporter mixed sources of different types (1. senior, 2. non-senior, 3. PR) and sectors in society (4. government, 5. politics, 6. private sector, and 7. private citizen) in the same item. Scores range between 1 and 7, with one point for no diversity and one additional point for each instance of source or sector diversity).

RQ3: Do print, radio, and online reporters address their sources with similar levels of skepticism? While reporters rely similarly on sources they trust highly,[26] they may differ from one medium to another in the frequencies with which they cross-check their versions with other sources and attribute their versions clearly in their final items, seeking to distance themselves from versions they consider less trustworthy.

RQ4: Do print, radio, and online reporters maintain a similar newswork structure?
This question addresses the extent to which reporters in different media maintain clear separation between two news phases in their news processes, thus affecting the active role of the reporter in building the news agenda, as research findings demonstrate.[27] During the news discovery phase, the reporter hears about the potential item for the first time, while during the subsequent news-gathering phase, s/he obtains the building blocks for the story. The discovery phase information itself may be too preliminary and fragmented to serve as the basis for a full-blown, publishable story. While clear separation between news discovery and news gathering occurs when the first source supplies only the discovery information, in a less structured and more rapid process the first source may supply at least some of the news gathering information as well.

Another aspect is the use of medium-specific features. The reporters were asked to state the number of features—such as photos, audio inserts, hyperlinks, and multimedia—that accompanied each item and the extent to which they were personally involved in their production and management (none/small/moderate/great/very great).

Method

The study uses a series of reconstruction interviews. Reporters from three media—print, radio, and online—representing ten different beats in each of nine leading Israeli national news organizations[28] were asked to detail, source by source, how they reported 841 recently published news items. The interviews took place during December 2006 and January 2007 and were preceded by three steps:

1. Random Selection of Beats and Reporters: To select reporters in proportion to their different beats, all reporting personnel were divided into three beat clusters known to use distinctive working patterns: politics and security, domestic affairs, and business affairs.[29] Then, ten specific news beats were chosen randomly from these clusters (2, 4, and 4 respectively), according to the proportion of the clusters among the overall reporting personnel. The study involved eighty reporters, because in one case (*Haaretz*), the same reporters worked for the paper and the website. Fourteen reporters were replaced with others from their beat cluster after refusing to participate or having published fewer than ten items per reporter.

2. Identification of All Published Items: The sampling period extended over four weeks (November 15 through December 15, 2006), reflecting an attempt to achieve a fair balance between variety among stories and use of material still fresh in reporters' memories.

3. Random Sampling of News Items: Ideally, we should have chosen one item per reporter and asked the reporter to carefully describe how he or she obtained the story. However, this would have exposed the precise manner in which a *specific* item was obtained, endangering the reporters' ethical demand for source confidentiality. Hence, we needed as many items per reporter as necessary to maintain the anonymity of any individual item and avoid matching reliably between the reconstructed items and the descriptions of their production processes. On the other hand, too many items per reporter would have taxed reporters' focus and patience. Ten items per reporter supplied the balance between both demands.

Seating was arranged to help maintain source confidentiality. Interviews were conducted face-to-face, but the reporter (with a pile of sampled stories) and the interviewer (with a pile of questionnaires) sat on opposite sides of a table. A portable screen was placed between them to supply a safe environment in which the reporter could choose each item and describe how it was obtained, while the interviewer could not see which item is involved. To avoid identifying details, the questionnaire used general categories, such as senior source (with specific defining criteria that were read to the reporter), government sector, etc. The questionnaires were filled out by the interviewer, who assigned interviewees' oral replies to *categories* in a closed-end quantitative questionnaire.[30] The questionnaire analyzed the production process of each item, addressing three chief aspects (the specific variables were stipulated in the research question descriptions, above):

News Sources. The total number of sources, their basic characteristics in terms of role, sector affiliation, etc.

Channels of Communication. Type of communication used to contact each source, e.g., landline and cellular telephone calls, e-mails, face-to-face interviews, etc.

Reporting Practices. Practice applied in the specific item, e.g., leaks, cross-checking, clear attribution of the source in the final item, separation between news discovery and news gathering (as explained in the research questions above), and employment of medium-specific features.

This method offers a perspective that traditional methods could not. For example, direct observation has yielded some of the deepest insights regarding newswork, such as criteria for selection of news sources and news items, the ways in which journalists employ technologies in different media, and their reliance on the accounts of "authorized knowers."[31] Nevertheless, direct observations may infringe source confidentiality, may miss many source-reporter exchanges that flow either outside the newsroom or through unobservable channels, such as telephone interviews, and may make it difficult to supply comparative evidence. Furthermore, observations cannot measure frequencies of phenomena as the current study sought to do. Content analysis studies can measure frequencies of phenomena, such as reliance on different types of news sources,[32] although they may be speculative here, as news products are often unclear and equivocal regarding the processes in which they were obtained.[33] Free-floating interviews and surveys can identify trends among journalists,[34] but they leave extensive room for journalists' bias by asking professional interviewers to evaluate their own work.

Findings

This study's data elucidate the extent to which different media obtain their raw information in generic or particularistic ways, based on a comparison of print, radio, and online reporters from comparable news beats. Data are based on detailed accounts of a sample of eighty reporters, regarding a sample of 841 news items published during a four-week period, in which they relied on a total of 2,045 contacts with different news sources.

While print items in the current study were one-shot publications, radio items included 2.74 versions and updates per item (some of which were reruns of the same item with minimal or no updating), compared with 0.52 updates per online item. To avoid unfair comparison, in which the final product of print might be compared to the *initial* output of their counterparts, online and radio reporters were asked to address their cumulative newswork for each item, including the most advanced update or version. Findings are displayed according to the four research questions, starting with **RQ1**, which addresses differences in reporting efforts (see Table 1).

According to Table 1, print reporters have an advantage over their counterparts in the number of sources per item—but even this difference is not significant. Radio reporters, on the other hand, initiate contacts to a significantly greater extent than their counterparts in both news phases. They also use the telephone more frequently. While in other media, the phone enables negotiation of source versions,[35] in radio it may represent a natural preference for an aural platform.

These differences are too small to mask the larger picture: reporters in the studied media invest strikingly similar reporting efforts to obtain their information. All tend to minimize their number of sources and their physical presence for coverage; all tend to wait for the initiative of their sources in the news discovery stage, but choose their news-gathering sources afterwards, obtaining their information primarily via the telephone.

RQ2 asked if print, radio, and online reporters maintain similar source relations. Data on source relations are presented in Table 2.

Print reporters have a clear advantage over their radio and online counterparts in important aspects of source relations. They rely substantially less on PR subsidies and substantially more on leaks, but do not use a significantly greater variety of sources. The combination of less PR and more leaks indicates more selective and independent source work, potentially yielding more

Table 1. Levels of Reporting Efforts Invested across the Studied Media

Medium Type	Print	Radio	Online	*N*	Sig.
Sources per Item[a]	2.59	2.51	2.52	841	NS
News Scene Attendance (% of contacts)[b]	7%	6%	8%	2,045	NS
Negotiation-enabling Contacts (Telephone) (% of Contacts)[c]	51%	67%	57%	2,045	**
Initiated Contacts: Discovery Stage (% of Contacts)[d]	24%	33%	27%	841	*
Initiated Contacts: Gathering Stage (% of Contacts)[e]	59%	74%	63%	1,823[f]	**

Notes:
* $p < .05$; ** $p < .01$

[a] $F_{(8.832)} = 1.71; p = .093$

[b] $\chi^2_2 = 2.20; p = .33$

[c] $\chi^2_2 = 36.33; p = .000$

[d] $\chi^2_2 = 6.02; p = .049$

[e] $\chi^2_2 = 28.27; p = .000$

[f] *N* is smaller, containing only gathering contacts.

exclusive and newsworthy information than routine news, probably thanks to a denser network of non-PR contacts. Higher leak rates may also indicate that news sources feel either greater trust in print reporters or higher esteem for their platform as a venue for highly sensitive, non-authorized disclosure of information.

Table 2. Source Relations across the Studied Media

Medium Type	Print	Radio	Online	*N*	Sig.
Mean Diversity of Sources [a]	2.05	1.87	1.96	841	NS
Reliance on PR and Spokespersons (% of Contacts) [b]	32%	43%	39%	2,032	**
Ordinary Citizens (% of Contacts)[c]	7%	3%	4%	2,032	**
Leaks (% of Items) [d]	35%	19%	25%	838	**

Notes:
** $p < .01$

[a] Index of variety in source type and sector in society. Ranges between 1 and 7. $F_{(2.838)} = 1.757$; NS

[b] $\chi^2_2 = 18.04; p = .000$

[c] $\chi^2_2 = 12.14; p = .002$

[d] $\chi^2_2 = 17.52; p = .000$

Table 3. Cross Checking and Attribution across the Studied Media

Medium Type	Print	Radio	Online	N	Sig.
% of Cross Checked Items[a]	48%	43%	46%	838	NS
% of Contacts that Were Clearly Identified (% of Gathering Contacts)[b]	40%	14%	31%	1,707[b]	**

Notes:
** $p < .01$

[a] $\chi^2_2 = 1.84; p$ NS

[b] $\chi^2_2 = 91.57; p = .000$

RQ3 asked whether the three types of reporters view their sources with similar levels of skepticism. Data regarding the levels of skepticism (in terms of cross-checking and attribution) regarding news sources across media are presented in Table 3.

Cross-checking was not found to be significantly different across the studied media. The striking finding regarding attribution of sources is the overwhelming presence of anonymity in radio items. In other media, however, less attribution means less transparency and less distance from non-trustworthy sources, whereas in radio, it may correspond to extremely short items, thereby reflecting a primarily stylistic convention rather than sourcing considerations.

Finally, **RQ4** asked about differences in structure of newswork. Table 4 data show that the separation between news discovery and news gathering was greater in print.

This may suggest that the process of obtaining news information in print is more "settled" than in radio and online news, allowing reporters first to receive and internalize the story leads and then to choose additional sources in a more "structured" manner.

Table 4. The Structure of Newswork across the Studied Media

Medium Type	Print	Radio	Online	*N*	Sig.
% of Separation between Discovery and Gathering Contacts per Item[a]	40%	25%	13%	841	**
Average Medium-specific Features per Item[b]	0.70	0.08	1.26	841	**
Reporter's involvement in obtaining these features[c]	19%	50%	26%	449[d]	**

Notes:
*** $p < .01$

[a] $\chi^2_2 = 51.19; p = .002$

[b] E.g., photos, video, and hyperlinks, added to the news item. $F_{(2.838)} = 116.69; p = .000$

[c] Percentage of interviewees who defined the extent of their involvement as great or very great. $\chi^2_2 = 20.61; p = .000$

[d] *N* is smaller, containing only items that included add-ons.

As could be expected, online news items are the richest in terms of medium-specific features, although reporters are rarely involved substantially in obtaining them. This is left inevitably to their editors, who not only insert the features into the final items, but also deal with their production in most cases. Radio reporters were substantially involved in obtaining medium-specific features, thanks to one station (*Galey Zahal*) that incorporated sound bites into its news bulletins. The reporters of this station were highly involved in recording the sound bites, although this reflects an organizational style rather than a medium characteristic.

Discussion

Although research usually seeks variance, the most substantial finding of this study is similarity as differences among media during the early stages of news reporting were found to be minor, nuanced, and not necessarily in the anticipated places and directions. Three explanations are suggested for the relative similarity across media:

Structural: News sources are considered "extramedia level" influences[36] and are generally perceived as more dominant than reporters,[37] leaving less room during the early stages of information production for adjustment to the "media routine level," that includes medium-specific procedures. Hence, when reporters from a new medium join the micro-culture[38] of an existing news beat, they have little room to adjust its already structured source relations, routines, practices, and norms to the preferences of their own medium.

Organizational: As the generic camp suggests, the similarity among media during the reporting stage is part of a set of converging forces, such as "isomorphism" among different media organizations, equivalent practices and routines, similar concepts of newsworthiness, "pack journalism," "homogeneity," etc.[39]

Occupational Standards: Similarity in reporting standards may suggest that despite their constraints, radio and online reporters cannot afford to rely on substantially fewer news sources and less cross-checking and legwork than their print counterparts, as they might thus jeopardize themselves and their organizations by publishing erroneous, one-sided, and fragmented information that would not be tolerated by their respective publics.

Obviously, the method used here, reconstruction interviews, is not entirely free of shortcomings. Although the interviews can cover an extensive variety of items, topics, organizations, and circumstances, and although they anchor the reporters' testimony in specific accounts of specific measures behind specific items, they are still highly dependent on journalists' self-reports and, consequently, are open to over- or underestimation. Some of this dependence was counterbalanced by alertness to inconsistencies in the interviewees' replies, such as between number of sources and number of communication channels. In any case, as there is no reason to believe that reporters from a specific medium are more prone than others to these potential biases, the findings across media may be considered comparable.

Conclusion

While the print, radio, and online news organizations studied here largely converge in the patterns of their news reporting, as the *generic* camp contends, they diverge substantially in the subsequent stages when items are accorded photos, video, hyperlinks, etc., as the *particularists* maintain. These findings suggest that the studied media are not unique factories of news, but rather unique packing and distribution houses of similarly obtained raw materials. Findings also suggest that the need for a particular sociology for online (as for print and radio) is less urgent than recommended, as far as news reporting in these media are concerned. It is important to note that the selected media were high-profile, competitive national news organizations, a decisive majority of which were employers of substantial reporting staffs.

A medium's uniqueness at the reporting stage manifests itself in subtle and not always expected facets of new production. For example, even if print reporters enjoy less-urgent deadlines,[40] they do not use substantially more sources per item, more legwork, more initiative, or more cross-checking; they do conduct a more "settled" reporting process, with greater differentiation between news discovery and news gathering, and they rely more on leaks and less on PR contributions.

This study focused entirely on process, whose impact on the quality of content might be indirect and complex. Naturally, the broad similarity of process across the three media must not be taken to suggest that the news products of each were of roughly equal value. Indeed, it might be hypothesized that because print items relied somewhat less on PR and somewhat more on leaks, on average, they had higher news value to some degree. To counterbalance that advantage, other media would have needed higher source work standards (e.g., more sources, more diversity, more firsthand witnessing). Our findings show, however, that the non-print media did not try harder.

Further research should explore whether medium divergence starts at the editing stage and culminates in the consumption stage, when each medium entails a unique "situation of contact"[41] and unique sensory, intellectual, and other experiences. Additional research should follow the web closely when it becomes a more mature news medium[42] and explore the incorporation of visual elements that are not only dominant in television news, but also increasingly present online.

In the future, news reporting will probably become more "generic," and the already minimal distinctions among media are likely to blur even more with the continuous decline in number of "non-converged" newsrooms and of editorial work forces, rising expectations of the remaining journalists to produce content for multiple platforms, intensifying trends of technological and organizational convergence, and the "homogenization" of news.

Notes

1. By "news media," we refer to a specific venture inside the news industry that specializes in production and distribution of news for specific audiences of readers, listeners, viewers, or users, employing specific channels, technologies, and platforms; John Hartley, *Communication Cultural and Media Studies: The Key Concepts* (London: Routledge, 2002); James Watson and Anne Hill, *Dictionary of Media and Communication Studies* (London: Arnold, 2000).
2. Pablo J. Boczkowski, "The Consumption of Online News at Work—Making Sense of New Phenomena and Rethinking Existing Concepts," *Information, Communication & Society* 13 (4, 2010): 470–84; Eugenia Mitchelstein and Pablo J. Boczkowski, "Between Tradition and Change: A Review of Recent Rresearch on Online News Production," *Journalism* 10 (5, 2009): 562–86; Michael B. Salwen, Bruce Garrison, and Paul D. Driscoll, *Online*

News and the Public (Hillsdale, NJ: Lawrence Erlbaum Associates, 2005); Miriam J. Metzger, Andrew J. Flanagin, Keren Eyal, Daisy R. Lemus, and Robert N. McCann, "Credibility for the 21st Century: Integrating Perspectives on Source, Message, and Media Credibility in the Contemporary Media Environment," *Communication Yearbook* 27 (2003): 293–335.

3. Mark Deuze and Steve Paulussen, "Research Note: Online Journalism in the Low Countries: Basic Occupational and Professional Characteristics of Online Journalists in Flanders and the Netherlands," *European Journal of Communication* 17 (2, 2002): 237–45; Mark Deuze and Christina Dimoudi, "Online Journalists in the Netherlands: Towards a Profile of a New Profession," *Journalism* 3 (1, 2002): 85–100.
4. Pablo J. Boczkowski, "The Development and Use of Online Newspapers: What Research Tells Us and What We Might Want to Know," in *Handbook of New Media,* ed. Leah A. Lievrouw and Sonia Livingstone (London: Sage, 2002), 270.
5. Mark Deuze, "Towards a Sociology of Online News," in *Making Online News: The Ethnography of New Media Production,* ed. Chris Pater-son and David Domingo (NY: Peter Lang, 2008), 199–209, 200; Laura Grindstaff and Joseph Turow, "Video Cultures: Television Sociology in the 'New TV' Age," *Annual Review of Sociology* 32 (2006): 103–25.
6. Tony Atwater and Frederick Fico, "Source Reliance and Use in Reporting State Government: A Study of Inter-Media Agenda Setting," *Newspaper Research Journal* 8 (1, 1986): 53–61; Charles R. Bantz, Suzanne McCorkle, and Roberta C. Baade, "The News Factory," *Communication Research* 7 (1, 1980): 45–68; Irving Fang, "Writing Style Differences in Newspaper, Radio and Television News" (a monograph presented for the Center of Interdisciplinary Studies of Writing and die Composition, Literacy and Rhetorical Studies Minor at the University of Minnesota, Minneapolis, MN, 1991); Emma Hemingway, *Into the Newsroom: Exploring the Digital Production of Regional Television News* (London: Routledge, 2008); Pamela J. Shoemaker and Stephen D. Reese, *Mediating the Message: Theories of Influences on Mass Media Content* (NY: Longman Publishers, 1996); Daya Kishan Thussu, *News as Entertainment: The Rise of Global Infotainment* (London: Sage, 2007).
7. The average radio item comprised 60–70 words (according to a count of a sample of 90 items, 30 from each of the studied stations)—far shorter than in print and online items that may be carefully estimated at least as double that amount for short items or triple for regular items.
8. M. David Arant and Janna Quitney Anderson, "Newspaper Online Editors Support Traditional Ethics," *Newspaper Research Journal* 22 (fall 2001): 57–69; David H. Weaver and G. Cleveland Wilhoit, *The American Journalist in the 1990s: U.S. News People at the End of an Era* (Hillsdale, NJ: Lawrence Erlbaum Associates, 1996), 61.
9. Rasha Kamhawi and David H. Weaver, "Mass Communication Research Trends from 1980 to 1999," *Journalism & Mass Communication Quarterly* 80 (spring 2003): 7–27; James W. Potter and Karyn Riddle, "A Content Analysis of the Media Effects Literature," *Journalism & Mass Communication Quarterly* 84 (1, 2007): 90–104.
10. E.g., David H. Weaver, Randal A. Beam, Bonnie J. Brownlee, Paul S. Voakes, and G. Cleveland Wilhoit, *The American Journalist in the 21st Century: U.S News People at the Dawn of a New Millennium* (Mahwah, NJ: Lawrence Erlbaum Associates, 2007); David H. Weaver, *The Global Journalist: News People around the World* (Cresskill, NJ: Hampton Press, 1998).
11. E.g., Donica Mensing and Jennifer D. Greer, "Above the Fold: A Comparison of the Lead Stories in Print and Online Newspapers," in *Internet Newspapers,* ed. Xigen Li (Mahwah, NJ: Lawrence Erlbaum, 2006), 283–302; Martin Engebretsen, "Shallow and Static or Deep and Dynamic? Studying the State of Online Journalism in Scandinavia," *Nordicom Review* 27 (1, 2006): 3–16.
12. Pablo J. Boczkowski, "Technology, Monitoring, and Imitation in Contemporary News Work," *Communication, Culture and Critique* 2 (1, 2009): 39–59; Edgardo P. Garcia, "Print and Online Newsrooms in Argentinean Media:

Autonomy and Professional Identity," in *Making Online News: The Ethnography of New Media Production,* ed. Chris Paterson and David Domingo (NY: Peter Lang, 2008).

13. David L. Altheide and Robert P. Snow, *Media Logic* (Beverly Hills, CA: Sage, 1979), 9; Peter Dahlgren, "Media Logic in Cyberspace: Repositioning Journalism and Its Publics," *javnost/The Public* 3 (3, 1996): 59–72; Deuze, "Towards a Sociology of Online News," 199–209.
14. Engebretsen, "Shallow and Static or Deep and Dynamic?" 3–16; Shoemaker and Reese, *Mediating the Message;* Pablo J. Boczkowski, "Affording Flexibility: Transforming Information Practices in Online Newspapers" (Ph.D. diss., Cornell University 2001); Boczkowski, "The Development and Use of Online Newspapers: What Research Tells Us and What We Might Want to Know," 270–86; Pablo J. Boczkowski, *Digitizing the News: Innovation in Online Newspapers* (Cambridge, MA: MIT Press, 2004); John H. McManus, *Market-Driven journalism: Let the Citizen Beware?* (Thousand Oaks, CA: Sage, 1994); Jane Singer, "Who Are These Guys? The Online Challenge to the Notion of Journalistic Professionalism," *Journalism 4* (2, 2003): 139–63; Paul Manning, *News and News Sources* (London: Sage, 2001); Vinciane Colson and Francois Heinderyckx, "Do Online Journalists Belong in the Newsroom? A Belgian Case of Convergence," in *Making Online News: The Ethnography of New Media Production,* ed. Chris Paterson and David Domingo (NY: Peter Lang, 2008), 143–57; Janet Kolodzy, *Convergence Journalism: Writing and Reporting across the News Media* (Lanham, MD: Rowman & Littlefield Publishers, 2006).
15. Dahlgren, "Media Logic in Cyberspace," 63.
16. Deuze and Dimoudi, "Online Journalists in the Netherlands," 96; John Huxford and Nancy Duda, "Cultures in Collision: Newspapers and the Internet" (paper presented at the annual conference of the International Communication Association, Acapulco, Mexico, June 2000); Kevin Kawamoto, "Conclusion," in *Digital Journalism,* ed. Kevin Kawamoto (Lanham, MD: Rowman and Littlefield, 2003), 167–82.
17. Kolodzy, *Convergence Journalism*, 54.
18. Lindsay H. Hoffman, "Is Internet Content Different after All? A Content Analysis of Mobilizing Information in Online and Print Newspapers," *Journalism & Mass Communication Quarterly* 83 (1, 2006): 58–76; Gaye Tuchman, *Making News: A Study in the Construction of Reality* (New York: The Free Press, 1978); Thorsten Quandt, "(No) News on the World Wide Web?," *Journalism Studies* 9 (5, 2008): 717–38; Herbert J. Gans, *Deciding What's News* (New York: Pantheon Boooks, 1979), xii.
19. Bartholomew H. Sparrow, *Uncertain Guardians: The News Media as a Political Institution* (Baltimore: The Johns Hopkins University Press, 1999); Rodney Benson, "News Media as a 'Journalistic Field': What Bourdieu Adds to New Institutionalism, and Vice Versa," *Political Communication* 23 (2, 2006): 187–202; Timothy E. Cook, *Governing with the News: The News Media as a Political Institution* (Chicago: University of Chicago Press, 1998).
20. Shoemaker and Reese, *Mediating the Message;* Michael Schudson, *The Sociology of News* (NY: Norton, 2003), 7.
21. Deuze, "Towards a Sociology of Online News," 199.
22. Barbie Zelizer, *Taking Journalism Seriously* (Thousand Oaks, CA: Sage, 2004), 68.
23. Pablo J. Boczkowski and Martin de Santos, "When More Media Equals Less News: Patterns of Content Homogenization in Argentina's Leading Print and Online Newspapers," *Political Communication* 24 (2, 2007): 167–80; Cook, *Governing with the News;* Mark Deuze, "What Is Journalism?: Professional Identity and Ideology of Journalists," *Journalism* 6 (4, 2005): 442–64; Denis McQuail, *McQuail's Mass Communication Theory* (London: Sage, 2000); Pablo J. Boczkowski and José A. Ferris, "Multiple Media, Convergent Processes, and Divergent Products: Organizational Innovation in Digital Media Production at a European Firm," *The Annals of the American Academy of Political and Social Science* (January 2005): 32–47; Susanne Bodker and Anja Bech-martn Petersen, "Seeds of Cross-Media Production," *Computer Supported Cooperative Work* 16 (6, 2007): 539–66.
24. John D. Peters, "Witnessing," *Media, Culture, and Society* 23 (November 2001): 707–24; Russell Frank, "You Had to Be There (and They Weren't): The Problem with Reporter Reconstructions," *Journal of Mass Media Ethics* 14

(3, 1999): 146–58; Barbie Zelizer, "On 'Having Been There': 'Eyewitnessing' as a Journalistic Keyword," *Critical Studies in Media Communication* 24 (5, 2007): 410.

25. Zvi Reich, *Sourcing the News: Key Issues in Journalism: An Innovative Study of the Israeli Press* (Cresskill, NJ: Hampton Press, 2009).
26. Gans, *Deciding What's News,* 144–45; Jim F. Detjen, Fred X. Lee, and Kim Yehoshim, "Changing Work Environment of Environmental Reporters," *Newspaper Research Journal* 21 (1, 2000): 2–12; Edie Goldenberg, *Making the Papers* (Lexington, MA: D. C. Heath, 1975); Zvi Reich, "Source Credibility and Journalism: Between Visceral and Discretional Judgment," *Journalism Practice* 5 (1, 2011): 51–67.
27. McManus, *Market-Driven Journalism: Let the Citizen Beware?;* Zvi Reich, "The Process Model of News Initiative: Sources Lead First, Reporters Thereafter," *Journalism Studies* 7 (4, 2006): 497–514; Reich, *Sourcing the News.*
28. The criteria for choosing organizations were as follows: (1) national news organizations; (2) market leaders; (3) employers of dedicated reporting staffs. Beats were selected from reporters' full lists, prepared by following the reporters' bylines over a three-month period according to the following criteria: (a) mainstream beats in each of the nine news organizations; (b) output published primarily in news and business sections; (c) covered by full-time reporters; (d) reporters who publish at least twelve items per month.
29. Reich, *Sourcing the News,* 163–67.
30. For a more detailed discussion of the methodology and a full version of the questionnaire, with minor modifications, see: Reich, *Sourcing the News,* 19–34, 195–200.
31. Daniel Berkowitz, "Refining the Gatekeeping Metaphor for Local Television News," *Journal of Broadcasting & Electronic Media* 34 (1, 1990): 55–68; Chris Paterson and David Domingo, eds., *Making Online News: The Ethnography of New Media Production* (New York: Peter Lang, 2008); Richard V. Ericson, Patricia M. Baranek, Janet B.L. Chan, *Negotiating Control: A Study of News Sources* (Toronto: University of Toronto Press, 1989); Gans, *Deciding What's News.*
32. Daniela V. Dimitrova and Jesper Strömbäck, "Look Who's Talking: Use of Sources in Newspaper Coverage in Sweden and the United States," *Journalism Practice* 3 (1, 2008): 75–91; Daniel C. Hallin, Robert K. Manhoff, and Judy K. Weddle, "Sourcing Patterns of National Security Reporters," *Journalism Quarterly* 70 (4, 1993): 753–66.
33. Jane Delano Brown, Carl R. Bybee, Stanley T. Wearden, and Dulcie Murdock Straughan, "Invisible Power: Newspaper News Sources and the Limits of Diversity," *Journalism Quarterly* 64 (spring 1987): 45–54; Hallin, Manhoff, and Weddle, "Sourcing Patterns of National Security Reporters"; Manning, *News and News Sources.*
34. Weaver and Wilhoit, *The American Journalist in the 1990s.*
35. Zvi Reich, "The Roles of Communication Technology in Obtaining News: Staying Close to Distant Sources," *Journalism & Mass Communication Quarterly* 85 (3, 2008): 625–46.
36. Shoemaker and Reese, *Mediating the Message.*
37. Gans, *Deciding What's New;* Reich, *Sourcing the Nexvs;* Jesper J. Strömbäck and Lars W. Nord, "Who Leads the Tango? A Study of the Relationship between Swedish Journalists and Their Political Sources" (paper presented to the Political Communication Division, International Communication Association, NY, May 2005).
38. Ericson, Baranek, and Chan, *Negotiating Control: A Study of News Sources,* 34.
39. Boczkowski and de Santos, "When More Media Equals Less News"; Cook, *Governing with the Nexvs;* Deuze, "What Is Journalism?"; McQuail, *McQuail's Mass Communication Theory;* Boczkowski and Ferris, "Multiple Media, Convergent, and Divergent Products"; Bedker and Petersen, "Seeds of Cross-Media Production."
40. Deuze, "Towards a Sociology of Online News," 205.
41. Eliot Freidson, "The Relation of the Social Situation of Contact to the Media in Mass Communication," *Public Opinion Quarterly* 17 (2, 1953): 230–38.
42. Ramón Salaverria, "An Immature Medium: Strengths and Weaknesses of Online Newspapers on September 11," *Gazette* 67 (1, 2005): 69–86.

Chapter Highlights

- It is important to be able to write basic news stories in print article format. This skill will translate well as the basis for all mediums.
- Asking whether newspapers will disappear is no longer the question to ask. It is a given that the mediums are changing, and a strong writer must know how to write for all mediums.
- A strong lead gives a news story the starting point it needs. The goal is to provide the news and leave the reader wanting to know more.
- Hard news leads and anecdotal leads are both important writing tools for the writer's toolbox.
- It is important to conduct research and to know what the facts of a story are before beginning to write the lead and news story.

For Discussion

1. What are the different styles of print articles? What do you feel is most effective for straight news writing? Do you like the inverted pyramid style? Do you like the anecdotal lead? What style appeals to you?
2. What's the story? Take a look at the headlines of the day and select a lead story. Read three full articles on that story from three different publications and compare and contrast them. Did the reporters capture the essence of the story? What is the story? Is it the same in each article, or did the coverage and angle change depending on the publication? Did anyone miss the story?
3. Let's take a few moments to talk about print journalism. We don't have to have all the answers, but it is a good discussion to have when we ask the questions. What is happening to newspapers? Do you ever read one? Where do you see the world of journalism going? Would you be interested in writing for a newspaper, or are you pleased with the direction of online journalism? Perhaps there is a new idea you will come up with (an invention or a new medium or mode of breaking news) for the future of journalism. Remember, you are the future writers and reporters!
4. What do you like to read? What newspapers do you read, if any at all? What magazines? Do you always go online, or do you sometimes buy a hard copy?
5. Does you want to be a features writer? What about the longer, thoughtful pieces appeals to you? We appreciate the longer form and especially enjoy news analysis articles. When you want to go deeper into understanding of a news story, how do you go about it in your own reading? Where do you look, and how do you conduct further research or go about information-gathering?

viii

Broadcast

The way we watch TV, if we watch TV at all, may change. The way we listen to news may change. We may get more tech-savvy and demand news how and when we want it. But good writing, broadcast-style, does not change. Whether you listen to the radio, live stream, program your DVR or On Demand, or stay current via Hulu, there is a demand for strong writing.

We want our news delivered, however we get it, in a clear and concise manner. We don't want to work hard at listening to find out the news of the day. A broadcast journalist's job, after seeking out the story, researching, collecting facts and information, conducting interviews, and confirming information with sources, is to write the news in a coherent manner.

Like any form of communication, the receiver wants to receive a clear message. This style of writing, broadcast journalism, offers a more conversational style of writing than print. In this chapter we will highlight a few broadcast scripts and provide relevant readings about TV and radio. In the exercises and discussion questions, you will have a chance to create your own mini-broadcasts. In this book, we will focus on strong writing, not necessarily on what video or digital content you will produce.

Using Writing as a Broadcast Journalist

What is broadcast writing, and what does it entail? A typical job description for a broadcast journalism job opening may read something like this (in fact, this is a recent job description from a posting for a broadcast journalist position).

Broadcast journalist research, investigate and present news and current affairs for television, radio and the internet. Their aim is to present information in a fair, balanced and accurate way through news bulletins, documentaries and other factual programs.

Broadcast journalists can fill a number of roles within the media including editor, reporter, presenter/news anchor, producer and correspondent.

Although exact duties and responsibilities will vary from role to role and between radio, television and the internet, broadcast journalists will generally be involved in many of the following duties on a daily basis:

- generating ideas for stories and features and following leads from news agencies, the police, the public, press conferences and other sources;
- pitching ideas to editors;
- researching and collating evidence and information to support a story using relevant information sources such as the internet, archives, databases, etc.;
- writing scripts for bulletins, headlines and reports;
- selecting appropriate locations, pictures and sound and exercising editorial judgment on the best angle to approach a story from;
- identifying necessary resources and deploying/managing technical crews for location shoots, including sound operators and camera crew;
- providing directorial input, advising crews on what to film or record;
- using portable digital video cameras and other equipment to record material and appropriate editing software to produce complete packages for broadcast;
- preparing, writing and presenting material "on air" for both pre-recorded and live pieces;
- identifying potential interviewees, briefing them, preparing interview questions and conducting both live and recorded interviews;
- preparing timings for each news item and monitoring these during broadcast;
- deciding on the running order for bulletins and making any necessary changes during broadcast;
- developing and maintaining local contacts and assuming a public relations role;
- understanding and complying with media law and industry codes of conduct.

As you can see, writing plays a strong part in being a broadcast journalist. Similar to how there are challenging changes taking place in the print medium, there are also challenges facing the broadcast medium, but no matter what technical changes take place, there will always be a need for content and good writing and clever video. Let's take a look at a well-crafted broadcast writing sample to give you an example of what to expect and strive for.

A note of thanks and acknowledgment to CNN for the open-source transcripts to use for our educational purposes within the university classroom. To find more CNN transcripts, please visit transcripts.cnn.com.

Here is one example to use in the classroom as an example of a current broadcast script. You will see a detailed and choreographed script, almost like a dance, between the newscasters, the interviewees, and the reporters. Because we are concerned with, in this book, the actual broadcast script and writing and not the video, we are including only the text. But students will be able to see how the stories and the newscast unfold and where video will be inserted. This is a fairly standard approach to broadcast writing. It will give you an idea of how scripts and news segments unfold, and the writing that is involved.

Aired September 11, 2013.

> **Quick Reference**
>
> *Anderson Cooper 360 Degrees.* "Striking Syria; President's Red Line; Interview with Paul Wolfowitz; Ariel Castro Kills Himself A Month Into Life Sentence; One Dead, Three Hurt In Stabbings At Texas High School; Oklahoma Governor Signs Extradition Order For Dustin Brown." *See* http://transcripts.cnn.com/transcripts/1309/04/acd.01.html.

The second example of broadcast writing is from a popular (and admittedly more liberal) show with well-known CNN host Anderson Cooper. You will notice that the writing is less hard news and more conversational. Depending on the show, the broadcast, and the news outlet, writing styles may vary. But this gives just another example of the creativity that comes with broadcast writing. Had the writers written in a stiff and overly wordy format, the host would appear as less conversational, which would result in a less friendly and approachable show. The goal of any broadcast writing is to convey the news effectively, but writers also need to consider the audience and the style. What else can be conveyed in broadcast writing? There is often a writing style or delivery approach that is sought. Anderson Cooper clearly has his own style of delivery, as do other host brands such as Larry King, Rachel Maddow, Bill O'Reilly, or Megyn Kelly. The broadcast writers need to be aware of the message as well as the branding when they write the scripts so that a coherent style is consistent.

> **Quick Reference**
>
> *CNN Newsroom.* "Pentagon Memorial for 9/11 Victims; Hearing Today for Admitted Drunken Driver; U.S. Postal Service's Cash Crunch; Video Could Crack Latest Zimmerman Case." *See* http://transcripts.cnn.com/transcripts/1309/04/acd.01.html.

Quick Tips for Writing Broadcast Copy

This is a wonderful quick guide, or a "cheat sheet" if you will. The material is culled from a well-liked textbook called *News Reporting and Writing* by Melvin Mencher 2010, and many journalism professors use these tips across universities. A special thanks to Stanford University Professor J. G. Willihnganz, who compiled the print versus broadcast tips on his Stanford website page. It is printed below for your educational reference.

Broadcast versus Print Copy

Since you will be writing for a weekly radio broadcast, you will need to know the differences in writing style for broadcast and print copy. When writing for broadcast, remember that listeners have only one chance to hear a story, as opposed to readers having limitless chances to study print copy. Keep the following broadcast writing guidelines in mind:

1. Use everyday language
2. Write short sentences
3. Use one idea to a sentence
4. Use the present tense if possible
5. Usually confine stories to one major theme

Most broadcast stories are two to five sentences running 10 to 30 seconds. The broadcast writer's job is to convey the story idea without detail.

Right or Wrong?

Anchor a story with present or present perfect verbs in the lead:

- WRONG: The state highway department **announced** yesterday that it will spend six million dollars this year improving farm-to-market roads. *(past)*
- RIGHT: The state highway department **says** that it will spend six million dollars this year improving farm-to-market roads. *(present)*
- RIGHT: The state highway department **has announced** that it will spend six million dollars this year improving farm-to-market roads. *(present perfect)*

Begin sentences with a source, with the attribution, if needed, and use paraphrased quotes:

- WRONG: "The city is going to need new traffic lights beginning right now," the mayor said.
- RIGHT: The mayor says the city needs new traffic lights.

Avoid starting a story with a participial phrase or a dependent clause:

- WRONG: Hoping to keep the lid on spiraling prices, the president called today for wage-price guidelines to keep prices down.
- RIGHT: The president is calling for wage-price guidelines to keep prices down.
- WRONG: When the bill was passed, he was absent.
- RIGHT: He was absent when the bill was passed.

Use ordinary, one- and two-syllable words whenever possible:

- WRONG: The unprecedented increase in profits led the Congress to urge the plan's discontinuance.
- RIGHT: The record profits led Congress to urge an end to the plan.

Use vigorous verbs:

- WEAK: She walked slowly through the mud.
- BETTER: She trudged through the mud.

Use active, not passive voice:

- WEAK: He was shown the document by the lawyer.
- RIGHT: The lawyer showed him the document.

Exercises

1. In the classroom, divide into broadcast teams. A small group of four or five is ideal. You will put together a twenty-two-minute broadcast with today's news. First, have a meeting to discuss the important stories of the day. Next, decide on the stories you will cover and pass out assignments. Remember that you will not be shooting footage; this is a broadcast writing exercise, so focus on the written word. One suggestion is to select a range of story ideas for a traditional nightly news broadcast in the areas of national news, international politics, local news, sports, weather, and any other topic areas your news team deems important. For fun, edit each other and read your broadcast scripts in front of the classroom, as if conducting a live broadcast.
2. Select a significant print story for the day. Find two to three sources and read each article. Then, in your own words, write a broadcast news story. Do this for television broadcast as well as radio. For radio, you will want to use more visual language to challenge the listener's ear. Use language that has a bit more imagery for the radio broadcast. After you read it to the class, ask your colleagues to describe what they saw as you read your script.
3. Brainstorm and create your own broadcast news segment. You get to decide what you cover, how you want to come across as the host of your own show, and what stories you cover. Assign stories to the class. Create your very own broadcast design. Use print resources and online stories to give headlines of the day, to do research, and to help you go in a certain direction for your show. Work together as a large newsroom team to create your own news show.

Reading List

We have selected the following readings to provide you with a foundation and background on broadcast journalism. The readings should expand on a definition of broadcasting (including radio history) to include the past and present.

CNN, the World's First 24-hour News Channel's 25th Year: The Challenging Times

By Sujatha Pampana

"We're gonna go on the air June 1, and we're gonna stay on until the end of the world. When that time comes, we'll cover it, play 'Nearer My God to Thee' and sign off."

—Ted Turner[1]

"Fox News Channel Continues to Crush CNN"

—Knight Ridder, Dallas Morning News[2]

Cable News Network (CNN), the world's first ever 24-hour news channel was launched in June 1980 with its headquarters in Atlanta. The brainchild of Ted Turner (an Atlanta-based business tycoon), CNN dominated the cable news market for nearly 15 years with its speed in news coverage. With its non-stop coverage of the Persian Gulf War, CNN attained the peak of popularity in 1991. CNN also launched other specialized channels dealing with sports and international news [Exhibit I] apart from related Internet sites. By 2002, CNN reached about 88 million homes in the United States and operated from 37 bureaus [Exhibit II] around the world. However, the advent of Rupert Murdoch's 'Fox News Channel' in 1996 triggered the downslide for CNN in terms of viewership. At the same time, many other cable networks also introduced round the clock news channels undermining the supremacy of CNN in cable news network. It was never the same for CNN thereafter, with Fox adopting novel approaches to draw audience away from CNN. CNN's viewership declined gradually to 52% in 2003, placing it second to Fox News in ratings. The gap between Fox's and CNN's profits which was 40% (CNN on the higher side) in 2003 also reduced to 20% by the end of 2004. After 25 years of existence, CNN in 2005 is working towards a reorganisation to improve the quality of its reporting, overcome the competition and countering the allegation of reflecting Liberal ideology[3] [Exhibit III].

CNN: The Initial Years of Broadcasting

Born in 1938 in Cincinnati, Ohio, Ted Turner (Turner) was a highly successful businessman in Atlanta. He had established Turner Broadcasting System (TBS) in the mid-1970s, which managed different Cable TV networks in USA. Turner nurtured a dream of launching an exclusive 24-hour news channel that would revolutionize the media world. Consequently, he negotiated with news veteran Reese Schoenfeld (Schoenfeld), who had by then developed the concept of 'all the news all the time' television. Impressed by Turner's ideas, Schoenfeld sold his news concept to him, and CNN as a 24-hour news channel was launched in June 1980 under the aegis of TBS. At the time of introduction, CNN not only was the first ever 24-hour news channel but also the first to launch televised news worldwide. While Schoenfeld was made CNN's first president, Turner took the responsibility of working with the news executives and dealing with the company's future strategies.

During the initial days of its launch, CNN reached 1.7 million homes in Atlanta which had access to the cable network, particularly appealing to the Conservative audiences. However, the revenue stream from the viewership was not sufficient to generate profits for CNN and for more than a year the channel incurred losses of about $2 million a month. The bigger players in the television industry and the critics had written off CNN and even nicknamed it the "Chicken Noodle Network." Yet, Turner did not lose heart. He employed more than 300 media professionals to improve the presentation and news reporting. Bureaus were also established in most of the places in United States and other parts of the world like Rome and London. Turner's efforts and investment seemed to pay off when CNN started gaining viewership. Encouraged by the results, Turner went on to launch CNN2, another news channel within the next two years.

However, even before CNN recovered its investment costs, Westinghouse Electric Company (Westinghouse) and American Broadcasting Company (ABC) together started a rival channel called the Satellite News Network. ABC was a television and radio network in America (acquired by Walt Disneyin 1996) while Westinghouse owned Columbian Broadcasting System (CBS). Between 1982 and 1983, CNN strived hard to prevent the financially strong rival channel to establish a foothold. CNN improved its news coverage by providing in-depth news from across the world and appealed to the cable operators to remain loyal. Cable operators in the US led by TCI's John Malone remained loyal because it was CNN and Turner who were instrumental in giving a boost to the cable business, which was started as a replacement to the traditional antenna system. Being a cable driven network, CNN had helped sell basic cable. "That's when we had that cable convention in Las Vegas, and I did that 'It was cable when cable wasn't cool. It never hurts to be popular with your customers," said Turner[4]. By October 1983, ABC and Westinghouse withdrew and sold their channel to Turner for $25 million, ending the only competition for CNN in the United States. CNN's reputation improved further when it covered round the clock proceedings of the Democratic and Republican conventions that took place in 1984. Also, CNN2 was renamed CNN Headline News.

By 1985, CNN was viewed in more than 30 million homes in the United States. During this time, to extend CNN brand, CNN International channel was launched. One year later, the channel became the exclusive one to air the live coverage of the explosion of "Challenger", NASA's space shuttle, which exploded just after 73 seconds of launch. Turner also added bureaus in Bonn, Moscow and Cairo. In 1987, CNN aired non-stop, the proceedings of the summit between the then US President Ronald Reagan and the then USSR President Mikhail S. Gorbachev, which was supposed to serve the purpose of putting an end to the Cold War between the two countries. CNN covered the summit by deploying seventeen correspondents at the venue of the event. Such news coverage helped CNN gradually climb the ladder of popularity by 1989. By the end of the 1980s, CNN reached audiences in 65 countries.

By the end of the decade, CNN and CNN Headline News accounted for about a third of TBS's $1.1 billion in overall revenues[5]. Special programmes, apart from the news, such as *Show Biz Today*, a daily entertainment report and *The World Today*, an evening newscast also contributed to an increase in CNN's viewership. Such was CNN's growing reliability and popularity that when the military troops of the United States attacked Panama in 1989, the Soviet foreign ministry instead of intimating its counterparts in the United States diplomatic corp., informed CNN's bureau in Moscow. Ted Turner had also often showcased global political figures like Margaret Thatcher, Francois Mitterrand and Fidel Castro as CNN's regular viewers. In 1989, CNN earned over $100 million in profits on revenues of

$315 million[6] and by the end of 1990, became the most popular source for breaking news in America and all over the world.

The live broadcasting of the 1991 Persian Gulf War, however, remained to be the milestone in CNN's path to glory. CNN was the only television network in the world that operated live from the very beginning of 'Operation Desert Storm'. CNN, with the permission of the military, covered everything from the first dropping of the bomb on Baghdad to the incidents that marked the end of the war. Bernard Shaw, Peter Arnett and John Holliman were the popular correspondents who reported live from Baghdad. But along with the achievements and even before the end of the war, Conservative audience began criticising CNN for its Liberal leanings. Saddam Hussein, the then President of Iraq, alleged during the war that the coalition forces had bombed the Baby Milk Factory in Iraq. To report on this issue, CNN sent its popular anchor Larry King; and he, instead of probing to find out the facts, spent time interviewing anti war propagandists. CNN's failure to eventually highlight the facts regarding the issue, invited the criticism of the audience who felt that the channel was biased in its reporting. Gradually, CNN began losing its Conservative audience. More problems also surfaced for Turner in the form of excessive coverage costs incurred in broadcasting the war. Turner could not compensate the expenses with the advertising revenues since CNN had pre-empted advertisements to enhance continuous coverage of war. Additional staff, additional satellite links and increased production costs also added to the budget and CNN reported that the channel exceeded its budget by $12 million[7].

In spite of being in financial doldrums in 1992, Turner went ahead and launched two more channels "Airport" and "Supermarket" to cater to the non-Conservative audiences and at the same time expand into new regions across the world. Airport channel broadcasted news on weather, stock market and airports across North America. The supermarket channel broadcasted news related to supermarkets, weather and current affairs at different supermarkets in America. But neither of the channels succeeded in terms of generating revenues as they failed to generate interest among the audience.

However, major events happening across the world such as the San Francisco earthquake, and the trial of O. J. Simpson helped CNN to remain competitive. During the broadcasting of these events and thereon, CNN strived to regain the trust of viewers by eliminating any trace of biased reporting. CNN's efforts paid off when the New York-based research firm Roper Starch Worldwide reported during the mid-1990s that the viewers ranked CNN as the 'fairest' among all channels. The Times Mirror's Center for The People & The Press also reported that the viewers trusted CNN more than any other news channel[8]. Moreover, CNN by then surpassed the 50 million household mark in terms of reach and celebrated 15 years of broadcasting in June 1995.

Troubled Times: The Competition

Concerns began for CNN after 1995 when the channel's growth rate of revenues stalled. Many of the advertisers withdrew their ads on the channel as they felt that CNN's audience was "too old" and "not as affluent" as could be found elsewhere[9]. Also, Turner sold CNN to media giant Time Warner for $6.2 billion in 1995. Experts opined that Time Warner being a corporate giant with numerous interests would not give CNN the due attention. After the purchase, Ted Turner was made the Vice Chairman of the Time Warner Group. The competition to CNN also increased during this time when Microsoft declared that it would form a joint venture with NBC to launch a news channel that would directly challenge CNN. The channel was later christened MSNBC. Furthermore, News Corporation

Inc. led by Rupert Murdoch and Capital Cities/ABC also planned a 24-hour news channel in the future to challenge CNN.

However, CNN continued to introduce specialized news channels and even launched its primary website. At the end of 1995 the financial network of CNN, CNNfn began its broadcasting in US and Australia. CNN/*Sports Illustrated* (CNN/SI), an exclusive sports network and CNN en Espanol (CNN in Spanish) were also launched during this time. CNN/SI was expected to be one of the most comprehensive sports news channel in America. By this time, Rupert Murdoch fulfilled his promise of starting a 24-hour news channel to compete with CNN and started Fox News Network.

Owned by the Fox Entertainment Group (FEG), Fox News (Fox) was launched in October 1996. FEG, the subsidiary of the News Corporation, one of the largest media conglomerates appointed Roger Ailes as the CEO, Chairman and President of Fox. At the same time many other channels such as MSNBC, CNBC, Bloomberg, Overseas BBC World Service and Deutcher Welle also started broadcasting round the clock news, thus posing a threat to CNN. "The network of record is in a bit of a slump, and rivals MSNBC and Fox News are waging vigorous challenges with fresh approaches to cable news," *reported American Journalism Review* about the competition to CNN.[10] At the time of launch, Fox News reached 17 million homes and slowly started making a dent in CNN's market share. In a day, Fox News broadcasted 15 hours of live programming from its headquarters in New York City targeting the Conservative audiences.

To establish itself and to improve its reach, Fox adopted a novel approach called 'cash-for-carriage', according to which, Fox offered local cable operators, a fee of $10 per every subscriber.[11] Fox anticipated that the 'cash-for-carriage' would help the channel in the long run to gain subscribers. And when it implemented the scheme, Fox earned 13 cents per every subscriber each month in return for $10 it paid.[12]

To counter the competition from Fox, CNN reinforced its reporting quality and coverage by including significant and special reports, documentaries and investigative programmes. Also, CNN pioneered the reporting on important environmental issues. CNN also developed a novel approach to cover the events, which became talk of the town and almost all other broadcasting channels followed suit. The idea initiated was that a well-known reporter would sit behind a desk at one of the news centres (Atlanta or London) while the cameras would continue to focus on the event to be covered. The channel would then shift the focus from the reporter on TV to the public at the event and then to reporters who are at the scene of the event. The reporter at the scene sometimes would take the help of a local expert to describe the cause or effect of an event. The coverage depending on the intensity of the issue was continued for hours together and also days when required. With such an expertise in live coverage, CNN gained the reputation as the *'voice and eyes of authenticity and truth'*.[13] On many occasions, magazines in US echoed the opinion that, "if one wants to get the best perspective on news of major importance, there is now the prevailing assumption that CNN will be the first to deliver that perspective, since what CNN relays is what is the most important news. News is what CNN broadcasts, and what CNN broadcasts is therefore news."[14]

Determined to survive the competition and on what he thought could attract viewers, Turner said, "I am one of those do-gooders and I am going to keep on doing. If the people don't watch the UN [coverage] this year, I am going to keep on running it. I am going to do the right thing. That's right. Shove it down their throats. I am going to keep on running it … "[15] While CNN remained popular, the effect of competition from Fox started to show on its ratings for the first time in 2000. One rating point is one percent of the total television households that viewed a program in consideration.[16] In that year, CNN's overall ratings decreased by 33% compared to the previous year's ratings. However, the slide in ratings was not only due to Fox's programmes but also due to lack of any major events happening during that period. This reinforced the opinion that CNN failed to keep the viewers glued to the channel in the absence of sensational or breaking news. According to *the News Republic*, "CNN hasn't done much with the opportunity. When the president is speaking, when major events are breaking, CNN's cameras and microphones are usually there, a notable asset if the moment is important, but what if the moment is not? This is where the quality of reporting and the level of imagination take over. And it is here that CNN suffers".[17]

A second ownership change for CNN came when the Internet giant America Online (AOL) acquired Time Warner in 2001. AOL Time Warner was created and Terence McGuirk replaced Turner, as the Vice Chairman of TBS. Turner was made the Vice Chairman and senior advisor for AOL Time Warner. After the creation of AOL Time Warner, are-organization took place resulting in 400 job cuts at CNN. Analysts viewed the exit of Turner from CNN's day-to-day affairs at a time of increasing competition as a blow to the channel. Jonathan Klien became CNN's president and under his leadership, in-depth storytelling on themes such as the stock exchange became the second priority at prime time to news. However, the shift could not bring any significant boost to viewership.

The competition brought to light, many flaws that CNN overlooked. One of the factors was the choice and the channel's little varied portfolio of programmes. Audience complained that CNN lacked variety in the programmes it aired and that they were being subjected to the same old series of shows on CNN such as *Crossfire*, *Capital Gang*, *Inside Politics* and *Reliable Sources*. On the contrary, Fox news aired diversified and novel programmes such as *Fox & Friends*, *Day Side*, and the top rated *O' Reilly Factor*. *O'Reilly Factor and Hannity & Colmes* were the two best-rated shows on Fox News because the discussions were conducted in an unbiased fashion. This attracted the Conservative audience who began to switch to Fox Channel. Such programmes also helped Fox News in attracting new subscribers who demanded cable operators to provide the channel in their households. During that time, the concept of digital cable boxes with fewer bandwidth restrictions on the number of channels a cable system could offer came into existence[18]. This worked to the advantage of Fox Channel as it helped the channel reach even more households.

Moreover, though CNN initiated measures to avoid biased reporting, the channel's inclination towards certain political parties reflected widely in its reporting [Exhibit IV]. This led to CNN being sarcastically referred to as the 'Clinton News Network'. Most of the time, CNN aired programmes in support of America and the then US President Bill Clinton in particular. One instance where CNN was said to have displayed its biased reporting was in March 1998, during the Clinton-Lewinsky scandal. CNN portrayed Clinton and Lewinsky to be 'a devoted and loving couple'. On another occasion, CNN aired a program on the Assault Weapons Ban, which immediately drew the criticism of National Rifle Association (NRA). NRA's Vice President Wayne LaPierre charging that the channel had presented a distorted view of the issue, said, "The only difference between CNN and the *New York Times* is that when a Times reporter lies, they fire him. CNN should fire the reporter and producer who produced this piece."[19] This further strengthened the accusations that CNN had Liberal leanings.

The industry analysts also observed that CNN had no programmes to compete against the most popular programmes of its rival channels such as the *Road to the White House* and *Booknotes*[20]. Due to such setbacks, the viewership ratings when calculated on an average ranked CNN in the second position. Fox News and MSNBC together attracted about half a million viewers in a day compared to just above three hundred thousand by CNN. When the Pew Research Center in US conducted a study to determine the partisanship percentages for the channels, Fox was reported to have 52% of the audience who were Conservative. CNN on the other hand had only 36% [Exhibit V].

The study by the Pew Research Center also mentioned about the declining credibility of CNN. According to the study, previously 32% of audiences believed what they heard on CNN compared with 25% for Fox. But the percentage decreased gradually since early 2000. According to Nielsen Media Research, in 2002 across the entire day, Fox averaged 831,000 viewers compared with CNN's 449,000 due to decreasing credibility of the channel. Also, CNN which fared on par with Fox in the daytime ratings was left wondering when Fox saw a 15% increase in its average prime-time viewership in 2002 from over the same period in 2001. Furthermore, in May 2002, CNN/SI also shut its operations, as it was unable to fight the competition against ESPN. CNN/SI reached only 20 million homes (unlike 86.5 million homes by ESPN) as reported by Nielsen Media Research causing the sponsors to ignore the channel. Also, in late 2004, CNN closed its CNNfn channel owing to its failure in attracting audiences[21].

Besides, CNN's interest in marketing itself rather than working on the quality of reporting also caused problems. Previously, CNN marketed itself with a background music and the tone of James Earl Jones announcing "This ... is CNN." But over the years, CNN prioritised marketing of the channel by roping in many celebrities to market its channel just by proclaiming, "I am watching you CNN ... ". The focus on marketing was what the analysts thought made CNN neglect its reporting quality.

Problems for CNN also originated from its failure to prioritise programmes that it broadcasted. Analysts opined that breaking news was not always important news and being live does not signify being serious. Such misjudgements were apparent in 1991 when CNN reported live the William Kennedy Smith rape trial, the Bobbitt trial, the Tonya Harding investigation and the Simpson case. The result of these telecasts was that the channel's producers found themselves trapped between what was exciting and what was important.

In 2003, CNN's Chairman and CEO Walter Isaacson stepped down from his post to be replaced by Jim Walton, who was already working as an executive at CNN. But a major transformation at CNN to improve the ratings was started by David Bohrman, the new head of CNN's Washington bureau, when he prioritised the telecast of breaking news stories before anybody did. He arranged his team in such a way that work was shared among reporters thereby decreasing the burden on each of them. While he reshuffled few of the jobs of the existing staff members, he fired some of them. Since then, although CNN managed to remain in the competition, it could not stop Fox from dominating the cable news network.

The Challenges

In June 2005, CNN celebrated its 25th year of existence as it unveiled many more changes to the network. Jonathan Klein, CNN's president announced that before anything there would be an evaluation of CNN's programmes. Further, he added one hour broadcasting of international news from one of CNN's sister channels to the midday schedule of CNN News channel. Jonathan Klein also worked on the 3 to 6 p.m. time slot and planned to do away with programmes such as *Crossfire* and *Inside Politic*. *Crossfire,* the long running programme on CNN had lost viewership after the host was replaced. He made plans for introducing a three-hour continuous telecast of news to be anchored by Wolf Blitzer, a professional journalist in Washington. But despite Jonathan Klein's assurance that hard-core news would remain to be CNN's mainstay, the revamping aroused in suspicion among CNN's employees. "It's safe to say there is at least a component of CNN employees, particularly those of long duration, who are still wondering what the sense of direction is," said Charles Bierbauer, dean of the

University of South Carolina's College of Mass Communications and Information Studies, and a CNN correspondent for 20 years[22].

CNN also worked towards starting non-talk shows, which would focus on topics of public interest such as security, health and employment. About the idea, Jonathan Klein said, "It's terrific that Americans know to run to CNN whenever there is breaking news. But we want to create a new habit, which is to turn to us every night before they go to sleep to find out what's going on in their world."[23] But can CNN wean away the audience from Fox with its financial might or will it bank upon its reporting strength is to be seen in the near future. Meanwhile, Fox continued to improve its average prime-time viewership. The number reached 1.5 million by mid-2005 while CNN's average remained 789,000, as per the Nielsen Media Research. Fox also proclaimed that its popularity over CNN was only increasing day by day on the strength of its news shows. MSNBC on the other hand was also emerging as a potential competitor.

Exhibit–I

CNN's Network

CNN airport network

CNN en Espanol

CNNfn (Financial Network)

CNN Headline News

CNN International

CNN Plus (CNN + a partner network in Spain, launched in 1999 with Sogecable)

CNN Sports Illustrated (a.k.a CNNSI), the network's all-sports channel, closed in 2002

CNN Turk

n-tv (CNN owns 27.5% of this news channel in Germany)

Source: CNN Specialized Channels, www.en.wikipedia.org

Exhibit–II
CNN's Bureaus by the end of 2002

CNN Domestic Bureaus	CNN International Bureaus
Atlanta	Rio de Janeiro, Brazil
San Francisco	Santiago, Chile
Boston	Rome, Italy
Miami	New Delhi, India
Los Angeles	Nairobi, Kenya
Detroit	Moscow, Russia
New York City	Mexico City, Mexico
Chicago	London, United Kingdom
Washington, DC	Lagos, Nigeria
Dallas	Seoul, South Korea
	Kabul, Afghanistan
	Jerusalem, Israel
	Jakarta, Indonesia
	Islamabad, Pakistan
	Hong Kong, China
	Havana, Cuba
	Dubai, United Arab Emirates
	Buenos Aires, Argentina
	Beijing, China
	Baghdad, Iraq
	Berlin, Germany

Source: Compiled by ICFAI Business School Case Development Center

Exhibit–III
Categorisation of Audience

Since the 1980s, the public's news viewing habits in America have reflected the polarisation towards particular political parties. Based on their political partisanships and ideologies, audiences have been categorised as the following:

Based on Partisanship towards a political party

Democratic

Republic

Independent

Based on Ideology

Liberal

Conservative

Moderate

It was observed that since 2000, increasing number of Conservatives and Republicans watched Fox News channel. By 2004, more than half of Fox audiences called themselves politically Conservative. CNN's audience on the other comprised of more Liberals and Democrats allegedly due to its biased programming. The news consumption survey conducted by the Pew Research Center for the People and the Press also traced out that ideology and partisanship contributed to the credibility of programmes. It was found out from a poll in the United States (conducted among 3,000 adults) that the Conservatives and Republicans preferred Rush Limbaugh's radio show and Bill O'Reilly's TV program on Fox channel because they triggered discussion on a certain event. In contrast, the Liberal and Democratic audiences preferred programmes like the News Hour because such programmes showcased news from one viewpoint.

Source: Compiled by ICFAI Business School Case Development Center

Exhibit–IV
Evidences of Biased Broadcasting by CNN

- The opening and closing montage of CNN's *Then and Now* shorts prominently feature mostly Liberal personalities such as Anita Hill and Janet Reno.
- During the first Gulf War, CNN reporters Bernard Shaw, Peter Arnett, and John Holliman refused to be debriefed by the US military concerning what they saw during their stay at the Al-Rashid Hotel in Baghdad during the initiation of the air campaign, citing themselves as belonging to an "international" news organization and stating it would compromise their journalistic principles.
- On August 16, 1997, Chief News Executive Eason Jordan gave a gift to North Korean leader Kim Jong-il in an attempt to improve CNN's access to North Korean affairs. (Jordan had been credited in 1996 with gaining exclusive access to North Korea for CNN reporters.)
- In January 1998, Lucia Newman, the bureau chief in Havana reported that Cuba's single candidate elections were better than the elections with "no dubious campaign spending" and "no mud slinging" in the United States.
- On March 10, 1999, while speaking at Harvard, Eason Jordan thanked Cuban President Fidel Castro for his comments instigating CNN's decision to broadcast in other countries, CNN International.
- In 1999, CNN, in partnership with corporate sister *Time* magazine, ran a report that Operation Tailwind included use of Sarin gas to kill a group of defectors from the United States military. The story proved untrue, CNN issued a public retraction.
- In 2000, Lou Dobbs left CNN, reportedly due to heated clashes with then-president, who was frequently accused of manipulating news programmes to present a Liberal slant. Dobbs returned the following year at the behest of CNN founder Ted Turner.
- On April 11, 2003, Eason Jordan confessed that CNN knew about human rights abuses committed in Iraq by Saddam Hussein since 1990, but the network abstained from coverage of them in order to gain better access to information on Hussein's government. Jordan maintained that complete reporting would have jeopardized the lives of Iraqi informants, and confidentiality was ensured to protect the lives of anti-Hussein Iraqi activists and translators.
- In November 2004 at the News Xchange conference in Portugal, Eason Jordan claimed that United States armed forces were arresting and torturing non-coalition Arabic journalists in Iraq. He also claimed that American troops were intentionally killing these journalists. Also at the conference, Chris Cramer, a CNN executive claimed that journalists were being "deliberately targeted (by the US military) for seeking out the truth." That month, al-Arabiya reporter Abdel Kader al-Saadi had been detained by US forces for 11 days during US-led attacks on Fallujah without comment on cause for his dentention.
- On January 27, 2005 Eason Jordan claimed 12 journalists who were killed were actually targeted by United States troops. He later tried to backtrack on his comments, but resigned from CNN on February 11, 2005 in an effort, he claimed, to spare the network from further controversy. Jordan's comments invoked outrage in the US, even among such "Liberal" politicians such as Sen. Christopher Dodd and Rep. Barney Frank.
- On March 24, 2005 in an interview with PBS' Charlie Rose, CNN President Jonathan Klein called FOX News Channel's audience "mostly angry white men [who] ... tend to be rabid." Klein then said a Liberal, progressive TV network would never be as successful as Fox because "progressives don't get too worked up about anything. And they're pretty morally relativistic."

Source: www. www.en.wikipedia.org

Exhibit–V
Fox Channel's Increasing Conservative Audience

Percent	1998	2000	2002	2004
who are ...	%	%	%	%
Republican	**24**	**29**	**34**	**41**
Democrat	36	32	35	29
Independent	33	29	22	22
Other/DK	7	10	9	8
	100	100	100	100
Conservative	**40**	**40**	**46**	**52**
Moderate	34	33	32	29
Liberal	20	21	18	13
Other/DK	6	6	4	6
	100	100	100	100

Source: "News Audience increasingly politicized", www.people-press.org, June 8th 2004

Notes

1. Schechter, Danny "CNN At 20: From Chicken Noodle Network To Global Media Power", www.alternet.org, June 8th 2000
2. Rendall, Steve "The Ratings Mirage", www.reclaimthemedia.org, March/April 2004
3. Since the 1980s, the people's news viewing habits in America have reflected the polarisation towards particular political parties. Based on their political partisanships and ideologies, audiences have been categorised under the following: Based on Partisanship towards a political party: Democratic, Republic, Independent; Based on Ideology: Liberal, Conservative, Moderate
4. Donnelly, Paul "Ted Turner: Cable When Cable Wasn't Cool", www.bcfm.com, April/May 2002
5. Konrad, Walecia and Hawkins, Chuck "The Scoop on CNN's Bottom Line", www.businessweek.com
6. Hogarth, David "Networks of recod", *Canadian Journal of Communications*, November 4th 1992
7. Hogarth, David "Networks of recod", *Canadian Journal of Communications*, November 4th 1992
8. Gomery, Douglas "Cable News Network", www.museum.tv
9. Ibid.
10. "CNN At 20: From Chicken Noodle Network To Global Media Power", op.cit
11. "Cable TV: Economics", www.stateofthenewsmedia.org
12. Ibid.
13. Edward "Public spectacle, public history" www.islamfortoday.com, February 24th 1999
14. Ibid.
15. Ibid.
16. "Television Advertising by the numbers", www.upn34.com, September 20th 2003

17. Rosenstiel, Tom "The myth of CNN: why Ted Turner's revolution is bad news", *The New Republic*, August 22nd 1994
18. "Cable News Network", op.cit
19. "Wayne V. CNN", www.nramemberscouncils.com, May 16th 2003
20. Book notes is the longest running book-based program on C-SPAN having completed 630 episodes. The concept of the interview show hosted by C-SPAN's CEO is 'one book, one author, one hour' where the author describes in detail about how and why he had written the book. 'Road to the white house' on the other hand is also a weekly show on C-SPAN which covers the events and issues that would continue till the 2008 presidential elections. These programmes gained popularity because of its distinctiveness from other regular shows.
21. "CNN", www.enwikipedia.com
22. Gold, Matea "25-year-old CNN reinventing itself", www.indystar.com, June 1st 2005
23. Gold, Matea "At 25, CNN is looking for a makeover", www.detnews.com, May 31st 2005

Chapter Highlights

- The way we watch TV, if we watch TV at all, may change. We are in an on-demand world where the news now comes to you. How we have our news delivered is changing.
- The job of a broadcast journalist is to report the news in a clear and concise manner.
- The broadcast journalist wears many hats, from editor and reporter to producer and researcher.
- A broadcast journalist should write in present tense. A broadcast journalist should not write in past tense.
- A broadcast journalist should use an active voice rather than a passive voice.

For Discussion

1. Take a look at the news of the day. What are the three top stories? Take a look at three different news broadcasts. Identify the writing style differences. First, see how the print stories differ from the broadcast stories. Next, look at the differences between the broadcast stories. How does one channel cover the story versus how another broadcast covers it?
2. Take one news story in the top of the news. Take a look at the way television broadcast covers the story, and then find a radio broadcast of the same story. How is the broadcast writing different, depending on the medium? Is there one you prefer? What appeals to you? What do you dislike about the writing?
3. Listen to one radio news broadcast today. This may be in your car commuting, or you may want to go online to find a radio broadcast and listen that way. One suggestion is National Public Radio's *All Things Considered*. Take a listen, and dissect the writing in a classroom discussion.
4. There was a time when print and broadcast journalism were separate paths. What has happened in recent years, and where do you see these styles of writing going? What is or is not effective?
5. What is the most compelling form of news writing to you personally? Be able to defend your answer, and reference three examples of strong news writing from examples that you find. If you find fault with broadcast writing as a whole, be specific in your criticism.
6. If you could predict the future, what would you say will happen to broadcast news with regard to television, radio, and the internet? Bring multimedia journalism into the discussion. How will you use writing effectively in this changing world?

ix

Online Journalism

The trend toward online news used to be a conversation piece in classrooms. Will online journalism crush print journalism? That question is old and outdated. We have proof positive that this generation gets news from online sources. As we begin to look at how to write online, we no longer need to consider whether online journalism is here to stay; of course it is. In fact, the trend now is to check the news from mobile apps; therefore, online news outlets are having to scramble and figure out revenue sources because the old advertising model (outdated and from print) no longer works.

But we are not here to solve the financial problems of newspapers, magazines, or online news sites; what we are here to do is to understand the context of writing across all media and learn how to write well-constructed news stories and clear and concise sentences in which to tell the news, no matter what the medium (websites or apps or other outlets not yet known).

One Idea per Paragraph

If there is one piece of information to walk away with, we want you to carry this: one idea per paragraph. Writing online is not dumbing it down, as some like to say; instead, it is putting news stories into a clear and concise format for readers to get quickly informed.

The rule of thumb is one idea per paragraph. Easy, digestible, quick, and in a format where writers can quickly go in and update. The 24/7 news cycle demands that online data be constantly updated and rewritten. New and current information must consistently lead the way and appear at the beginning of an online article, or in the headline for apps. Therefore, writing in simple and easy-to-understand and digestible sentences is a must. This does not mean to dumb it down; it simply means to write clearly.

One idea per paragraph. Some even say one idea per sentence, but we don't believe that readers are that simple. Offer the crux of the story up front and explain why it is relevant or put it into context. Drop the use of an inverted pyramid style here, because readers are less patient than online readers. Answer the question—what's the story?—right off the top.

Something else to consider: online writing adds up to be approximately half the word count of conventional writing. Also, visually you will want to incorporate lists that are appealing to the reader. Let's call them bulleted lists, or some way of breaking out information from the main online text, similar to a sidebar in traditional print writing. In addition, the online writer will want to include hyperlinks that make sense for the reader as well as related and interesting graphics.

If this were a history of journalism class, we would dive into how online journalism came to be, but writing about the origin of what was once termed the World Wide Web (thus the www history) might put us all to sleep. Instead, let's focus on how to write online articles. Not only do we see one idea per paragraph; we see one sentence per paragraph, which is a contrast from print journalism.

Online Sites that Work

A couple of good news sites for checking out breaking news follow. One observation you will make is that all of the sites write in short, clear, and concise sentences and all add the latest and greatest and breaking news to the leads, and they update frequently. Take a look at these sites:

- www.drudgereport.com
- www.huffingtonpost.com
- www.npr.org

Top-Twenty Lists

For a more official list, we turn to a valuable Internet resource found at news.nettop20.com. It is a site that has top-twenty lists of all things on the Internet:

1. CNN.com
2. CBS News
3. ABC News
4. Google News
5. Reuters
6. Yahoo News
7. BBC News Online
8. World News
9. MSNBC
10. Fox News
11. USAToday.com
12. CBC News Online
13. Time.com
14. The Associated Press
15. Guardian Unlimited
16. NewsLink
17. *The New York Times*
18. EmergencyNet News
19. Consortium News
20. News.com.au

We also cut and pasted from The Drudge Report to offer a quick list of additional range online news sources for student journalists to refer to. We've found that a lot of students aren't reading as much as they should be and we believe strongly that in order to be a strong write you must be a daily and consistent news reader. So find something you like to read or watch and take in all the news you can. It's a fun list, so enjoy:

- ABC News
- Access Hollywood
- Ad Age Deadline
- Adweek
- BBC
- BBC Audio
- Bild
- Billboard
- Blaze
- Boston Globe
- Boston Herald
- Breitbart
- Broadcasting & Cable
- Business Insider
- Buzzfeed
- CBS News
- C-SPAN
- Chicago Sun-Times
- Chicago Tribune
- Christian Science Monitor
- CNBC
- CNN
- CNN Political Ticker
- Daily Beast
- Daily Caller
- Daily Kos
- Daily Swarm
- Daily Variety
- Deadline Hollywood
- Der Spiegel
- E!
- Economist
- Editor & Publisher
- Emirates 24/7
- Entertainment Weekly
- Esquire
- Financial Times
- Forbes
- FOX News
- FOX News Nation
- France 24
- Free Beacon
- Free Republic
- Gawker
- Hot Air
- HELLO!
- Hill
- Hollywood Reporter
- Huffington Post
- Human Events
- iAfrica
- International Herald Tribune
- Infowars
- Investor's Business Daily
- Jerusalem Post
- Los Angeles Daily News
- Los Angeles Times
- Lucianne.com
- Media Week
- Mother Jones
- MSNBC
- Nation
- National Enquirer
- National Journal
- National Review
- NBC News
- New Republic
- New York Magazine
- New York Daily News
- New York Observer
- New York Post
- New York Times
- New Yorker
- NewsBusters
- NewsBytes
- Newsmax
- Newsweek
- People

- Philadelphia Inquirer
- Philadelphia Daily News
- PJ Media
- Politico
- Radar
- Real Clear Politics
- Reason
- Red State
- Roll Call
- Rolling Stone
- Salon
- San Francisco Chronicle
- Seattle Times
- Sky News
- Slate
- Smoking Gun
- Splash
- Star
- Sydney Morning Herald
- Talking Points Memo
- Time Magazine
- TMZ
- [UK] Daily Mail
- [UK] Daily Mirror
- [UK] Daily Record
- [UK] Evening Standard
- [UK] Express
- [UK] Guardian
- [UK] Independent
- [UK] Sun
- [UK] Telegraph
- US News & World Report
- USA Today
- Vanity Fair
- Verge
- Village Voice
- Wall Street Journal
- Washington Examiner
- Washington Post
- Washington Times
- Weekly Standard
- World Net Daily
- wowOwow
- X17

Blogs

Another form of online writing that cannot be denied is blogging. The one-sentence history is that blogs morphed out of what were once called web logs. Often the first-person, journal-style blogs are not considered to be mainstream media, and they shouldn't be. Many blogs ramble, have weak sources (or none at all), and are opinion-driven. But there are a chunk of blogs out there that should be read and taken seriously written by media influencers. Bloggers are often separated from members of the media, which makes sense to us. But there are some key bloggers who are considered to be influencers, and those bloggers are strong writers; they have solid sources, and they break news.

A Back-in-the-Day Story

One of the first examples of an online blog that worked and broke news was a news project developed by Yahoo and one of the first backpack journalists named Kevin Sites. He is sometimes referred to as the granddaddy of backpack journalism. Sites covered wars and conflicts around the world on his own and reported back to his blog, which was called *In the Hot Zone* (2007).

This was such a far cry from what other journalists were doing at the time; it was considered innovative and unheard of. Sites ended up breaking news on his blog that got picked up by mainstream press. Sites took all he needed to report in one backpack (thus the name "backpack journalism") into the field, and he was one of the first who shot footage from a small camera, conducted interviews, did the editing, the writing, and the reporting, and filed stories via a blog, plus appeared on camera on some evening news shows. This is considered commonplace today, and it is expected that you will know how to do several forms of writing and reporting; as we've discussed, no longer are broadcast and print separate—the lines are completely blurred and overlapped today. Backpack journalism is a style of reporting that is often called "mobile reporting."

To better understand his background, take a look at Sites's bio from Wikipedia and think about what entrepreneurial ideas you may have for your own blog reporting. Remember, when Sites started this project, it had not been done before; it was an idea he had, and he took it to fruition. He turned his blog reporting ideas into a book. What ideas do you have?

An Early Backpack Journalist

Kevin Sites is an American author and freelance journalist. He has spent nearly a decade covering global wars and disasters for ABC, NBC, CNN, and Yahoo! News. Dubbed by the trade press as the "granddaddy" of backpack journalists, Sites helped blaze the trail for intrepid reporters who work alone, carrying only a backpack of portable digital technology to shoot, write, edit, and transmit multimedia reports from the world's most dangerous places. His first book, *In the Hot Zone: One Man, One Year, Twenty Wars* (Harper Perennial—October 2007), shares his effort to put a human face on global conflict by reporting from every major war zone in one year.

In 2009, Sites was one of four cast members of the reality television series *Expedition Africa* on the History channel. The eight-part series followed Sites and three explorers as they retraced the journey of Henry Morton Stanley in his quest to find David Livingstone. It was this journey that allegedly ended with the famous phrase, "Dr. Livingstone, I presume?"

While Sites spent most of his early career producing and reporting for television network news with staff positions at ABC, NBC and CNN, he left the networks for the Internet in 2005, hired by Yahoo! to be its first correspondent for Yahoo! News. He spent one year traveling to all the major war zones in the world, reporting for his website *Kevin Sites in the Hot Zone*, unique at the time for its multimedia mix of text, video, and still images in its storytelling.

As a pioneer of the "SoJo" method of solo journalism/video journalism, or backpack journalism, Sites helped to galvanize the idea of the modern, mobile digital correspondent, traveling and reporting without a crew, carrying a backpack of portable digital technology to write, videotape, and transmit his multimedia reports.

Sites's assignments have brought him to nearly every region of the world, including Africa, the Middle East, Southeast Asia, Central Asia, South America, and Eastern Europe.

Sites grew up in Ohio and currently lives in Hong Kong. He was a professor at the Journalism and Media Studies Centre of the University of Hong Kong teaching bachelor's and master's programs. His most recent book is called *The Things They Cannot Say: Stories Soldiers Won't Tell You about What They've Seen, Done or Failed to Do in War.*

To read more about his work, please check out www.kevinsitesreports.com.

Blog Assignment

Your blog is your chance to show off all you have learned about writing across the media from the semester. While this assignment has become a favorite of students in past semesters, it is also challenging because a strong adherence to solid writing is expected.

Do not simply write in whatever online style you seem to think will work. This is not Facebook or a personal journal. A blog is still journalism. You are writing and reporting and creating. Do so responsibly. Find your "voice" but also write professionally, as if you were a journalist.

This assignment is much more than pasting photos you like and adding your personal commentary. Research and report. Use the AP stylebook. Conduct interviews. Write well. Discover your own blog voice. Each post is two hundred words. You will write five blog posts.

Your grade will reflect organization, presentation, visuals, a theme, professionalism, use of videos, layout, links, content, strong emphasis on writing style, use of the AP stylebook, reporting, research, use of interviews (ideally each post will have a quote from an interview you conducted), and use of attribution and quotes. Avoid typos. Avoid grammatical pitfalls. Think of each blog post as a print article. It must be in final form and should be well researched and edited.

Again, a minimum of five blog posts is required, with at least two hundred words each. Your blog should have a minimum of one thousand words. Do not interview family members or friends.

Deadline: Your blog is due in final form at deadline.

Your deadline is ______________________________.

We may have a blog "show and tell" to showcase your work. Work hard, but enjoy the process!

Enjoy! Consider using this blog on your résumé as a writing sample. Your blog should be professional and well written. Aim for work that could be published.

iPhone Reporting

Digital reporting, mobile journalism, backpack journalism—whatever you want to call it—this is a tool in your toolbox, and you must pay attention to this changing media world and adapt to changing technology. Decades ago, when Sites started out solo in the field, his equipment was very different for reporting than it is today. We are not spending time on the technology tools, because they will continue to change, but let's address what won't change—and that is coherent storytelling and clear writing.

To highlight iPhone reporting, let us take a look at the writing and work from one Washington, DC–based reporter named Neal Augenstein, who currently uses an iPhone to report for WTOP radio. He was one of the first reporters to do this nationally, and his radio station has done a superb job of transitioning from just radio broadcasting to multimedia journalism, including online journalism and iPhone reporting. We pulled a quick list off Augenstein's website to give you resources if you are interested in learning more about this form of writing and reporting. Please refer to iphonereporting.com for detailed and current information.

iphonereporting In The News www.iphonereporting.com

- **Poynter:** WTOP "Mojo" Pioneer Donates iPhone to Newseum
- **Talkers:** WTOP Reporter Does All Field Reports on iPhone or iPad

- **Journalism.co.uk:** Five Tips from a Radio Journalist Who Reports Solely from an iPhone and iPad
- **Poynter:** Radio Reporter Covers DC with an iPhone Only
- **TBD:** The Best #DCjournotweep Covering Local News
- **It's All Journalism Podcast:** Taking Old School Radio, Mobile—WTOP Reporter Neal Augenstein Shares How
- **Nieman Lab:** Your Handiest Reporting Tool May Be the Smartphone in Your Pocket
- **Web Video Chefs:** iPhone Reporting: A Lesson from Neal Augenstein
- **Reynolds Journalism Institute:** Expert Interview—Neal Augenstein
- **International Journalists' Network:** Eight Tips on Using the iPhone for Reporting
- **Journalism.co.uk:** 50 Blogs by Journalists, for Journalists
- **Reynolds Journalism Institute:** Mobile Reporting Apps

We wanted to highlight this reporter as an example of someone who has changed his work and writing focus from radio-specific broadcast writing to more of a multimedia approach to journalism, which is exactly what could be expected of you in your career.

This is his bio as written by WTOP news, his employer:

Ever since 1997, when Neal Augenstein kept nudging the then–news director to hire him as a part-time weekend reporter, he's had the great pleasure of being a reporter for WTOP.

Things have changed in many ways. When he walked in the door, the newsroom was still equipped with reel-to-reel tape recorders, and the portable bag phones that weighed as much as a bowling ball. Today, Neal is the first major market radio reporter who does most of his field production on an iPhone.

Through the years, Neal has covered many of the crimes and trials that have gripped the Washington community—including the Beltway Snipers, Chandra Levy, and, of course, Sept. 11, 2001. But ironically, listeners seem to remember the lifestyle and feature reports—cooking food on the dashboard of his car in 100-degree weather, butt-lifting underwear and pole dancing for guys.

Neal's been pleased to receive awards over the years for hard news, feature reporting, use of sound and sports. However, he's most proud when people he reports about tell him they believe his reporting is accurate, fair and in context.

Neal's ultimate honor is having listeners trust him and the WTOP team to provide information they need and enjoy in their life.

You can email Neal at naugenstein@wtop.com or follow him on Twitter @AugensteinWTOP.

To view Augenstein's iPhone reporting tips, visit: www.iphonereporting.com.

Exercises

1. Find five blogs or columns online to read and follow. Deconstruct one article from each site. Discuss how the sentences are short and the paragraphs are limited to one idea (or a few ideas).
2. What's happening is often what is written online. Details are often elaborated on in print. Take a look at both styles of writing, online and print. See which writing style holds your interest longer. What is done well? What would you do differently?

3. View *All the President's Men* in class or watch the movie (or read the book) on your own. Discuss how reporters Bob Woodward and Carl Bernstein found the story and how it unfolded, slowly, in *The Washington Post*. Discuss how this same story would unfold if it were breaking online.
4. Come up with a fun news story to break online. Write it up as if it were going to be published online. Experience writing as if you were an online journalist and try the one-idea-per-paragraph approach.
5. Take the same fun news story from exercise four and write it up as if it were going to appear in an online blog. Experience writing as if you were an online blogger with major influence.
6. Take a print article and rewrite it for online publication. Your goal will be to cut the article in half and keep only one idea per paragraph. Give yourself one class period to do this as your deadline.

Reading List

Writing Web Copy

By Janet Mizrahi

Today a website is as important as a company logo. Often a website is a member or customer's first impression of an organization, so a professional, easy-to-navigate, well-designed, and clearly written website is a basic business necessity. But because reading on a screen differs from reading on a printed page, web writers face distinct challenges.

Web writing differs from print writing in several significant ways. First, when writing for the web, the writer is typically part of a team. Websites integrate technology with copy, so writers collaborate with web designers, software engineers, and other members of an organization who have input into the site's content and usability. Another difference is that web writers use media such as sound and video as well as two-dimensional graphics and integrate these elements into copy. This blending of technology with words requires writers to think about their task in new ways.

Web Audience Analysis

Sites are designed with a specific audience in mind, whether it is broad (such as the audience for CNN.com) or specific and narrow (such as a site geared to cardiac surgeons or IT specialists). So as with every writing task, writers must consider their audience. Are the readers teenagers who have grown up with a mouse in hand or are they elderly people who have trouble reading small print? To best provide a site's readership with an optimal experience, the writer must know readers' limitations and expectations.

All web readers share a few common needs: They visit a site for information, whether that is a treatment option or an exercise regimen. And they all expect to access that information fast. If readers don't find what they need quickly, they will leave a site.

But beyond those similarities, readerships will vary greatly. A detailed reader's profile will help a web writer create a site that will be more successful in attracting and keeping readers. Begin the audience analysis portion of the first stage of the writing process (assessing) by completing Table 1.1 in chapter 1. But when writing for the web, go beyond those basic steps and create several *personas*[1] using the facts you've gathered about the site's readership.

A persona takes demographic data and actually creates a narrative about the typical user. This persona may include a photograph of a representative user, information about why the user visits the site, quotes gathered from interviews about using the site, and the user's web habits. A persona is similar to a novelist's character sketch and can be very useful when thinking about who is reading a site's copy. Use the "Persona Template" at the end of this chapter to help you create a persona for your user.

Many organizations conduct *usability* tests to assess a site's effectiveness. These tests are designed to measure the user's experience, including ease of use, error frequency, and satisfaction. Conducting a usability test can be as simple as sitting down with a user and watching how he or she navigates a site or as complicated as conducting surveys or focus groups. The savvy writer will consider usability test results when evaluating web copy.

A final point: It is important to remember that the web is indeed "worldwide." Audiences from Japan to Jamaica can access an organization's website. So while we may have a specific reader in mind when we write copy, we must also be aware that our readership is entirely out of our control unless a site is password protected. If you are writing sensitive material, be aware that anyone, anywhere can—and likely will—read it.

Determining Purpose

As we have discussed, websites primarily provide information, which calls for an objective, clear, and concise writing style. Yet many sites are also designed to persuade visitors to purchase a product or service. Visitmexico.com (http://www.visitmexico.com/wb/Visitmexico/Visi_Home?show=regions) is clearly a site dedicated to providing information to potential tourists. But that information is designed to persuade readers to choose Mexico as a vacation destination. It does so by offering complete, factual information arranged in layers that are intuitively organized and written in a concise, easy-to-read format.

Some sites exist solely to entertain and are written in a distinct style to serve the site's audience. For example, the mock political news site *The Onion* is sarcastic; the entertainment site *E! Online* is gossipy. When a site's audience expects an attitude or voice, the writer must deliver.

Reading on the Screen versus on the Printed Page

Reading on a printed page differs from reading on a computer screen. Reading on a screen takes nearly 25% longer than reading a printed page.[2] Most traditional print copy is read in a linear fashion, from beginning to end. But because of a website's interactivity, readers jump from page to page. This type of reading is called nonlinear—readers select a section and click to read it.

Readers tend to scan web pages and sites, focusing only on what interests them. To organize a website to meet this expectation, writers categorize copy into a series of headings in an organization style called *hierarchical branching*,[3] which can be likened to an outline with headings and subheadings.

As readers scan, they have definite expectations about web copy, the most basic of which is *speed*. They want to "get it" as fast as possible, so web prose needs to be clear and concise. Speed also refers to the length of time a page takes to load; as broadband capabilities have improved, readers have come to expect pages to load almost instantly. If a page takes too long to appear, readers quickly lose interest and click away, often out of a site entirely.

Web readers also expect a site to have *visual logic* and *organization*. Although usability experts do not agree about how many clicks is too many to find a piece of information, they do agree that a site's organization must be intuitive—that is, readers must be able to seamlessly access information. Readers access information in layers, so the writer must organize web pages accordingly. Finally, web readers expect information to be updated regularly; sites with stale information lose credibility with today's readers.

Web Writing

A writing strategy called *chunking* works best when composing for nonlinear reading. As was discussed in chapter 4, chunking arranges information into bite-sized portions of about one hundred words so they can fi t on one computer screen without requiring scrolling. Chunking is typifi ed by abridged paragraphs and short, easy-to-follow sentences. To appeal to web readers' need for speed, web copy must be tightly edited for conciseness and efficiency. A basic rule to follow is to halve what would be written for print.[4]

Site organization. A website's "face" is the *home page*. The home page should immediately express the site's purpose and set its tone or personality with colors, graphics, writing style, and visual elements. Readers don't spend much time on a home page, so its material should be organized intuitively, allowing visitors to quickly access information or begin tasks. The example of the home page in Figure 9.1 illustrates this organizational approach.

The home page provides links to *destination* or *information* pages, often via a *pathway* page.

A destination page (sometimes called an information page) contains the information the reader seeks. Each destination page should have a clear title so when visitors arrive, they

Figure 5.1. Home page.

Montecito Bank and Trust's home page provides a clear snapshot of the site's offerings.

immediately know they are in the right place. Figure 9.2 is a destination page from the same organization previously illustrated.

A *pathway page* is an intermediary page that guides readers to a specific information page. This type of page can be likened to a table of contents[5] and is often just specific headings containing links to information pages. Often this approach is used by large organizations whose websites contain many layers of information.

When developing web copy, it's important to have a clear picture of the site's organization. A *site map* is a graphical overview of a website, showing hierarchical relationships between pages. Before writing website copy, create this map and define the routes your readers will have to take to obtain specifi c information.

Most websites are arranged with *navigation tabs* on the top of a page. For example, on the home page for Visitmexico.com, we are greeted with colorful tabs labeled "About Mexico," "Destinations," "Activities," "Vacation Theme," "Travel Experiences," and "Events." The left side of the home page has links to both the same destinations as the tabs and additional ones. When the visitor clicks "Activities," a destination page with four subheadings lists 30 options. The reader may choose to delve deeper into any one of them by clicking. Each clickable, descriptive subheading contains another layer of information that is obtainable by clicking the specific page.

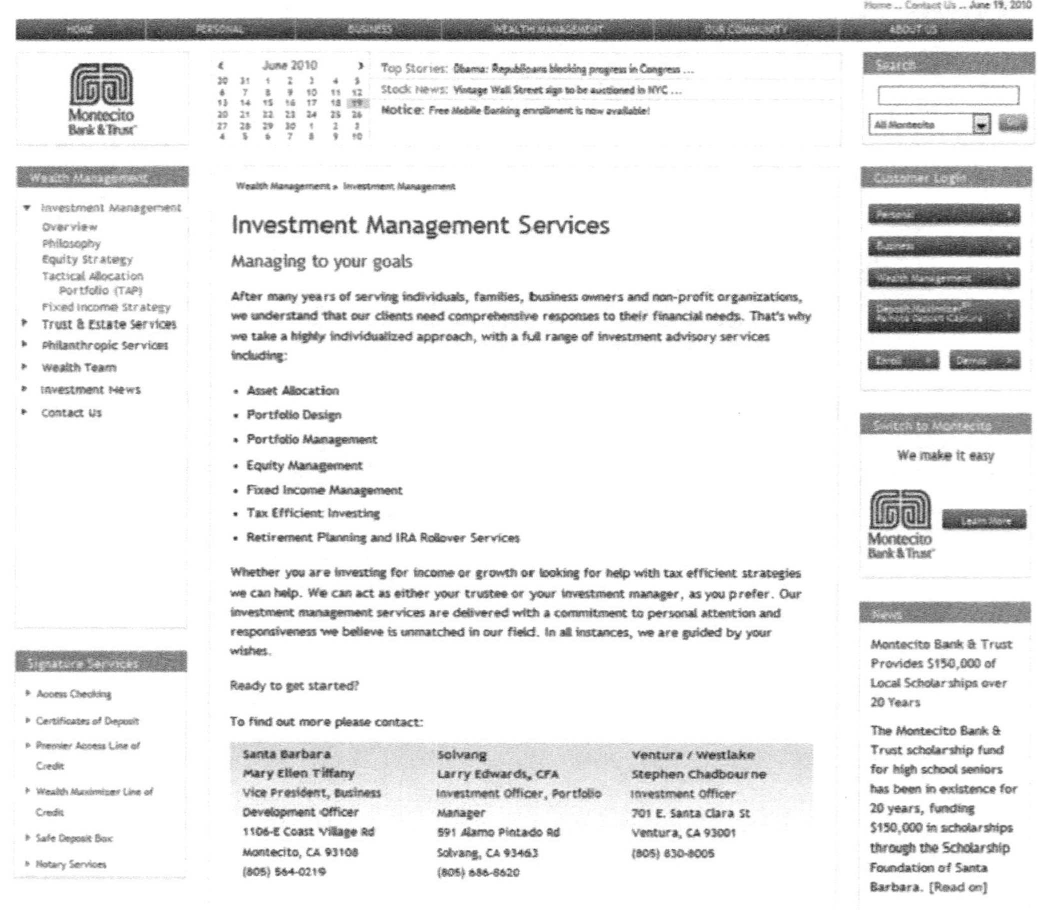

Figure 5.2. Destination page.

Source: http://www.montecito.com/Depts/Wealth/Default.aspx

A well-organized site is key to its success and includes the following elements.

Scannability. Because web readers scan rather than read word for word, effective web copy is written to meet this need. To create scannable copy, highlight words that capture main ideas. That being said, too many highlighted words create a blur that will confuse rather than aid readers. Avoid long blocks of type; keep paragraphs short, aiming for no more than eight lines. Limit the number of characters per line to 70 for optimum scannability (a character is a letter, punctuation mark, or space); lines longer that those with 70 characters are hard for the eye to track.

Another technique to make text scannable is to use *bulleted points* and *headings*. Bulleted lists make text scannable because readers can glance down a list much faster than they can read a dense paragraph containing the same information. For example, look at the difference in scannability in the two paragraphs that follow. The fi rst is a paragraph intended for the printed page. The second is that same information written for the web.

> Santa Barbara's temperate weather and unique history make it an ideal destination. Just 150 miles north of Los Angeles, Santa Barbara boasts many cultural and recreational

> attractions for the whole family to enjoy. Begin with a tour of the historical landmarks in the downtown area and take in the Presidio and Mission, both built in the 18th century. Santa Barbara's Botanical Gardens feature native plants and magnificent vistas, and the harbor offers whale watching cruises. Enjoy the outdoors on pedal go-carts, or take a kayak off Stearns Wharf. Surf, golf, or horseback ride, or take a day trip to Santa Barbara's picturesque wine country or nearby, Dutch-themed Solvang.

Santa Barbara's ideal weather and history make a great destination, with cultural and recreational activities such as:

- Historical tours of Presidio and Mission
- Botanic Gardens
- Harbor cruises and whale watching
- Biking
- Golf
- Kayaking
- Horseback riding
- Day trips to Solvang or wine country

Each bulleted point in the second paragraph would be a link that the visitor could click to obtain another layer of information. Notice the number of words in the second paragraph is reduced by more than half, and the selection is easy to scan.

Headings and *subheadings* also help readers scan text. By breaking text into blocks labeled with a heading that summarizes the content, the reader can easily focus on specific areas of interest. *Subheadings* are miniheadings[6] that break up long text, mostly to enhance visual appeal. Headings and subheadings should be short and indicative, explaining the subsequent content with specificity. Use nouns and verbs, and avoid cutesy headings meant to entertain rather than inform. Many headings and subheadings omit articles (a, an, the) if doing so does not compromise meaning.

Interactivity. Integrating various media into a website can make it dynamic and interactive. When composing web copy, the writer should think about how words can mix with visuals to enhance meaning. Various media are available: sound, video, animation, or images. All are accessed using links. Links are similar to visual aids used in a speech or items in an appendix of a written report. It's worth noting that too much media interspersed within text can detract from meaning. Graphics and sound should be inserted to enhance meaning, not simply because it's technologically possible to do so.

Interactivity poses another challenge. If you provide a link that takes users outside of your site, they may never find their way back. Another negative of links that send readers out of your site is that some sites evaluate their effectiveness by "stickiness," or how long a user stays on a page or in a site. If a link sends readers away from the site, the stickiness factor decreases.

Page length. Because web readers are typically in a hurry, they're less likely to scroll down a page to read more information. If you cannot limit a web page to one screen, consider providing *anchors*. Anchors are headings that appear at the top of a page and link to sections or subheadings within a long page. Anchors provide another way to help web readers get where they want to go faster.

Web Writing Style

Web writing demands economy above all. Impatient readers have millions of website choices, so websites need to be concise and clear. The following elements should be considered as you write web copy.

Inverted pyramid structure. When writing web copy, organize material according to the inverted pyramid style we discussed in chapter 3. Begin with the most important information, which is summarized in the first paragraph. Arrange subsequent information in descending order of importance. Since readers may not scroll down, keep critical information to one screen and be aware that only readers who are very interested in a topic will stick with it long enough to scroll down several panels.

Paragraph length and style. While all writers need to be aware of how words appear on a page, web writers must be particularly sensitive to the visual aspect of their copy. Keep paragraphs short to avoid dense blocks of text. Break up paragraphs with bulleted lists and use highlighting to emphasize key words.

For maximum usability, build paragraphs written for the web around one idea. And just like your English teacher taught, begin the paragraph with a topic sentence. The reason is simple: Often web readers will only read the first line of a paragraph.

Web writers sometimes use spacing to emphasize a point. For example, to draw attention to an important idea, the writer may use a one-sentence paragraph. This journalistic technique works well on the screen but should be used sparingly.

Sentence length. It may be surprising to learn that a sentence of as few as 20 words is considered diffi cult to read; a sentence of seven words is considered easy. Knowing that web readers are busy and impatient, writers need to be aware of sentence length as a way to simplify web copy. Aim for sentences of between 10–20 words at the most. Avoid long, rambling sentences with embedded phrases such as this:

> A person working out for the first time should be monitored by an experienced trainer, who has either been licensed or who has been involved in the exercise business for a long enough time to be knowledgeable about the body, and should be aware that muscle soreness and aches are to be expected.

The sentence revised should read as follows:

> People new to exercise should be monitored by an experienced, licensed trainer and can expect some muscle soreness.

While web copy should aim for shorter rather than longer sentences, your writing still needs to be rhythmical and conversational. Avoid series of short, choppy sentences, and always read web copy aloud to make sure it flows and just sounds right.

Professionalism. A site with grammatical errors and typos screams *unprofessional.* One of the first things teachers warn students to watch for when analyzing a website's credibility is typos. Other signs of unprofessional (and therefore noncredible) sites are broken links, dated information, and authors who do not provide their credentials. Professional sites are carefully edited, and any errors are fi xed immediately.

Tone. A site's personality is reflected in its writing voice or tone. A key characteristic of web copy is its conversational tone, so it's entirely appropriate to use "you" when talking to your user. In so doing, you will also avoid passive voice and extra words.

A website's tone depends on its level of formality. For example, a site for a global organization would demand a professional tone with precise, correct English. Such a site would avoid fluffy language, rambling sentences, and words with emotional connotation or denotation. A small, local business might emphasize a more casual, neighborly tone to appeal to nearby residents.

Sites dedicated to selling a product may use a persuasive, marketing-style approach that relies on exaggerated claims, generalizations, high-pressure language, and superlatives.[7] Websites using these strategies abound, and many are probably successful. Some consumers undoubtedly respond to high-pressure techniques ("Buy now—limited time offer!") and overthe-top claims. Here's a perfect example taken from Hoodia.com.

> Make your brain think your [sic] full with Hoodiamax and lose 1–6 lbs per week!

The fact that the claim includes the wrong form of a word ("your" instead of "you're") might turn off some readers, but many will ignore or be unaware of the error and be taken in by the unsubstantiated claim. Still, savvy web users would click away from such a site quickly; more and more users are knowledgeable about how to evaluate web content for accuracy. Additionally, many people find "salesy" language a turnoff and prefer objective explanations of a product or service when conducting research. Use caution with obvious sales-driven phrasing.

Word choice. Simple, well-known words work best for web copy. If text requires technical language and a portion of the intended audience is nontechnical, defi ne the jargon. For example, if writing about a medical condition for a lay audience, the writer might word an explanation like this:

> Cardiac infarction—also called a heart attack—is the number one killer of women.

When in doubt, choose the simpler word or term.

Conclusion

Web writing requires understanding the unique needs of web readers. Because the web audience needs to access information quickly, the writer must be especially sensitive to clarity and conciseness. Web writers must also be familiar with basic usability strategies to create meaningful, effective websites. The web also provides writers with almost endless possibilities to embed other media within their words. This unique capability makes web writing distinct from other media we've discussed.

Persona Template

Name	
Photo	
Occupation	
Web habits	
Quotes	
Knowledge level (specific to product/organization)	
Goals (specifi c to product/organization)	
Needs/wants	
Skills	
Narrative	

All the News Fit to Post? Comparing News Content on the Web to Newspapers, Television, and Radio

By Scott Maier

A content analysis of 3,900 news stories examined how online news differs in coverage from newspapers, network television, cable television, and radio, finding that 60% of the top stories on news Web sites covered the same topics as covered by legacy media. But fewer than a third of news stories hyperlinked by blogs and social media corresponded with mainstream media top stories. The results indicate that journalism's agenda-setting role, though dissipating, remains viable in the fragmenting media universe. Audiences turning to news Web sites will find the dominant stories of the day plus fresh perspectives on national and world events.

The migration of news consumers to online sources has arrived at a pivotal juncture. While most media continued to see audiences shrink, only two platforms experienced growth in recent years. One was cable news, reaping a surge of viewers tuned into a lively presidential election. The other was online news. "We may well look back at 2008 as [a] milestone in the history of the Web as a news destination," the Project for Excellence in Journalism reported in its annual *State of the News Media*. "As a source for national and international news, according to survey data, the Web surpassed all other media except for television."[1]

As underscored by layoffs and other desperate cost-saving measures by newspapers and other news operations, the growing migration to online news sources has contributed to traditional media's economic turmoil.[2] But does the shift also represent a sea-change in news content? If news stories found online are essentially the same as news presented in newspapers and electronic media, then the transformation represents little more than a move to an all-digital format of news. But if news coverage is substantially different, then online news represents not only a change in medium but also content. This is more than an academic distinction. Online news adds little breadth to the media mix—or the public's access to diverse news perspectives—if the medium basically covere the same stories as its traditional counterparts. Journalism's agenda-setting role, focusing people's attention on a small number of issues, would be largely unaltered.[3] At the other extreme, journalism's role in society as information provider and community builder is diminished if online news coverage lacks scope and depth, or if the public's world view—as represented by the news—is largely based on the news medium each audience reads or tunes into.

In a secondary analysis of data collected in 2008 and the first half of 2009 by the Project for Excellence in Journalism (PEJ), this study examines how news Web sites compare to traditional media in story choices and depth of coverage. PEJ's annual *State of the News Media* identifies the year's top news stories and provides instructive analysis on how news media differ thematically (i.e., the percentage of international news coverage carried by each type of news outlet). This study provides a different perspective by asking, in any given week, to what extent would audiences find the same stories online as they would in newspapers, on television, or on radio? In doing so, this study seeks to determine what proportion of the top national and international news stories covered by traditional media—newspapers, network television, cable television, and radio—also were the focus of online news services.

This study also evaluates the depth of coverage. To what extent do online news sites and traditional media go beyond summary "headline news" in covering their top stories? In addition, this study analyzes how news stories hyperlinked by blogs and social media correspond to mainstream media's top stories. The results provide a baseline measure of Internet news scope and depth for this pivotal time of transition to online news.

Changes in news consumption have far-reaching implications. If media fragmentation accelerates political polarization, with audiences narrowing their news focus to match their personal views, the role of mass communication in nurturing a civic agenda is potentially transformed.[4] As audiences increasingly customize their news choices, Chaffee and Metzger contend in a provocatively titled article, "The End of Mass Communication?," people isolate themselves from the larger public discourse and, "in the process, undermine the very notion of a larger public discourse."[5] While a common agenda may be diminished, new communication technologies also could increase diversity of news content, broadening the information flow and giving greater voice to people whose agendas are often overlooked by mass media.[6]

Background and Related Studies

News consumption has been undergoing change for decades as audiences shift from newspapers to network television to cable TV and more recently to online news—or tune out altogether from mainstream news outlets. The Pew Research Center for the People and the Press, which has been tracking these changes, reports that since the 1990s the proportion of Americans who say they read a newspaper on any given day has declined about 40%, while regular network television viewing has fallen by half. By contrast, online news consumption has grown at an accelerating pace, with six in ten Americans now getting some news online in a typical day.[7]

Research has shown that the loss of newspaper and network television audiences can be attributed, at least in part, to gains in online news consumption,[8] though displacement may be a recent phenomenon.[9] "The trend is unmistakable," the Pew Research Center reports. "Fewer Americans are reading print newspapers as more turn to the Internet for their news. And while the percentage of people who read newspapers online is growing rapidly, especially among younger generations, that growth has not offset the decline in print readership."[10] Nonetheless, a sizable segment of the population—about 23%—tends to get its news from both traditional and online sources.[11]

New Media. In recent years, Weblogs and social media also have captured new audiences, with a quarter of U.S. adults now saying they read blogs,[12] and more than a third of American adult Internet users claiming they maintain a profile on an online social network site (up from 8% in 2005).[13] Despite the growth of blog use, Hargrove and Stempel found that blogs in their early years were not a major source of news. In their 2006 national survey, only 12% of respondents reported they had obtained news from a blog in the past week; by contrast, 34% got news from a Web site at least once in the week.[14] John Kelly, founder and chief scientist at Morningside Analytics, contends that the "blogos-phere" and mainstream media are complementary players, with blogs commonly linking back to newspaper sites and other legacy media outlets.[15] This supposition is also supported by Singer[16] and Reese et. al[17] in studies that indicate a symbiotic relationship in which blogs and traditional journalism rely on each other for source material.

News Content Researchers have sought to evaluate differences between Internet news and mainstream media, though the focus has tended to be on how the message is delivered rather than what is communicated.[18] In a study of print and online versions of six Colorado newspapers, Singer documented that online content provided a stronger "local" orientation than its printed counterparts, but overall, online material was "shovelware" repositioned from print.[19] A content analysis of news coverage in 2007 showed that newspapers and five prominent news Web sites shared similar news judgments regarding story topics and story prominence, but newspapers offered depth and breadth unmatched by the online sites.[20] Two other studies also highlighted media homogeneity: A content analysis by Just, Belt, and Crigler found online and legacy media coverage of the 2008 presidential campaign to be similar in tone and content[21] Hoffman reported that mobilizing information—information aiding people to act—was no more prevalent in Web newspapers than in their print counterparts.[22]

News Consonance. A long line of communication scholarship supports the proposition that news story selection is determined by professional "gatekeepers" who hold similar news values, resulting in a more-or-less standardized media agenda.[23] Numerous studies have documented that network television newscasts and, to a lesser degree, newspapers are highly similar in selection of news topics.[24] News consonance, in which media tend to cover the same issues or events, is not necessarily a negative phenomenon. As noted by Riffe and his colleagues, "Story duplication is arguably functional, by focusing a pluralistic public's attention on common threats, and in some cases building consensus. ... And agenda-setting is enhanced by consonance, wherein different media or channels repeatedly emphasize the same issues."[25]

As media options grow, the question is raised whether the public still consumes a common diet of news.[26] In an analysis of national survey data, Hollander found that the fragmented media marketplace has contributed to political polarization in which partisans increasingly seek news sources compatible with their beliefs, while others turn to more entertainment-oriented fare.[27] Hollander observed: "A fragmented media marketplace is one full of choices, a buffet from which individuals can choose sources more in line with their closely held beliefs or avoid those they see as threatening their core values. ... But choice for many, when it comes to the news means not necessarily tuning in, but instead tuning elsewhere."[28]

Changes in news consumption have generated competing theories as to whether fragmentation of media audiences undermines public discourse.[29] One hypothesis suggests that fragmented news audiences weaken the media's ability to provide a common public agenda—that is, a shared basis of information on which to think about and act.[30] Another hypothesis suggests that online news and information may be so highly redundant with mainstream media that the agenda-setting role of media persists despite audience fragmentation.[31] Testing these competing theories, Lee conducted a content analysis of blog posts and mainstream media news stories during the 2004 presidential campaign. His study found the blog news agenda was similar to that of mainstream media, "indicating a fairly stable agenda across mainstream and Internet news outlets, despite the diversification of information channels."[32]

Hypotheses and Research Questions

In summary, the Internet clearly has accelerated the fragmentation of the mass media audience as more people turn to Web sources for news, opinion, and entertainment. Migration of audiences to the Internet poses an economic threat to legacy news media, but less evident is how the transition affects the public's perspectives on the news. Whether news online differs substantially from other media is a threshold issue in agenda setting. As McCombs posits, media fragmentation will lead to the demise of journalism's agenda-setting role only if "the agendas to which people are exposed to on the Web are highly divergent, rather than the highly redundant agendas found in the traditional news media."[33] This study seeks to evaluate how different the storylines on news Web sites are from news storylines provided by their "legacy" counterparts—newspapers, network television, cable television, and radio. In addition, the study examines differences in news topics between institutional news Web sites and "new media" as represented by blogs and social media. The following hypotheses and research questions are posed:

H1: Top national and international stories covered by news Web sites correspond to a large extent with the top stories covered by newspapers, network television, cable television, and radio.

H2: News coverage by news Web sites is similar in breadth and diversity of story topics to news coverage by newspapers, network television, cable television, and radio.

H3: When reporting on the same news topics, news Web sites provide similar depth of coverage as do newspapers, network television, cable television, and radio.

RQ1: What news stories do blogs and social media sites most frequently hyperlink to? To what extent do news topics focused on by new media correspond with the leading storylines of mainstream media?

Method

This study builds on the Project for Excellence in Journalism's News Coverage Index, which examines in real time what is being covered by the U.S. news media. A listing of top stories by five news sectors is provided by PEJ in a weekly report posted at www.journalism.org. The news index, analyzing about 70,000 stories a year from forty-eight news outlets, is considered "the largest effort ever" to measure the content of the news media on a continuing basis." In addition, this study uses the results of the New Media Index, a companion index launched by PEJ in January 2009 to identify what news stories bloggers and social media Web sites, herein defined as new media, most closely follow.

Sectors and Units of Study. The News Coverage Index tracks the five main sectors of mainstream media: newspapers, network television, cable television, online news, and radio. The sample is purposive, designed to be "illustrative but not strictly representative of the media universe."[35] For example, the print sector includes a selection of first-tier newspapers (i.e., *New York*

Times and *USA Today*), second-tier newspapers (i.e., *Kansas City Star* and *San Jose Mercury News*), and third-tier newspapers (i.e., [Spokane] *Spokesman-Review* and the *Anniston* [Alabama] *Star*). Only national and international stories that begin on A1 arc included in the sample. Network news includes the major broadcast news shows on ABC, NBC, CBS, and PBS, as well as the news segments of network morning talk shows. The cable news sample includes daytime and prime-time cable news on CNN, Fox News, and MSNBC. The radio news sample includes National Public Radio's morning news, talk shows, and headline feeds from national radio organizations like CBS and CNN.

Online news—the fulcrum of this study's focus—includes five prominent Web sites: Yahoo News, MSNBC.com, CNN.com, AOL News, and Google News. Starring in 2009, the online sector was expanded to include seven more top-viewed news sites: NYTimes.com, BBC News (international version), Reuters.com, Foxnews.com, USAToday.com, Washingtonpost.com, and ABCNews.com. The online sector purposely includes a mix of online news sites that produce their own content and those that aggregate news from throughout the Web. For each site, content is captured each week day on a rotating time schedule.

The index's primary variable, topic of the story, is quantified by the percentage of the news that the storyline consumes in any given week. The measurement used to determine top stories in broadcast and cable is time, and in text-based media, words. As explained by the Project for Excellence in Journalism, "The industry term for this is 'newshole'—the space given to news content. ... This way all media are represented in the same measurement—percentage."[36] For example, broadcast coverage of ground events in Iraq is measured by the time allocated to the story over a week divided by the total time of all of the week's stories analyzed; newspaper coverage is measured by the number of words given a story over a week divided by the total word count for the week's front-page stories analyzed. Intercoder agreement on this variable is 87%.[37]

New Media Index. To better understand how social media shape public interaction with the news, the Project for Excellence in Journalism introduced in 2009 a companion index that tracks what news stories bloggers and other online commentators discuss. PEJ researchers use two Web-tracking sites, Technorati and Tcerocket, to monitor links to news articles embedded on the more than 100 million blogs and 250 million pieces of social media tracked by the two sites.[38] Percentage of links provides a gauge of news influence. "Each time a news blog or social media Web page adds a link to its site directing its readers to a news story, it suggests that the author places at least some importance on the content of that article. The user may or may not agree with the contents of the article, but they feel it is important enough to draw the reader's attention to it," PEJ says in describing its method.[39] The New Media Index uses percentage of links, rather than newshole, because Web sites have essentially no limits in terms of length or space. A list of the top five linked-to stories is compiled Monday through Friday, followed by a content analysis using the same coding method applied to tracking mainstream media with the News Coverage Index.

Secondary Analysis. To provide a timely perspective of differences in news content between online news and other media, this study required building a database drawn from the weekly News Coverage Index posted on the PEJ Web site. An electronic copy was made of each of the weekly reports from the first week of January 2008 through June 2009. These copies were converted into an Excel spreadsheet and a unique identifier was assigned for each medium and story. The completed Excel file yielded 3,900 cases, providing a database of each medium's top ten stories for each week during the year and a half studied.

The Excel file was imported into SPSS 16.0 for data aggregation and statistical analysis. Evaluating the extent that online news sites cover the same stories as other mainstream media required reorganizing the data to track common storylines week by week. To achieve this analysis, a separate database was created for each medium, followed by a merge with the online news index matching cases by week and by story ID. The resulting four databases yielded week-by-week data of online's top news stories in side-by-side comparison with the top story lines of newspapers, network television, cable television, and radio. For example, in the first week of January 2008, seven of the top ten stories dominating online news sites were identical in topic to the top ten stories found on newspaper front pages. To conduct further analysis, additional variables were computed to measure percentages of newshole in common and their differences, as well as to count the number of news stories covered online in tandem with another medium in any given week. A similar process of data aggregation and analysis was used to examine the New Media Index. Because the New Media Index was introduced in the final six months of this study, this data set consists of a relatively small sample of 110 cases.

Results

H1 predicted consonance in story selection by news Web sites and legacy media. The hypothesis was supported. The study of eighteen months of news coverage documented that major news Web sites more often than not concur with legacy media as to the major news stories worth covering. In a week-by-week analysis of each medium's top ten news stories, this investigation found that 59% of the storylines on Web news sites covered the same topics as those covered by newspapers, television, and radio. The online news mix was most similar to network television, in which 63.1% of the same top news stories were covered, compared to 58.3% same-story coverage by radio, 58.2% by newspapers, and 56.3% by cable television. These figures are in line with differences in the selection of stories among traditional media. For example, newspapers and network television covered the same story lines almost in identical proportion with each other as with online media.

The commonality of news agendas is even more pronounced among the top ten news storylines across the eighteen-month period studied, 2008 and the first half of 2009. Of the ten stories receiving the most coverage by news Web sites, eight stories also ranked among the top ten stories covered by newspapers and network television; cable TV provided top coverage for seven of the same ten stories; radio's top ten overlapped with six of the Web's top ten story topics. All but newspapers, which focused most heavily on the U.S. economy, devoted the year's top coverage to the 2008 campaign. In fact, the top six stories for the eighteen months studied were nearly identical among all five media sectors, though not ranked in the same order (see Table 1).

H2 predicted that online news coverage is similar in breadth and diversity to news coverage by legacy media. This hypothesis was supported in part. Diversity is evaluated by how widely dispersed or concentrated news coverage is among story topics.[40] In this study, diversity is assessed by two measures: space (how much of the total newshole is consumed by the top ten stories) and story count (the number of times that the story made the Top Ten list). By both measures, a small number of top news stories dominated news coverage, regardless of medium. In fact, two story topics—the 2008 campaign and the troubled economy— accounted for more

Table 1. Comparing Online's Top 10 News Stories to Story Rank by Legacy Media, January 2008 through June 2009

Storyline	Web News Top 10	Newspaper Story Rank	Network TV Story Rank	Cable TV Story Rank	Radio Story Rank
2008 Campaign	1	2	1	1	1
U.S. Economy	2	1	2	2	2
New Obama Admn.	3	4	3	3	3
Iraq War	4	3	5	8	5
Auto Industry	5	6	4	6	6
Terrorism	6	5	7	4	4
Pakistan	7	8	18	40	14
Iran	8	13	9	7	11
Afghanistan	9	10	11	15	12
Olympics	10	12	8	52	18

Bold = Ranked a Top 10 story

than a third of the newshole for the eighteen months studied. Relative to other media sectors, online news was a leader in diversity of news coverage, but the differences were generally small. In terms of newshole, coverage was least concentrated at Web news sites (with the top ten stories representing 44.4% of coverage), followed by network TV (47.7%), newspapers (48.4%), radio (53.4%), and cable TV (64.6%). Network TV devoted the smallest proportion of its story count to the top ten stories (40.9%i), followed by online news (43.7%), cable TV (45.3%), radio (45.4%), and newspapers (53.8%).

H3 predicted that when news topics converged, Web sites provided as much depth of coverage to these stories as their mainstream medium counterparts. The hypothesis was generally supported. As shown in Table 2, the correlation of depth of story coverage (measured by percent of newshole) by news Web sites in relation to every other medium studied is strong and statistically significant ($p < .001$). For example, the correlation of newshole devoted to stories covered by both news Web sites and newspapers is 0.89. This indicates that online news sites not only often reported the same stories as legacy media, but when they did, they provided a similar degree of attention in terms of frequency and depth of coverage.

Paired-sample *t*-tests were conducted to further evaluate stories covered in tandem by online news sites and other news media (see Table 3). The results of this week-by-week comparison show that Web news sites devoted a larger portion of newshole to these stories than newspapers, but the differences were small (on average, less than 1% of news-hole). Web news coverage was slightly less extensive than offered by network television or radio, but, again, the differences were less than 1% of newshole. Only cable television news, which on average devoted three percentage points more of its newshole to these top stories, offered substantively more coverage than online news.

Table 2. Pearson Correlation Coefficients for Depth of News Coverage by News Web Sites in Relation to Mainstream Media

	Correlation with Web News Coverage	*n*	Sig.
Newspaper	.889	454	<.001
Network TV	.904	492	<.001
Cable TV	.808	439	<.001
Radio	.826	455	<.001

When mainstream media and news Web sites covered the same news topics (*n* = number of stories in common), the proportion of newshole devoted to these stories tended to be similar.

Table 3. Paired Samples *t*-Test Comparing Differences in Depth of News Coverage (Percentage of Newshole) of Stories Covered both by News Web Sites and legacy Media

	Mean Difference	*t*	df	Sig.
Online—Newspaper	0.59	2.58	453	0.010
Online—Network TV	–0.30	–1.21	491	>.05
Online—Cable TV	–3.04	–1.72	438	0.001
Online—Radio	–0.55	–1.40	454	>.05

Online news devoted a similar proportion of newshole to top stones as traditional media covering the same story topics.

R1 asked whether news topics focused on by new media correspond with the leading storylines of mainstream media. In late January 2009, the Project for Excellence in Journalism began tracking news links that appeared in blogs and social media Web pages. An analysis of the initial data suggests that these new media sites concentrate on news topics substantially differently than mainstream media (including news Web sites). Only 29.1% of the 110 top news story topics identified by the New Media Index were the same as identified by PEJ's News Coverage Index tracking mainstream media—starkly different from the 59% overall story match among Web news sites and newspapers, television, and radio news. When both mainstream and new media platforms focused on the same storylines, coverage was slightly more extensive in blogs and social media, though the differences were not statistically significant in this small sample (t [31] = .664, $p > .05$). As with legacy media and news Web sites, new media devoted more attention in the first half of 2009 to the nation's economic crisis and to the new Obama administration than any other story. But the remainder of the top ten news topics converged only in shared attention to news developments in Iran and the outbreak of swine flu. Examples of news topics that dominated new media—but didn't even make any other media top weekly story lists—include government torture policies, a reported decline in organized religion, and the right-ward turn of a European parliamentary election.

Discussion

This study indicates that, in any given week, news consumers who turn to major news Web sites are more likely than not to get a mix of national and international news that follows the storylines covered by legacy media. In this regard, online news media are similar to their mainstream counterparts. Just as one wouldn't expect to see exactly the same lineup of stories on the front page of newspapers as on the network news, the match-up is imperfect: On average, about six in ten of the top news stories on news Web sites correspond with the storylines found on the front pages of newspapers, an national television, or on radio. The strong correlation of storylines covered by news Web sites and other news media indicates that online news outlets not only tended to choose the same top stories as legacy media, but when they did, they often shared strikingly similar news values in how each storyline is played in terms of frequency and depth of coverage. For example, the troubled economy, the Iraq war, and the new presidential administration universally received abundant coverage, yet news consumers would have to go online to find as much coverage of political unrest in Tibet or the Georgia-Russia conflict (both covered extensively by Web news sites) or turn to newspapers to learn as much about immigration issues or troubles with the Federal National Mortgage Association (both of which were top newspaper weekly stories).

In a time of media turmoil, these are important and reassuring findings: Online news services cover the mast important news stories (at least as defined by conventional media) with depth that goes well beyond cursory "headline news." Yet news Web sites also offer an independent view of what is newsworthy, providing a news mix in which four of the week's ten top stories differ, on average, from those covered by mainstream media. This indicates that major Web news sites today do not simply mirror the selection of news stories leading in print and broadcast. In the fragmenting media universe, audiences turning to news Web sites will find the dominant stories of the day, as well as a selection of news reports offering fresh perspective on events shaping the nation and the world.

It is also noteworthy that online news media offered greater news breadth than any other media sector. But it is a dubious honor, considering how highly concentrated all media were in their news coverage. Whether online, in print, or on electronic broadcast, the top ten stories consumed about half of coverage for the eighteen-month period studied. The story topics dominating the news—economic turmoil, 2008 campaign, and political violence in Iraq, Iran, and Pakistan—all are worthy of attention. Nonetheless, these results underscore prior research that the news agenda remains quite narrow, even though there are more choices than ever to find the news.[41]

To some degree, these results give weight to McCombs' proposition that journalism's agenda-setting role is retained as long as online news tends to mirror legacy media. Homogeneity of news agendas, McCombs wrote in an essay on the future of agenda-setting research, would "hardly be surprising," given how professional norms, economic incentives, and organizational influences transcend media formats.[42] These tendencies are likely accentuated because online news pulls stories from legacy media, compounding the overlap of news stories. But with 40% of online's top stories taking a different cast than mainstream media (and new media even more divergent), evidence also supports the counter-hypothesis that fragmented news audiences are weakening the media's ability to provide a common public agenda. Story consonance likely will dissipate as news Web sites become less dependent on "shovelware" of stories replayed from newspapers and other mainstream media. In short, journalism's agenda-setting role, though evidently still viable in a fragmenting media universe, is tenuous and should be closely monitored.

While coverage by news Web sites resembled traditional media, blogs and social media concentrated on news topics sharply distinct from mainstream media—including online news. For example, traditional media focused overwhelmingly in early 2009 on the economy and the new presidential administration; new media followed these stories, too, but also paid considerable attention to such topics as a mock "zombie attack," a corn syrup study, and Catholic indulgences.[43] In the first half of 2009, fewer than a third of the top story topics identified by the New Media Index overlapped with the News Coverage Index tracking mainstream media.

Overall, hot-button news topics, such as same-sex marriage and abortion, dominated new media. Even when the subject matter was shared, bloggers diverged from mainstream media. In January 2009, for example, both bloggers and the mainstream media dwelled on President Barack Obama's inauguration, but their news frames were quite different. "In the new media, seemingly every aspect of the ceremony was critiqued, often quite passionately, the emotions ranging from euphoria to dread," the Project for Excellence in Journalism reported. "In the more traditional press, the inauguration disappeared fairly quickly, and the focus moved onto the politics of the stimulus package and other Administration business."[44]

That blogs and other social media resemble talk radio in temperament and content does not undermine public discourse if they are used primarily to extend debate or to articulate a shared point of view. But their idiosyncratic personal agendas are worrisome if social media become a person's primary, if not sole, source of news. Further study of newly collected data for the New Media Index should help illuminate how news stories frame the increasingly influential realm of blogs and social media.

This study, relying on pre-existing data, evaluates only national and international news coverage. But, as noted by Singer, the success of many online news operations hinges on their ability to provide highly localized news.[45] Needed is a news index that tracks what is arguably the media's strongest asset—local coverage of their communities. Another limitation of this study is its sole focus on *what* is covered by the news media—leaving largely unaddressed *how* each story is reported. Depth of coverage is mechanically assessed by percentage of newshole, but length is only one dimension of how thoroughly a story is reported. Important analysis remains comparing online and legacy news coverage in terms of accuracy, balance, context, independence, and other fundamentals of journalism.

This study contributes a baseline measure of scope and depth of coverage by news Web sites at a time when the Internet is emerging as the primary information source. Longitudinal studies are needed to track changes that inevitably will occur as the transition from legacy to new media continues to evolve. Such scholarly pursuits promise not only intriguing empirical results, but also will make an important contribution in understanding how the (new) media agenda influences the public's agenda.

Notes

1. Project for Excellence in Journalism, "Press Alert," *The State of the News Media: An Annual Report on American Journalism,* March 23, 2009, http: //www.stateofthenewsmedia.com/2009/press_online.php.
2. See, for example, John Nichols and Robert McChesney, "The Death and Life of Great American Newspapers," *The Nation,* April 6, 2009. Available online at http://www.thenation.com/doc/20090406/nichols_mcchesney?rel=hp_picks.

3. For further discussion on how the Web potentially affects agenda setting, see Maxwell McCombs, "A Look at Agenda-setting: Past, Present and Future," *Journalism Studies* 6 (November 2005): 543–57.
4. See, for example, Steven H. Chaffee and Miriam Metzger, "The End of Mass Communication?" *Mass Communication & Society* 4 (autumn 2001): 365–79; Barry A. Hollander, "Tuning Out or Tuning Elsewhere? Partisanship, Polarization, and Media Migration from 1998 to 2006," *Journalism & Mass Communication Quarterly* 85 (spring 2008): 23–40; David Tewksbury, "The Seeds of Audience Fragmentation: Specialization in the Use of Online News Sites," *Journal of Broadcasting & Electronic Media* 49 (3, 2005): 332–48.
5. Chaffee and Metzger, "The End of Mass Communication?" 375.
6. Chaffee and Metzger, "The End of Mass Communication?"
7. The Pew Research Center for the People and the Press, "Key News Audiences Now Blend Online and Traditional Sources," August 17, 2008, http://pewresearch.org/pubs/928/key-news-audiences-now-blend-online-and-traditional-sources. Also see Project for Excellence in Journalism and the Pew Internet & American Life Project, The State of News Media (2010), April 1, 2010, http://www.stateofthemedia.org/2010/online_summary_essay.php.
8. Carolyn Lin, Michael B. Salwen, and Rasha A. Abdulla, "Uses and Gratifications of Online and Offline News: New Wine in an Old Bottle?" in *Online News and the Public*, ed. Michael B. Salwen, Bruce Garrison, and Paul D. Driscoll (Mahwah, NJ: Lawrence Erlbaum Associates, 2005), 221–36.
9. A national survey of media use in the late 1990s indicated that the Internet was not the cause of the decline in use of other media. See Guido H. Stempel III, Thomas Hargrove, and Joseph P. Bernt, "Relation of Growth of Use of the Internet to Changes in Media Use from 1995 to 1999," *Journalism & Mass Communication Quarterly* 77 (spring 2000): 71–79.
10. The Pew Research Center for the People and the Press, "Newspapers Face a Challenging Calculus," February 26, 2009, http://pew research.org/pubs/1133/decline-print-newspapers-increased-online-news.
11. Pew, "Key News Audiences."
12. Pew Internet and American Life Project, "New Numbers for Blogging and Blog Readership," July 22, 2008, http://www.pew internet.org/Commentary/20G8/July/New-numbers-for-blogging-and-blog-readership.aspx#.
13. Pew Internet and American Life Project, "Adults and Social Networks," January 14, 2009, http://www.pewinternet.org/Reports/ 2009/Adults-and-Social-Network-Websires.aspx.
14. Thomas Hargrove and Guido H. Stempel III, "Use of Blogs as a Source of News Presents Little Threat to Mainline News Media," *Newspaper Research Journal* 28 (winter 2007): 99–102.
15. John Kelly, "Mapping the Blogosphere: Offering a Guide to Journalism's Future," *Nieman Reports* 62 (winter 2008): 37–39.
16. Jane B. Singer, "The Political J-blogger," *Journalism* 6 (May 2005): 173–98.
17. Stephen D. Reese, Lou Rutigliano, Kideuk Hyun, and Jaekwan Jeong, "Mapping the Blogosphere," *Journalism* 8 (August 2007): 235–61.
18. Lindsay H. Hoffman, "Is Internet Content Different After All? A Content Analysis of Mobilizing Information in Online and Print Newspapers," *Journalism & Mass Communication Quarterly* 83 (spring 2006): 59.
19. Jane B. Singer, "The Metro Wide Web: Changes in Newspapers' Gatekeeping Role Online," *Journalism & Mass Communication Quarterly* 78 (spring 2001): 65–80.
20. Scott R. Maier, "Newspapers Offer More News Than Do Major Online Sites," *Newspaper Research Journal* 31 (winter 2010): 6–19.
21. Marion Just, Todd Belt, and Ann Crigler, "New Media, Old Media: The Same Old Story?" (paper presented at the annual meeting of the American Political Social Science Association, Boston, August 2008).
22. Hoffman, "Is Internet Content Different," 58–76.

23. This line of scholarship is rooted in several classic theories of mass communication: consonance, gatekeeping, and agenda setting. See Elisabeth Noelle-Neumann, "Return to the Concept of Powerful Mass Media," *Studies of Broadcasting* 9 (1973): 67–112; David Manning White, "The Gatekeeper: A Case Study in the Selection of News," *journalism Quarterly* 27 (fall 1950): 383–90; Max E. McCombs and Donald Shaw, "The Agenda-Setting Function of the Mass Media," *Public Opinion Quarterly* 36 (summer 1972): 176–87.
24. See, for example, Guido H. Stempel III, "Gatekeeping: The Mix of Topics and Selection of Stories," *Journalism Quarterly* 62 (winter 1985): 791–815; Daniel Riffe, Brenda Ellis, Momo K. Rogers, Roger L. Van Ommeren, and Kieran A. Woodman, "Gatekeeping and the Network News Mix," *Journalism Quarterly* 63 (summer 1986): 315–21; Guido H. Stempel III, 'Topic and Story Choice of Five Network Newscasts," *Journalism Quarterly* 65 (fall 1988): 750–52; Daniel Riffe, "Conflict and Consonance: Coverage of Third World in Two U.S. Papers," *journalism Quarterly* 59 (winter 1982): 617–26.
25. Riffe et al, "Gatekeeping and the Network News Mix," 315.
26. Tewksbury, "The Seeds of Audience Fragmentation."
27. See, for example, Hollander, "Tuning Out or Tuning Elsewhere?"
28. Hollander, "Tuning Out or Turning Elsewhere?" 33–34.
29. These competing hypotheses are articulated in an article by Jae Kook Lee, "The Effect of the Internet on Homogeneity of the Media Agenda: A Test of the Fragmentation Thesis," *Journalism & Mass Communication Quarterly* 84 (winter 2007): 745–60.
30. See, for example, Chaffee and Metzger, "The End of Mass Communication?"
31. See, for example, McCombs, "A Look at Agenda-setting," 543–46.
32. Lee, "The Effect of the Internet," 745.
33. McCombs, "A Look at Agenda-setting," 545.
34. Project for Excellence in Journalism, "About the News Coverage Index," March 23, 2009, http://www.journalism.org/about_news_index/overview.
35. Project for Excellence in Journalism, "Methodology," March 23, 2009, http://www.journalism.org/about_news_index/methodology.
36. Project for Excellence, "Methodology."
37. In intercoder reliability tests, the level of agreement for other key variables was 91% for geographic focus, 94% for story placement, and 100% for story date and media source. Project for Excellence in Journalism, "Methodology, State of the News Media 2008," http;//www.stateofthemedia.org/2008/methodology, php.
38. Project for Excellence in Journalism, "New Media Index Methodology," March 23, 2009, http://www.journalism.org/commentary_backgrounder/new_media_index_methodology.
39. Project for Excellence in Journalism, "New Media Index Methodology," March 23, 2009, http://www.journalism.org/commentary_ backgrounder / new_media_index_methodology.
40. This method is adapted from a technique used by the Project for Excellence in Journalism. However, the data universe differs; this study tracked news storylines, while the PEJ used a broader thematic study of news topics.
41. Project for Excellence in Journalism, "A Year in the News," *The State of the News Media 2008,* March 2008, http://www.stateofthemedia.org/2008/narrative_yearinnewsjntro.php?media=2.
42. McCombs, "A Look at Agenda-setting," 545.
43. Project for Excellence in Journalism, "Bloggers Ponder Every Aspect of Obama's Inauguration," New Media Index: January 19–23, 2009, http://www.journalism.org/commentary_backgrounder/bloggers_ponder_every_aspect_obama%E2%80%99s_inauguration.
44. Project for Excellence, "Bloggers Ponder."
45. Singer, "The Metro Wide Web," 77.

Chapter Highlights

- Writing for online publications is not considered "dumbing it down." But sometimes less is more.
- With the 24/7 news cycle, online writing is constantly updated and rewritten.
- One idea per paragraph is a good rule of thumb for online writing.
- Backpack journalists, bloggers, and media influencers are several types of positions that are available to writers today who can write online. These positions once did not exist when the world was solely inhabited by print and broadcast journalists. Many more writing avenues are available today.
- iPhone reporting is a valuable tool a journalist today has as a resource for covering breaking news. An online journalist should be able to write, report, do voiceovers, and broadcast using an iPhone to be more competitive in today's environment.

For Discussion

1. Find a story online. Turn it into a multimedia project. Use a smartphone and Augenstein's tips for quick reference.
2. Take a look at online layouts that include graphs and bullets. Why do you think this appeals to the reader?
3. Take a look online and select three articles to discuss in class that specifically use the listing format (or bullets) to highlight important facts from the article. Why does this work well for online writing?
4. Bring in a current newspaper or hardcopy magazine. Find a current article and read the first five graphs. Now, take a look online at the same news topic and find out what has been added to the article's timeline. Can you find specific examples in the updated facts that improve the article from the print version? Does the print version seem dated? How did the online journalist update the online article? Is there more analysis or simply newer facts added to the lead and the first few graphs?
5. If more and more readers are getting their news from mobile apps, and less from computers (PCs and laptops), how do you see the role of news changing—and, therefore, how will writing change as a result?

X

Social Media

There is no denying that social media is here to stay. Learning to have a command of the language on social media is a skill that will serve you well. We won't spend a lot of time talking about the specific social media sites you should write for, because there are hundreds you will come across, and what may be trending today may be less popular tomorrow. This style of writing is short (we all know how many characters Twitter allows for), creative, and current. Social media is defined as the plethora of online multimedia tools that bring together online communities to disseminate information and exchange ideas. In other words, social media gets people talking—breaking news, discussions, and branding all take place in a tweet on Twitter, a Facebook wall or newsfeed post, an Instagram photo, or a pin on Pinterest, just to name a few.

Social Media as a News-Gathering Tool

Here is a brief snapshot from a short online article we liked from Radio Television Digital News Association—we appreciate this association as a resource for journalists and for our educational purposes in our classrooms. You can visit www.rtdna.org for more information on this organization. Let's explore more in an online article by Lynn Walsh, an investigative producer at WPTV, News Channel 5 in West Palm Beach, Florida.

Leveraging Social Media in Your Reporting: Followers Can be Great Resources

Tweeting, pinning, liking—we are all using social media. We share our stories, spread the word about breaking news developments and more. But what about using it as a news-gathering tool?

I am sure many of you do this every day without even realizing it. Here are some ways I use social media to develop and find new stories.

1. Finding victims. This can work well on Facebook and Twitter. Let's say you have a story about a company that is scamming people out of money and you want more victims; you could easily post to Facebook or Twitter about the company and have them contact you. (I do this on my personal page first, before going to the station page, just because there is some fear of the competition picking the story up. But, normally when I am posting something this publicly, we are close to ready to go to air.)
2. Tracking stories. I use social media all the time to track stories on topics our team may be interested in. I primarily use Google Alerts, but also create lists on Twitter that are specific to topics we have covered and want to continue to cover. This allows me to see the stories about the topic that are happening worldwide. I also use this tool as an opportunity to re-share a link to the stories we worked on.
3. Showing connections. This comes into play a lot while trying to work on an investigation. Sometimes you can use sites like LinkedIn and Facebook and Twitter to show how closely connected individuals are to one another. LinkedIn is a great source to show where someone went to school and when they graduated. I always verify this independently as well with schools and organizations, but it is a great starting point and this information is self-reported and can be hard for someone to deny when approached about.
4. Finding experts. Just like finding victims, social media can be a great resource for finding experts. I am usually more successful using this technique to get experts than victims. You would be surprised how willing people are not only to be interviewed but to have a conversation about the topic itself. It provides great insight and can really help with the next steps in an investigation while you are gathering information and planning your story.
5. Developing relationships. I do not think we can be reminded of this enough. While it is important to follow topics and know what is going on in our communities, we also have to take the time to get to know the people in our communities. It takes time and it can be difficult but social media can make it a little bit easier.

Take the time to respond to those who tweet to you, leave comments on Facebook posts and on the web. As you meet people in your area, add them to your social networks and continue to interact with them and share stories that you think they may be interested in. Creating the connections will lead to stories and relationships!

Mashable

One of the most notable social media sites today is Mashable. Take a look at www.mashable.com. Pulling directly from the site description, Mashable is a leading source for news, information, and resources for the Connected Generation. Mashable reports on the importance of digital innovation and how it empowers and inspires people around the world. Mashable's twenty million monthly unique visitors and six million social media followers have become one of the most engaged online news communities. Founded in 2005, Mashable is headquartered in New York City with an office in San Francisco. With more than forty million monthly page views, Mashable is the most prolific news site reporting breaking web news, providing analysis of trends, reviewing new websites and services, and offering social media resources and guides.

Mashable's audience includes early adopters; social media enthusiasts; entrepreneurs; influencers; brands and corporations; marketing, PR, and advertising agencies; Web 2.0 aficionados; and technology journalists. Mashable is also popular with bloggers as well as Twitter and Facebook users—an increasingly influential demographic. In other words, if you are part of the Connected Generation (yes, that's you), you will want to be familiar with what Mashable covers and why it is important to the social media world you are writing for.

Here's an example of what Mashable provides to online readers for resources:

- 10 Ways Journalism Schools Are Teaching Social Media
- How Social Media Is Radically Changing the Newsroom
- 10 Must-Haves for Your Social Media Policy
- The Journalist's Guide to Twitter
- Everything I Need to Know about Twitter I Learned in J School

Two Books from Mashable: 101—*The Basics* and *the Journalist's Guide to Facebook*

Mashable editors have also written and released two social media books that deal directly with writing and branding on the popular social media sites Facebook and Twitter.

According to Mashable, "Twitter is an entirely new way to communicate, and for new users it can be a bit daunting. Let these guides show you the ropes." Here is how one of the books breaks down and what it covers as important to social media knowledge for the budding journalist. You can access the books or the chapters you are interested in easily online at the Mashable website www.mashable.com

What is Twitter?
Twitter Video Tutorials
What is a retweet?
How can I customize my Twitter background?
What is a #hashtag?
How can I build my personal brand on Twitter?
Twitter terms to know
tweet this
Chapter 2
Building Your Twitter Community

Twitter is all about facilitating conversations, so learning how to build your community is vital to getting the most from your experience.

Tips for building your Twitter Community

What is #followfriday?

How to find people on Twitter

How do I find Twitter users in my town?

Why aren't people following me?

What to do when you've followed too many people

What's a tweetup?

tweet this

Chapter 3

Twitter for Business

It's not all play on Twitter—there's serious business being done as well, and this guide will teach you how to put Twitter to work.

Finding a job using Twitter

Twitter tips for executives

Twitter best practices for brands

40 of the best big brands on Twitter

Using Twitter for customer service

The media maker's guide to Twitter

tweet this

Chapter 4

Sharing on Twitter

One of the greatest aspects of Twitter is that it's a global platform for sharing information, images, and video. We'll show you how.

Sharing music on Twitter

Sharing video on Twitter

Sharing images on Twitter

Get your questions answered on Twitter

tweet this

Chapter 5

Managing Your Twitter Stream

For the uninitiated, the speed at which information flows on Twitter can be overwhelming. Learn how to manage your Twitter stream.

Tools for organizing your Twitter community

Twitter from your iPhone

Managing multiple Twitter accounts

Managing Twitter on your desktop

Filtering your Twitter stream

Creating groups on Twitter

tweet this

Digital Storytelling

One valuable online writing resource for journalists who wish to engage in digital storytelling is Storify. This tool for writers is available to (as Storify explains) make the web tell a story, collect media from across the web, publish on Storify, embed anywhere, share and notify sources, and go viral. Check out www.storify.com to learn how to do it step by step. This storytelling tool is one example of how journalists can tell stories and use social media to go viral and connect people with ideas.

Totally Cool Social Media Campaigns

Some of the very best social media campaigns are highlighted on a fun site called Social Media Today. Love! In other words, we like. #creative

Every single campaign presented below can be used as an excellent case study to highlight short, creative, and current writing. We are appreciative to Social Media Today for highlighting these campaigns to use in our classrooms for educational purposes, and we acknowledge their creativity. Below is a link to an online article that specifies some of the best social media campaigns and excellent writing, from the social media blog Cygnis Media, as well as a link to the Social Media Today site:

- www.cygnismedia.com/blog/best-social-media-campaigns/#ixzz2hzKTI6jN
- socialmediatoday.com/syed-noman-ali/1638021/best-social-media-campaigns-brands

Exercises

1. Select one popular brand today and create one new social media promotional idea. How would you incorporate short, creative, and current writing into your social media idea?
2. Take a look at the news today. What do you see in print or online journalism that needs to break on a social media outlet? Next, follow the news. Do you see it breaking anywhere? If so, how and where? What would you do differently? Write it up in one paragraph and share with class.
3. Select a fun product that you discover. Make sure it isn't too popular yet. Come up with three ideas for promoting this product to help it trend by using social media. Specifically, how would you use writing for your new idea?
4. Take a look at the brand Dove. In a recent campaign, "realistic models" were used instead of size-zero models. Was this effective? Interview two "normal-size" women to get their reactions. Did it work? How did Dove use clear, creative, and current writing in the branding campaign?
5. Pepsi versus Coke is an old rivalry in the media. Take a side. Pick a brand. Divide the classroom into Coke versus Pepsi. Each team should come up with three ideas to beat the other brand. What are the three ideas? How is strong writing incorporated into this new social media campaign?

Reading List

Writing for Social Media: Blogs and Microblogs

By Janet Mizrahi

The new world of social media has added another layer to the marketing and public relations mix. With the proliferation of social networking and video-sharing sites, blogs, and chat rooms, the web is crawling with online commercial communication. Successful marketers have caught on to the enormous potential these new media platforms provide and are making social media a vital part of their marketing mix.

This chapter will focus on two arenas of social networking: *blogs* and *microblogs*. Blogs—short for web logs—are sites written by an individual with a special interest in a topic as a way to share that interest and point of view with others.[1] Blogs provide interactivity by allowing readers to post comments in response to what the blogger writes, thus creating community. Organizations use blogs to communicate directly with consumers, bypassing the established media entirely.

Microblogs are shorter than traditional blogs. They may be published using technologies other than the web-based methods and include text messaging, instant messaging, email, or digital audio. Among the most notable microblog services are Twitter, Tumblr, Plurk, Emote.in, Beeing, Jaiku, and identi.ca.

The popular Twitter microblogs called "tweets" are limited in length to 140 characters. With 75 million users and counting, Twitter has become increasingly popular with organizations as a way to reach a network instantly, thus creating word-of-mouth publicity. Social networks allow a message to be viewed immediately by thousands and thousands of readers, making the posts invaluable—when they work.

Audience Analysis

Social networking has two main audiences: customers and clients and the media.

Customers and clients. Current or potential customers and clients are a primary audience for blogs and tweets. People interested in an organization, a product, an issue, or a person form the target audience for many content-specific blogs and tweets. These readers are a niche audience who are actively looking for input.

Since a majority of blogs and tweets are aimed at an organization's current customers or clients, these readers should be well defi ned, whether the posting organization is a global leader such as Starbucks or a start-up looking to attract new customers. As with all writing tasks, writing for social media will be most effective if the content fits the needs and wants of the target audience.

To create a more intimate and successful relationship with readers of blogs and tweets, the writer should create one or several *personas* for these messages. As we discussed in chapter 5, a persona is a profile or an invented biography of a typical user or buyer. For example, a PR professional working for a university might create several personas as targets for social networking that could include newer alumni, older alumni, prospective students, or parents. Each persona has specific needs that could be targeted in the posts.

It's also a good idea to monitor the activity of your competitors' blogs and tweets to understand your audience. By watching the discourse between a competitor and its audience, you may gain important feedback that will influence your communication.

Use Table 1.1 and the Persona Template in chapter 5 to help define your audiences for blogs and tweets.

Media. The media is the second audience for an organization's social networking efforts. Editors and writers comb the web in search of ideas for stories, interesting people, and news about organizations. Social networking conversations provide the media with fodder for good copy, thereby allowing an organization to reach an otherwise fickle audience. And for unknown organizations, using free networking can be a way to attract the media's attention. By following a social media community's comments about a product or an organization, the "legitimate" media can pick up on a new trend and write about it. In the eyes of the media, simply having an audience validates an organization or its product.

Determining Purpose

Blogs and microblogs are designed to provide useful, consistent, and interesting updates that create and engage a community of people who share a concern or need. The goal of these media is to establish a readership that ultimately becomes an audience for a product, provides immediate customer feedback, and creates a communication tool for handling any negative news. In this way, social media is similar to direct mail campaigns—but without the cost of postage.

The following provides an example of how an organization might use social media as part of its public relations campaign. Say a bicycle shop owner in Portland, Oregon, starts a blog geared to bicycling enthusiasts. One blog post might include a link to a video from the *Tour de France* simply to share with like-minded enthusiasts. Our bicycle shop blogger might post another blog that offers news about an upcoming local bike race with links for more information about how to participate. To announce the blog, the shop owner might send a tweet informing its network that a new blog has been posted with a link to the post. And finally, when the bike shop has an upcoming promotion, the blogger will inform the community of the opportunity with a blog post and a tweet. The blogs would reside on the bike shop's website with archived older posts.

Interactive and informative blogs and tweets can be highly effective channels of communication that produce a lot of bang for a relatively low cost.

Content

As we've discussed, blogs and microblogs must be informative to attract savvy readers. Therefore, content must appeal to the readership's interests. The information in a blog might be news or commentary, but readers of these messages always expect an interactive experience. Therefore, part of each message includes a link to video clips, photographs, other blogs, publications, or websites. Unlike a website, however, a blog is dynamic, changing several times each week.

Characteristics of blog writing. Because blogs are a way to humanize the dialogue between a company and its potential users, their writing voice is extremely casual. Blogs should read like a conversation with someone who has a distinctive voice. Consequently, any graphical element (such as underlining or italics) or turn of phrase that helps the blog "sound" like a conversation is not just allowed—it's expected.

Before jumping in and writing, spend some time observing the online community's conventions. Look for commonly used acronyms, jargon, and stylistic elements such as tone and language use. If you're going to become a member of a group, you don't want to stick out—you want to fit in.

The following are some of the basic characteristics of blog writing:

- Catchy, intriguing headlines
- Keywords that contain the blog's main idea; searchable words for search engine optimization (SEO)
- Graphical devices such as *italics*, dashes (—), and punctuation marks (!) for emphasis or to emulate a real conversation
- Length of several paragraphs to 300 to 400 words
- Short sentences that avoid long introductory phrases or dependent clauses
- One-sentence paragraphs or very short paragraphs
- Questions sprinkled throughout
- Pull quotes to highlight a theme or catchy phrase to draw in readers
- Links to other sites
- Casual tone with relaxed adherence to conventional grammar
- Careful balance of information share and self-promotion
- Artwork or some sort of graphic for visual interest
- "About Me," a brief author bio, and a photo or other icon representing the organization

Note: Although blogs take a relaxed approach to correctness, no organization wants to be considered sloppy or careless. At the very least, make sure to spell check a blog post!

Characteristics of tweets. Tweets help an organization or an individual create an online presence. Those who follow a Twitter account are interested in a particular subject and therefore anticipate tweets as a way of keeping posted and up to the minute. But because tweets are limited by length, they share certain characteristics:

- No headline
- Profile picture, company logo, or a photo of an individual's face or a product (subject to change if one doesn't produce results)
- Questions to prompt engagement

- Length of up to 140 characters, or roughly 12 words
- Truncated language that omits articles ("a," "an," "the") and abbreviations
- Link to a recommended URL; using a URL shortener such as bit.ly
- Content containing a response to another tweet, a recommendation, or a link to an item of interest
- Exclamation points (!) and question marks (?)
- Writing style similar to news headlines

Interconnectivity of Social Media

The various elements of social media—blogs, tweets, and social networking sites—can work in tandem and with the organization's other marketing tools. For example, the organization's website will have a tab to its blog and a link to sign up to receive the group's newsletter. The organization will notify its network of new blog posts or other news via tweets. Still another social media tool that is quickly gaining popularity is a social network page, with Facebook being the current favorite choice. Other popular social networking websites include MySpace, LinkedIn, and XING, with each having its own microblogging feature, better known as **status updates**.

Facebook pages allow organizations to create an online presence that engenders interactivity among "fans" or readers. Organizations are increasingly using this free new media device to keep a community engaged. Smaller organizations especially can make use of the free analyticals Facebook provides that measure traffic and reader demographics. Facebook pages help brand an organization and are yet another way to communicate with potential clients. They mirror blogs and tweets in that they too are conversational and interactive and provide pertinent information to readers. Writers should use the same language on all social media for branding purposes and to stay on message.

Conclusion

Social media is quickly becoming an essential part of every organization's marketing mix. But because it's a fast-growing, new PR tool with no fixed model to follow, newcomers may be wary of jumping in. The upside is that nothing created in social media is etched in stone. A tweet can be deleted; a fan post can be edited; a comment on a blog can be taken down. In the interactive world, nothing is forever, so mistakes can be covered up.

One thing is for certain. Writers who master the language and technology of social media will have an increasingly valuable part to play in the organization's public relations strategy.

Facebook Messages: Changing the Face of Online Communication?

By Saradhi Kumar Gonela

On November 15, 2010, Facebook Inc,[1] considered by many as the most popular social networking website[2] (facebook.com) with its more than 500 million subscribers,[3] announced the launch of a new product 'Facebook Messages'. The launch intensified competition in the free Internet e-mail market—dominated by a few global players, particularly Google,[4] Yahoo!,[5] and Microsoft.[6] Facebook announced the launch of Facebook Messages as an integrated platform for online chat and text messages (from mobiles) with traditional e-mail services. Till then, other e-mail providers had been offering all these services as independent products and users were unable to access one service from another. Highlighting this fact during the launch of the new product, Mark Zuckerberg, CEO of Facebook, said that the traditional e-mail services no longer appealed to the younger generation of Internet users as they were too slow.

Subscribers of Facebook were to be provided with a facebook.com personal e-mail address that would integrate all services. The new feature was expected to simplify communication through text, instant messages, online chat, or email by offering all these communiqués from one single feed known as a 'social inbox'. Users would be allowed to reply in any mode they wanted i.e., a user could, for example, reply to a chat through e-mail, through text messaging, or through chat itself. Observers opined that Facebook aimed to make the new product a one-stop-shop for all Internet-based communication related services, a major step in the progress of a company that had started as a social networking site.

Another Enterprise from Harvard Dorm-Room

In 2002, after graduating from a prestigious private school, Phillips Exeter Academy,[7] Zuckerberg joined Harvard to study computer science and psychology. On the Harvard campus, he was actively engaged in building easy to use websites for students.[8] In the process, he launched thefacebook.com site from his Harvard dormitory room on February 4, 2004. It was believed that the name had been taken from Phillips Exeter Academy's student directory, The Photo Address Book, which students referred to as 'The Facebook'. Many private schools in the US published photo directories, which students used to list attributes such as their class years, their friends, their telephone numbers, and other related information. It was said that thefacebook.com was an extension (and also digitalization) of these directories using the Internet.

On the Harvard campus, thefacebook.com was an instant hit as all students were expected to know all other students on campus. In the first 24 hours of the launch, 1,200 Harvard students had enlisted, and within one month, half of the undergraduate students of Harvard had a profile.[9] Students and faculty at Harvard were required to enlist themselves on thefacebook.com site with a Harvard e-mail address along with their personal profile, on receiving an invitation from an existing member (The invitation-only method was adopted to restrict member listings and thereby ensure hardware functionality). The personal profiles were then made visible to all others with a Harvard e-mail address. In this way, thefacebook.com enabled everyone with a Harvard email address to know about everyone sharing the same e-mail address. Analysts opined that the social necessity of knowing about others on the Harvard campus and technical filtering using the Harvard e-mail address were two key factors for the early success of thefacebook.com.

Boosted by its success at Harvard, Zuckerberg[10] introduced the website to other universities with the help of roommate Dustin Moskovitz (Moskovitz, was later to own a stock in Facebook Inc. As of 2010, his net-worth was calculated at around US$1.4 billion by *Forbes*).[11] To begin with, they introduced thefacebook.com at Stanford University, Dartmouth College, Columbia University, New York University, Cornell University, and Yale University. Once the website proved successful in these universities, it was introduced in other universities that had social contacts with Harvard. By mid-2005, thefacebook.com had become a fad among students in American universities and having a profile on the site had become almost a social compulsion.

The site was rechristened facebook.com in August 2005 and the address was purchased for a reported amount of US$200,000. One of the early investors was co-founder of PayPal,[12] Peter Thiel. The site was made open to US high schools in September 2005. In the following month, it was made open to UK universities. Yet, it still followed the invitation-only member enlistment method. During this time, MTV Networks[13] was reported to have offered US$75 million for Facebook, but the offer was declined.[14] On his declining the offer, Zuckerberg said, "It's not because of the amount of money. For me and my colleagues, the most important thing is that we create an open information flow for people. Having media corporations owned by conglomerates is just not an attractive idea to me."[15]

From late 2005, Facebook began spreading worldwide and by mid-2006 it started accepting members beyond the educational fraternity, allowing entry to any individual across the globe with an active e-mail account.[16] During this period, it was reported that many technology companies, including Google and Microsoft, had made futile attempts to take over Facebook for undisclosed amounts. Yahoo! was said to have offered US$1 billion during 2006 but was turned down.[17] However, Facebook sold 1.6% stock to Microsoft for a sum of US$240 million to fund its growth during 2007.[18]

From 2007, the company expanded the breadth of its offerings to its members, accommodating gifts and presents to friends, placing classified advertisements (for free), and developing personalized applications. Of all the offerings, personal posting on an individual's facebook.com page (called the wall) was particularly popular, for it offered a stage for an individual's expression and also enabled friends of the respective person to leave comments. The ease with which a Facebook account could be used, with no emails having to be sent back and forth for communicating with friends—caught the imagination of users. Analysts opined that 'the wall' was the most appealing factor of Facebook, as it enabled people to communicate with multiple friends and stay in touch with them all the time without having to mail or text. Some observers even commented that Facebook had become a real substitute for e-mail providers and that the emphasis on networking with multiple friends and acquaintances was the unique selling proposition (USP) of Facebook. By 2010, around 400 million people were visiting facebook.com per month.[19] In

September 2010, *The New Yorker*[20] reported that at least one out of every fourteen people in the world had a Facebook account.[21]

Analysts believed that Facebook's revenue was generated through targeted advertisements, where sellers could use personal information provided by its members to pick potential buyers. Facebook allowed third party players (essentially sellers) access to the personal information of its members along with their posts on the wall. Sellers would then place an advertisement on the wall of an individual whom they deemed to be a potential customer and Facebook made revenue out of these advertisements. *The Daily Mail*, a UK-based daily newspaper, explained ". . . . if you were in America and visited Pandora, an Internet radio station not yet available in the UK, Facebook would allow Pandora software to whizz around your Facebook account to read what music you have told your friends that you like and then serve it up to you."[22] The daily further stated that Facebook had, over the years, changed its privacy policy to allow sellers to view the private information of its members. According to *New York Times*, the company's privacy policy had grown to 5,830 words by 2010—more than 1,287 words longer than the US constitution (not taking amendments into account)—from 1,004 words in 2005.[23] Facebook stated that members could place restrictions on making private information public by changing the privacy settings. However, *New York Times* pointed out that a member had to click through more than 50 privacy buttons and choose from among over 170 options to block most information from public access.[24]

Industry observers felt that by holding personal information of about 500 million people from across the globe in terms of tastes, interests, likes (dislikes), preferences, habits, social and marital status, profession, personal e-mail address, networks, personal communication links, and a host of other relevant information for marketers, Facebook had become one of the most valuable companies for advertisers. As the company's subscriber base swelled, the number of minutes spent by each subscriber on the site increased (Refer to Exhibit I for number of minutes spent by users on Facebook in comparison with Google and Yahoo); and as the number of messages transmitted from the site reached 4 billion per day,[25] its valuation also increased. By the end of 2010, Facebook's value was estimated at around US$40 billion.[26]

Facebook Messages—What Message Would it Deliver?

At a time when the four biggest players on the Internet[27] were battling out for every minute spent on the Internet by users, Facebook announced the launch of its Messages service in November 2010. The company said that the service would be launched gradually on an invite-only basis, i.e., a new member would be allowed to join only on accepting the invitation sent by an existing member. And each member would have only a limited number of invitations to share. Analysts predicted that with this method it would take several months for all the 500 million existing Facebook users to avail of the new service and that the method would provide ample time for Facebook to augment its hardware and requirements.

The new service was modeled more on chat than on traditional e-mail which meant there would be no subject lines, or cc or bcc fields—but it would operate through a @facebook.com e-mail address. Users could mail their friends by clicking the respective receiver's name and not have to type subject lines. Three major features of the new service that were different from traditional e-mail were 'Seamless Messaging', 'Conversation History', and 'The Social Inbox' (Refer to Exhibit II for operating model).

Seamless Messaging referred to the system of sending and receiving messages via SMS, chat, or e-mail. The sender would have to choose a name and type a message and the receiver would receive the message through whatever medium or device was convenient to him/her. Further, the receiver and sender could have a conversation in real time. In the traditional system chat, SMS and e-mail operated on different technologies with different procedures and hence had to be operated differently. For instance, e-mail opened only through an Internet browser either on a computer or on a mobile phone and SMSs could be exchanged only through mobile phones. Analysts observed that the new method would be more user-friendly and would reduce the time taken to send an e-mail or a chat message or an SMS.

Facebook's Conversation History was devised to store all the messages exchanged between two users through various platforms, whether sent through chat, email, or SMS. Further, all the conversations with each person would be stored as a single conversation. In contrast, a traditional storage mechanism stored all similar messages on the respective arena. For instance, all e-mails were stored at one place, chats at another, and SMS on mobile phones. Also, each message was stored separately depending on date and time. This made checking e-mail, chat, and SMS history a tedious task for users.

The Social Inbox was designed to distinguish messages of friends from messages from other sources. It segregated messages from friends into one folder and the other e-mails in a separate folder. "It seems wrong that an email message from your best friend gets sandwiched between a bill and a bank statement. It's not that those other messages aren't important, but one of them is more meaningful,"[28] wrote, Joel Seligstein (Seligstein) , a Facebook engineer on the Facebook blog. The company stated that The Social Inbox would also allow the users to choose from whom they wished to receive messages; the rest could be blocked. This way, the company said, users could control spam themselves and could manage their inbox better.

By building the new system around the convenience of users and breaching technological barriers, observers said, Facebook was trying to strike an emotional chord with the users and thereby win customer loyalty. Industry watchers were of the opinion that the company wanted to differentiate itself from the competitors by focusing more on user convenience, while others were more technology driven. Seligstein, during the launch of Messages, stated how Facebook was different, "Relatively soon, we'll probably all stop using arbitrary ten digit numbers and bizarre sequences of characters to contact each other. We will just select friends by name and be able to share with them instantly. We aren't there yet, but the changes today are a small first step."[29] Andrew Bosworth, director of engineering at Facebook, added, "We really want to enable people to have conversations with the people they care about. It sounds so simple. We have all this technology that should be enabling that but it's not. It's fragmenting that. So I have one conversation on email with my grandfather and another with my cousin on sms and all these things don't work the same way. I shouldn't have to worry about the technology. I should just have to worry about the person and the message. Everything else is just getting in the way."[30]

Though Facebook said Messages was meant to eliminate differences between different media, analysts thought that Facebook was trying to catch up with the reach of e-mail users. Research carried out by Forrester Research[31] showed that while 90% of adults in the US had an e-mail account, only 59% of adults maintained a profile on any social networking site. Industry analyst Augie Ray of Forrester Research pointed out that e-mail had a far higher reach compared to the reach of social networking sites.[32] It was believed that Facebook was trying to lure the e-mail account holders to its site by providing them with superior experience. Charlene Li, social media analyst and founder of Altimeter Group[33], opined that with the launch of the Messages service, Facebook would become a web portal on the level of Google, Yahoo!, and Microsoft.

A number of analysts also felt that Facebook's new services were an attempt to get the younger generation on to the Internet. Some studies found that text messaging had become the preferred means of communication among US teens.[34] Analysts opined that this may have prompted the company to include SMS also on its Messages platform. Adding strength to this argument, Zuckerberg, on announcing the new service revealed that his conversations with high-school students—who said that they preferred SMS and chat to e-mail, which was too slow and more formal—had inspired him to build Messages.[35]

Wall Street Journal[36] noted that Facebook's entry into the new service was to tap the US$26 billion, briskly growing online advertisement industry in the US.[37] Experts opined that online advertisement was the prime reason why Facebook had built the ability of communicating with any e-mail account. They said that by this, Facebook expected to keep as many users on its site as possible and gradually to make e-mail an insignificant service. A columnist in *Washington Post*[38] wrote that in a year or two after the full fledged launch of Messages, some Facebook users might consider e-mail not as important as it was before. When 500 million-plus users (about 350 million of whom used Facebook's existing messaging system) made Facebook an epicenter for their online correspondence, Facebook would inevitably displace e-mail—one of the oldest standards on the Internet.[39] But other analysts said that might take a longer time for that to happen. Robert Scoble,[40] technology writer, said Messages was a new product but it might not sound the death knell for Yahoo!, Microsoft, and Gmail as users would take a fairly long time to stop using traditional e-mails, and this would give these companies enough time to retort by building their strength in online social space.[41]

Ramping up Rivalry with Google, Microsoft, and YAHOO!

While Facebook had been building Messages from early 2009, the traditional e-mail providers had been rolling out services synchronized with social networking from mid-2010. Targeting the needs of younger generation Internet users, the major players started offering integrated and easy-to-use services (similar to social networking sites) on existing e-mail platforms using cloud computing[42] technology. While doing so, the providers also focused on reducing spam, saving storage, and increasing the speed of services.

Microsoft upgraded the services offered through its Instant Messenger (IM), its chat service. With the aim of keeping its users glued to IM for most of the time, Microsoft enhanced its IM to display updates from its online partners such as Facebook and around 80 other social network sites. With this service, a user could virtually look at his/her friends' profiles on other sites, without moving away from IM and could also send messages to those profiles. In addition, the company had introduced video sharing facility through which an online video link could be pasted on the IM to watch it together with a group of friends on the IM. The service supported videos from YouTube, Vimeo, DailyMotion, Break.com, and Wat.tv. IM had also introduced video chat facility, which could be used by installing the required hardware. To offer photo and video sharing, the company had introduced SkyDrive, a service through which photos and videos could be uploaded (also a 10 GB mail could be composed) utilizing cloud computing. Once photos were uploaded, they could be viewed as a slideshow by anyone with whom the link was shared. SkyDrive would provide 25GB space for every individual user through cloud computing.

Yahoo! had updated its mail architecture after nearly a decade of its initial launch and launched a beta version in mid-2010. In addition to the new version reportedly being faster than the older version, Yahoo! provided unlimited mailbox size to users. Yahoo! Messenger, the chat service of Yahoo!, also had been updated to track users and switch the medium from computer to mobile phone depending on the user's presence. Yahoo! Messenger had also been upgraded to access social networking sites to enable users to post comments on their friends' profiles on other sites by not logging off from Yahoo! Messenger.

Meanwhile, Google had ugraded its free e-mail, Gmail, by enabling data storage through cloud computing. This allowed multiple users to access data for working on it instead of the data having to be sent back and forth among the users. Google also launched Google Buzz (Buzz), a built-in social networking tool in its Gmail. Buzz users could access various websites such as Picasa, Flickr, Twitter, Blogger, YouTube, and Google Reader. Buzz could also be used to share links and conversations (either publicly or with a group of known friends) by its members. The company also enhanced its chat, Google Talk, by installing automatic translators. This made chatting between two Google Talk users in different languages possible.

Analysts opined that while all the major players were upgrading their services to make every user stick to their site as long as possible and provide marketers with potential customers, the introduction of Facebook Messages had augmented competition in social networking. They added that while competition could help users by providing better services, it would affect the bottom lines of all the players and might make such services unviable in the long run as marketers would constantly keep looking for better avenues for spending their advertisement budgets. Further, it was also believed that users might get irked by the intrusion into their privacy by these companies and that this might result in an exodus of users from the social networking sites.

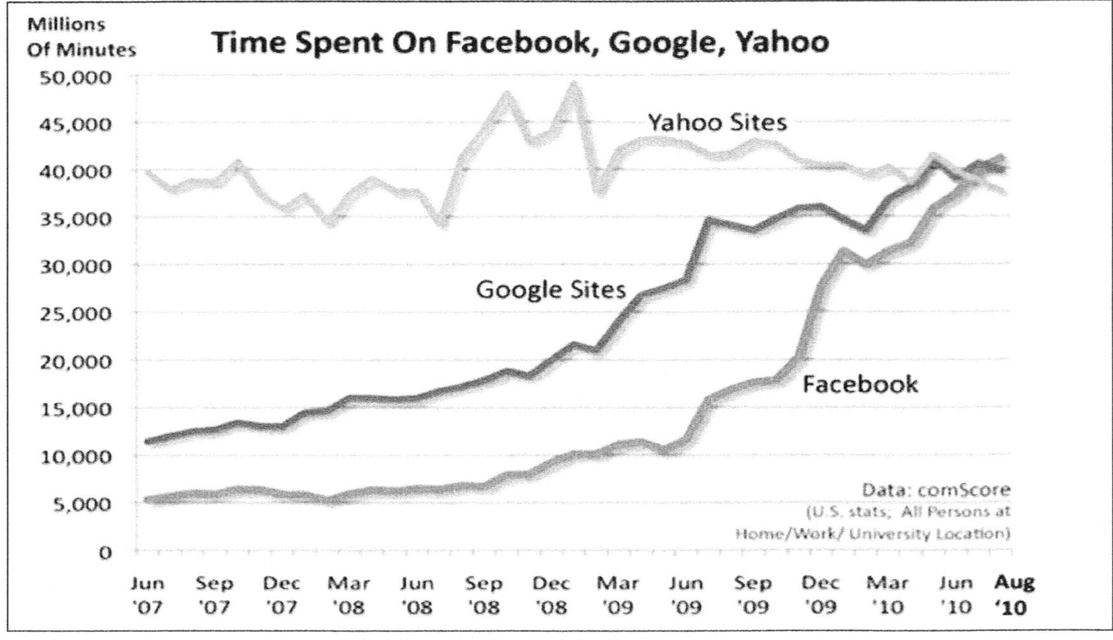

Source: Mark Suster, "Social Networking: Past, Present, Future," http://docs.docstoc.com/orig/2971317ccc4b39-5b8e-436c-a2e1-10743ed3157b.ppt,

Exhibit II

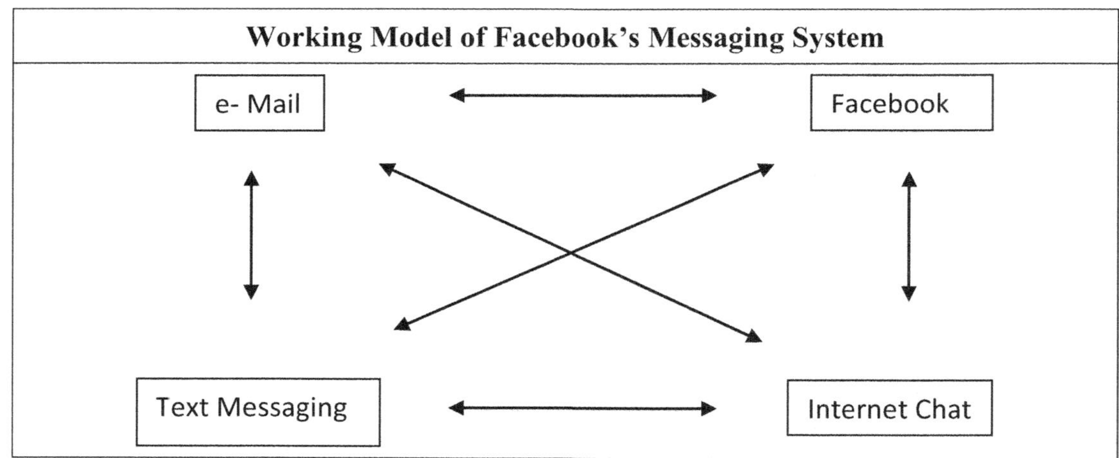

Source: "Facebook Unveils "Modern Messaging System"," www.dbswebsite.com, November 17, 2010

Notes

1. Facebook, Inc, a privately held company, operates the largest social networking website, facebook.com, with more than 500 million subscribers as of the end of 2010. The company was founded in 2004 and is based in Palo Alto, California, with an operation in Hanoi, Vietnam.
2. A social networking website is an internet-based service platform, manifesting the relationship between its members, as for example students of an academic discipline, or people who share an activity/interest, or individuals who know each other and so on and so forth. These websites generally enable members to exchange/share ideas/opinions or simply to communicate in the form of instant messages, to look up a friend's web pages, share photos and videos, and a host of other services. Members can avail of these services from a webpage dedicated to each of them—often called profile/account—which contains personal information about the individual along with web-links of other members with whom a member linked. They are different from common e-mail providers in the sense that they do not allow communicating with non-members.
3. Maggie Shiels, "Facebook Ramps Up Competition With a New Message System," www.bbc.co.uk, November 16, 2010
4. Google, Inc. is one of the most popular high-tech companies with operations in internet searching, free e-mail, cloud computing, video sharing, digital maps, a social networking site, and advertisement technologies. The flagship service of the company is its internet search technology with operates on a page-rank algorithm. The search technology is so effective that it earned the title of "Gateway of Internet" for the company. Google's free e-mail, called Gmail, had around 190 million subscribers in November 2010.
5. Yahoo! is a web portal offering a host of internet services including news, free e-mail, search engine, Yahoo! Directory, advertising, online maps, video sharing, and social media websites and services. It is reckoned to be the most visited website. Its free e-mail called Yahoo! Mail had around 270 million users at the end of 2010.
6. Microsoft, one of the first software companies in the world, develops, licenses, and supports a plethora of software products and services for a huge variety of computer devices. The most popular product of the company is the Windows Software Suite for personal computers. Its free e-mail Windows Hotmail was one of the first e-mail providers and it had around 360 million subscribers at the end of 2010, which made it the largest e-mail provider.
7. Phillips Exeter Academy (PEA) is one of the prestigious co-educational independent boarding schools for grades 9–12 and postgraduates. It is located in Exeter, New Hampshire, USA.
8. Before launching the facebook.com he launched a number of websites on the Harvard campus. Two of the most popular were 'CourseMatch', which allowed users to choose a course by tracking the choices of others, and 'Facemash', where students could be rated (by fellow students) on physical attractiveness.
9. Sarah Phillips, "A Brief History of Facebook," www.guardian.co.uk, July 25, 2007
10. Mark Zuckerberg is famous as the youngest billionaire with a net worth of US$6.9 billion as of September 2010 (calculated by *Forbes*), by virtue of holding a 24% stake in Facebook Inc. He attended Harvard University and studied computer science before moving the company to Palo Alto, California.
11. "Forbes 400 Richest Americans," http://www.forbes.com/fdc/welcome_mjx.shtml
12. PayPal is an e-commerce site, which allows payment and receipt of money electronically (through the internet). It is an alternative to the paper method of money transfers such as checks and money orders. PayPal earns revenue by charging the parties involved a proportion of money being transferred through the site.
13. MTV Networks is a division of Viacom, the media conglomerate. MTV Networks operates a number of music television channels and internet brands. MTV Networks focuses on offering music to western music fans in their teens and twenties.
14. Jose Antonio Vargas, "The Face OF Facebook," www.newyorker.com, September 20, 2010
15. "Face-to-Face With Mark Zuckerberg '02," www.exeter.edu, January 24, 2007

16. Sarah Phillips, "A Brief History of Facebook," www.guardian.co.uk, July 25, 2007
17. Jose Antonio Vargas, "The Face OF Facebook," www.newyorker.com, September 20, 2010
18. Rahul Thadani, "History of Facebook," www.buzzle.com, March 11, 2010
19. Nicholas Carlson, "At Last—The Full Story Of How Facebook Was Founded," www.businessinsider.com, March 5, 2010
20. *The New Yorker* is an American weekly magazine published by Condé Nast Publications that reflects popular culture of New York, with a mix of reporting of politics, humor, cartoons, fiction, poetry, reviews, and criticism.
21. Jose Antonio Vargas, "The Face of Facebook," www.newyorker.com, September 20, 2010
22. Steve Boggan, "The Billionaire Facebook Founder Making a Fortune From Your Secrets (Though You Probably Don't Know He's Doing It)," www.dailymail.co.uk, May 21, 2010
23. Guilbert Gates, "Facebook Privacy: A Bewildering Tangle of Options," www.nytimes.com, May 21, 2010
24. Nick Bilton, "Price of Facebook Privacy? Start Clicking," www.nytimes.com, May 12, 2010
25. Maggie Shiels, "Facebook Ramps Up Competition With a New Message System," www.bbc.co.uk, November 16, 2010
26. Ian Burrell, "Mark Zuckerberg: He's Got the Whole World on His Site," www.independent.co.uk, July 24, 2010
27. According to the three-month Alexa global rankings of "The Top 500 Sites On the Web," Google Facebook, YouTube (a subsidiary of Google), Yahoo!, and Microsoft Live occupied 1st, 2nd, 3rd, 4th and 5th places respectively, as of December 2010. On the same list MSN (a portal of Microsoft that provides Hotmail—free e-mail—along with a host of online services) was positioned 11th.
28. Joel Seligstein, "See the Messages that Matter," www.facebook.com, November 15, 2010
29. Joel Seligstein, "See the Messages that Matter," www.facebook.com, November 15, 2010
30. Maggie Shiels, "Facebook Ramps Up Competition With a New Message System," www.bbc.co.uk, November 16, 2010
31. Forrester Research, Inc. is an American research company that provides advice to corporations in business strategy and technology. The company's products and services are targeted to 19 specific roles, including senior management in business strategy, marketing, and information technology.
32. Maggie Shiels, "Facebook Ramps Up Competition With a New Message System," www.bbc.co.uk, November 16, 2010
33. Altimeter Group is a strategy consulting firm that advises companies on emerging technologies. It focuses on four areas: leadership and management, customer strategy, enterprise strategy, and innovation and practice.
34. Pradeep Nair, "Will Facebook Sound Death Knell for Email?" http://timesofindia.indiatimes.com, November 17, 2010
35. Caroline McCarthy, "Facebook Unveils E-mail, the Sequel," http://news.cnet.com, November 15, 2010
36. *The Wall Street Journal* is a leading international daily newspaper primarily covering international business and financial news.
37. Geoffrey A. Fowler and Amir Efrati, "Facebook's New Front in Google Rivalry," http://online.wsj.com, November 15, 2010
38. Founded in 1877, *Washington Post* is the oldest and largest selling daily newspaper of Washington DC, covering primarily political news.
39. Rob Pegoraro, "With 'Messages,' Facebook Tries to Run the Switchboard," www.washingtonpost.com, November 16, 2010
40. Robert Scoble is an American blogger, technical evangelist, and author. Scoble is best known through his blog, Scobleizer, which came into prominence during his tenure as a technical evangelist at Microsoft. He is credited by *The Economist* as being one of the most influential technology writers. He also the coauthored *Naked Conversations: How Blogs are Changing the Way Businesses Talk with Customers* with Shel Israel.

41. Maggie Shiels, "Facebook Ramps Up Competition With a New Message System," www.bbc.co.uk, November 16, 2010
42. Cloud computing is an Internet-based computing technology where resources aka hardware, software, and processers are shared and are provided to individual users, companies, and all others in need of computing on demand. Services are delivered through common centers and servers and are charged depending on the usage (pay-as-you-go basis). The system functions more like an electricity grid. Major corporations involved in cloud computing are Microsoft, Google, HP, IMB, Amazon, Salesforce, and Dell along with all other big names in the IT space.

References and Suggested Readings

1. **"Facebook Unveils "Modern Messaging System","** www.dbswebsite.com, November 17, 2010
2. Pradeep Nair, **"Will Facebook Sound Death Knell For Email?"** http://timesofindia.indiatimes.com, November 17, 2010
3. Maggie Shiels, **"Facebook Ramps Up Competition With a New Message System,"** www.bbc.co.uk, November 16, 2010
4. Rob Pegoraro, **"With 'Messages,' Facebook Tries to Run the Switchboard,"**
5. www.washingtonpost.com, November 16, 2010
6. Geoffrey A. Fowler and Amir Efrati, **"Facebook's New Front in Google Rivalry,"** http://online.wsj.com, November 15, 2010
7. Caroline McCarthy, **"Facebook Unveils E-mail, the Sequel,"** http://news.cnet.com, November 15, 2010
8. Joel Seligstein, **"See the Messages That Matter,"** www.facebook.com, November 15, 2010
9. Jose Antonio Vargas, **"The Face OF Facebook,"** www.newyorker.com, September 20, 2010
10. Ian Burrell, **"Mark Zuckerberg: He's Got the Whole World on His Site,"** www.independent.co.uk, July 24, 2010
11. Steve Boggan, **"The Billionaire Facebook Founder Making a Fortune From Your Secrets (Though You Probably Don't Know He's Doing It),"** www.dailymail.co.uk, May 21, 2010
12. Guilbert Gates, **"Facebook Privacy: A Bewildering Tangle of Options,"** www.nytimes.com, May 21, 2010
13. Nick Bilton, **"Price of Facebook Privacy? Start Clicking,"** www.nytimes.com, May 12, 2010
14. Rahul Thadani, "History of Facebook," www.buzzle.com, March 11, 2010
15. Nicholas Carlson, **"At Last—The Full Story of How Facebook was Founded,"** www.businessinsider.com, March 5, 2010
16. Sarah Phillips, **"A Brief History of Facebook,"** www.guardian.co.uk, July 25, 2007
17. **"Face-to-Face With Mark Zuckerberg '02,"** www.exeter.edu, January 24, 2007
18. **"Forbes 400 Richest Americans,"** http://www.forbes.com/fdc/welcome_mjx.shtml
19. http://investing.businessweek.com
20. http://en.wikipedia.org
21. www.nytimes.com
22. www.livemint.com
23. www.facebook.com
24. www.washingtonpost.com

Chapter Highlights

- Learning to have a command of social media language is a skill that will serve journalists well.
- Leveraging social media in your reporting is part of being a solid journalist today.
- Mashable is a notable social media site that you will want to get to know as an online resource for journalists.
- Understanding the world of digital storytelling is a must for our media environment today.
- Branding is a part of the role of a well-rounded journalist today.

For Discussion

1. Discuss what you see working on current social media sites and what falls short. What are old ideas, and what are new ideas?
2. Take a look at current social media sites that seem to work. Select six examples of strong writing that help promote a product or brand or cause. Discuss why they work.
3. Take fifteen minutes of class time to peruse social media. What news is breaking? Or what's trending? Are credible sources attributed? How often do social media posts attribute a credible source when breaking news? Or, are you finding a lot of gossip and sloppy reporting? What would you do differently?
4. Spend a few minutes in class researching old examples of breaking news. Come up with a top-five list of hard news stories that broke on social media. To get you started, Google the following phrases: "Newtown, Connecticut" and "Boston Marathon terrorist attack." Discuss in class how the stories broke and whether the reporting was well done or where there was room for improvement. Did any reporters get facts wrong? If so, what do you think about that?
5. If you thought analyzing breaking news via social media was fun, next let's take some time to go way back. Can you discover the very first breaking news story on social media? When and where did this take place? Why was this moment so profound for journalists? At the time it was unheard of and hard to believe. Compare and contrast the news via social media then and now.

xi

Legal Challenges

Everyone has rules by which they have to play or behave. There are no exceptions. For writers, this is particularly true. Think about it. There are the rule of grammar, punctuation, and spelling to which one must adhere. And then there are various style rules, such as ones set by the Associated Press, that writers cannot ignore. Furthermore, when a writer puts pen to paper, he or she is writing about another person or a topic that others will read. Readers will draw from what they read, utilizing the information to make decisions that affect their own lives and interactions with those with whom they connect on both personal and professional levels. Thus, what they and all of us read makes a difference in the well-being of our days. Consequently, it is extremely important that what writers write be accurate and understandable. The quality of what they do makes a difference. Big time.

Writing may seem like an act of isolation, but the fact is that it is not. Writers write to be read. People read to learn and be entertained. They then take that knowledge to further their own goals or agendas in ways that affect others. And so it goes. This process all begins with those men or women who may be alone in some isolated part of the house or faraway corner of a public library. While those people may be off by themselves, the writer casts what has the potential of becoming a giant shadow. Struggling writer J. K. Rowling, now internationally known as the author of the incredibly popular Harry Potter books, spent quiet mornings at local coffee shops putting together those stories of a boy wizard. Before going off to work each morning, the unknown John Grisham set aside a minimum of fifteen minutes each day to put down as much as he could about stories running through his head that needed to come out. These moments of isolation gave Rowling and Grisham what they needed to compose stories that went on to touch the hearts and minds of millions. Their performed acts of isolation resulted in the unprecedented inclusion of others.

Granted, what the average public relations writer pens has nowhere near the cultural and financial impact of Rowling, Grisham, and countless other successful authors. This, however, does not detract from or minimize the importance of what they do and the potential impact it has on others, many of whom they do not or never will know. A great burden that professional communicators carry with them is the fact that their acts of communication—specifically, writing—do, in fact, influence the actions and thoughts of men and women whom they in all likelihood will not only never know, but never know of. This, then, points to just how vital it is that what the so-called average professional communicator writes be accurate and not misleading or deceitful. We are speaking here of both public relations professionals and journalists, two professions that revolve around the art and craft of writing. Journalists, ideally, strive to report news in a straightforward, objective manner. Again, ideally, they do so beholden only to the information itself rather than to a specific client or organization. Regarding the public relations professional, either directly or indirectly, this person's job and focus is to help establish and maintain relationships with an array of publics on behalf of a client. To enjoy any degree of success, then, what the public relations practitioner communicates is as important as how he or she communicates. The how of this equation includes the numerous communication tools we mentioned earlier in the text. The what, however, is a never-changing constant: the truth.

Why is this important? The answer is both simple and profound. While the average journalist or public relations practitioner may never have the name recognition of J. K. Rowling or John Grisham, what these professionals do have is impact. Their work affects the day-to-day lives of others. This is no small thing. Because those in each profession perform work that is visible to others—made available for public consumption—it is essential that their efforts be carried out with pure intention. By that, we mean not to do harm but, rather, to enlighten and inform. A mistake can cause financial damage, great disruption, and personal harm. For instance, if one morning parents, students, and teachers wake to find that heavy snow is falling, they naturally wonder whether school is going to be open that day or, at the very least, open late. What happens if the school system's chief communicator announces that schools are open when in fact they are not? What happens if the journalists reporting the decision by the school system get the decision wrong? We, of course, could go on and on with examples of situations where incorrect information is communicated and the disruption this can cause. The point is that the work of writers is serious because these professional communicators do not perform in a vacuum. Thus, in the world of communication, accuracy is nonnegotiable.

Obviously, no one is perfect. People do make mistakes, simply because none of us are programmed for perfection. (Perhaps sometime in the future this will change, but, for now, in our lifetimes, we can all assume that each of us will mess up from time to time.) Innocent mistakes, though unfortunate, happen. When they occur, steps such as corrections and apologies can be made to address them. Still, the professions of journalism and public relations as well as the federal government of the United States have guidelines and laws in place to ensure that professional communicators, particularly when they write, adhere to the truth. The primary purpose of this chapter is to identify and discuss those guidelines and laws to help writers fully understand the parameters in which they are working. The bottom-line message of these various tenants is that journalists are not free to include any tidbit they wish about a person or topic without first ensuring that it is accurate; nor are public relations practitioners free to say or write whatever they wish on behalf of a client. Straying from the truth has consequences.

Super-secret agent James Bond may have a license to kill, but in the real world writers who dwell in the world of fact and information do not and never will have a similar license to communicate false information. In this case, what they say is as important as how they say it.

To more fully explore this important topic, we look at (1) the ethical guidelines of the journalism and public relations professions and (2) key communication laws that have been challenged, tested, and debated in courts at all levels and reinforced by elected officials for the protection of individuals from all walks of life. Collectively, they point to the most fundamental values of a democratic society: openness and honesty. While it remains legal for people and organizations to share their perspectives or opinions on specific people or issues, doing so on the wings of purposeful falsehoods that do harm to a person or entity's character, reputation, or ability to function in society places the communicator of such outpourings in jeopardy of becoming the subject of legal actions. In other words, one spreads lies or unsubstantiated charges against another—either verbally or in writing—at his or her own risk.

The Canons of Journalism

In 1923, the American Society of Newspaper Editors (ASNE) adopted what it called the "Canons of Journalism," a series of seven principles to which it said all media reporters should subscribe in carrying out their day-to-day responsibilities. At the time, of course, television with its various news and talk programs did not exist. Furthermore, KDKA-AM, the nation's first commercially licensed radio station, was only three years old. It had no news department at the time. Obviously, in 1923 the so-called radio industry had no impact on news. As newspapers were the only meaningful agents of covering and reporting news to the masses on a daily basis, these canons were placed on the shoulders of those working in the print media. Now, more than ninety years later, they remain viable yet are more widespread, as they do touch on those who report for broadcast media.

The seven canons are as follows: responsibility; freedom of the press; independence; sincerity, truthfulness, and accuracy; impartiality; fair play; and decency. Following is a brief discussion of each.

Responsibility—

Journalists are looked on as being agents of the public, professionals whose job it is to provide information to a general public not able to do so themselves. As a result, journalists operate on behalf of the public welfare. Failure to do so results in a population cloaked in ignorance of events and decisions by powers, including the government, that might affect their well-being.

Freedom of the Press—

The first amendment of the United States Constitution prohibits the making of any law respecting an establishment of religion, impeding the free exercise of religion, abridging the freedom of speech, infringing on the freedom of the press, and interfering with the right to peaceably assemble. The canons say that journalists should defend and support this amendment, particularly regarding its endorsement of a free press. Such an amendment is vital to the welfare and existence of a free society.

Independence—

Journalists must be able to carry out their jobs free from the improper influence of sources, politics, and advertisers. If, for instance, a reporter uncovers information reflecting negatively on one of a paper's advertisers, the reporter should be free and encouraged to print it, regardless of the financial consequences it might have on the paper or actions taken by the advertiser. The public's right to know trumps any threats or actions by advertisers, politicians, or sources against the story itself.

Sincerity, Truthfulness, and Accuracy—

These tenants speak for themselves. They represent the basic standards by which members of the press should pursue and write stories. Whether the story is deemed positive or negative, it will remain credible so long as it has been pursued in an sincere and professional manner and contains information that is accurate and presented truthfully.

Impartiality—

All stories should be free from bias and opinion. While reporters may have their perspectives or views on various issues or individuals they cover, such thoughts should not enter into or be reflected in what they actually write. It should be the job of the press to simply report what has happened, been done, or been said. The public, then, is free to make up its own mind or draw its conclusions on this information. This, of course, does not apply to opinion pieces such as editorials that all media outlets print. It is vital, however, that the media outlet distinctly differentiate between its editorials and its so-called straight news sections.

Fair Play—

As part of being unbiased and impartial, it is essential that journalists be fair in their coverage of public issues and accusations. Doing so requires that they present opposing views in their stories or, at the very least, provide those representing opposing sides or views the opportunity to speak out. In addition, exhibiting fairness calls for the press to print corrections when there are errors in their stories.

Decency—

This canon calls for reporters not to pander to what the ASNE labeled the "vicious instincts of society" by printing graphic and/or unnecessary information regarding matters of crime and vice. While people may want to know such details, journalists should refrain from catering to such demands that add little, if anything, to the primary content of the story. This canon speaks to the judgment of a reporter regarding what might or might not be deemed to be in the best taste.

When speaking of the seven canons, a key word to remember is "guidelines." The canons are not in and of themselves legal laws. Writers cannot be arrested should they violate any of them. When composed by the ASNE, the canons were presented more as philosophic ideals to which reporters could and even should prescribe while carry out their out their duties in a manner deemed to serve the best interests of the general public. The ASNE viewed reporters as being objective chroniclers of events and decisions of the day. They were not necessarily viewed as being part of the news or news stories. Rather, members of the press were seen as being carriers of information from a source to the public. Now, of course, more than four score and twenty years later, reporters are much more engaged in what they cover than ever before. How much this has benefited the profession or the public which its practitioners seek to serve remains a topic of debate. Whether this is a good or bad change is one topic. Perhaps a more engaging one revolves around the impact this change has had and continues to have on the canons of journalism and the ASNE's original vision of them.

Public Relations Society of America's Code of Ethics

The Public Relations Society of America (PRSA) is the largest professional association for public relations practitioners in the world. It boasts more than twenty-one thousand members and more than one hundred chapters in the United States and other countries throughout the world (Guth & Marsh, 2009). Also, the PRSA has a number of student chapters located at various colleges and universities throughout the United States. In 2000, the PRSA's general assembly approved a code of ethics that included a listing of professional values and principles of conduct. In passing this comprehensive code, the PRSA reaffirmed its commitment to ethical practices and to retaining what it terms a "level of trust" between its members and the public these practitioners seek to serve. For the purposes of this text, we present the code's professional values and then its principles of conduct, along with a brief description of each.

Statement of Professional Values

Advocacy—

This refers to providing the best and most responsible service to who or whatever the practitioner represents. Doing so includes giving the client—an individual or organization—a voice in the marketplace of ideas or financial competition.

Honesty—

Though practitioners are representing a specific perspective, this should not be an excuse for not maintaining the highest standards of accuracy and truth in advancing or promoting the interests of those they represent.

Expertise—

Practitioners communicate for a living. They are professionals. It is vital that they maintain a high level of knowledge about the field and continue to remain as proficient as possible in their ability to perform the various communication tasks their job requires.

Independence—

Though practitioners are advocates on behalf of their clients, the counsel they provide should be objective. At times, this requires telling clients things they may not want to hear. Practitioners are accountable for their actions. Thus, being anything less than truthful with a client is as much of a disservice to that client as it is to the practitioner.

Loyalty—

This represents a dual track for practitioners. They are to be loyal to their clients and those they represent. This means that practitioners should not represent clients who happen to be on the opposite side of an issue. An example would be working on behalf of two political candidates who are running against each other in an election. That aside, practitioners should also be loyal to the overall public interest. This means being honest and truthful in all they communicate and advising their clients to behave in a like manner.

Fairness—

A fundamental tenant of the United States is that everyone is equal. Some may have more money than others. Some may hold a higher station in society than others. Nevertheless, the United States functions on the principle that all are equal in the eyes of the law and that one person's vote is of no greater or lesser importance than another's. It is under this umbrella that public relations practitioners are called on to treat everyone, including clients, employers, employees, competitors, peers, vendors, and members of the general public, fairly and with respect. Practitioners should also actively recognize that all have a right to their opinions as well as a right to free expression. Therefore, any strategies that they help devise should support those beliefs.

Principles of Conduct

In addition to being communicators of high quality, public relations practitioners are viewed by the PRSA as being advocates and proponents of the ideals that distinguish the United States and the freedoms it guarantees under the Constitution. The principles of conduct, generally, are designed to do more than simply call on practitioners to conduct themselves in a certain way when working with clients. The principles call for these professionals to constantly present them as advocates for the standards listed below that support both the profession of public relations and U.S. ideas. Following is a summation of these principles.

Free Flow of Information—

This principle speaks to protecting and advancing the free flow of truthful and accurate information.

Competition—

This principle calls for the promotion of healthy and fair competition in an ethical climate.

Disclosure of Information—

In a democratic society, open communication is key to maintaining necessary transparency. This includes correcting any misinformation as well as building trust among participants in any communication effort or process.

Safeguarding Confidences—

Practitioners need do all they can to protect the privacy rights of clients, including individuals and organizations. An example of improper conduct under this principle would be intentionally leaking sensitive information that is detrimental to some other party.

Conflicts of Interest—

By building on the trust and goodwill of clients, colleagues, and the general public, practitioners can help avoid real, potential, or perceived situations where a person or entity's personal and public obligations bump heads.

Enhancing the Profession—

Above all, practitioners represent the public relations profession itself. For better or worse, how they conduct themselves reflects on the profession and the level of confidence and trust others have in it.

Is living up to these values and principles a tall order? Perhaps. Theoretically, they put practitioners in the position of occasionally being their clients' "fly in the ointment." By this we mean that the practitioner may be the one who reminds the client what is ethical and/or legal when it comes to communicating information about its product, cause, or competitors. Sometimes people in power do not like being told "no" or that their ideas may need to be turned down several notches. At times, it falls on the practitioner to do this. On the flip side, it can be tempting for practitioners to support ideas with which they may not be totally comfortable when they believe that to do the opposite would affect their employment. A classic example is the moral crossroads on which Jerald ter Horst, press secretary of president Gerald Ford, found himself when Ford announced his decision to pardon former president Richard Nixon, who had resigned from the presidency over the Watergate scandal. ter Horst disagreed with the decision. Rather than defend Ford's action to the media as his job called for, he resigned. While this example did not involve any writing, it nevertheless pertained to communication and ter Horst's belief that he could not communicate something that he did not or could not support. For him, it was an ethical dilemma.

While the great majority of professional communicators do not find themselves at the kind of crossroads that ter Horst faced, it is important to note that these scenarios do happen. The challenge is one that is not so much legal as it is moral. Such an area as represented in journalism's canons and the public relations profession's values and principles of conduct speaks to those unique challenges where communicators—writers—contend with matters of conscience. In this area, choices are not necessarily right or wrong or black or white. Rather, they are more gray, thus making them matters that can be decided only on an individual basis. This, however, is not to be confused with the law itself. Here things tend to be more definitive in terms of the parameters of behavior and what one is allowed to communicate, orally and in writing. Once a final decision on a point of contention or issue has been rendered, the matter is settled. Regarding situations where ethical choices are faced, choices may be made, but final assessment on the actual merit of the decision may continue to be the subject of debate. An example is the ter Horst decision. Even now, more than forty years after the fact, his choice still ignites discussion and disagreement. When the courts become involved, however, the great majority of their decisions, even controversial ones, carry with them a weight of finality that ethical choices often do not. Thus, it is this field—the law—on which we now focus.

Communication and the Law

We begin with a question: In terms of writing copy, are professional communicators, such as public relations practitioners, responsible for their own actions? Can the courts hold writers accountable if their boss instructs them to write something that is proved to be libelous? If such a person appears in court, can the writer claim innocence by simply declaring that he or she was only following orders? To answer that, we note that as visible members of an organization's team, it is not uncommon for practitioners to be part of lawsuits or litigation when people take exception to the employer's behavior or actions (Guth & Marsh, 2009). While we cannot say that practitioners are necessarily always "guilty by association," we can observe that it does happen that they are charged based on their associations. A second key reason—perhaps more important than the first—is the reality that free speech is not unlimited. Yes, all of us consider America to be a free, democratic nation, but the reality is that our nation is neither totally free nor totally democratic. Laws, no matter how well intentioned or wise, by definition are geared to place limits on behavior and help ensure that people conduct themselves within what are viewed to be reasonable parameters.

Though we live in a free society, none of us are "free" to drive a car without wearing a seatbelt. If we do and are caught by authorities, we will be penalized. Furthermore, while America is considered to be among the oldest democracies in the history of mankind, those democratic principles go only so far. Not everyone can vote, for instance. Ten-year-olds are not eligible to vote. Furthermore, only those people born within the United States are eligible to run for the office of president of the country. We mention these truisms to drive home the point that even free societies have their limitations. As this pertains to professional communicators, particularly those who write, even free speech has boundaries. Writers cannot say or write anything they want or are instructed to write as it pertains to other people or products. Making false claims regarding a product or charges against another person can and often does put those who make these statements on very thin ice.

These reasons, then, are why all communicators, regardless of their specific profession, need to be well versed in matters of the law. As wide open as the act of communication might be, it behooves all who do write professionally to be well versed in the rules of the game. Thus, we delve into the primary aspects of the law that most apply to communicators and look at how courts in the past have addressed questions regarding these areas. For the purposes of simplicity, we have identified four primary categories or areas with which professional communicators should concern themselves. They are libel, malice, privacy, and copyright.

Libel

Zelezny defines *libel* as a false communication that wrongfully injures the reputation of others. (1997). Following this definition, it does not matter whether the mistake was intentional. If one's reputation has been damaged or compromised, that person has grounds for suing those who communicated the hurtful information. Regarding libel, there are several aspects that pertain to the burden of proof that must be addressed by a person claiming that he or she was damaged. They are called defamation, publication, identification, damage, and fault. Following is a quick summation of each.

Defamation—

This is any communication that unfairly injures a person's reputation and/or ability to maintain social contacts. An example would be calling a person a child molester without proof.

Publication—

This is the communication of a defamatory statement to a third party. This applies not just to publications as we traditionally think of them, but to all communication channels. Even repeating a defamatory statement, unless it is before an official government body or in court, can make one vulnerable to charges of libel.

Identification—

This refers to a person or organization, even though not mentioned specifically by name, that claims that any reasonable person knows that it is the object of defamatory comments.

Damage—

There must be evidence that the aggrieved party suffered damage. Examples range from financial loss, losing a job, or even losing all social contacts or friends.

Fault—

The person claiming that he or she was grieved—the plaintiff—demonstrates or proves that the defamatory statement or communiqué against him or her was false.

Malice

Any discussion of actual malice must include one of the most famous U.S. Supreme Court cases of the twentieth century: *The New York Times v. Sullivan.* This case revolved around public officials, individuals who voluntarily step into the public arena. In 1964, the high court ruled that public officials had a greater burden of proof than those who do not hold positions of great visibility. These individuals have to demonstrate not only that statements about them were not true but that the sources of the statements actually knew—or should have known—they were not true. "Actual malice" is the term attributed to this higher burden of proof. This term, as defined by the court, is viewed as a knowing falsehood or reckless disregard for the truth.

Since that ruling, courts have initiated efforts to further clarify the question of public officials and public figures. Public officials have been defined as people elected to public office or anyone who has significant public responsibility and/or who is involved in policymaking. Public figures such as celebrities or professional athletes, according to the courts, are those individuals who have widespread notoriety or have injected themselves into a public matter in order to influence a particular outcome. All this points to the cliché "the price of fame." When people are well known, no matter the reason, they have a difficult time winning libel cases. To professional communicators, this may make famous folks easier targets for criticism, but such a realty should not be an encouragement for or give license to any journalist or public relations practitioners to stray beyond what is ethically acceptable.

Privacy

Just because people are famous or well known, it does not mean that they walk around with a bulls-eye on their backs. Their fame does not make them target practice for writers wishing to take pot shots at them without consequences. In other words, the famous have just as much right to their privacy as anyone else. Having said that, however, this does not mean that laws regarding privacy issues are less complicated. To help add some degree of clarity to this issue, the law recognizes what it calls "torts," or wrongful acts that compromise invasion of privacy. These acts are intrusion (improper and intentional invasion of a person's physical space or private affairs), false light (purposely presenting someone in a false light), publication of private facts (public disclosure of personal information that is embarrassing and/or offensive), and appropriation (commercial use of someone's name, voice, likeness, or other defining characteristics without consent).

The above topic generally speaks to journalists. But privacy issues also pertain to public relations practitioners in that they help produce a large volume of communiqués for public consumption, including press releases, photos, videos, and websites. Collectively, issues revolving around matters of dispute over privacy speak to the matter of differences between private individuals—most of us—and those who dwell in the limelight,

Copyright

As we have alluded to previously, writers, particularly those in the promotion business, produce numerous publications or make use of ones that previously exist. This aspect of the law speaks to the protection of original works from being used without the proper authorization. Specifically, it speaks to "intellectual property," which the federal government defines as "original works of authorship that are fixed in a tangible form of expression." This covers a range of types of communication, including works largely from the arts: musical compositions, literary works, sculptural artwork, motion pictures, sound recordings, dramatic pantomimes, choreographed dances, and audiovisual media. It is a matter of protecting one's property. Those making use of the work of others must be careful to gain the proper permission of the material's authors or owners.

Fair Use

Of course, there are exceptions to this rule. This, then, speaks to what is known as "fair use." In this regard, courts have ruled that making use of copyrighted material is OK so long as it is for purposes of "criticism, comments, news, reporting, and teaching." The upshot here is that writers should be given a say on whether their work, published in one form, may be used in another, such as an online database. In terms of using the work of others, fair use enables public relations practitioners to use a quotation from a copyrighted publication. Examples here would be using a quote from an earlier president and incorporating it into a press release, brochure, or speech. However, this is acceptable only when the author of that quote is properly recognized.

Wrap-Up

Writing within the law is not as freewheeling as one might think or perhaps wish. Journalists and public relations practitioners are wise to draw from their own levels of creativity and depth of knowledge when composing stories. On those occasions when they are drawing from the work or insights of others, they must give credit where it is due. To do otherwise not only puts writers in jeopardy of violating the law but places them in direct conflict with the canons and ethics of journalism and public relations.

How well one adheres to ethical standards and stays within the boundaries of the law defines his or her quality as a professional. This is true in the routine aspects of individuals' writing efforts as well as in those times when their professional challenges are anything but that. What happens, for example, when a journalist quotes a source in an article only to find later that source was not telling the truth? What should this person do? And what should the public relations practitioner do when a client is on trial for a serious crime it claims it did not commit, only to find out in private conversation that the client actually is guilty? Such ethical and professional dilemmas are from far easy. Then there is the matter of a crisis. Communication during times of unexpected turmoil and disruption is particularly vital. It is in such scenarios when people feel most vulnerable yet have the most need for information that is timely and accurate.

Depending on the circumstance, the communicator may be dealing with information that he or she is told should not be shared with the public. The disclosure of such information, for instance, may impede a criminal investigation or compromise the lives of people. When this happens, what is a journalist or public relations practitioner to do? On the one hand, these professionals have agreed to be agents of truth, as one of their core values is to be open with the public. On the other hand, they are told by authorities that being totally open might actually do the public harm. Is the public's right to know completely open-ended? Does a dishonest client deserve public relations representation? As is the case in many such instances, there is not always an easy answer to these kind of questions. Communicators are gatekeepers of information. To contend with space and time constraints among their routine deliberations is to decide which information to share with others and which not. In times of crisis, such determination takes on greater significance. Often the answer is found in the moral code of the communicator.

Without question, writing is a form of intellectual creativity. For professionals in both fields, communicating well is their most demanding challenge. Not only is writing itself difficult; doing so day in and day out makes it even more daunting. Given the prospect of having to climb such a steep mountain on such a regular basis, it is certainly understandable if writers are tempted to draw from the works or thoughts of others. In fact, it is even acceptable, so long as they do not claim what they are borrowing as their own. Thus, when it comes to writing, how they play the game is as important as the game itself.

Reading List

Much has been and continues to be written about ethics in regard to journalism and public relations. How those working in these fields meet their responsibilities, particularly regarding the written word, dominates many scholarly works. The following articles speak to several aspects of this important topic:

Journalism, Politics and Public Relations: an Ethical Appraisal

By Brian McNair

Introduction

At the end of the twentieth century the citizens of western democracies have access to more information about politics than at any previous time in human history. Journalistic media proliferate, and politics is high on their agenda. Politicians are acutely aware of this, and work hard to influence public opinion through those media. A supporting network of professional communicators strives to ensure that political messages are accurately and widely disseminated, in the face of a journalistic profession which becomes more aware of, and resistant to, such efforts by the year.

Through print, television and radio, with mass access to digital broadcasting and the Internet now imminent, we—the electorate, to whom all this communicative activity is ultimately directed—have access to a continuous flow of political information in all its forms—news, current affairs, debate shows, phone-ins, commentaries, satirical comedy—from early in the morning until late at night.

Are we then, as a consequence, more knowledgeable about politics, and thus more powerful as citizens (assuming that Francis Bacon was right and knowledge is still power) than ever before? Or are we merely passive witnesses of a media spectacle beyond our control, in which the quantity of information communicated is high, but its quality as a resource in opinion-forming and political decision-making is low?

In posing the question in these terms we enter a debate which is not new, but which has acquired new urgency as the sheer quantity of political communication in circulation increases, and the debate about its effects on the democratic process intensifies. In both Britain and the United States in recent years the role of political communication in electoral victory and defeat has been crucial. Quantifying that role is difficult, but it is beyond dispute that effective political communication played a large part in saving Bill Clinton's second term, and that it greatly helped the British Labour Party to its first government in eighteen years.

If few would challenge the underlying truth of these observations, many are concerned about their implications for the conduct of democratic politics. Three general concerns are voiced:

- first, that the style and content of political journalism is not, as it should be, supplying the citizenry with useful information, but on the contrary is actually obstructing the communication of political messages;
- second, that political actors no longer formulate their policies on grounds of principle and rational argument, but do so in consideration of the perceived need to 'play well' in the media, and to please 'public opinion', itself often argued to be largely a media creation;
- and third, that the communicative work of both journalists and politicians has become distorted by the influence of what Edward Bernays in 1923 called 'press counsellors', and who are better known today as 'spin-doctors', 'communications advisers', 'media consultants' or 'PR gurus'.

Taken together, it is argued, these developments have undermined the integrity of the public sphere, and rendered the late twentieth century's apparent participation of the masses in the democratic process illusory. Worse, they have encouraged mass apathy and growing non-participation in politics, as exemplified by the American case[1]. Such criticisms identify three groups of actors whose communicative ethics we should be concerned with:

- the politicians, in and out of government, for whom information flows are important power resources;
- the journalists who monitor, report, scrutinise and analyse the politicians' actions and rhetoric;
- and the group occupying a place in the communicative process somewhere between the first two: the aforementioned public relations advisers and spin-doctors.

Political communication is, to a large extent, both the process and the result of interaction and negotiation between these groups, each of which has its own ethical codes, defined in relation to the normative principles of liberal democracy. Politicians in a democracy are supposed to communicate (professionally, at least) for the purpose of ensuring good government, presenting citizens with political choices, laying claim to political power, and informing citizens honestly and openly about the administration of government.

The public relations practitioner (whether in the guise of lobbyist, spin-doctor, or Whitehall press officer) aspires to facilitate the effective communication of a message from a political actor to a wider public, in most cases through the media, since these are the channels through which the vast majority of people receive their political information. He or she also communicates in the other direction, lobbying politicians on behalf of organisational clients such as companies, trade unions and single-issue pressure groups. Because the public relations industry (including its political wing) is young (very much a twentieth-century phenomenon) it has developed ethical codes and practices which are designed to enhance its status and prestige as a *profession*, and thus to legitimise its existence as a necessary and worthwhile element of the contemporary media environment. The deliberate telling of lies on behalf of a client, for example, is not regarded as ethical.

Journalists, finally, are considered a key source of the information on which the integrity of the public sphere depends. But they are also expected to monitor the political environment on the citizens' behalf, and keep a watchful eye out for the abuse of power. This has been their 'fourth estate' role since the time of Edmund Burke.

These roles and functions are, of course, ideals. They describe things as they should be, and not necessarily as they are. But they are ideals taken seriously by all three professional groups, and reflected in standards of communicative behaviour which we as citizens are entitled to see applied, even if imperfectly. When they are not, then the democratic condition of an authentic public sphere, supported by rational information flows, through channels open and accessible to all, is called into question. This essay assesses the form and content of contemporary political communication from the perspective of the politician, the public relations professional, and the journalist respectively, in the context of the ethical standards which they have set themselves, and of the ongoing debate about these issues which so occupies academic and professional observers at the present time.[2]

Communicating Politics

We begin with the politicians, since it is they who stand at the apex of the communicative pyramid, and compete most aggressively for the prizes awarded in the game of democratic politics. They do so, at this point in capitalism's evolution, in a uniquely public way, subject to the approval of a genuinely mass electorate. It is, after all, only eighty or so years since women were excluded from this electorate, and not too long before that, that men without the approved wealth and education qualifications were also deprived of the vote. Now, regardless of class, sex, ethnic or religious background, all are equal in the privacy of the polling booth. Politicians must compete for our support, using the channels of mass communication at the centre of our cultural lives to project their ideas, values and policies. To the extent that politicians require public support political communication is largely about publicity. Where feudal lords (and their contemporary counterparts in China, Iraq and elsewhere) imposed their will on powerless subjects, politicians who claim to be democratic leaders must win popular consent, and be seen to have won it. They must have *legitimacy*, or they cannot govern.

There are two stages to winning legitimacy. One is to be seen and heard in the public sphere, by securing a requisite *quantity* of media coverage. As one observer notes, 'the struggle for visibility is at the centre of all politics'.[3] Civil servants and party functionaries prefer anonymity and secrecy, but the ambitious politician must be seen and heard, if the highest reaches of office are to be his or hers.

As many politicians know to their cost, however, not all publicity is good publicity. A second stage in winning democratic legitimacy in today's political environment is to secure *qualitatively* favourable coverage, which accentuates the positive and downplays negative features of a politician's or a party's public identity. This fact has led politicians to develop increasingly sophisticated means of managing the media so as to secure such coverage. In the process, argue the critics, the communication activity of politicians has become artificial, manipulative, even deceitful. The rational content of political discourse has been subordinated to the needs of public opinion management.

Jurgen Habermas's framing of the argument continues to be influential. For Habermas, 'publicity' as we understand the term today is the harmful by-product of democratic politicians' perceived need for favourable media visibility. Because *favourable* publicity is desired, the presentation of information tends to be selective and dishonest. As he puts it, 'publicity work is aimed at strengthening the prestige of one's own position without making the matter on which a compromise is to be achieved itself a topic of public discussion' (1988, p. 200). Publicity seeks to divert the attentions of the public from critical debate about the real business of politics (the issues), and towards passive consumption of symbols (personality and style). If publicity is, in normative terms, the process of informing the public on important matters, in current conditions of mass mediatised politics it has lost its educative and critical functions. Through publicity 'arguments are transmuted into symbols to which one does not respond by arguing but only by identifying with them' (p. 206). Political decisions are made 'for manipulative purposes and are introduced with consummate propagandistic skill as publicity vehicles into a public sphere manufactured for show' (p. 221).

Habermas wrote these words in the 1960s, but recent events lend support to his central argument. Bill Clinton's political resurrrection and eventual victory in the presidential election of November 1996 was the result not least of his highly public, highly visible abandoning of some hitherto cherished policies, and the adoption of others previously associated with the US right. As Clinton's communications adviser Dick Morris (1996) boasts in his account of the Clinton first term, this 'positioning' of the president in a place somewhere between traditional notions of left and right was done deliberately to attract voters, a strategy which—despite Whitewater, Hillarygate, 'Slick Willie' and all the other personal scandals which afflicted his first-term administration—was successful, if measured by the proportion of votes cast. Clinton's ideological principles and instincts were sacrificed to the greater goal of retaining political power, much to the anger of ordinary Democratic party members who, despite their pleasure at the prospect of a second Clinton term, accused him of betrayal of the causes on which he had first been elected in 1992.

In Britain, similar accusations have been made of the Labour Party since the election of Tony Blair as leader in 1994. Here, too, it is alleged that political principles have been sacrificed in the pursuit of power; that policy has been formulated and communicated with an eye on public opinion rather than what is right for the country; that 'New Labour' is all style and no substance, masking what amounts to a historic betrayal of British socialism and of the British working classes. The fact that New Labour won a General Election in 1997 does not invalidate the criticisms of those who hold such views, nor mollify their feelings of betrayal since, they would argue, a left-of-centre party in power without a principled approach to government is hardly a better prospect than another Conservative term of office.

Elsewhere I have argued that criticisms of this type are naïve, betraying a romanticised, patronising view of both the social democratic left (which has by definition never been 'socialist' in any theoretically rigorous sense) and the working classes, who have consistently rejected 'authentic' socialist policies and who, on the contrary, have sustained right-wing governments in Britain for most of the century (McNair 1995, 1996). Intepretations of policy aside, however, can the politicians who have led these 'betrayals' be fairly accused of unethical behaviour in their ever more managed and calculated approach to the communication of their messages?

An answer to this question can only be given on the basis of specific circumstances. If politicians, in the content of their communication, knowingly deceive the electorate, then we are certainly entitled to criticise their ethical standards. When politicians, in government or opposition, lie about their motives, ambitions and decisions; when they suppress information which the public has a right to receive; when they 'leak' aggressively and unfairly against opponents and colleagues, they are behaving unethically, and there have been instances of all three in recent

British history, on all parts of the party political spectrum. If, on the other hand, they are simply using the available repertoire of communicative techniques and instruments to project ideas which may deviate from traditional norms, but which are a sincere response to changed political and socio-economic circumstances, then the charge of ethical violation seems excessive. No individual politician, or party, can be blamed for the fact that considerations of image and style are today as important to political success as the detail of policy, and none can be blamed for participating enthusiastically in 'the game' as it is now played. On the contrary, failure to do so, in the manner of the Labour Party before the arrival of Peter Mandelson as communications director in the mid-1980s, might be viewed as a greater evil, since it deprives the electorate of meaningful choice and makes minority government more sustainable. Commentator Anna Coote, paraphrasing the French sociologist Pierre Bourdieu, points out that

> as traditional differences between left and right break down, so the notion of faith [in politicians] becomes increasingly important: what matters to voters is not what politicians promise, or even what they stand for, but whether they can be trusted. That, in turn, depends on the personality of the politician and the character of the relationship with the voter. These are expressed largely by means of image and style.[4]

Greater emphasis on 'image and style' is, in short, the price of mass democracy in a late capitalist, post-Cold-War environment, whether one likes it or not.

Managing Political Communication: The Ethics of Political Public Relations

Whether politicians are ethical or not, the design and execution of their media performances are increasingly delegated to professional advisers and consultants: specialists in political public relations, marketing, lobbying and advertising who are employed, usually behind the scenes, to advise on and manage the communication process. The names of the best-known members of this profession—George Stephanopoulos, James Carville, Dick Wirthlin and Dick Morris in the United States; Brendan Bruce, Tim Bell, Peter Mandelson, Alistair Campbell in Britain—have become, for their critics, emblems of the ethical decline in political life, and generated a major sub-genre of political journalism devoted to the discussion of their alleged crimes. These include manipulation and intimidation of the media to advance the politicians' publicity goals, pressurising politicians to denude themselves of principle and integrity in deference to presentational gloss and, in the worst cases, of usurping the place of the politician and becoming major political players in themselves. The worst offenders in this regard are said to be the 'spin-doctors', a new breed of communicator who does not facilitate the flow of political information (a long-standing and respected function ideally carried out in a disinterested manner by civil service functionaries and other 'apolitical' staff) so much as 'doctor' it for media, and then public consumption. Journalist Simon Heffer contrasts the more traditional function of press officer with that of the spin-doctor in the following terms:

> The press officer, even if he was a party rather than a government employee, would mainly concern himself with the provision of facts and background information ... The

> spin doctor is concerned mainly with spin. His role goes beyond the facts; it is to outline to journalists exactly what he feels the thrust of their story should be; it is to persuade them to accentuate the positive and ignore or at least play down the negative.[5]

The term was imported from the United States in the 1980s, and has since come to be used as a form of mild abuse, surrounding those to whom it is applied with a slightly sinister air of magic and mystery. Spin-doctors seek to manipulate press coverage by controlling access to senior politicians and, in particular, denying it to journalists who do not seem amenable to the 'persuasion' mentioned by Heffer. Their main weapon is aggressive lobbying, accompanied by punitive action against dissenting journalists. They are often accused of being arrogant and overbearing. Columnist Iain MacWhirter complains that the 'media minders cruise the lobbies these days like celebrities. No longer are they the servants of the press, whose function it is to get the party message across as clearly and as widely as possible. They now regard themselves as players in their own right'.[6] Labour's Peter Mandelson and Alistair Campbell have been the most frequently attacked in these terms, most famously in relation to the fax sent to the BBC newsroom when the verdict of the O. J. Simpson trial was announced. They were concerned about the possibility of having a Tony Blair speech driven down the BBC's running order by the news from Los Angeles, and the fax was a blatant attempt to influence editorial policy.

The attempt failed, in so far as the fax became a news story in itself, making more transparent and newsworthy the process of political news management. In October 1996 the *Panorama* current affairs magazine marked the Labour conference by devoting an entire edition to the work of spin-doctors, much to the anger of Campbell and Mandelson. The fax incident, and others like it, thus led to a new policy of increased vigilance on the part of BBC producers, reducing the ability of political news managers of all parties to influence journalistic agendas.

In his defence, Alistair Campbell has repeatedly maintained that the notoriety of the Simpson fax shows how rare is conflict of this kind between journalists and party news managers and that, in any event, the activity of 'spinning' is not a qualitatively new or unethical feature of democratic politics. 'Spinning' may have grown in importance and visibility alongside the growth of the political media, but it dates back at least as far as the reign of Charles II, who employed Samuel Pepys to act as his 'press handler'. Responding to the *Panorama* programme in which he featured prominently as one of Clare Short's 'people who live in the dark' Campbell pointed out that:

> We live in the media age. There are more newspapers, magazines, television and radio stations than ever before. They all have space to fill, and they look to politics to fill a good deal of it. The political party that does not understand the needs of the media is doomed. Much of the work involves ensuring all outlets are spoken to, a consistent line is taken, and our central points communicated. None of that stifles debate.[7]

This seems reasonable, provided that it is communication rather than intimidation to which journalists are exposed. If Campbell, Mandelson and their colleagues can be blamed for a bullying and over-zealous approach to ensuring 'consistency' of policy presentation—and even they admit that they *have* been guilty of this on occasion[8]—then they should also be given the credit for instilling professionalism and coherence in their employer's communication management, with all that has subsequently flowed from this in terms of electoral success. Whether the price of this success has been too high will perhaps be clearer at the end of Labour's first term.

Lobbying

One branch of the political public relations industry whose ethical standards have been most directly and deservedly challenged in recent years are the lobbyists. Such organisations as Westminster Strategy, the Communication Group, Government Policy Consultants, and the now infamous Ian Greer Associates, exist to advance the interests of extra-parliamentary clients in the House of Commons. They 'lobby' for some acts of legislation and against others, by using a variety of formal and informal communicative tactics. In the case of Ian Greer Associates and certain Conservative MPs, as was revealed by the press in 1995 and 1996, this involved passing brown envelopes full of money in exchange for said MPs asking official questions of ministers. The 'cash for questions' scandal, and other examples of 'sleaze' documented in the early 1990s were clear violations of the ethical standards of the professions involved.

On the other hand, most political lobbying companies do not seek to bribe politicians, and most politicians would not accept bribes if they were offered. That some do, have then been exposed by the press, and have seen their careers damaged by the resulting waves of criticism, might be interpreted to mean that the British political system is not yet in the same league of corruptibility and criminality as those of many other comparable countries. Nevertheless, this dimension of the political communication process requires continued monitoring, not just by the various parliamentary committees and watchdogs which have been set up in the wake of the 'sleaze' scandals of the 1990s, but by the political media. In this respect the *Guardian* and the *Sunday Times*, which led the investigative reportage of the Hamilton affair, have played an exemplary role, and one which should be viewed as a model for the role of the 'fourth estate'.

The Ethics of Political Journalism

Unfortunately, the praise which legitimately accrues to some newspapers for their exposure of unethical practices in the political arena is more than matched by persistent criticism of the media's role in degrading and trivialising the democratic process. Some of these criticisms raise the issue of ethical standards, since they concern features of political journalism that are deliberate and intentional. Others highlight trends which are the product of factors beyond individual journalistic control but which, intentionally or not, are alleged to damage the quality of public political discourse.

The press and political bias

In relation to the press, two ethical criticisms are made most frequently. The first concerns the long-standing issue of bias, and the tendency of so many newspapers to act as propagandists for right-of-centre political masters. This bias results, it is argued, not only in editorial support for the ideas and values of the right, and against those of the left, but dishonest and inaccurate reportage. Well-known examples include the 1980s coverage of the activities of the 'loony left' in London, the *Daily Mirror's* false accusations of Arthur Scargill's 'links' with Libya in its coverage of the 1984–5 miners' strike, and a succession of British General Elections in which the Labour Party was unable to secure a fair hearing from the vast majority of the press. Although empirical evidence for a pro-Tory effect of this coverage is difficult to assemble, many commentators have argued that the seventeen-year hold of the Conservative Party on government was not unrelated to the degree of unquestioning support which it enjoyed from all but a few broadsheet and tabloid newspapers over this period.[9]

Former Conservative minister Lord Wakeham is among those in his party who frankly concede that the role of the press was crucial in securing electoral victory in 1992. In his view, 'the sharpness of the pro-Conservative newspapers' comments and the depth and breadth of their reporting undoubtedly helped to ensure some of the movement towards us in the last weeks of the campaign' (1995, p. 5). The 'sharpness' and 'depth' referred to by Wakeham included such stories as the *Daily Mail's* 'tax bombshell' coverage, and the *Sun's* day of-poll headline, 'If Kinnock wins today, will the last person to leave Britain turn out the lights'.

Anti-Labour press bias was not new in 1992, but it reached unprecedented heights and may, in the view of many observers, have made a crucial difference to the result. For leading Tory fundraiser Lord McAlpine, writing in the *Sunday Telegraph* a few days after John Major was returned to office, the press were 'the heroes of [the 1992] campaign'.

> Never has the attack on the Labour Party been so comprehensive. They exposed, ridiculed and humiliated that party, doing each day in their pages the job that the politicians failed to do from their bright new platforms. This is how the election was won.[10]

The press in a democracy has, of course, the right to say what it likes within the law, but the self-proclaimed ethical standards of the journalistic profession may be thought to preclude efforts to 'fix' elections by the deliberate distortion and misreporting of political information. There is, as Noam Chomsky and others have persuasively argued, little difference between the Soviet-era propaganda sheets and those newspapers of the 'free press' which volunteer themselves as cheerleaders of one political party over another, irrespective of 'the truth'. The fact that the period between 1992 and 1997 saw a decline of pro-Conservative press bias, attributable in large part to sustained and skilful courting of the Murdoch titles by the Labour Party, does not alter the underlying argument: that journalists in a democracy—even those working on tabloids—have a responsibility to pluralism and diversity of political debate, and to refrain from peddling myths and lies about groups who may be viewed in certain quarters as 'subversive'. The fortunes of the Labour Party in government will be significantly shaped by how seriously the British press take this responsibility in the coming years.

The Tabloidisation of Political Journalism

If the period between 1992 and 1997 was one in which the press became less like the collective house organ of the Conservative Party, it was also one of unprecedented reportage of political scandal, much of it affecting the Conservative Party itself. It may be that the two phenomena are related, and that Messrs Murdoch, Black, Montgomery *et al.* found it increasingly difficult to give unbending support to a party so apparently prone to moral lapses. In vigorously reporting the numerous cases of alleged ethical misconduct amongst politicians which have been revealed in recent years, however, the press has been accused of undermining faith in the political system itself, and of itself behaving unethically.

I referred above to the 'cash for questions' scandal, and the widely welcomed reportage of those newspapers which exposed it. Less welcome, for many observers, have been the many exposures of alleged sexual and 'lifestyle' misconduct amongst MPs. These have included serial philandering (Steven Norris), bizarre sex practices (the tragic death of Stephen Milligan), closet homosexuality (Jerry Hayes), alcoholism and drunk driving (Nicholas Scott). Almost all of these accusations involved the Conservative Party, and many required ministerial resignations, contributing much to the decline of the government's poll ratings after 1992. In reporting these stories, newspapers have been accused of masking the pursuit of commercial advantage (in an extremely competitive press market) behind pious concern for the nation's morals. Politicians, it is argued, have a right to privacy in so far as their private activities do not interfere with their public duties. What, for example, has Jerry Hayes's sexual preference got to do with his parliamentary life, given that he has been a liberal on gay rights in any case?

The royal family, too, has seen its private problems and difficulties relentlessly exposed in the press, leading to a climate in which its future as the pillar of the British constitution is under serious threat.

The ethical defence of such expository journalism is usually presented as follows. Regardless of the motivations behind it (and there can be little doubt that commercial rather than public interest considerations have been prominent in the thinking of tabloid editors) the press has a right, indeed a responsibility, to expose hypocrisy in public life. When politicians who on conference platforms preach about the social evils presented by single motherhood, or who choose to campaign around 'back to basics' moral values, turn out to be unfaithful to their wives, or neglecting their illegitimate children, the voters have a right to know. The conduct of private life in such cases has a clear relevance to public policy, and contradictions between the two are the proper subject of political journalism.

Revelatory coverage of the royals also has a public interest defence. Andrew Neil justified the *Sunday Times* serialisation of Andrew Morton's biography of the late Princess of Wales by arguing, firstly, that it was the product of Diana's own desire to have her side of the story reported, and furthermore, that the public has a right to know of matters which have serious constitutional significance, even if these are painfully private. He favourably contrasted the media visibility of the Charles–Diana marital split with the secrecy and widespread public ignorance which surrounded the abdication of Edward VIII in 1936.

The above justifications for a political journalism which is, whatever else it may be, undeniably titillatory, voyeuristic, and commercially successful, are indeed consistent with the ethical standards of a profession which since its emergence from the ruins of feudalism in early modern Europe has aspired to watch over the powerful. If the public's estimation of the political class suffers as a result, we might argue, then whose fault is it but their own?

Some media sociologists complain that the resulting coverage is 'part of a tendency to distract the public from matters of principle by offering voyeuristic pseudo-insights into individual matters' (Gripsund, 1992, p. 94). Others positively welcome the (unintentionally) subversive effect of such material appearing on our breakfast tables each morning, creating as it does an 'informed popular scepticism' (Fiske, 1992, p. 61) towards the powerful.

Readers of this book will have their own views on the impact of 'sleaze' journalism on our political culture. There are, clearly, some cases where the revelatory reportage of élite misbehaviour is consistent with the ethical codes of liberal journalism, and others where it is not. Distinguishing between the two is the task, firstly, of the journalists themselves, if they do not wish their already low reputation as a professional group to sink even further; of those who buy the newspapers concerned, and who give such coverage commercial value; and of the industry regulators, the Press Complaints Commission, whose judgements on these matters have not always been consistent or effective, prompting demands for legal measures to prohibit the worst excesses. Most journalists, including those who would not touch a toe-sucking royal story if it were handed to them on a plate, agree that it would be a pity if these demands led to legislation, since the law would be used most aggressively by the powerful to censor the legitimate, wholly ethical exposure of élite corruption and abuse.

Broadcasting

Broadcast political journalism has, until relatively recently, avoided the ethical challenges confronted by the print media. In Britain and many other countries, broadcast journalism has been strictly regulated to ensure that it is not biased towards one political party or another, and serves the public as a whole with political information and analysis of the quality demanded by modern democratic procedures. As a consequence, even in countries with almost entirely commercial systems, such as the United States, broadcast news has an image of neutrality and non-partisanship—a reputation for standing above and back from the party political fray—which gives it a distinctive role in the public sphere. Increasingly in the 1990s, however, broadcast journalists have been accused of abusing this role, and of damaging the political communication environment in the process.

Referring back to an earlier stage of the discussion, the growth of broadcast media, and television in particular, has been held responsible by many for the ascendancy of political style as an element in voter decision-making. Broadcast journalism, because of its space limitations and the brevity it imposes on political discourse, has produced what the senior BBC correspondent Nicholas Jones describes as 'a media environment habituated to the relentless pursuit of the soundbite' (1995, p. 51). The American James Fallows, editor of *The Nation,* accuses his colleagues in broadcast news of 'a relentless emphasis on the cynical game of politics' (1996, p. 31) which 'threatens public life itself'. Although individual broadcasters can hardly be blamed for an environment which they confront as a pre-given of their work, broadcasters as a group are the third essential strand of the politician–spin–doctor–journalist web, and as such implicated in the transformation of political communication into the deployment and manipulation of neat catchphrases (soundbites) and pleasing images (photo-opportunities).

Many variants of these criticisms exist in the literature, but they can perhaps be summarised in the claim that, for reasons of commerce, technology and professional vanity, the style of political journalism has gradually come to take precedence over substance. As the quantity of broadcast political communication available to viewers and listeners has grown exponentially, its quality has declined.

The Ethics of Broadcast Style

Walter Cronkite, for example, has attacked what he sees as 'the trend towards trivialising "infotainment"'.[11] The increasingly revelatory and voyeuristic content of press journalism about politics was discussed earlier. Now, the argument goes, as broadcasting systems become more commercialised and competitive, similar features are becoming apparent in television and radio journalism.

Cronkite's reference was to America, but it applies also to Britain where, with cable, satellite and digital technologies quickly coming on stream, broadcasting is undergoing rapid change. Will this be accompanied by a 'tabloidisation' of broadcast journalism? If so, for Jon Snow of Channel 4 News, 'the whole fabric of democracy is threatened. In a world in which debate is replaced by exchanged seven second soundbites, the content of politics falls victim to the more easily communicated evidence of human frailty'.[12]

Criticism is focused not only on the familiar evil of 'tabloidisation'. Broadcast political journalism also stands accused of developing a repertoire of stylistic traits which, though intended to connote authority, balance, neutrality, and so on, actually inhibit the communication of substantive information. The media analyst Bryan Appleyard observes of television news that 'the cult of seriousness has become a style in itself ... there has been an extraordinary blooming of technical and representational style, driven by a highly competitive market that demands the maximum impression of significance and sensation'.[13]

Nowhere is this more apparent than in the 'cult' of the 'star' presenter, exemplified in Britain most notably by Jeremy Paxman and John Humphrys and, on occasion, Sue MacGregor, James Naughtie and others who have acquired reputations for increasingly aggressive adversarial interviewing styles. At regular intervals in recent years these individuals have been accused of being excessively confrontational in their dealings with politicians, and of turning political interviews into sterile exchanges of accusation and counter-accusation which may entertain, but do not inform. The interview, it has been argued by politicians and broadcasters alike, becomes a test of a politician's ability to engage in verbal jousting rather than the articulation of policy.

The subject of political journalism becomes the *game* of politics, rather than the issues; the *process,* rather than the policies. As James Fallows observes, the 'context that gives meaning to information' (1996, p. 130) is sacrificed to make way for ratings-friendly drama.

For the 'stars' themselves, on the other hand, hostile interviewing is wholly consistent with their ethical responsibilities to the audience. John Humphrys, in rejecting politicians' criticisms of his style, has argued that broadcasters like himself play a key role in exposing the gap between what politicians say and what they do. In an increasingly managed communication environment, the in-depth political interview allows an element of unpredictability and challenge to be re-introduced, to the benefit of the citizen. The results may often lack rationality and coherence, but 'interviewing politicians is an important bridge between the electorate and their political leaders. We have to distil the national argument, to represent the voters' concerns'.[14] Michael Cockerell agrees that while Humphrys (and the other 'star' interviewers) 'may sometimes deploy a terrier-like persistence in his interviews that can sometimes be counter-productive ... his aim is to strip away the public relations gloss and use his own sharp teeth to counter pre-rehearsed soundbites'.[15]

The ethics of political interviewing is a subject which, perhaps understandably, has mainly preoccupied the politicians who are most regularly subjected to the techniques developed by Humphrys and his colleagues. For that reason alone, we should be cautious before endorsing calls for a journalistic retreat from the confrontational style. Occasional examples of presenter-vanity and 'hyperadversarialism' (as James Fallows calls it) are a small price to pay for a journalism which is not intimidated by the powerful.

Conclusion

Each of the three groups whose communicative behaviour we have examined in this essay is participating in a competition—a game, to use the metaphor frequently applied in this context. The politicians and the journalists compete to set the news agenda, and to have their perspectives on events reported. The spin-doctors act as coaches and managers on behalf of the politicians, and as technical assistants in realising the desired communicative effects. We, the voters, are positioned as spectators, with occasional walk-on parts. At the end of each electoral cycle we are asked to choose whom we think has performed best during the preceding period, and who is likely to perform best in the forthcoming one.

The politicians ask us to make that decision on the basis of the policy options which they lay out before us. Their spin-doctors and communication advisers operate on the assumption that we will also be influenced by the presentation, as well as the policy content of the message, a consideration which places great emphasis on the political performers' style and image. The journalists, meanwhile, probe this confection of policy-substance and image-surface, exposing and widening the gap between rhetoric and reality, laying bare the contradictions, drawing our attention to the existence of the game and the artifice employed by its participants.

None of this is incompatible with the respective ethical standards of each group. Politicians advocate, media consultants advise, journalists scrutinise. They are all, in that sense, merely doing their jobs. The difference between now and earlier times—and what has made this such a burning issue—is principally that the game is, from the viewpoint of the players, more competitive and managed. For us as spectators it is more omnipresent, even intrusive, than ever before. At times we come to feel that we have overdosed on politics. We grow weary with the politicians' posturings, the journalists' probings, and the spin-doctors' efforts to pull the wool over our collective eyes. Yet the luxury of excess is not one which we should take for granted. Less than one hundred years ago, as was noted above, women did not have the vote in Britain. Free from the gaze of electronic media, politicians and other élite groups could pursue their business relatively free from journalistic intrusion. As recently as the 1950s the journalistic norm in dealing with politicians was (as seen from this distance in hilarious black and white newsreel footage) embarrassing, laughable deference. As for the world beyond the countries of advanced capitalism, many populations still live under criminally corrupt or authoritarian regimes, where a Jeremy Paxman, a James Naughtie, and even a Kelvin Mackenzie would not last ten minutes.

Of course there are excesses, and none of what has been said thus far is intended to lessen the significance of ethical lapses when they occur. Politicians lie. Journalists pursue confrontation for confrontation's sake, and expose the private failings of public figures for no more noble cause than the commercial advantage of their proprietor. Spin-doctors overdo it with threatening faxes and bullying phone calls.

The encouraging thing in all this, however, is how often we come to know about these abuses of the political communication machinery, how often they are exposed and themselves become part of the evidence and information on which we make our political judgements. This essay on the ethics of political communication could not have been written without reference to the vast quantity of media debate about— the ethics of political communication. We exist—largely thanks to the media—in a state of informed 'knowingness' which does much to protect us from the politicians' tendency, assisted by their professional media advisers, to dissemble, deceive and manipulate. And, of course, we have our own reservoirs of experience against which to compare everything that the political communicators say and do. The media supply a large part of the information on which we base our political behaviour, but by no means all.

We cannot reverse the communicative trends discussed in this essay, nor, I would argue, should we wish to. We inhabit the most media-literate, information-rich society in human history, where it is ever more difficult for élites to keep secrets, and to suppress debate, should ethical failings predispose them to do so. We *are* probably overloaded with political information, much of it trashy and superficial, but better that than the inhibited, boot-licking media of a few short decades ago.

As we enter the era of digital television and the Internet, we face another expansion of the political media, as hundreds of new channels come on air or on-line with space to fill. In meeting that challenge we as citizens should be vigilant, and ensure that our journalists are vigilant on our behalf, maintaining their own ethical standards, those of the politicians on whom they report, and the spin-doctors who seek to influence their coverage. We should encourage media education in schools and universities, so that the citizens of the twenty-first century learn the skills of critical reading and viewing as part of their preparation for civic responsibility. We should demand freedom of information and governmental openness. We should support appropriate restrictions on media ownership, so that the means of political communication are not open to monopolisation by wealthy individuals, and the potential for one-sided press bias is minimised. We should defend public service broadcasting, while accepting that it must adapt to meet the demands of new technologies and new viewing and listening patterns. And if all of that is not enough, we will simply have to exercise our right not to play the game: to switch off, withdraw our support, and call it to a halt.

Notes

1. The French philosopher Jean Baudrillard says, for example, that 'for some time now, the electoral game has been akin to TV game shows in the consciousness of the people. The people enjoy, day to day, like a home movie, the fluctuations of their own opinions in the daily opinion polls. Nothing in all this engages any responsibility. At no time are the masses politically engaged in a conscious manner', in *In the Shadow of the Silent Majorities … or the End of the Social* (New York: Semiotext, 1983), p. 38.
2. Although the opinions expressed are entirely my own, the argument draws on work funded by the Economic and Social Research Council on political communication and democracy currently being undertaken by the author in collaboration with colleagues at the Stirling Media Research Institute of Stirling University, Scotland.
3. M. Woollacott, 'When invisibility means death', *Guardian,* 27 April 1996.
4. A. Coote, 'Labour puts its neck on the line', *Sunday Times*, 29 September 1996.
5. S. Heffer, 'Spinning for a living … who cares?', *British Journalism Review* 6/4 (1995).
6. I. MacWhirter, 'Not what the spin doctor ordered', *The Scotsman*, 9 August 1996.
7. A. Campbell, 'Auntie's spinners' , *Sunday Times*, 22 September 1996.
8. In an interview given to the *Guardian* in February 1997 Campbell conceded that his and his colleagues' response to Clare Short's 1995 statements on tax had been inappropriate and unfair (J. Mulholland, 'Labour's Mr Media', *Guardian*, 17 February 1997).

9. See Martin Linton's *Guardian* lecture, 'The battle for Jennifer's ear', given at Nuffield College, Oxford, on 30 October 1994. In it he asserts that 'Labour has never won an election when it was more than 18 per cent behind the Tories in press share' (reported in M. Linton, 'Sun-powered politics', *Guardian*, 30 October 1995).
10. Quoted in D. McKie, 'Fact is free but comment is sacred', in I. Crewe and B. Gosschalk (eds) *Political Communications: The General Election Campaign of 1992* (Cambridge: Cambridge University Press, 1995), p. 128.
11. W. Cronkite, 'More bad news', *Guardian*, 27 January 1997.
12. J. Snow, 'More bad news', *Guardian*, 27 January 1997.
13. B. Appleyard, 'Please adjust your mind set', *The Independent*, 9 February 1994.
14. J. Humphrys, 'In the firing line', *Guardian*, 24 May 1995.
15. M. Cockerell, 'Whose fingers on the mike?', *Guardian*, 27 March 1995.

Journalism and Ethics: Can They Co-Exist?

By Andrew Belsey

Introduction

Both the image and the essence of journalism are hard to pin down because each appears to contain contradictory strands. By 'image' I mean the way in which journalism is generally regarded by the public. By 'essence' I mean the reality that lies behind (or apart from) the image. It is well known that journalism has a poor image with the public. They do not regard it highly. They are suspicious of journalists and the way they practise their trade. Journalists are regarded in much the same way as politicians, as disreputable, untrustworthy and dishonest, pushing a personal or sectional interest rather than the facts of the case. If people are told that the essence of journalism is truth-telling, they will react with some scepticism or derision. If they are told that the practice of journalism is founded on ethical principles they will either laugh or, if they are prepared to take the matter seriously, point out that the typical tabloid story is trivial, scurrilous or invented.

But all this is contradicted by another image of journalism, illustrated by the most extraordinary event of the British General Election of May 1997. This was the election of Martin Bell as Member of Parliament for the Tatton constituency. Until about a month before the election,

Mr Bell was a television journalist—a respected journalist, let it be said—working for the BBC, reporting from the war-torn zones of the world with an immediacy and an integrity that made a considerable impact. To cut a long story short, Mr Bell stood as an anti-corruption (or as the media put it, 'anti-sleaze') candidate against Neil Hamilton, the previous MP for the constituency, who was alleged to have been involved in financial dealings ethically incompatible with the status of a Member of Parliament. When Mr Hamilton refused to stand down and was renominated by his party, the candidates of the other major parties withdrew to give Mr Bell a clear run, and he was elected as an Independent with some ease.

This was an unusual situation. It is unusual for non-party candidates to be elected to the House of Commons. It is even more unusual for major parties to stand aside to assist a non-party candidate. But what was most unusual was that this non-party candidate, standing on a platform of public and political honesty, was a journalist, a member of a profession usually mistrusted as much as politicians themselves. But here was the public, or at least that part of it represented by the electors of Tatton, putting their trust in Mr Bell as the right person to stand up against political corruption, or any suspicion of it.

Part of the reason for this is the character of Martin Bell himself, as he is well known to the television audience who have been able to assess him as a person of integrity. But there is more to it than this. It is not that there is a general mistrust of journalists, but with Martin Bell as the sole exception. There is a different and competing image of journalism, which can indeed be focused on reporters like Martin Bell. Journalists who, for example, stand in bullet-strewn areas at considerable risk to themselves, telling the viewers via the camera what exactly is going on, are regarded as brave and honourable, and almost certainly doing their honest best to present an objective and truthful account of what is happening and why.

There is, perhaps, a difference between television and newspaper journalism here. Many people rely on television as the main source of information for news, current affairs, world events, consumer matters and the like. Being able to see the journalist or presenter and whatever else is on the screen means that the audience can to some extent trust its eyes rather than rely solely on the word. Of course, in one sense this means that there is even greater scope for manipulative propaganda if the control of television broadcasting is in the wrong hands, so the audience will also take the source into account. In the United Kingdom the BBC is more trusted than channels with purely commercial (profit-seeking) interests, which is one reason why the maintenance of public service broadcasting is socially and politically important. Still, although of course anyone would be foolish to place absolute trust in anything that appears on television, there is a contrast with the newspaper world, where there is the suspicion among readers, justifiably based on actual cases that have been exposed, that journalists sit in their offices and invent stories. Newspapers are also known to be politically biased and to treat their readers unscrupulously, so why should they be trusted? But it is not just intentional bias that is regarded as a danger. Although both television images and written stories are taken in through the eyes, there is an enormous difference in their reception, for words are known to be deceptive, always at a remove from a reality that can be depicted directly.

It would, however, be a mistake to rely on there being an intrinsic difference between television and newspaper journalism. Although stories have been invented by some newspapers, it is usually other papers that have exposed these deceptions of the public. And the alleged corruption against which Martin Bell offered himself as a symbol was brought to light by a lengthy and sustained campaign by newspaper journalists, and one that was legally dangerous, given the severity of British libel law. And as for the deceptiveness of the written word, this is not the place to go into this ancient and extraordinarily deep philosophical issue, so let me just say that it is a problem that we mostly manage to overcome at a pragmatic level in our daily lives. Whenever we are offered information, whether by newspapers, television, the Internet or any other source, we have no option but to use our everyday intelligence to assess it for reliability. This applies as much to a depiction as to a word or written text.

There is then no general assurance of the soundness of journalism. Just as nowadays the practice of television journalism is satirised on television, so there is a long tradition of satire against the foolishness of the newspaper industry before the television age (Evelyn Waugh's *Scoop*, for instance). But there have always been journalists who have stood out from the crowd because their virtue (if not always their judgement) seems unimpeachable. There are examples this century from George Orwell and James Cameron down to the investigative journalists of recent years, who have recognised that the proper practice of journalism must sometimes be subversive and anti-establishment, and expose what those in power would rather keep concealed from the public to whom they should be accountable.

The point, however, is not that there are exceptional individuals like Orwell, Cameron and Bell who escape the public suspicion and distrust of journalists. It is rather, as I have already hinted, that there is a different and competing image of journalism, one that contradicts the low esteem in which journalism is held. No doubt there is a good deal of Hollywood in this image, but it is more than a myth. This alternative image presents the journalist as the fearless investigative reporter standing up against the mob or the dishonest city boss, determined to expose the corruption because 'the public has a right to know'. More generally this is an image which sees journalism as serving a useful, even indispensable function in society, providing the information, the analysis, the discussion and the comment without which a modern complex society could not operate. This takes us straight to the underlying political justification for the existence of journalism and for such notions as 'the freedom of the press', that the free circulation of news and opinion is a requirement of a democratic society.[1]

Journalism as an Industry

Corresponding roughly to the double image of journalism is a two-sided reality but one in which the two sides contradict rather than complement each other. On the one hand journalism is an industry, a major player in the profit-seeking market economy, and journalists are merely workers in that industry, driven by the need to make a living. On the other hand journalism is a profession, a vocation founded on ethical principles which direct and regulate the conduct of the practitioner. Since trying to live in both these realities is difficult, if not contradictory, deeper explanation and analysis is called for.

There is no doubt that journalism is a major industry. Indeed, journalism is too narrow a term: this is the age of the media. The media are multifarious, transnational and interlinked: newspapers, magazines, television, radio, film, video, cable, communication satellites, the Internet are increasingly coming under the control of a handful of corporations which are based nowhere and everywhere and which seek greater market share, greater profits and greater global influence. In spite of the variety the media is, in defiance of grammar, a singular phenomenon, and one which has universal effect. Once upon a time social theorists were concerned with material production and with the means of production, the farms, forests, factories, fleets and mines which constituted the economy. Today we are sometimes urged to forget these old-fashioned concerns and to realise that this is the age not of production but of information, and that it is the means of information that now dominate economic and social life and provide an insight into its heart and mind.

In such an industry media workers are like any other workers. They are concerned with getting a job, job security, working conditions, future prospects, and, quite rightly, personal satisfaction. They are under the usual pressures of work in the 1990s: line management, downsizing, deskilling ('shorthand not required') and reskilling ('Windows 95™ and PageMaker™ required'). It is market share and the 'bottom line' that rule, and sales figures, circulation figures, audience figures and keeping the advertisers happy dominate the thoughts and actions of the executives who manage the various branches of the corporation. This ethos soon permeates the whole structure of the media industry, including, it must be stressed, that part of it still theoretically devoted to the public service. In a competitive market audience figures and the urge towards growth are as inescapable in 'non-commercial' organisations as in the explicitly profitseeking ones.[2]

Let me admit that this is not the whole story, for, whatever other age we live in, it is also nominally the ethical age, not just in medical ethics and other traditional areas of moral concern but in environmental ethics, professional ethics, business ethics. Corporations—not necessarily from the best of motives but because they recognise and fear the power of the concerned consumer—include ethical objectives in their statements of principle, and emphasise their commitment to environmental responsibility, the rights of indigenous people, meeting the needs of the customer, personal (or personnel) development, parental leave, crèches, and all the other symbols of the modern caring corporation. But while admitting all this it is not too much of an exaggeration to say that overall it has little effect against the overwhelming demands of competition and the requirement for growth as the only means to survival in a heartless world. The market is either amoral or immoral (or perhaps both at different times), and this affects the media industry as much as any other.[3]

What then of ethics in the media? Inasmuch as workers of all sorts are required to 'perform', financial objectives predominate and there seems to be little scope for ethics, irrespective of the worker's own personal motives and desires. Perhaps it could even be argued that in journalism the situation is worse, because the doctor who exploits a vulnerable patient for sexual favours can be struck off and lose the privilege of practising, and an accountant who steals from clients can be sent to prison, but a journalist who misbehaves may get a scoop and a promotion. The theoretical and practical difficulty, however, lies in deciding what constitutes journalistic misbehaviour.

There are two contradictory pressures on journalists. On the one hand they are subject to the attention of the lobbyists and the publicity-seekers, who not only want their story told but want their own slant on it. This is an ethically-fraught area (especially if the lobbyist happens to be also the owner of the newspaper or television channel). But it is the other hand which is even more ethically interesting and puzzling here, because a lot of journalism consists of discovering and printing information about something or some situation that those involved in would rather keep secret. (Sometimes, of course, the two hands come together: journalists are deliberately given a misleading story to print but recognise it for what it is and have to investigate for themselves what the real story is.)

To make the situation even more complicated, this second aspect of journalism can itself be divided into at least two parts. First, much of the practice of discovering and printing information that some people would wish to keep secret is absolutely and legitimately central to journalism. Investigative journalism, finding out what is really going on in society, keeping people well informed about political, economic and other matters, providing information, analysis and comment, is precisely what a responsible press is supposed to do in a democracy in order to serve the public interest. But where are the boundaries of the public interest? That is the question. They do not coincide, as has often been pointed out, with what the public is interested in.

The second part of discovering and printing what some people would prefer to keep secret often involves information that the public is interested in, but should not be, from an ethical point of view. This is what is not legitimately part of journalism. This can involve any combination of ethically dubious content, presentation and investigation. The content may be what is properly secret, or at least private (the two are not the same).[4] Thus personal privacy should be respected, and although it is difficult to draw the line, there are some things clearly on the wrong side of it, like invasions of private grief and suffering. But well beyond this private people are entitled to a private life; the difficulty is always in deciding who are these 'private people'.[5] Then there is the question of presentation. Dubious material is usually presented in dubious ways, involving trivialisation, sensationalism, obscenity, vulgarity, racism, sexism and homophobia. But even legitimate material can be presented in ways that are ethically offensive, a point often overlooked in discussions of media ethics.

Methods of investigation have traditionally received more ethical attention. There are technological aids, like long-range cameras, telephone taps and electronic eavesdropping devices of all sorts, used to spy on people and pry into their affairs. Of course, modern technology cannot be blamed for unethical journalism, since deception, lying and trespass have always been open to journalists. We know, of course, that journalists often behave in such unethical ways, and if it is unethical, then they should not do it. It is as simple as that.

If only it were as simple as that! The point is that words like 'deception', 'lying' and even 'spy' and 'pry' have the ethical evaluation, the condemnation, built into them. But should activities like this, only without the condemnation, be contemplated by journalists? Let us revisit the distinction between the content, the material of journalism, and the method of investigation. Could the end justify the means? In the investigation of crime or corruption, or just incompetence, perhaps the journalist has to resort to some deception.[6] These are areas where the people involved would rather keep things secret but where the public really does have a right to know. There is a long and honourable tradition (perhaps dying now) of investigative journalism, in which the journalist cannot come straight out with the questions. Much investigative journalism (like much police work) is not glamorous but consists of the minute analysis and comparison of thousands of documents. But then some first-hand investigation might be called for, in which a bit of deception, a touch of electronic eavesdropping, is the only available means—but with words like 'deception' and 'eavesdropping' shorn of their condemnatory ethical undertones.

But can we play about with the meanings of words like this? In this context the question is part of a much larger and central ethical issue about the relation of ends and means, and the related problem of dirty hands. Can we do good by doing bad? If we are doing good, then perhaps we are not doing bad. The issue usually comes up in discussions of issues much more difficult than journalism, like war and violence. Is bombing a city justifiable if civilians will be killed? Is it morally right to assassinate the evil dictator?[7] (It is worth remembering, however, that for journalists not lucky enough to work in liberal democracies, this last question might be practically pressing rather than merely theoretical, especially when the dictator is not only willing and able to assassinate them, but preparing to.) But even in liberal democracies journalists can find themselves investigating evil and ruthless people, when prudence if not morality calls for deception. But how can the gangster, the drug pusher, the corrupt politician, the fraudulent businessman be exposed, except by methods which in other contexts would be questionable? Perhaps in these journalistic contexts such methods are morally required.

So far in this section I have been concerned with 'industrial' journalism, in which journalism is just a job and the journalist is subject to all the usual pressures to 'perform' for the sake of the corporation. I have already strayed into ethical matters but will postpone further discussion of them until the next section, when I shall deal with them more directly. Before that, what can we conclude about industrial journalism? Corporate pressures, the search for sales, the search for audience, promote the production of material that the public is interested in, rather than that which is in the public interest. So as not to appear too unconspiratorial, I should say that 'what the public is interested in' is not fixed, a given, eternal, immutable fact of nature. The appetite is rather, and largely, constructed by the very media that feed it, in a glorious circle of supply creating demand and demand creating supply.

One symptom of the resulting trivalisation of social life and the representation of it in the media is the failure to distinguish between secrecy and privacy, and a resulting failure to understand the ethical significance of the distinction. Neither term is well defined, and I do not intend to stipulate once-and-for-all definitions of them, but instead to try to bring out the differences significant in the context of journalism. Although private individuals can have secrets, I take secrecy in the political sense to be the concealing of information by those public individuals and organisations with power, when it ought to be available to ordinary people as part of the democratic process, for reasons of accountability. Privacy, on the other hand, although the term is often misused in connection with what organisations try to keep hidden,[8] is something that only individual persons can have, and only in so far as they are engaged in private and not public activities.

These definitions solve few problems; there is an element of circularity, and they do not provide criteria for distinguishing what may be kept hidden legitimately, whether it be a matter of secrecy or privacy. Just as there are no doubt legitimate areas of privacy for individuals so no doubt there are legitimate areas of secrecy for organisations, but they are much smaller than is often taken for granted. (Consider the long struggle in the United Kingdom against official secrecy and for freedom of information.) But industrial journalism, in league with supposed public demand, too often confuses the two areas, and connives with the powerful to keep secret what ought to be exposed, while invading the privacy of those who neither wish for nor deserve such treatment. This is an over-generalisation, of course. Lots of individuals love the attention of the media and are quite willing to be on the receiving end of the publicity. And at the other end of the scale there is still serious journalism dedicated to serving the public interest and to keeping the public informed as part of the democratic process. But the reality of industrial journalism is to be found largely inhabiting an ethics-free zone.

Ethical Journalism

So journalism is just a job in a market economy in which the usual pressures of work discourage practice based on ethical principles. But there is another reality in which journalism is a profession based on ethical principles, indeed constituted by ethical practice. However exaggerated the claims about this reality have sometimes been, it is not just a myth, a self-serving piece of propaganda put about by those with lots to hide and lots to gain. Nor is it just an ideal, never to be attained. It is a reality illustrated (rather than proved) by the experience of Martin Bell in Tatton, a journalist getting the support and confidence of the public in direct competition with a politician. Ethical journalism even has a sort of physical embodiment in the *Code of Practice* issued by the Press Complaints Commission (as well as in similar codes all over the world), even though such codes fail to be sufficient from an ethical point of view.[9]

But before fully considering the claims of journalism to have an ethical existence, we should look at the question of professionalism.[10] Ethics and professionalism are often seen as co-requisites. What then is a profession? Traditionally a profession involved the giving of a service by a certified expert to an individual client, for a fee and on the basis of mutual trust and respect. In areas like law and medicine the client has to trust the expertise and the good faith of the practitioner, who in turn respects the needs and vulnerability of the client. The professions are policed in the sense that a practitioner who transgresses against the ethically based standards of practice is punished in some way, with expulsion from the profession as the ultimate sanction.

On this account journalism doesn't sound like a profession, but then neither do many other occupational areas that today claim professional status. (Almost every occupational area claims professional status.) Even the traditional professions often fail to match their traditional image, as social, economic and technological changes alter the relationship between the service-seeker and the service-provider. Perhaps then the emphasis should be on the ideas of ethical practice and adherence to an ethical code. Indeed, it is the proliferation of such codes among occupational groups that is used to justify the claim to professional status. Presumably, the spread of such codes, inasmuch as they have a genuine and serious effect, should be welcomed, as it means that the idea of ethical practice permeates further into society. But if all occupational groups are code-based professions, professional status no longer points to any significant ethical distinction between one occupation and another.

A further (yet related) account of professionalism is in terms of each profession's essence, which links the practice of the profession to the attainment of some intrinsically worthwhile end. Thus it is claimed that the essence of medicine is the promotion of health, of accountancy the insistence on financial probity, of law the pursuit of justice, of social work the enhancement of client autonomy, of the Church the cure of souls, etc. On this approach the essence of journalism is telling the truth, or, to put it in different terms, journalism is constituted by truth-telling. Essentialism of any sort is not these days universally popular as a method of explanation and illumination, and these examples show some of the reasons why. For a start, we might expect all the transactions of everyday life to be based on telling the truth, so there is nothing distinctive about journalism on these grounds. Furthermore, while we might be able to deal with the truth and nothing but the truth, the whole truth is altogether more difficult. All information is selected from an infinite whole, and all information has to be presented in one way or another. And then much journalism is concerned with opinion, argument, debate and discussion, where notions of objectivity and fairness are central, rather than truth. Furthermore, essentialism of this sort is not very helpful because it is over-general and thus somewhat vague. It provides no way forward when the rights and interests of different people conflict. There is a very great deal in the practice of medicine, for example, which is not illuminated by generalities about the promotion of health. This so-called essence does not help much on questions about abortion and euthanasia. Similarly, the notion of truth-telling in journalism does not answer the problem, already discussed, of using dubious methods to obtain the truth. This does not, of course, suggest that telling the truth is not important in journalism.

We have not, so far, tracked down what is meant by speaking of journalism as a profession, except in so far as ethical practice is necessary, but not sufficient, for a profession. But this should be of little concern, as it is the ethical practice and not the designation 'profession' that is important. So long as any occupation, or indeed any activity, is based on sound ethical principles, why should we worry whether it is a profession or not? As I have already suggested, professional status tends to be a self-awarded honorific these days, a fact that is of more sociological than ethical significance. What clearly is of ethical significance is the ethics of the activity, whether it be journalism or anything else.

What then of the reality of ethical journalism? Analogies with traditional professions obstruct rather than assist understanding. A journalist is not (except perhaps in a very few, exceptional cases) an individual service-provider with an individual client. Nevertheless, journalism can best be thought of as providing a service. Journalists provide a vital service to society as a whole, but it is a political service. Journalism is part of the political process. Now of course there are dangers in such a statement. Journalists are not legislators and neither are they governors. It is bad for society and for journalism if journalists are tempted to be either. They should be considered, rather, as facilitators, to use the jargon of the modern age to make a very traditional point.

They facilitate the democratic process. It is not true that we have just moved into the information age, because even the drafters of the American Bill of Rights recognised that information oils the wheels of democracy when they laid down that 'Congress shall make no law ... abridging the freedom of speech, or of the press' (First Amendment to the Constitution of the United States of America (1791)). Autocratic governments control information, and regard secrecy as a important weapon—and not only autocratic governments. But if a government is to be accountable to the people it must know what is going on; if the people are to cast their votes wisely and rationally they too must know what is going on. Information is necessary (though not of course sufficient) for a successful democracy, inasmuch as it requires the free circulation of news, opinion, debate and discussion. Hence the incorporation of freedom of expression and freedom of information in international charters like the Universal Declaration of Human Rights. A democratic necessity is transformed into a human right.

As commentators on the American Constitution have pointed out, the traffic is not one way, and the privileges guaranteed to journalists by the First Amendment should be reciprocated by the responsibilities of journalists.[11] The privileges are granted to enable journalists to facilitate the democratic process without hindrance, and so they license conduct which is directed towards actually facilitating it, and not just any old conduct. It is in this political area that the reality of ethical journalism is located, since journalism as part of the democratic process can only be ethically informed journalism. The point is obvious, in that the ends of democracy cannot be served by media that are full of untruths, lies, invasions of privacy, scurrility, obscenity, triviality, distortion, bias and all the other sins that industrial journalism actually exhibits. All the virtues associated with ethical journalism—accuracy, honesty, truth, objectivity, fairness, balance, respect for the autonomy of ordinary people—are part of, and required by, journalism as located within the democratic process.

If the media are to be part of the democratic process because of their role in the origination and circulation of information and opinion, then the quality of that information and opinion is going to be a vital issue. Quality here is meant in a typically ethical sense, so that the ethics and the politics of the media are not really different or separable issues. Ethical journalism serves the public interest. One good reason for putting the point in terms of virtues is that although virtues might become ingrained dispositions they are not arbitrary or irrational but based on sound ethical principles. Virtues are not algorithms, but the very nature of their principle-based flexibility enables them to deal more successfully with novel situations than can a set of rules embodied in a code of practice. And a democratic society, especially one in a technological age, will constantly produce situations and opportunities which are ethically novel.

This then is the reality of ethical journalism, journalism based on the idea of virtuous conduct, facilitating the democratic process and serving the public interest. Cynics will say that this is myth-making and that there is no reality behind it. The less cynical might say that it is an ideal of what ought to be, and a long way in advance of what actually is, although we might aspire to make some further progress towards the ideal. The cynic, I wish to argue, goes too far, although given the nature and power of industrial journalism one can understand why there is an apparent justification for such cynicism. The lesser cynic is correct in approach, although, as I have argued, ethical journalism is not just an ideal but a reality, just as much a reality as industrial journalism.

Journalism is a two-sided reality, in which the two sides contradict rather than complement each other. Is this a helpful way of putting the point? I hope so. Industrial journalism exists, and so does ethical journalism. They both co-exist and contend, battling for supremacy in a recreation of an ancient and eternal struggle. Each is armed with different weapons. Industrial journalism can call on the amoral power of the transnational corporation, but ethical journalism is undefeated, being able to rely on the undiminished strength and perennial appeal of virtue.

Co-Existence?

But enough of these Manichean metaphors! What is the ordinary journalist to do in his or her everyday working life? No doubt journalists, especially when young and entering the profession, wish to be good journalists, to do a good job, and to obtain at least some degree of personal satisfaction. But they will have mixed motives and expectations, some material, some ethical. It is unlikely that many journalists are motivated directly by a desire to serve the public interest, yet they are likely to have some such notion occupying an underground area of their thoughts.

The pressures of work keep it underground, mostly. Journalists do behave unethically. Yes, they have invented stories, invaded privacy, harassed the unfortunate, used sexist images and generally behaved badly. The image of journalism held by the public, according to which journalists are a shifty, untrustworthy bunch of unprincipled self-servers, has plenty of justification. And yet not all journalists suffer from this image, as is shown by the example of Martin Bell, not only in his habitual role of respected journalist but also in his unexpected role of victorious politician. There is a delicious irony in the fact that it was a journalist who stood for and was elected to Parliament on an ethical ticket.

The pressures of work that prevent ethics from having a firm place in journalism are not all that different from the pressures on anyone else. There is a job to be got, promotion to be obtained, so the story has to be written and the methods necessary to obtain the story used. The story must sell, the managers must be satisfied, the growth targets met. The market must be chased, so there is a constant temptation (more than a temptation) to print trivial stories, salaciously presented and obtained by suspect methods. Personal beliefs and desires do not come into it. Journalists are often thought to be hypocrites when those who are committed Labour voters work for or even edit newspapers that are little more than Conservative Party propaganda sheets. This has happened, and probably the other way round as well. How can they do it, people wonder, failing to recognise that the necessity of making a living makes a mockery of most people's highest ethical aspirations. Compromise is part of living in the world as it now is.

Does this mean that there is no place for moral integrity in journalism? No, I am far from arguing that, having claimed that ethical journalism is as much a reality as industrial journalism. But of course ethical journalism is under pressure, as is ethics in almost any walk of life, because we live in a world dominated by economic considerations and an economy driven by market forces. Moral motivations and moral intentions are good, but they can be powerless in practice, or misled. They are powerless when the pressures of the system are too great for them to prevail against. They are misled when, for example, journalists find themselves justifying their unethical conduct in terms of their own unblemished intentions to do good, though employing dubious means. This is the doctrine of the double effect, and it is as fallacious in journalism as it is everywhere else.[12]

But fortunately it is not necessary to draw a totally pessimistic conclusion. In spite of all the pressures ethics is entrenched in journalism, and so it will never disappear completely. There is a tradition of truth-seeking, objective reporting and fair and reasonable presentation which is sufficient to challenge if not to defeat industrial journalism. There is also a tradition, though not one that is as strong as it should be, of reasoned discussion of such matters. It is an interesting coincidence that the same Martin Bell, shortly before his sudden transformation into a successful politician, was attracting media attention not because of his own work in the media but because of his theoretical discussion of some of the principles on which it was based. The point he was making was that there is not the conflict that many people assume must exist between objectivity in reporting and commitment to values, because journalists should not try to take a neutral stand between right and wrong. The war reporter in the world of today cannot avoid witnessing an appalling collection of atrocities, massacres, torture and other crimes, and must not pretend that these are neutral events of no moral significance. Such pretence involves a failure to be objective.

This is surely correct, and it illustrates some of the problems of ethical journalism. It is relatively easy for journalists based in liberal democratic countries to be objective about unsavoury military dictators in other parts of the world, but objectivity does not come so easily when the unsavoury character is your own boss. The case of Robert Maxwell demonstrates both the farcical and the tragic side of this. The sight of the sycophants of the living Maxwell intoning moral condemnations over his corpse was amusing for the uninvolved spectators but not for those whose pensions disappeared with Maxwell over the side of the boat.

But there is, I fear, no resolution of the contradiction, no solution to the paradox of industrial journalism co-existing with ethical journalism. Yes, good intentions are fine, but they can only operate within the existing system. But systems are rarely monolithic and thus they fail to be monopolistic. There is scope for good intentions, after all. But good intentions are not sufficient, as they need to be matched by corresponding good actions. This is why I put the emphasis on virtue in journalism, as virtue is a disposition to act in ethically correct ways, even in novel situations. And whatever the difficulties caused by co-existing with industrial journalism, there is still scope for the tradition of ethical journalism to live and develop.

Notes

1. See Judith Lichtenberg (ed.), *Democracy and the Mass Media* (Cambridge: Cambridge University Press, 1990).
2. For a wide-ranging discussion of the issues raised in this paragraph, see James Curran and Jean Seaton, *Power without Responsibility: The Press and Broadcasting in Britain,* 4th edn (London: Routledge, 1991).
3. The current state of business ethics is surveyed in Peter W. F. Davies (ed.), *Current Issues in Business Ethics* (London: Routledge, 1997).
4. See Sisela Bok, *Secrets: On the Ethics of Concealment and Revelation* (Oxford: Oxford University Press, 1982); and F. D. Schoeman (ed.), *Philosophical Dimensions of Privacy* (Cambridge: Cambridge University Press, 1984).
5. This is discussed further in my article 'Privacy, publicity and politics', in Andrew Belsey and Ruth Chadwick (eds), *Ethical Issues in Journalism and the Media* (London: Routledge, 1992), pp. 77–92.
6. See Bok, *Secrets,* pp. 249–64; and Jennifer Jackson, 'Honesty in investigative journalism', in Belsey and Chadwick, *Ethical Issues in Journalism,* pp. 93–111; and on the wider issues, Sisela Bok, *Lying: Moral Choice in Public and Private Life* (Brighton: Harvester, 1978).
7. Jonathan Glover provides an illuminating introduction to such moral issues in *Causing Death and Saving Lives* (Harmondsworth: Penguin Books, 1977). See also Richard Norman, *Ethics, Killing and War* (Cambridge: Cambridge University Press, 1995).
8. See Bok, *Secrets,* esp. p. 13.
9. Press Complaints Commission, *Code of Practice* (London, Press Complaints Commission, September 1994). There is an analysis of the PCC Code in Andrew Belsey and Ruth Chadwick, 'Ethics as a vehicle for media quality', *European Journal of Communication* 10 (1995), pp. 461–73. See also Nigel G. E. Harris, 'Codes of conduct for journalists', in Belsey and Chadwick, *Ethical Issues in Journalism,* pp. 62–76.
10. See Ruth Chadwick (ed.), *Ethics and the Professions* (Aldershot: Avebury, 1994).
11. This issue is discussed in Stephen Klaidman and Tom L. Beauchamp, *The Virtuous Journalist* (New York: Oxford University Press, 1987), esp. pp. 5–14. My thinking on ethics and journalism owes a great deal to the clarifications and insights of Klaidman and Beauchamp's book.
12. See Glover, *Causing Death and Saving Lives,* esp. pp. 86–91.

Chapter Highlights

- The work of professional writers, particularly journalists and public relations practitioners, affects others. Thus, it is essential that what they do adheres to the highest standard of accuracy.
- For journalists, the primary guidelines of ethical conduct are outlined in the Canons of Journalism (adopted by the American Society of Newspaper Editors). For public relations practitioners, comparable guidelines are found in the Public Relations Society of America's Code of Ethics.
- The best defense for any journalist or public relations practitioner facing charges of libel is the truth.
- Libel is a false communication that wrongfully injuries the reputation of others.
- Writers are responsible for their own actions in terms of what they write. Should they be sued, they cannot defend their actions by claiming that they were following instructions.
- It is ethically and legally improper for writers to use the ideas or words of others without using proper attribution.

For Discussion

1. From the perspective of a writer, can you think of a situation where something could be legal yet ethically or morally improper?
2. Is it appropriate that journalists and public relations practitioners be held to the same legal standards?
3. Compare and contrast the American Society of Newspaper Editors' canons of journalism and the Public Relations Society of America's code of ethics.
4. Who do you believe the public holds to a higher standard of behavior: journalists or public relations practitioners? Discuss your reasons.

xii

Effective Communication and Writing Skills in the Job Market

Can we all agree right up front that there are few things in the world less fun than looking for a job? This is because, in part, you can do everything well and correctly and still not get the result you wish and never know why. How frustrating is that? It is one thing to apply for a job that you know you may not quite be qualified for, or go into an interview and give answers that are poorly worded or do not quite address what the interviewee is asking. This is all disappointing, but at least in those situations you have a good idea as to why another candidate was selected. But then there are those prospective jobs when your background and qualifications perfectly match what the employer is looking for and when the interview goes extremely well. At those times, you practically tap dance out of the office. As you go home, you can't help but start thinking about life at this new job and the new friends and colleagues you will be making. It is a great feeling. Then, two days pass. Another couple of days go by. A week. Still no word. Finally, an impersonal letter arrives thanking you for your interest but informing you that someone else has been selected. Describing such an experience as not fun does not do it justice.

Most everyone who puts in enough time in the professional world has this experience. It is almost a rite of passage. Yet such a reality does not lessen the frustration and disappointment that comes from the experience. Unfortunately, nothing we say or share in this chapter will guarantee that such a scenario will never happen to you. Our purpose here is to help provide you with a particular perspective as to how to approach a prospective job and then how best to frame your letter of application. Such communiqués are vital in the job-hunting process. Often they spell the difference between being called in for an interview and not. Our goal is to help better the odds of your getting that interview.

Not-So-Conventional Wisdom

One of the age-old questions in life is "What comes first, the chicken or the egg?" When it comes to job hunting, a similar question is "What comes first, the application or the job announcement?" In other words, does the job seeker and his or her interest in a particular job or field come first, and then the fortuitous job announcement follows—or does the job announcement precede people seeking a new job who shape or frame their skills and experience to fit this prospective opportunity for employment? Our answer is "neither." The whole process begins with the individual and what he or she brings to the table. This includes a skill set, employment record, education, experience, and vision. Vision is an important element because it represents the direction in which the job seeker wishes to go. What do job seekers see for themselves? What are their professional hopes and dreams? How can they best intersect with others in order to advance their own career trajectories while providing assistance to those for whom they work?

Conventional wisdom suggests that job hunting is about the job seeker. Their job quest is about seeking to fulfill or meet their own professional needs and wishes. This is true. Conventional wisdom also suggests that how one presents themselves to a prospective employer—both in writing and in person—is about that individual as well. This is only partially true. It goes without saying: everything we do, including how we dress, behave, and communicate, says much about us. In the context of job hunting, however, it is the "other guy"—the prospective employer—who primarily drives the train. Companies, organizations, and even individuals advertise open positions because they have a need they want met. They have a hole in their operation that needs to be filled and duties that need to be performed. Thus, employers are seeking someone who can meet their needs. Any desire the employer might have to help a prospective employee fulfill his or her needs is secondary to what the employer wants for himself or herself and the organization.

Thus, applying for a job—any job—is more about the employer than it is about the applicant. That potential boss wants to know what you can do for him or her. Make no mistake, when you are writing a cover letter, filling out an application, and even being interviewed by a prospective boss or a search committee, you are not just talking or writing about you. To put it bluntly, the interviewers and people who ultimately decide whom or whom not to hire are assessing all applicants primarily on the basis of what they can do for the organization and not what the organization can do for them. If an employer is going to give another person—the applicant—a salary and then provide that person with an array of benefits, including vacation time, you can bet that the organization is assessing what hiring a particular person will do for them.

While this may seem obvious, nevertheless many applicants and job seekers make the mistake of couching their cover letters and résumés and then presenting themselves in interview situations as if this experience is totally about them. "Of course," the applicant assumes, "they want to learn more about me because they have invited me in for an interview." Such an understandable conclusion is only half-true at best. That prospective employer only wants to learn more about the applicant in the context of how he or she can help the company. The hiring manager wants to know what you—the applicant—can do for him or her. Therefore, if applicants in their cover letters or interviews do nothing else but sing their own praises, they are being shortsighted and making a mistake. The prospective employer wants to know how all the skills, talents, and attributes a person claims to have can and will be used to help the employer meets its needs.

What, then, does this mean for applicants or job seekers, particularly in terms of how they present themselves in writing? They answer is simple: they must frame their "wonderfulness" in the context of how that brings the most benefit to the employer. For example, when any of us go to a department store to buy a new suit or dress, we do not want to just hear the salesperson talk about all of his or her past sales. Instead, we want to learn about that new sports coat or dress and how it showcases our good looks. To make the sale, the salesperson needs to promote the clothes in a way that speaks to our wishes and needs. Applying for a job is no different. Thinking "What's in it for me?" does not make any of us bad people. It is an aspect of human nature that more often than not our actions are driven by self-interest. Even when we decide to help that little old lady across the street, we do so in part because it will make us feel better. For job applicants, however, it is important that they (1) put themselves in the shoes of prospective employers and ponder "What's in it for them?" and (2) come up with answers to that basic question.

The dynamic between the applicant and the prospective employer is akin to the beginning moments of any relationship, with one notable exception. Yes, the two individuals are taking a step forward to familiarize themselves with the other. They have information to share and information to obtain. Both are on their best behavior—or should be. They are also weighing the pros and cons of a long-term commitment with the other. It is time of assessment, negotiation, and judgment. It is at this point, then, where the exception we mentioned kicks in. This budding relationship is not balanced. The applicant is after something, and the employer is trying to decide whether he or she wants to give it up to that person. This is why applicants often come across as being very eager, while the employer is more reserved and noncommittal. It is a dance unique to the circumstance. Only when the employer makes a decision and actually selects a particular applicant does the balance between the two begin to shift and become more equal.

Thus, it is the answer to the question of "What's in it for them?" that needs to drive how applicants present themselves both in writing and in person. They need to connect the dots between their qualifications and the employer's needs. For applicants, it is not enough to be wonderful. Rather, they must be wonderful in the context of the one doing the hiring. Making that connection is a challenge, but the good news is that it is doable. The basic elements needed to make this happen include research, empathy, creativity, and a good sense of direction. Before discussing them, we share examples of what helps application letters be strong and appealing to prospective employers.

One relevant point, however, pertains to the length of a cover letter. There are many who emphasize that cover letters should never, ever be longer than one page. Anything longer, they say, and those reviewing your application will simply stop reading. The thinking is that those prospective employers are busy people and simply do not have time to devote to any communiqué of this nature that go beyond one page. Maybe. Our thinking, however, is a bit different. If what you have to say takes more than one page, by all means make it a two- or even three-page cover letter. The cover letter is about you and why you are perfect for a particular job in the context of the employer's needs. By all means, take the space that you need to make a case for yourself. However, if you do go beyond one page, be certain that the points you are making are strong and relevant. Cover letters should not include any superfluous information. While it is commendable that you won your second-grade spelling bee, how does that relate to this current job to which you are applying? More to the point, the cover letter should include those items about yourself that most directly relate to the job, your perspective as to why you are the most qualified candidate, and your vision as to what your priorities would be, should you be the one who is hired.

Tone/Content of the Cover Letter

Applying for a job is serious business. However, this does not necessarily mean that the letter of application should be written in a tone that is solemn. Generally, such communiqués should be upbeat and positive and exhibit energy. Ideally, the underlying message the writer should communicate is that this job is just the opportunity he or she has been waiting for to showcase his or her skills and abilities, be part of an exciting organization, and grow as a professional. Beyond that, the applicant should give those reviewing the application the sense that he or she has the enthusiasm and insight to make a positive difference in the organization's growth and overall progression. Does that seem to be asking a lot of a cover letter and its author? Let us answer that question this way: if applicants are going to have any kind of viable chance of being called in for an interview, they must do what they can to make prospective employers see what they see. Applicants must strive to give their possible bosses the sense that choosing them for a job is virtually a no-brainer. It is just a matter of having the in-person interview and then making a job offer.

Achieving such an objective may not be completely realistic, but it is a star worth shooting for. People—even prospective bosses—want to know that people care about what they do. A good way to do this is to exhibit enthusiasm about something that the boss cares about. In this case, it is the position for which the applicant is applying. Demonstrating genuine interest and enthusiasm in that prospective job is a positive step in the right direction. Doing so in a way that is believable to that prospective boss is an important goal to achieve. Following are several examples.

Demonstrating Enthusiasm

Example 1

Dear Hiring Managers:

I am very interested in the position of director of public relations for the XYZ Company. As a long-term resident of Northern Virginia, I have been very familiar with the important role your company has played in helping the entire region maintain its reputation as a strong economic engine for the state. Stepping into the role of public relations director would give me an opportunity to be part of an organization I greatly admire as well as help it continue to grow and maintain its most positive reputation.

Example 2

Dear Hiring Manager:

I am writing to apply for the position of director of public relations. Being part of the XYZ Company has long been a goal of mine. As one who has been active in the communication profession for many years, I have admired the reputation you have cultivated and maintained throughout our entire region and beyond as an entity that cares deeply about its customers and those it seeks to serve. This, in part, has been the result of a dynamic and strong public relations effort that, in many ways, has been a beacon in the communication industry. I am very excited about the prospect of joining your team in such a valuable capacity.

Comparison/Analysis

The challenge in any professional setting—and this includes a formal letter of application—is to maintain a balance between being respectable in tone and demeanor and over-the-top in that regard as to be off-putting and disingenuous to the reader. The above examples strike that balance. Furthermore, in each letter the applicant performs a nice hat-trick: the applicant praises the organization, suggests that he or she has broad knowledge of the organization, and introduces his or her goal of helping the organization build on its past successes. Presumably, what follows in each letter are specifics that support these initial comments or claims.

Showcasing the Résumé

As good or strong as a letter of application might be, the candidate must have the professional chops to support his or her claims of being "right" for a job and the one to hire to help bring the organization to even greater levels of success and respectability. In other words, their résumé needs to be appropriately substantial. Just as a product such a new car or a toothpaste must do all that its sellers claim it can do, the applicant must have everything he or she claims in an interview or application letter. This includes academic credentials, professional successes, and work history. Assuming the applicant does, in fact, have solid and appropriate credentials for a given job, presenting the résumé or work history in the best possible light becomes even more critical.

Two of the primary purposes of any letter of application are to introduce the applicant and then showcase his or her résumé. Together, the bottom-line objective is to garner an invitation for an interview. (At that point, of course, it is up to candidates to win over those doing the hiring via the power of their personality, how well they speak, and their ability to handle themselves in that pressure situation known as the job interview.) While the application letter is extremely important in the job-hunting process, it is the résumé that is the ultimate deal-maker or deal-breaker when it comes to determining whether a candidate will be invited in for an interview. Thus, the role of the application letter is to showcase the best part of one's résumé, particularly as it relates to the job opening. The question is how best to do this. Does the applicant (1) simply list his or her academic degrees and various places of employment, for instance, or (2) allude to certain aspects of his or her professional background that are most applicable to the qualifications the prospective employer expects all candidates to at least match? For those of who answered "option two," go to the head of the class.

The next question is, specifically, what parts of your résumé do you highlight? One response revolves around the one or two aspects of your professional life in which you take the most pride. If, for example, you graduated first in your class from college, by all means mention that. While this tidbit may not be completely relevant to the job to which you are applying, if you nonetheless believe that it showcases something important about you that you want others to know, you do not have to be shy about bringing it to the attention of those who are reviewing your application. The second response pertains to those items that are directly germane to the desired job. For instance, if candidates are required to have a minimum of five years' experience and a master's degree, and you, the candidate, have them, include this information in your cover letter. Also, if you actually have ten years' professional experience and a doctorate, definitely highlight these facts about yourself.

In bringing this type of information to the attention of your prospective employer, try to couch it in such a way that drives home the point that you are the strongest possible candidate for this position. Why, for instance, is it a good thing that you have ten years' professional experience when the employer is asking for a minimum of five? Address that point in your cover letter. Do not assume that those reviewing your application and cover letter will see this fact in the same way you do. With each piece of information about yourself that you include in a cover letter, you should be able to answer the question "So what?" For example, "So what that you have ten years' professional experience?" Spell it out for the potential boss.

Before moving onto the key elements of a cover letter, following are examples of ones in which the candidate articulates his or her vision for the position and the organization.

Emphasizing a Vision

Example 3

Dear Sirs:

As your company's public relations director, I would focus my energies on developing a detailed, well-coordinated media relations plan designed to increase your visibility in a way that enhances your image. My objective would be to work closely with a handful of reporters—print and electronic—to educate them about the company's priorities and overall mission.

Example 4

Dear Sirs:

As your primary communication officer, my initial steps would be to establish a good working relationship with your top officers and other key individuals, as well begin making myself known throughout the various layers of the organization. Following that, I would focus on establishing myself with various external publics, including the media and prospective supporters.

Comparison/Analysis

Putting aside the merits of the vision identified in the above samples, examples three and four illustrate an attempt by the candidates to give the prospective employer a strong and more clear sense of what the applicants would be focusing on initially when they are hired. Obviously, in actual cover letters applicants would provide a greater, more detailed explanation of their vision and couch their explanation in the context of conferring closely with the chief officer to ensure that he or she is comfortable with how they will begin their new job.

In outlining an initial vision, it is not necessary that candidates go overboard with specifics. Until they are hired, applicants will be able to talk only in general terms. Employers understand this. The mere fact that candidates have given this job enough thought to lay out a general vision is no small thing. It demonstrates that they are serious about this job. Thus, they deserve the utmost consideration.

A word of advice: the more research candidates do on their possible place of employment, the better they will be able to produce a logical, coherent, and pertinent vision.

Connecting the Dots

The above examples and discussions of an application letter's content and tone serve as a helpful lead-in to an explanation of those key elements that help connect the dots between interests and needs. These elements are research, empathy, creativity, and sense of direction. Following is an explanation of each.

Research

It is difficult to put yourself in the shoes of another if you know little or nothing about that other person. Thus, you must take steps to find out as much as you can about the person who one day you may call "boss" and the company or organization for which that person works. What is that person's background? Has he or she been at the company long? What kind of boss is that person? Answers to these questions may not be easy to find, but that does not make them any less worthy of answering. The Internet is a good place to start. Google the person and see what pops up. Such information might be of interest and, more important, of use. Also, you may see some aspects of that person's career that are similar to yours. Such commonalities may help make your initial meetings more comfortable. Then there is the company or organization's own website. Perhaps there may be information about this person and his or her staff that you can use in your communiqués with him or her.

The Internet is also very useful when it comes to learning about the company or organization. Among the questions an applicant might try to pursue in putting together an application for the desired position and possible interview are the following: What are the organization's goals? What is its mission? What is its organizational structure? Where does the position in which you are interested fall within that structure? What is the company's history? Even if you cannot find answers to these and other related questions, it is helpful to be prepared to ask them, should you be invited in for an interview. The fact that a candidate has taken the time to prepare a number of thoughtful and stimulating questions reflects well on him or her.

Following is a partial list of points of information the applicant should seek to collect in preparation for submitting a thoughtful and stimulating application:

- The history of the company or organization
- Its primary annuals goals
- How well the organization or company did this past year. Was it successful in meeting its goals for the year? Why or why not?
- Employee turnover—is this a problem?
- The history of the position for which you are applying—why is it vacant?

Empathy

As we mentioned earlier, the more an applicant can and does view the desired position from the perspective of the person or people attempting to fill it, the better able he or she will be to frame his or her background, qualifications, and interest in the position. While the applicant is interested in a specific position, on a larger scale he or she is looking to become part of a team or conglomeration of people. Exhibiting empathy is a way of visualizing yourself as a member of the group. Becoming knowledgeable about the organization or company in which you are interested and finding out what you can about your prospective boss is complimentary to both entities, yet it represents flattery that is meaningful rather than frivolous.

Creativity

A little later in this chapter we will be providing examples of application letters that display a level of creativity geared toward generating interest from a prospective employer. In using the word "creativity," we are calling on writers to be original in their how they link their background and qualifications with the needs of their hoped-for employer. Often, when employers review résumés or applications, they do not always recognize on their own any tie-in between the two. It therefore falls to applicants to point this out. In fact, they should emphasize it. Writers should do this in a way that is straightforward and precise. They should not attempt to be so clever or creative as to make their primary points difficult to understand. Thus, the creativity about which we are speaking needs to be found in the directness of the text of the cover letter of application.

Sense of Direction

What is it you want? What is your immediate goal? What are your long-range plans? Prospective employers are not guidance counselors. Consequently, they are not interested in or wish to take the time to help applicants identify a career path for themselves. They are looking for a person with a precise understanding of what he or she wants and why he or she wants it. Cover letters should reflect this. However, it is important for applicants to state what they want but—again—in the context of what the employer needs. That is one of the essentials of any solid cover letter. (It is also one of the points the applicant should make in the course of any interview opportunity.) In this sense, the applicant is a matchmaker—but instead of pairing two people, the applicant is connecting or matching his or her strengths with the employer's needs.

Following is a partial list of points that applicants should raise in their letters of application:

- Professional experience as it relates to the job opening
- Education as it relates to the profession and the job opening
- Several career highlights that relate to the job opening
- Overall career interests or path as it relates to the job opening
- General observations about the company

Personalizing the Appeal

Example 5

Dear Hiring Manager:

I am writing to apply for the position of director of public relations. I believe that with my background, education, and track record of success, I can add much to your organization.

Example 6

Dear Hiring Manager:

I am writing to apply for the position of director of public relations. Over the past year, I have been extremely impressed with your company's creative and imaginative outreach program. I believe that with my background in advertising, strengths as a writer, and ability to work well with others, I can help you maintain the momentum you have generated as well as add to the overall effectiveness of your efforts.

Comparison/Analysis

There is nothing wrong with example one. In it, the applicant outlines his or her interest in a straight-forward manner. Where it is weak is that such a statement could apply to any job and any company. It is not personalized. There is nothing in this sentence to suggest that the applicant has made any effort to learn about the company or organization that he or she supposedly wants to join. Furthermore, such a statement is about the applicant and not the company. In example two, the applicant has at least taken a stab at demonstrating some knowledge about the company as well as introducing the notion of how he or she can help the organization.

Speaking to the Employer

Example 7

Dear Hiring Manager:

As a professional with over ten years' experience in public relations, including supervising a team of highly diverse people, directing an award-winning publicity campaign, and overseeing a budget of more than $1 million, I can introduce your growing organization to strategies designed to increase its visibility and enhance its already impressive reputation.

Example 8

Dear Hiring Manager:

One of the qualities I have most admired about your company has been its ability to connect with its customers while serving as a positive force within our region. Becoming part of such a company is a major goal for me. As your director of public relations, I would do much to help you continue to succeed and remain a viable force in the region.

Comparison/Analysis

Once again, neither of these versions are bad. However, the applicant in example seven does a far better job of personalizing his or her interest. In it, the applicant provides a snapshot of his or her background while making a general statement about what he or she can do for the company. Ideally, the applicant would follow up such a statement—later in the letter, in an interview, or both—with specifics on what strategies he or she has in mind. In contrast, example eight is the case of another letter that says, "Look at me!" The applicant does touch briefly on one of the company's qualities, yet then immediately reverts back to talking about himself or herself without properly touching on the company's needs or characteristics. Again, neither of these versions is bad. However, it is a matter of presenting yourself in a way that results in genuine interest on the part of the prospective employer.

Wrap-Up

Whenever an applicant applies for a job, the goal is two-fold: to be invited for an interview and then, of course, to elicit a job offer. The challenge is found in how best to get to those points. In the job search process, what the candidate has going for him or her is the cover letter and résumé. Thus, it is essential that both be strong, positive, personalized, relevant to the desired position and its company, and readable. They need to be door-openers, deliver the one-two punch that instills enough interest in those who are reviewing all candidates, including that person's future boss, to think, "We really need to meet this person." Granted, even under the best of circumstances, this is not easy to do. In the current climate of today, when it is common to have more than one hundred applicants for a single job, the challenge is even more daunting. But the good news is that people—candidates—climb that mountain every day. You can, too! Make no mistake, the tips and perspectives identified in this chapter will still not make the experience fun. There will still be frustrations, disappointments, and the stress from waiting—and hoping—to get a call back from that prospective boss. But by focusing on that person's needs and wishes, learning more about the organization you wish to join, and presenting yourself as a thoughtful, creative, and empathetic candidate and professional, the odds of being invited for an interview will be much greater. These ingredients contribute to making communication that is effective and communicators who are successful.

Reading List

Pursuing a career in the media is not without challenges. That the competition is heavy and the fields of journalism and public relations are continuing to evolve contribute to the size of the hurdle one must jump to achieve sustained employment and professional growth in these areas. Nevertheless, opportunities exist for those able to fine-tune their communication skills and project the direction in which the media is heading. Furthermore, what will those who depend on the media for information and enlightenment need from their newspapers, magazines, radios, television, Internet providers, and so forth, and what could they possibly want in the months and years to come? Answers, including educated guesses, to those questions shed light on job opportunities that lie ahead for those whose desired careers include communicating via the written word. The following articles provide insight into possible upcoming opportunities:

The Top 20 (Plus 5) Technologies for the World Ahead

By James H. Irvine and Sandra Schwarzbach

Breakthroughs now emerging in biotechnology, robotics, and other key areas bear the potential to reshape life on Earth. Two military analysts describe the 20 innovations that will have the biggest impacts in the near future, plus five prospective technologies that could have major repercussions in the longer term.

About 10 years ago, we at the Naval Air Warfare Center in Southern California set out to determine how emerging technologies might change armed conflict over the next 25 to 50 years. We selected 200 new technological applications, projecting out their growth and how they might influence future military strategy and warfare.

Our conclusion: These technologies would be major drivers of not only future military affairs, but of virtually all of human life. From these 200, we examine here what we consider the top 20 innovations that will have the greatest effect in the near term; in addition, we've selected five other feasible technological developments that could significantly change our world in the more distant future.

1. Computer Technology

Computing power has increased by a factor of 10^6 since 1959. Based on present-day central processing technology, we can expect a 10^8 further improvement in the next 30 to 40 years. Advances of up to 10^{18} (100 quintillion) could result, if any of the following innovations (which already exist at the laboratory level) undergo further development:

- Parallel processing.
- Advanced computer architecture.
- Special function processing chips.
- Special function analysis chips.
- Such a level of enhanced computer performance would require much more advanced production technologies, including new chip production technologies; new types of computer chips, circuit elements, and computer architectures and software; and a projected 10^5 improvement in telecommunications-transmission rates over the next 25 years.

2. Ubiquitous Computing

Household appliances and many other items in our everyday lives will be embedded with cheap and barely detectable microchips, sensors, microcontrollers, and microprocessors that sense our presence, anticipate our wishes, and read our emotions. Imbued with these tiny yet powerful computing components, appliances and consumer products will become "intelligent." They will interconnect and communicate with each other via network grids.

The ubiquitous-computing phenomenon will be further enabled by three new technologies:

- **MEMS.** Micro-electro-mechanical systems integrate items such as sensors, computers, data storage, and transmission systems onto a single computer chip. MEMS are small, low mass, lightweight, low power, and easy to mass produce. They also measure a wide range of physical phenomena, such as acceleration, inertia, and vibration. They can be analytical instruments to measure biological or physical states and can also be active response systems.
- **Bots.** Formally known as *semi-intelligent specialized agent software programs*, bots can automatically sort data based on set preferences, keep track of specific dynamic data sets (such as checkbook balances or inventories), maintain schedules and calendars, and track movement of things and people while integrating them with outside events. Bots are also capable of interacting with other computer software and other bots on their own initiative to accomplish tasks independently of a human user.

  The general deployment of bots is projected to occur in the next seven to 10 years, pending the rollout of more advanced processor hardware. Masses of bots and bots-inhabited equipment will work together without human initiative—or even human knowledge—to automate large portions of society's routine activities. Bots will also manage computer networks. By 2025, the Internet will have evolved into a bot-coordinated, bot-directed "information grid" that connects billions of devices, nodes, and sensors to each other. Under bot management, the Internet will be much more dynamic than it is today.
- **Swarm technology.** Network command-and-control system architecture will be very unlike that of networks today. The ability to understand and manage the collective movements, reactions, and interactions of masses of interconnected items will be critical. Swarm technology—i.e., decentralized arrays of agents or programs interacting locally with one another and with their surroundings, thus carrying out "intelligent" large-scale behavior (much like an ant colony, bacterial culture, or school of fish)—will be important in the near future for controlling and managing this new system.

3. Human Language Interface for Computers

Another great technological advance of the next 20 years will be the development of computers with human-language interfaces that fully comprehend human words—both spoken and written—and their meanings and that will talk, listen, and read aloud in humanlike voices. Some applications will permit information retrieval using natural language and automated foreign language translation for print and voice. Also, semi-intelligent personal search agents will use human-language interfaces to search the Internet's databases and archives to compile information in specialized fields of knowledge and areas of interest based on the human user's specific interests and wishes.

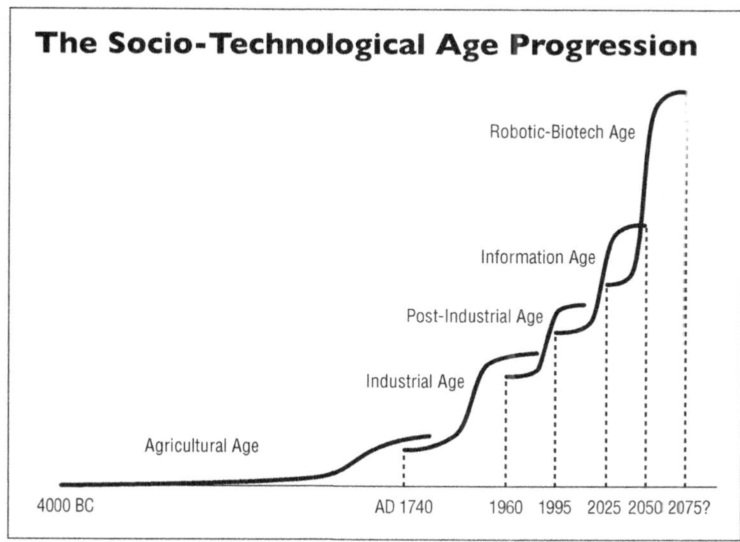

The human language computer interface could potentially transform society from a written culture to one relying more on verbal interactions. This interface will also automate a large number of voice-based activities, such as placing orders, asking directions, and executing verbal instructions to perform complex tasking. The education system and service area will both become more automated.

4. Machine Vision

Machine vision that will become available in five to 15 years will grow more sophisticated over time. Developed machine vision will have capability far beyond the range of the human eye (infrared, ultraviolet, multispectral). Robotic systems equipped with machine vision will recognize, classify, sort, and manipulate objects and respond to changes in their environments in unique ways. They will be put to a wide variety of industrial, laboratory, and surveillance uses, such as automatic guidance systems for vehicles and accident avoidance systems for machinery.

5. Robot Technology

We are now in the process of developing human-directed, virtual presence machines capable of remote-controlled movement and manipulation of objects. These devices are often called robots, which they are not. The technology to build real robots is on the way, however.

In the near-term future, our world will be driven by two emerging technologies that are advancing simultaneously: robotics and biotechnology. These technologies will overtake information technology and give us a new Socio-Technological Age around the year 2025. This new age will continue for 50-plus years.

The technologies needed to build robots that can perceive their surroundings, move themselves, and perform tasks without human oversight should reach fruition between 2015 and 2025. By 2040, robotlike machinery will inhabit the world alongside people, doing much of the work.

As robots enter the mainstream, they will probably exert major economic and societal impacts. On the positive side, labor productivity will vastly increase, which could be lifesaving as populations of retirees will swell in the developed world. Replacing the retiring labor force with high-tech robotic equipment will ensure that economies remain productive enough to support their retirees. Additionally, hundreds of thousands of new jobs could become available for human professionals who possess the skills to program robot-tohuman interface systems, movement control, harm-avoidance systems, vision packages, tasking systems, and speech-recognition programs.

At the same time, major disruptions of the world's workforces could result. Studies estimate that robots could replace as much as one-third to one-half of human labor in some industrial and service sectors. Additionally, robot technology could almost completely take over agriculture and displace most, if not all, of the world's farm workers. Even worse, this precipitous fall in human labor will probably occur at a rapid pace: in about a five-to seven-year period.

6. Telecommunications Revolution

Mass interconnection of computerized data systems has enabled people and machines to talk to each other at high data rates. These data rates will get progressively higher over the next half century. Optical fiber network transmission systems will continuously increase their capacities and reach transmission capabilities as high as 100 terabytes per second once new photonics switches, photonics circuit elements, optical routers, and plasmon switches—all now under development—go into widespread use. This will ultimately produce a seamless, all-optical network for data communications four to five times more powerful than the current one.

The next telecommunications revolution will offer mass sharing and transfer of databases, unrestricted worldwide communications and an ability to locate and communicate with anyone, a much higher diffusion of work via telecommuting, rapid and widespread dissemination of knowledge (unlimited access for everyone to the sum total of knowledge of the human race), and a much wider variety and availability of education and entertainment.

7. Fullerene Chemistry

In September 1985, Nobel Prize–winning chemist Rick Smalley discovered the original C_{60} molecule, buckminsterfullerene ("buckyballs"), which comprised 60 pure carbon atoms. In 1990, a means to mass produce buckyballs was discovered, making them available for large-scale study and establishing the new field of fullerene chemistry. Since then, chemists have learned not only how to form fullerene molecules, but also how to attach other kinds of molecules to them and build new structures and materials, such as *nanotubes* and *graphene*.

Nanotubes are hollow, tubelike structures composed of carbon atoms. They are very strong under linear tensile loads, conduct electricity with little resistance, can store items in their hollow interiors, can filter substances that pass through them, and conduct heat better than any other known material. Researchers are exploring carbon nanotubes' potential commercial uses as fiber in composite structures, as superconductive wire, and as a storage medium for hydrogen fuel. Other uses may include transport mechanisms for fluids in and out of the body, as molecular sieves and filters, superconducting interconnections on circuit chips, computer memory storage devices, thermal regulators, and small electric plasma guns.

Graphene, first produced in a lab in 2004, is a flat, two-dimensional carbon fullerene consisting of a carbon sheet just a few atoms thick that can be extended indefinitely along its edges. It is an amazingly good conductor of electricity and has many potential uses in the electronics and semiconductor industries. Graphene ribbons made on an industrial scale, for example, could be used as connectors on computer chips. An experimental nanoscale graphene transistor was first demonstrated in a laboratory in April 2008.

Large-scale production of graphene wafers could produce a new class of semi-superconducting substrate with which to build computer chips. This would make possible several revolutionary advances in chip technology: development of a superconducting substrate layer to connect components, processing elements, and multiple core dies and development of graphene-based superconducting transistors.

Graphene wafers might also make Johnson junctions, induction switches, and "Y" switches work at room temperature. These three devices are three times faster than transistors, but at present they only work at cryogenic temperatures. If, by using graphene wafers, engineers successfully made them work at room temperature, they could create extremely efficient electrical networks that would not require active switching—i.e., fewer moving parts and fewer resources required.

Emergence of the New Social Structure

Agricultural Age Social Structure
- Aristocracy
- Intellectuals & Artists
- Merchants
- Artists & Craftsmen
- Agricultural Workers

Industrial Age Social Structure
- Upper Class
- Intellectuals & Knowledge Workers
- Merchants
- Industrial Workers
- Agricultural Workers

Post-Industrial Age Social Structure
- Upper Class
- Intellectuals & Artists
- Merchants & Entrepreneurs
- Urban Bohemians
- Skill & Knowledge Workers
- Retirees
- Industrial Workers
- Service Workers
- Working Poor
- Agricultural Workers
- Social Wards

Information Age Social Structure
- Upper & Ruling Class
- Intellectuals
- Developers of Intellectual Goods
- Cultural Sycophants
- Entrepreneurs
- Knowledge Workers Sub-Class
- Skill & Knowledge Workers
- Bio-Med Sub-Class
- Retirees
- Industrial Workers
- Agricultural Population
- Service Workers
- Working Poor (unskilled but trainable for routine tasks)
- Social Wards
- Under Class

Robotic-Biotech Age Social Structure
- Upper & Ruling Class
- Intellectuals
- Developers of Intellectual Goods
- Cultural Sycophants
- Entrepreneurs
- Knowledge Workers Sub-Class
- System Knowledge Workers Sub-Class
- Skill & Knowledge Workers
- Bio-Med Sub-Class
- Retirees
- Industrial Workers
- Agricultural Population
- Service Workers
- Working Poor (unskilled but trainable for routine tasks)
- Social Wards
- Under Class

8. Multi-Level Coding System in DNA

Scientists now recognize that DNA has at least six levels of coding. Some birth defects, cancers, and other genetic disorders may not actually be the result of genes themselves, but of coding errors in these outer layers of the DNA system. Some of the "non-gene" control layers may be easier to manipulate than the classic, first-line gene layer. Recent discoveries have opened several new lines of genetic research, making this the dawn of a new era in molecular genetics.

9. Biotech Analysis Instrumentation

Development of new instruments to examine biological phenomena is revolutionizing the fields of biological research and medicine. One of the most important new instruments is the DNA microarrays, which are compact robotic systems that detect DNA and other biochemical matter. Modern microarrays' detector systems are made with postage-stamp-sized coated glass wafers. Each wafer includes a grid of strands of DNA that only bind to their complementary DNA matches (or alternatively, dots of some biochemical reagent).

> "Biochemists' ultimate goal—of a full-scale biochemical computer model of human genetics, biochemistry, and all their interactions—will be available within 10 to 20 years."

The grid elements can measure the presence and level of a given gene or gene product (mutants, abnormal variants, dysfunctional genes) in a sample. These wafers can also find and analyze chemical and biological compounds within the body. Current machines are only capable of statistical samples. Scientists would like a machine capable of analyzing the entire human genome and its biochemical environment with all its variants in a single pass. It will probably be the late 2020s before a full human body biochemical scan can be performed.

At present, however, our greater challenge is not how to detect the chemicals, but how to interpret the results. Too few tests have been conducted to establish the normal level of most of these chemicals in the human body. By the mid-twenty-first century, we will have enough data analyzed to tell what chemicals, proteins, and enzymes are normal in the human body; whether their physical form is a mutation or merely a normal statistical variation; and whether certain measurements are metabolic disorders or just normal variations of human metabolism. This information will have a significant impact on health.

10. Human Biogenetic– Chemical Computer Model

New biotechnology and computer science breakthroughs are revealing the body's biochemical secrets and spurring creation of new methods for attacking metabolic and genetic disorders. We have begun to examine the body's biochemical nature to determine whether it is functioning correctly and is in balance and to determine what effect this balance or imbalance has on health.

Biochemists' ultimate goal—of a full-scale biochemical computer model of human genetics, biochemistry, and all their interactions—will be available within 10 to 20 years. The amount of data and calculations involved will require a larger computer than available today, but this deficiency will be overcome within that time.

By the mid-twenty-first century, we will have a working computer model of human genetics, biochemistry, and major portions of their interactions. This will permit the modeling of an individual's genetics and biochemistry, which can be used to diagnose and isolate individual biochemical deficiencies, including a number of conditions that today may be considered psychological but are actually statistical variations in metabolism. This will also be used to determine the effect of drugs and nutrients.

11. Treatment of Hereditary Diseases

The human race is now afflicted by some 4,000 hereditary diseases caused by genetic abnormalities. These diseases have until now largely been untreatable. However, the new knowledge of gene structure and function could possibly lead to new treatments. Eventually, genetic intervention could prevent or treat a large number of diseases. More successful treatments might be possible via selected artificial protein therapy and/or micronutrients.

It is also possible that this new biotech knowledge will uncover a variety of "minor" genetic diseases that people haven't recognized or have assumed to be normal variations. Since these minor diseases affect a larger portion of the working population than the major hereditary disorders do, mitigating or curing them could lead to bigger increases in workforce productivity and performance.

12. Control of Bio-Metabolic Disorders

New means will arise to measure how the body is working at a biochemical level and to assess the body's biochemicals (types and amounts) and whether the body metabolism displays proper balance. Biochemical "retuning" will treat a number of chronic, long-term conditions—including Parkinson's disease, Alzheimer's, and possibly even the aging process itself—by supplying chemical compounds that the patient's body does not have in order to realign the biochemical functions.

13. Blood and Tissue Matching of Drugs

At present, only about 40% of the population reacts favorably to a new drug. The rest have either minimal reaction or adverse reactions. As knowledge of human bio-metabolism advances, however, clinicians will learn to group patients into bio-metabolism classes and tissue-type groups to determine who will benefit from a specific drug and who will have adverse reactions. Use of bio-metabolism classes and tissue-type groups will be widespread by 2050 and result in increased drug effectiveness, fewer negative drug reactions, and lower drug-treatment costs.

14. Tissue Engineering

The creation of self-replicating bio-materials for healing wounds and bone fractures, including the combining of synthetic materials and structures with living cells, is another area of scientific exploration. Tissue engineering will revolutionize body and wound repair, organ transplantation and surgery in general.

> "Understanding how the brain operates on an individual basis will permit society to match the individual to task performance, to individualize educational programs, and to identify and mitigate mental illness."

New polymers that satisfy safety and effectiveness requirements are being researched and developed for many surgical uses, including tissue scaffolding, bone grafts, cartilage repair, tissue regeneration, wound repair, and tissue joining. Soon, artificial organs and body parts will be available for replacement surgery. Research programs are now under way to develop artificial ears, hearts, pancreases, lungs, kidneys, livers, and legs.

15. Neurotechnology

Neuroscientists have developed a set of scanners capable of determining how and where the brain performs specific functions. The new brain-scanning and brain-mapping tools are opening up a whole new understanding of how humans think and act. Using them, researchers can observe brain activity, measure its intensity, chart the general pattern of brain operation, and identify the type of chemical reactions occurring in the brain.

Brain-scanning technology will soon be upgraded by the use of atomic magnetometer sensors—a new magnetic sensor technology that uses cesium vapor as a sensing element. These devices are 100 times more sensitive and 1,000 times faster than present sensor elements. They will, with time, better discern how people think, how the brain performs tasks, how thought processes differ among individuals, and what those differences mean in relation to task performance and personality.

The new knowledge of brain operation and its effects will be one of the major, socially transforming events of the twenty-first century. Understanding how the brain operates on an individual basis will permit society to match the individual to task performance, to individualize educational programs, and to identify and mitigate mental illness.

16. Neuropharmacology

We can now see the operation of the brain. We can also systematically study and measure the effects of nutrients, micronutrients, and drug treatments on the brain and on various mental conditions. This has led to the new science of *neuropharmacology*—the study of how we change the brain's operation through the use of drugs, food, and other nutrients, micronutrients, and proteins. Over time, this field will apply knowledge of the brain's biochemical operations to systematically treat mental disorders and mental conditions pharmaceutically, as well as enhance people's natural mental abilities.

17. Cellulose-to-Glucose Process

One of the major goals of the biotech and chemical industry is the production of glucose, the principal food of many microorganisms, from cellulose. If cheap, plentiful glucose were available, microbes could be genetically engineered to make almost anything. An economical cellulose-to-glucose process would revolutionize the world's chemical industries and allow the conversion of much agricultural cellulose-based waste into useful raw materials.

18. Nanotechnology

Instrumentation has begun to permit us to see and manipulate matter at a nano level—10^{-6} to 10^{-9} meter—the level of atoms and molecules. This has created the new field of *nanotechnology*. The ability to create smaller structures using modern chip-manufacturing technology will permit us to change and modify materials one atom or molecule at a time and to develop super-fine powders, quantum dots, and nanotubes. These capabilities have now started to shrink things into the "upper nano" range—a range that advancements in production technology will push us into over the next 10 to 15 years. The scale of objects will continue to shrink, and some useful upper-nanoscale devices and phenomena will be developed and deployed.

19. Chaos Theory and Complexity Models

Our world is much more complex, interconnected, and dynamic than we once thought. New mathematical concepts are challenging the rationalized, deterministic, scientific models of the Industrial Age. The Industrial Age paradigm held that there is one best way to organize a given thing and that, in all cases, a given "rational" outcome is predetermined by nature. The new scientific paradigm will ultimately replace this older mentality.

The new Information Age is being driven by applied technology and by two major advances in theoretical science that are altering our view of how the world works: an ecological/ecosystem model, which supports ecological and environmental diversity, and modern chaos and complexity theories, which emphasize unpredictability, self-organizing systems, and the coexistence of the linear and the random. In the near term, this paradigm shift will significantly change people's views of society, of themselves in relation to society, and of how the world and the greater universe work.

20. Fuel Cells to Allow Deep-Sea Habitation

A major effort is under way to develop advanced fuel cells for cars. The greatest social effect of fuel cells will not be in automobiles, however, but in the opening of the undersea world to exploration and habitation. Fuel cells that produce electricity directly, without producing toxic fumes as a byproduct, will bring down the costs of submarines and keep them running for days as opposed to hours. This will permit human exploration and—eventually—colonization of the continental shelves and the shallow oceans.

Fuel cells will lead to the development of extensive deep-sea business sectors and myriad human habitations out in the ocean. Mining operations to exploit the shallow ocean floor's mineral wealth, as well as commercial aquaculture enterprises to exploit the ocean's biological resources, will follow. Earth's available resource base will expand significantly, and Earth's population—which could reach more than 9 billion people by mid-century (or even 11 billion if medical advances extend average life spans)—will have much more room to grow.

Five Future Technologies and the Problems They Could Solve

Several technologies yet to come could significantly affect the nature of our world. Our top five are as follows:

1. **Superconductivity at room temperature.** When certain metals and ceramics are cooled to ultra-low temperatures, they become *superconductive*—i.e., they can carry huge amounts of electrical current for long durations of time without losing any of the current's energy as heat. Diverse work is going on in making materials superconductive at room temperature. If it succeeds, we could substantially increase the efficiency of electrical machines and power grids and also develop new types of computer chips, improved medical-imaging devices, and high-efficiency ion drives for space vehicles.
2. **Low-cost space lift.** Lifting objects into orbit is expensive—a problem that slows human improvement in space capabilities. The advent of a cheap space lift would allow exponential growth, and perhaps a new technological age. It would be attainable either by politicians agreeing to the massive funding needed for such a development or by some unforeseen, dramatic technological breakthrough. Neither, however, can be guaranteed to happen within the next 25 years.
3. **Artificial intelligence of human-level capability in computers.** The development and widespread use of AI of human-level capability in computer systems stands to be one of the major advances in computer technology over the next 75 years. AI claims have been made for 40 years, but to date, they have not delivered. Furthermore, there appears to be no current, fundamental breakthrough that will alter this in the near future. However, research grants bolster those who think that the big breakthrough is right around the corner.

> "A successful low-grade, agricultural-product-to-fuel path would enrich agricultural economies throughout much of the world."

4. **Cellulose-to-liquid-hydrocarbon path.** A number of new, synthetic fuel processes can produce diesel fuels from agricultural products. The means now exist for converting vegetable oils into biodiesel fuel, protein matter into diesel oil, various agricultural substances into synthetic oil, and sugars and starches into fuel-grade ethyl alcohol. Unfortunately, all these biosynthetic fuel processes are much more expensive than fossil-fuel generation, largely due to the costs of harvesting and processing. One lower-cost option may exist,

however: converting low-end agricultural waste (largely cellulose) into synthetic oil. A number of experimental processes to derive fuel from cellulose waste are now in R&D. A successful low-grade, agricultural-product-to-fuel path would enrich agricultural economies throughout much of the world, and in addition make energy independence more attainable for communities everywhere.

5. **Improved medicine and life span.** The question is not whether we are going to get some life-span extension, but how much: Will the extension be a moderate increase in life expectancy of 100 to 120 years, a significantly increased life expectancy of 150 to 170 years, or a very significant life extension of 250 to 300 years? Conversely, radical life extension could lead to life spans of 1,000-plus years.

Life extension has both positive and negative social implications. It will alleviate suffering caused by age deterioration and will result in a longer-lived, more productive workforce. On the other hand, it may cause issues with pension plans, Social Security, life insurance, and other retirement programs. It could result in overpopulation, food shortages, pollution, wars for resources, and extinction of species. Another important consideration is that of control: Who would determine how this precious technology would be shared?

The Effects of Emerging Technologies on Society

As the technology areas covered in this article advance along their individual development curves, their combined effect will remake society as we know it. Ultimately, they will give humankind two new socio-technological ages in the first half of the twenty-first century: the Information Age and the Robotic-Biotech Age. The current Information Age, which should continue for the next 20 to 40 years, is being driven by advances in computers, telecommunications, and electronic instrumentation, plus major advances in materials, space, energy, and manufacturing.

The Robotic-Biotech Age will follow at around 2025, driven by the simultaneous advances of robotics and biotechnology, and reinforced by advances in nanotechnology, materials, and manufacturing technology. The Robotic-Biotech Age will continue for 50-plus years, until another great technology emerges as a new force in the world.

The Information Age came on very quickly and will be relatively short-lived (about 50 years). Society and social structure will not have had the time to fully adjust before the next wave of technological innovation comes along. This speed of change is going to continue for the next 50 to 75 years as the current wave of emerging technologies matures.

In the twentieth century, many people viewed the philosophical movements to which they belonged (communism, fascism, various radical nationalisms, socialism, social democracy, liberalism, etc.) as belief systems that would and should govern how the world runs. In the name of these systems, 500 million people died by war, genocide, war-related famine and disease, politically motivated terror, and régime-based terror.

Members of the emerging generation, operating under the new paradigm, are much more likely to see themselves as cellular automata—trying to optimize themselves in their environment—rather than as governors of the universe. Whether this is good for society as a whole is not yet known, but it will represent a new social viewpoint.

New socio-technological ages tend to produce new social structures and new social mores. Historical precedent suggests that this new age will also produce a new and different societal basis for war and the use of military force, along with a new social perception of the legitimate application of war.

> "Technological progress alone is relatively slow at driving social change. However, the near future will see society change markedly as a result of new emerging technology and demography."

It is possible to project with some certainty the social structure of both the new Information Age and the Robotic-Biotech Age (see graph on page 19). With each transition to a more advanced stage of civilization, certain things transpire:

- The social structure acquires an increasingly large number of small, specialized niches.
- There is a significant increase in the number of players in the political power structure.
- There is an increasing spread of knowledge out to the masses.
- The average person's standard of living goes up.
- Human control over nature increases.

As society has advanced, class structure has become more complex. In the later Information Age and Robotic-Biotech Age, there will be simply too many classes for a dominant one to emerge. The complexity of the new social structure, coupled with the rise in general knowledge level, will require recognition that specialized knowledge is necessary and that all classes serve useful functions and are needed for society to operate properly.

It is usually hard to change the direction of society, absent great social perturbations, such as war or economic disaster, which can force rapid social change. In an age of peace and prosperity, it takes a long time to modify social norms, regardless of the level of new technological progress that occurs. Technological progress alone is relatively slow at driving social change. However, the near future will see society change markedly as a result of new emerging technology and demography.

This need not be any cause for alarm. With some exceptions, most of the changes described portend to be highly positive. Barring bad luck and bad management, the world will—when all the technologies are deployed—be a better place to live in.

What Does Success Look Like for Your Company: Social Media Starting Points with Measurable Returns

By Anne Berkowitch

We've all read conflicting reports about how to enact social media inside a company—the questions the discussion raises loom large. Do we ease into social media? How prepared do we need to be when we open up the floodgates? What platforms do we try first, second or third? Do we need to hire someone to manage social media? How do we measure the value of our efforts and demonstrate that value to executives?

The answer to all of these questions lies in what our business objectives are for social media activity. Social media is no longer separate from marketing, branding, public relations, human resources, lead generation, customer service or any other facet of a business. It has the potential to be an integral part of each of those departments' daily activities and play a critical role in their success.

The questions we should be asking before any others include:

- What do we hope to gain from engaging in social media?
- Does our business lend itself to being social intrinsically?
- What does success in social media look like for our business?

And most importantly:

- How will we measure social media ROI?

When it comes to HR, social media should not be tapped only as a way to identify future employees, but also as a driver for attracting them to our business, retaining them moving forward and leveraging their own networks for further growth. Let's consider for a moment an integrated social media plan for a company's HR department that would help practitioners find quality talent via the assets they already have on staff. Not only can a strong understanding and use of social media in business be an influential selling point for job seekers, but it also allows people to maximize their own personal networks to drive business growth. Growth generated via referrals is the best kind, especially when it comes to recruiting—referred candidates outperform job board candidates more than threefold in terms of retention and termination rates, not to mention that a referral candidate is 54 times more likely to result in a hire than a job board candidate.

Anne Berkowitch, "What Does Success Look Like for Your Company: Social Media Starting Points with Measurable Returns," *People and Strategy*, vol. 33, no. 3, p. 10.

While the solution to creating a social media strategy may not seem clear, it is necessary to be able to measure the success and engagement of the actions a company takes online so that future decisions can be made. Deciding on an initial goal that aligns with business aims first, tracking its impact on the bottom line, and expanding from there is a recipe for success. Also, when it comes to corporate networking online, understanding the viral power of those networks is integral to one's own success—referrals bring in 25 percent of recruits at 50 percent savings per employee. Thus the impact can be enormous.

So as we start to think about creating a social media plan, let's keep this outline in mind:

- Evaluate where the company is in terms of social media activity—even if it feels like square one, it might not be.
- Who in the company is involved personally?
- Do they identify as part of the organization?
- Decide on initial and projected social media goals that align with current, overall business goals.
- How can social media and referral networking be leveraged — for recruiting, business development, branding?
- Benchmark where competitors are in this process.
- What platforms have they adopted?
- What level of activity are they maintaining?
- What other technologies might they be using?
- Test the social media waters via internal-facing social media vehicles.
- Internal chatting tools
- Private micro-blogging platforms
- Corporate referral networking solutions

> When it comes to HR, social media should not be tapped only as a way to identify future employees, but also as a driver for attracting them to our business.

A goal as simple as driving recruitment initially allows social media activity to be internally focused. By creating a channel for employees to leverage their personal networks, help their connections as well as their business, and potentially earn a bonus in the process engenders positive employee sentiment and will drive measurable returns for the organization as well.

Chapter Highlights

- One primary purpose of letters of application is to showcase the highlights of your résumé.
- Parts of a résumé that should be highlighted include the information most relevant to the requirements and needs of the job.
- In any letter of application, it is not enough for the job seeker to simply showcase his or her strengths and background. The letter of application is not simply about the applicant.
- In applying for a job, applicants should focus on the needs of the prospective employer. Applicants should strive to match their qualifications with the needs of the employer.
- To prepare a strong letter of application, the applicant must research the company or organization and develop a solid understanding of its mission and goals.
- Letters of application should be creative, enthusiastic, and empathetic.
- Letters of application provide applicants with the opportunity to do more than express their interest in a job. They also allow applicants to share their vision of what they would do if the job was theirs.

For Discussion

1. Put your hands on an older letter of application you have written. In the context of this chapter, critique it. What changes, if any, would you make to it?
2. What is your dream job? What company or organization would you love to be part of? Prepare a letter of application for a job with that company.
3. What aspects of your background are you most proud of? What are effective ways to incorporate them into your letter of application?
4. Ask a friend or fellow student to share with you a letter of application he or she has sent out previously. Critique it and, where appropriate, offer suggestions as to how it might be improved.
5. Discuss in detail the relationship between the application letter and the résumé

References

Adams, J. (2010). The sharpened quill. *The New Yorker,* November.

Aristotle. (1954). *Rhetoric.* (W. Rys. Roberts, Trans.). New York, NY: Moderr Library.

Augenstein, N. In the news. Retrieved from iphonereporting.com.

Baker, B. Retrieved from www.newsthinking.com

Barnlund, D. C. (2008). A transactional model of communication. In C. D. Mortensen (Ed.), *Communication theory*. New Brunswick, NJ: Transaction.

Bernstein, W. J. (2013). *Masters of the word: How media shaped history from the alphabet to the internet.* New York, NY: Grove Press.

Berger, C. R., & Calabrese, R. J. (1975). Same exploration in initial interaction and beyond: Toward a development theory of communication research. *Human Communication Research, 1*, 99–112.

Bosco, R. A. & Myerson, J. (2010). The later lectures of Ralph Waldo Emerson, 1843–1871, vol. 2. Atlanta, University of Georgia Press.

Botan, C. H. (2006). Grand strategy, strategy, and tactics in public relations. In C. H. Botan & V. Hazelton (Eds.), *Public Relations Theory II* (pp. 223–247). New York, NY: Lawrence Erlbaum Associates.

Botan, C. R., & Hazelton, V. (2006). *Public relations theory II.* New York, NY: Lawrence Erlbaum Associates.

Broom, G., Casey, S., & Ritchey, J. (1997). Toward a concept and theory of organization-public relationships. *Journal of Public Relations Research*, *9*(2), 83–98.

Cameron, J. (1999). *The right to write: An invitation and initiation into the writing life.* New York, NY: Putnam.

Canary, D. J., & Cody, M. J. (2000). *Interpersonal communication: A goals-based approach.* New York, NY: Saint-Martin's.

CNN Newsroom. (2013, September 11). Broadcast script.

Cooper, A. (2013, September 4). 360 degrees broadcast script.

Crable, R. E., & Vibbert, S. L. (1985). Managing issues and influencing public policy. *Public Relations Review, 11*, 3–16.

Darwin, C. (1958). *On the origin of species by means of natural selection, or the preservation of favoured races in the struggle for life*. New York, NY: Signet Classics. (Original work published 1859)

Dewey, J. (1927). *The public and its problems*. Chicago: Swallow Press.

Dozier, D. M. (1995). *Manager's guide to excellence in public relations and communication management*. Mahwah, NJ: Lawrence Erlbaum Associates.

Drower, M. S. (1985). *Flinders Petrie*. London, England: Victor Gollanz.

Echeveste, J. (2009). Interview. In D. W. Guth & C. Marsh, *Public relations: A values-driven approach*. Boston, MA: Pearson Education, Inc.

Ehling, W. P. (1992). Estimating the value of public relations and communication to an organization. In J. E. Grunig, D. M. Dozier, W. P. Ehling, L. A. Grunig, F. C. Repper, & J. White (Eds.), *Excellence in public relations and communication management*. Hillsdale, NJ: Lawrence Erlbaum Associates.

Farhi, P. Article about the Associated Press style. *The Washington Post*.

Ferguson, M. A. (1984). *Building theory in public relations: Interorganizational relationships*. Paper presented to the Association for Education in Journalism and Mass Communication, Gainesville, Florida.

French, H. W. (2011). E. I. Wilson's theory of everything. *The Atlantic, 308*(4), 70–82.

Geisel, T. (1986, May 21). On becoming a writer. *The New York Times*.

Goldman, E. F. (1948). *Two-way street: The emergence of the public relations counsel*. Boston, MA: Bellman Publishing Company.

Grunig, J. E., & Hunt, T. (1984). *Managing public relations*. New York, NY: Holt, Rinehart and Winston.

Guth, D. W., & Marsh, C. (2009). *Public relations: A values-driven approach*. Boston, MA: Pearson.

Houston, S. D. (2004). *The first writings: Script inventions as history and progress*. Cambridge, England: University Press.

Janssen, J. (1896). The invention of printing and its spread till 1470: With special reference to social and economic factors. *The Library Quarterly, 2*(3), (July, 1932), 180.

Klein, K. L. (2008, June 9). A practical guide to branding. *Bloomberg Business Week*.

King, S. *On writing*.

Lake, L. (2013). What is branding and how important is it to your marking strategy? Retrieved from marketing.about.com.

Ledingham, J. A. (2001). Government-community relationships: Extending the relational theory of public relations. *Public Relations Review, 27*, 285–295.

Ledingham, J. A. (2006). Relationship management: A general theory of public relations. In C. H. Botan & V. Hazelton (Eds.), *Public Relations Theory II*. New York, NY: Lawrence Erlbaum Associates.

Maslow, A. (1954). *Motivation and personality*. New York, NY: Harper & Row.

Mencher, M. *News reporting & writing*.

Minthorn, D. AP Article, a Grammar Expert. *The Washington Post*.

Mitchell, A., Jurkowitz, M. & Guskie, E. (2013). The newspaper industry overall. Pew Research Journalism Project, www.journalism. org./2012/02/.

O'Neill, K. (1991). U.S. public relations evolves to meet society's needs. *Public Relations Journal, 28*.

Oursler, F. (1964). *Behold this dreamer*. Boston, MA: Little Brown.

Pressfield, Steven. *The war of art*.

Salinger, J. (2010). Thomas Paine's continental mind. *Early American Literature, 45*(3), 593–617.

S. E. & Copeland, D. (2003). *The function of newspapers in society*. Santa Barbara, CA: Praeger Publishing.

Sites, K. (2007). *In the hot zone: One man, one year, twenty wars.* Harper Perennial.

Social Media Today (with Cygnis Media) Branding examples.

Spitzberg, B. H., & Cupach, W. R. (1984). *Interpersonal communication competence.* Beverly Hills, CA: Sage.

Strunk, W., & White, E. B. *Elements of style.*

Walsh, L. Radio Television Digital News Association Online Article. Investigative Reporter, Florida.

Weaver, W., & Shannon, C. (1963). *The mathematical theory of communication.* Urbana, IL: University of Illinois Press.

Willihnganz, J. G. Stanford University Press. Stanford faculty webpage.

Zelezny, J. D. (1997). *Communications laws: Liberties, restraints, and the modern media.* Belmont, CA: Wadsworth.

About the Authors

Beth Jannery

Professor Jannery has been in the communication field for more than twenty-five years. She is the director of the journalism program at George Mason University. This consists of the journalism minor, the sports communication minor, and the journalism concentration within the Department of Communication. She teaches journalism courses full-time and is a former journalist who covered the Pentagon. Jannery was the communication officer for Harvard University's John F. Kennedy School of Government with the Belfer Center for Science and International Affairs. She is author of several nonfiction books in the Simple Grace book series, including *Simple Grace: Living a Meaningful Life*. Her latest book is a novel titled *The Admiral's Daughter*.

Jannery started her journalism career at age twenty-one at CNN's Investigative Reporting Unit. She went to Boston University for graduate school, earning a master's degree in broadcast journalism. She worked for the largest English-language newspaper in Bangkok, Thailand, called *The Nation*. In Bangkok, she wrote feature articles and covered politics. She was on the first writing/producing team for Southeast Asia's *Face the Nation* and *Good Morning Thailand*. She has a writing and editing communication business called Jannery Communications. She taught writing and communication for American University in Washington, DC, and Marist College in New York. Jannery lives in Northern Virginia and has two daughters, Skye and Tess, and a golden retriever named Bella. You can connect with her on LinkedIn.

Daniel L. Walsch

Dr. Walsch has been part of the communication field for more than forty years as a journalist, public relations professional, press secretary, speechwriter, instructor, and author. Among his most recent books are *A Strategic Communication Approach to Crisis Situations: A Case Study Analysis of Transformative Events at George Mcson University and Northern Illinois University* (published by Lambert Academic Publishing) and *Communication Wars: Our Internal Perpetual Conflict* (published by Cognella). He also maintains a blog, *Why Communication Matters*, which may be accessed at www.myskeets.blogspot.com. He is an accredited public relations practitioner as certified by the Public Relations Society of America. He earned his PhD in communication at George Mason University. Dr. Walsch resides with his wife in Fairfax, Virginia.

CPSIA information can be obtained at www.ICGtesting.com
Printed in the USA
LVOW03s1800080715
445327LV00002B/2/P